Nothing has puzzled the mind of modern man more that *the confusing paradigm of fourth-dimensional physics. For millennia, the ignorance of these truths has culminated in countless suffering for humanity through different means which have included religious persecution, various forms of mind-control, and unbridled torture of the human soul. The most soul-wrenching of these abominations included the Montauk Project, a vast mind-control project which included the manipulation of individuals across different dimensions.*

The Montauk Book of the Living pursues the quantum *residue of the Montauk Project which leads to cohesive pathways of synchronicity and the eventual discovery of a quantum relic. This relic opens the door to understanding the greatest mysteries of history and heralds a new time period once prophesied by native elders as the Second Coming of the Pharoahs.*

The artifacts of history point to a mysterious Blue Race *which founded the Egyptian culture and honored the feminine principle through the star Sirius which was known as the Star of Women. The descendants of these people are the Tuareg, or Blue People, who reside in one of the most mysterious and intriguing strongholds left on Earth: the Ahaggar Mountains in southern Algeria.*

The Montauk Book of the Living explores these artifacts *as well as the doctrines of the ancient Kabbalists and breaks new ground with regard to the occult biology of the Virgin Birth, the Blue Race and the mystery religions of antiquity. In the background of these remarkable discoveries lies the everlasting guiding force of the universe. In these pages, you can expect the unexpected.*

Cover Art by Jill Bauman

Artistically inspired rendition of
Queen Antinea of Atlantis, the Mother of the Blue Race
who gave Mankind wisdom and sustenance
through the gift of the olive tree

THE MONTAUK BOOK OF LIVING

BY PETER MOON

NEW YORK

The Montauk Book of the Living

First printing, January 2009

Cover art and illustration by Jill Bauman
Medicine wheel (back cover) designed by Artie Crippen
(color rendition by Rick Smith)
Typography by Creative Circle Inc.
Published by: Sky Books
Box 769
Westbury, New York 11590
email: skybooks@yahoo.com
website: www.skybooksusa.com

Library of Congress Cataloging-in-Publication Data

Moon, Peter
The Montauk Book of the Living
by Peter Moon
384 pages
ISBN 978-0-9678162-6-5 (13 digit)
ISBN 0-9678162-6-2
1. Body, Mind & Spirit/Magick Studies 2. Occultism 3. Healing
Library of Congress Control Number 2008936721

This book is dedicated to
Olive Pharoah and Louise Boyd

Other titles from Sky Books

by Preston Nichols and Peter Moon

The Montauk Project: Experiments in Time
Montauk Revisited: Adventures in Synchronicity
Pyramids of Montauk: Explorations in Consciousness
Encounter in the Pleiades: An Inside Look at UFOs
The Music of Time

by Peter Moon

The Black Sun: Montauk's Nazi-Tibetan Connection
Synchronicity and the Seventh Seal
The Montauk Book of the Dead
Spandau Mystery

by Joseph Matheny with Peter Moon

Ong's Hat: The Beginning

by Stewart Swerdlow

Montauk: The Alien Connection
The Healer's Handbook: A Journey Into Hyperspace

by Alexandra Bruce

The Philadelphia Experiment Murder:
Parallel Universes and the Physics of Insanity

by Wade Gordon

The Brookhaven Connection

CONTENTS

Acknowledgements

Kenn Arthur, Howard Barkway, Tantra Bensko, Gail Boyd Evening Star, Techumseh Brown-Eagle, T. Buddha, Hamza Sid Catlett-Bey, Robert Cooper, Artie Crippen, Cat Crippen, Roosevelt Gainey, Charlotte Henderson, Dennis Marshall, The Montauk Nation, Robert Pharoah, True Ott, Penelope, Mark Roberts, Joy Sackstein, Vicki

PREFACE

This book is not for the average person. If you are average and want to stay that way, this book is not recommended for you. On the other hand, if you have an adventurous state of mind and would like to discover new ways of looking at the universe, I invite you to try reading this book. It is based upon the principle of quantum synchronicity. Before we go into the narrative of the book itself, it is advisable to first have a look at exactly what is meant by the term "quantum synchronicity."

The word *quantum* derives from the Latin root *quanta* which means "how much" or "quantity." In the subject of physics, *quantum* refers to quantum mechanics which is the study of the underlying principles of atomic physics. Quantum mechanics was pioneered and codified by a scientist named Wolfgang Pauli in the 1920's. Pauli encountered or precipitated so many strange coincidences in his life that his colleagues began to refer to these occurrences as the "Pauli effect."

Pauli's work was revolutionary because his theories took physics out of the realm of what might be considered "pure physical analysis" and put it into the realm of the observer. Although many physicists would hate to admit it, an observer is nothing more nor nothing less than a spirit. The two terms are synonyms for each other. The fact that some physicists might "hate" this says a lot about their own powers of observation.

In modern-day colloquialisms, the word *quantum* is often used to refer to spiritual events or paradigms or to situations that reach beyond the boundaries of ordinary physical reality. This is a bit of a misnomer that has already been ingrained into popular consciousness. Quantum mechanics is called such because it is concerned with the principles or mechanics that underlie the quantitative nature of reality.

When we consider the Latin root of the word *quantum*, we find that the prospect of the observer is precipitated in the very etymology itself. The word derives from the Latin *kwo* which means "who or what." The word *qualify* has a similar root and is derived from the Latin *qualis* which means "of what kind" plus *facere* "to make fact." *Qualis* derives from *kwi* which, once again, means "who." In both cases, the observer is being invoked.

There is yet deeper symbolism when we relate *kwi* and *kwo* to *kwa,* a Chinese word which represents the emanation of the energy being. In martial arts, the kwa refers to the energy triangle upon and around which the genitalia is situated. It is not only considered to be a point of maximum vulnerability but a point from which power is generated.

Further exploration of the word *quantum* takes us to yet another vista. The phoneme or root *qua* is also intrinsically connected to the word or prefix *quad* which means "four." The number four is very significant with regard to the quantum observer because it is a direct reference to the Hebrew four-letter expression for the Creator: *YHVH* or *Yod He Vau He*. This is also an expression for the four elements known as fire, water, air and earth. It should be noted that introducing elements to the equation accents the proposition of quality in the universe. All of creation can be identified by which of these elements are represented in the various constituents we know as matter. Quantity and quality are both fundamental expressions of the universe.

Kwa, kwi and *kwo* are also close cousins to *queen* which essentially means *quintessence* and refers to the essential ingredient or essence of something. I could go far deeper into these associations and write an expounded essay on these and other relationships, but that is not the point of this preface. The point I am making is that a very deep and fundamental expression of the universe is housed in the word *quantum*.

The pioneers of quantum mechanics had opened up a significant gate of consciousness in this regard. In addition to this, they also experienced the phenomena of quantum participation in the universe. At least that is true in the case of Wolfgang Pauli. As a scientist, Pauli surpassed his colleagues by reaching beyond the conventional means of correlating scientific data. He was experiencing and not just idly sitting by. As a colleague and patient of psychologist Carl Jung, the two men explored the associations and meaning of what became known as synchronicity.

Synchronicity is a word coined by Carl Jung which refers to the phenomenon of coincidence. Jung also apologized that he could not find a better word and described *synchronicity* as a "poor man's Tao." Jung also stated the following. "Tao can be anything, I use another word to designate it, but it is poor enough. I call it synchronicity."

The Tao is an ancient Chinese word for the fundamental and mysterious principle underlying creation, yet it cannot be confined to that definition because it is, by definition, without definition. In other words, "the Tao that can be defined is not the true Tao." In this respect, it is no different from the Judaic concept of God as "the name which cannot be named." More constructively, the Tao could be defined as the phenomenon that one expects to encounter when one reaches the Tao. In many respects, the Tao is similar or identical to the root expressions and etymologies underlying the word *quantum*. Once again, we have arrived at the proposition that underlies quantum mechanics, but this time it is through an Oriental flavor and not through the predicaments or propositions of early 20th Century scientists.

When one approaches either the cutting edge or pinnacle of scientific knowledge, one of two things might happen to an individual. Most people will be crammed with so much information that they will shut down and go about their business in overload mode. Most humans are already in this condition and they are the ones referred to at the beginning of this preface as "average." There is another alternative besides shutting down which is that one will experience quantum phenomena. By this, I am referring to becoming conscious of associations and coincidences presenting themselves from out of the blue. This is what Carl Jung referred to as synchronicity.

Synchronicity has not only been the hallmark of my writing career, it is the currency through which I survive. Whether you are aware of it or not, it also the currency upon which you survive. It is how you associate with the universe. My experiences with quantum synchronicity were precipitated by my personal investigation of the Montauk Project. This not only involved the cutting edge of science and technology, it has created a profound legacy of experiences which still echo across the world today.

INTRODUCTION

This story begins in the early Nineties with the unveiling of the Montauk Project, a colloquial name for a series of bizarre and secretive experiments that occurred at or near the Montauk Air Force Station which is located on the extreme eastern end of Long Island, New York. Just a short distance from Montauk Point and its famous lighthouse, the Montauk Air Force Station is located on grounds that have considerable historical significance. During World War II, huge bunkers were constructed that featured deep underground storage. Known as Camp Hero, the top part of the base was contoured so as to appear to be a sleepy fishing village. With the advent of the Cold War, a new use was found for Camp Hero in the Fifties when a huge SAGE radar system was installed in order to monitor incoming aircraft or missiles. Known as the Eastern Defense Shield, this was America's first line of defense against enemy attack. A huge underground complex was constructed in order to record and relay the radar signals that were received. As the personnel and equipment were of vital importance to the defense of the country, additional precautions were made to make these underground complexes impenetrable. Just in terms of national defense alone, this complex had to be state-of-the-art when it came to issues of security.

Not far from where Camp Hero sits today is a structure called Third House which is surrounded by many tiny cabins. This is the area where Colonel Theodore Roosevelt took his troops to recuperate after being exposed to malaria and different tropical diseases after the Spanish American War. For many people, this put Montauk on the map. Thc land, however, has an even richer and far more significant history than all of the above, but we will address that later.

The Montauk Project itself was a secretive black-budget operation that was run outside the controls of our regular government but used the Government in the process. It is a complex array of research that reaches across a wide strata of military and industrial associations. The most sensational and colorful associations tied to the Montauk Project are the Philadelphia Experiment and the secret Nazi technology.

In popular culture, the Philadelphia Experiment is a hybrid of legend and truth that revolves around various experiments conducted aboard various destroyer escorts, the most notable being the DE-73 *U.S.S. Eldridge* while it was docked at the Philadelphia Naval Yard. The Navy was then experimenting with degaussing techniques in order to demagnetize the ship for various reasons. Effective degaussing could possibly make the ship invisible to radar and sonar but could also prevent underwater mines from exploding. In conjunction with the degaussing, however, sophisticated techniques in "field rotation" were employed which resulted in literal invisibility which also had disastrous effects upon the crew. Returning from a hyper-dimensional field, the crew were either mentally unbalanced or physically compromised in some way. Some suffered spontaneous combustion while others returned to this dimension literally inserted into the bulkhead of the ship itself. The crew were sent to different hospitals for further study, one of which was at Camp Upton, New York which was destined to be the future site of Brookhaven Labs.

The aftereffects of the Philadelphia Experiment resulted in a massive human factor study which was, at least in part, designed to understand why men suffered when subjected to different dimensional fields. After the war, this data was combined with the Captured German Documents confiscated from the Third Reich which included the empirical data collected from the experiments of Joseph Mengele and other Nazi doctors.

Besides being affiliated with the Philadelphia Experiment and Brookhaven Labs, Camp Upton also had a colorful association with the Nazis themselves, if only by reason of its location. It was adjacent to Camp Siegfried and German Gardens, the home of the Nazi Bund in America. During the Thirties, this area housed the largest compound of Nazis outside of Germany itself. This association of Germans and Americans might seem strange to the uninitiated, but prior to the war, German scientists had participated in invisibility studies with the Americans. It was only natural that the Americans and Germans would reunite after the war.

As this exotic and highly interesting research carried forward, avant garde experiments were conducted which included linking the mind and thoughts of man with radio waves and with early computing devices. All of this experimentation occurred around the same time as and was blended with the infamous MK-ULTRA program, a continuing series of mind-control experiments that included drugs, psychic driving and an assortment of invasive and barbarous methods of abusing human beings. MK-ULTRA centered around Dr. Donald Ewen Cameron. His abusive treatment methods of psychic and mental torture have been well documented and even acknowledged by the Government.

Over the years, funding was cut for these heinous projects and the operators were forced to rely on their old Nazi connections and resources. This took the whole operation from the frying pan and put it into the fire. Further funding came from mysterious sources and is said to have included Nazi gold.

As the thought and mind-control experiments developed, the issues of extra-sensory-perception and psychic abilities came to the forefront. Eventually, in the most dramatic unfoldment of events that might be imagined, the Montauk Project resulted in a painstaking campaign to understand and manipulate the constructs of time itself. The more sensational legends include the creation of vortexes that allowed for actual time travel.

While all of the aforementioned information might seem rather unbelievable to the average mind, the data presented appears as a logical progression of events. We would know none of it, however, if not for Preston Nichols, my coauthor of *The Montauk Project: Experiments in Time*, who came forward and told the truth as he knew it. This was a rather brave act in the early years of his disclosure as their were many factions who harassed him and fought dearly in order that this information would not be released.

If you want to read more details about the Montauk Project, you can read the above book as well as the host of websites that have arisen on the subject. Most of the websites are not very good and will misdirect you. One of the reasons for this is that virtually all of the documentation on the project has been deliberately obliterated by the perpetrators. This leaves the area open to opinions and emotions which, of course, have little to do with facts. Another factor that has undermined the efforts of others to look into the Montauk Project has to do with a factor that is endemic to the human condition. Most people look at the phenomena associated with the Montauk Project either as spectators looking at a train wreck or as victims of the train wreck itself. One has to get beyond the initial ontological shock of the data presented. Instead, one might find it more beneficial to become interested in the railroad tracks, how the train got there, and the railroad company that put it on the tracks in the first place. The Montauk Project is like a gaping wound in humanity. Gawking at the blood rushing out is somewhat understandable, but it is not very productive.

Earlier in this narrative, I alluded to a richer history and deeper significance to Montauk Point than its military history. This, to say the least, is one of the missing ingredients in the aforementioned websites but, like the Montauk Project itself, data on the subject has been virtually obliterated. There is a logical reason for this. The Montauk Project is ultimately tied to the ancient history of the locale. It would therefore make sense that one obfuscation would lead to another.

In this book we are not going to deal with the electronic widgets and exotic antennas of the Montauk Project but the antecedents of the human condition and circumstances that allowed it to take place. According to Chinese medicine, you can heal the body by restoring the energy channels of the body. Unblock the energy and there will no longer be any gaping wound to look at. In this book, we are going to explore the original template upon which the Montauk Project was based. By that, I am referring to the consciousness of that locale itself and how it ties back into ancient antiquity. Further, we will examine how these ties to antiquity predisposed Montauk to be used as a mind-control center as well as a depot to harvest souls and regulate consciousness. In its most exotic aspects, this includes the manipulation of time itself.

Keep in mind that as you read this book, all of the information was discovered through the principle of synchronicity.

THE DREAM — PART I

Submerged beneath the water, I found myself in the clutches of a naked blue lady, the Blue Lady of the Lake who had just pulled me under. Just previously, I had lectured the entire day to an assortment of magical creatures who came from every corner of the world to hear my story, a story which was summated in *The Montauk Book of the Dead.*

Finishing that story, I saw a warm bon fire in the distance. Festivities were starting and I wanted to be a part of them. The Blue Lady, however, had something else in store for me. She clutched me and held me tight. The water was cold, but I could not feel the cold. Her body and the lake were slimy, like primordial slime. In her grip, I could not escape; but I could not even think about escaping. She was directing me in some mysterious way.

Still feeling submerged, I was somewhat helpless. I then heard her voice, but it was not coming through the water. It was her voice, but it was coming into my brain as if she was sending me thoughts.

"Remember!" she exhorted.

Having no idea what she was talking about, I was perplexed. I had just lectured all day to these Celtic people and fairy folk as well as my dead ancestors. What did she want me to remember?

"Remember!" she commanded again. "Focus on the Saracen!"

As I had spoken to the group earlier that day, the two most outstanding characters in the group were the Saracen and the Bard of Bards. The Bard of Bards was the great storyteller who had come to listen and relay my story as he saw fit. Wearing a colorful fool's cap, he was most interesting in his appearance. The Saracen, however, was majestic. His skin was black, but only his face was visible as he wore shining armor. As I focused on the Saracen, the Blue Lady eased her vice-like grip and I began to remember something from my actual life. It was the first time I had ever heard the term *Moor*.

The year was 1964, and I had just seen *The Long Ships*, a movie starring Richard Widmark and Sidney Portier. It was a story about a rogue Viking, played by Widmark, who landed upon the shores of Morocco where he was engaged by the warriors of a Moorish king, played by Portier. I was very familiar with Vikings but had never heard of the Moors. What intrigued me most was that the Moorish warriors were both black and white. There was no distinction. Was this lazy Hollywood casting I wondered? Besides that, I had never heard of or seen movies where black people were portrayed as civilized, particularly with white people living amongst them as apparent equals. And all ruled by a black king! As Hollywood is often careless with facts, I did not know what to think. All I knew was that I found the movie enjoyable.

The next day, my father was home and I told him all about the movie but also had a lot of questions. A fan of history, my father told me that the Moors had the greatest civilization in known history. Crediting them with reviving the ancient knowledge of the Greeks, my father told me that they had developed the sciences which included astronomy, algebra, and chemistry, just to name a few. He also told me that there was no distinction of race or color in their civilization. As I told him about the movie, he said there was at least one point that was wrong. The movie had portrayed the Vikings as superior sailors and the Moors as people who were landlubbers. This was not the case, he said. The Vikings were great sailors, but he said no one surpassed the Moors in this field. They were the greatest sailors in history and could travel around the world. After all, this is why tying up a ship to a dock is referred to as *mooring*.

After that day, and for the rest of his life, my father would infrequently remind me that "the Moors are very important, son. Study the Moors." There was no apparent rhyme or reason to it. It was just something he said every once in a while. Perhaps he did not say it that often. What is important is that I remember him saying it at all. If he only said it two or three times, I remember it as if he said it once a month.

The Blue Lady now seemed pleased. She had successfully jogged my memory. Still under water, she turned me around to face her and gripped me with one hand on my shoulder. I could see her eyes and they were beckoning me to remember once again.

"Remember!" I heard her voice again within my skull. This time, however, I could see her as I heard her commanding voice.

Her lips did not move, but I knew it was her. I could not help but notice her beautiful naked body. In some way, I felt as if she was offering me a reward if I could remember specifically what she wanted. It was clear that this would be a new memory and not the one I had just drudged up beforehand. I had no idea what the reward would be — only that it would be something very good. She then let go of me with her hand, and she began to descend deeper into the water. As she did, her hair extended upward and she looked outrageously beautiful.

"Remember!" I heard the voice again.

It was now the summer of 1972, and I had suddenly and unexpectedly found myself in the land of the Moors. To be more specific, I had just landed at the airport on the outskirts of Casablanca, the largest city in Morocco. I was there to join the crew of the *Apollo,* also known as the mystery ship of Scientology founder L. Ron Hubbard.

I was going to the *Apollo* to learn what I knew to be the most advanced techniques ever discovered for the transformation and exaltation of the human spirit. In my own experience, I had already used these techniques successfully to the point where I had achieved what the Scientologists call a full out-of-body exteriorization. In other words, I could see my body from ten feet over my head. I could also see my friend who was sitting next to me and all the various activity in the room. This was incredible, but it was only the beginning as I was just getting started in Scientology. The best was yet to come, but that is another story.*

Morocco was also another story, but the Moors depicted in *The Long Ships* were very far from my conscious mind. As I rode a bus to the dock where the *Apollo* was moored, I got a good glimpse of daily life in Casablanca. The city was huge and labyrinthine. Wearing American clothes, one stood out like a sore thumb. The women wore veils, but I did not have too much time to think about culture shock. I was on my way to the *Apollo* where everyone spoke English as well as Scientologese, a technical slang that only Scientologists speak and a slang that I had mastered in the last year. I would soon be in familiar surroundings.

Morocco, and later Portugal, were only background props to what the Scientologists were trying to accomplish. In my case, I

* This subject is fully covered in *The Montauk Book of the Dead.*

was focusing on the technical applications of Scientology to better understand the out-of-body state I had already experienced several times. The whole idea was to make it more permanent and help others in the process as well. Only on rare occasions would I have time to contemplate the circumstances and culture of Morocco.

One such time was during an evening voyage from the port of Tangier to Casablanca. Sailing down the coast, I could see many lights emanating from what appeared to be houses. If I were in America, I would assume such lights to be suburban settlements. This country, however, was completely different, and I could not help but wonder who the people were who lived in those houses. What was their day-to-day life like? I knew they were not watching NFL football or the steady diet of television that Americans watch. I wondered if they had any television at all.

When we finally approached Casablanca, I saw one of the most inspiring sights I have ever seen and that is the great mosque that towers above the city with lights shining upon it as if it was the greatest spectacle in the world. I could not help but think that no matter how inspiring their mosque might be, these people probably knew very little, if anything, about exteriorization and certainly did not have techniques for dealing with such phenomena. The Moors and their ancient culture, however, had made a definite impression on my psyche and one that I would never forget.

The Blue Lady of the Lake now smiled at me. It was clear that I had made the connection she wanted me to make. The Moors I saw in Casablanca might not have had the inside track on exteriorization, but there was something special about the Moorish culture that was very important. The people on the shore had very different customs, but inside, they could not be too much different from Americans. They ate, slept, experienced joy, and endured grief. I would eventually learn that these people were far closer to me that I could possibly have realized at the time. Events and circumstances would eventually make that very clear. The most obvious aspect of the Moors, however, is that they represent a gateway. Morocco, by reason of synchronicity alone, was to be my gateway to higher realms.

Having clearly made her point, the Blue Lady disappeared — at least for the time being.

1

A QUANTUM TRAIL

After having been subjected to the data you have just read in the introduction, I essentially ghostwrote *The Montauk Project: Experiments in Time* for Preston Nichols. We are listed as coauthors, but that book is Preston's story, not mine. In the process of writing that book, however, I was exposed to many more details and also some of the players involved in the Montauk scenario.

Knowing there was considerable truth in what could only be considered fragmented stories from Preston, I sought out on my own in an attempt to verify whether or not the Montauk Project did, in some form or another, actually exist. My initial forays in this regard were nothing more than what might be considered an ordinary journalistic approach. The paper trail, however, was virtually destroyed and various people who could have offered clues were unwilling to help. Worse than that, these unwilling people seemed to suffer from an ominous quality suggesting a fear of repercussions that might include death or something yet worse.

What I did find in the way of help primarily came in a different form entirely than what is usually chronicled in mundane journalism. Various psychics and clairvoyants happily offered their assistance. This, in conjunction with my own detective work, developed a saga, legacy, and adventure that has turned out to be either unprecedented or at least remarkable in terms of regular human endeavor. The Montauk Project, after all, was a quantum event and was therefore subject to all of the laws, discovered or not, that apply to the entire field of quantum physics. If you take away the paper trail, there is still going to be a quantum residue and a quantum trail. For the most part, that is what there was to follow.

At this writing, it is now seventeen years since my original forays into this subject so I can speak with the advantage of considerable hindsight. The Montauk Project was a quantum holocaust. As an archetypal representation, it is somewhat akin to the original Fall from Grace except that it is far worse. The Fall from Grace implies a mistake or unwitting departure from a divine state. The Montauk Project and all of its implications suggest a deliberate and premeditated effort to take "fallen" souls and imbibe them with "divine" powers so as to use them in a manipulative and twisted fashion. Such an endeavor seems not only designed to reinforce the Fall from Grace but also to perpetrate the lowest common denominator that can emanate from creation.

It was thus that I found myself investigating a quantum event that, by the very nature of its own description of itself, not only embraced the predicament of God and Man, but surpassed all known limits of historical consciousness. For me, the description was highly theoretical, but I had seen too many people with personal involvement in this so-called Montauk Project. Despite the absurdities involved, there was a haunting thread of logic between the victims of the Montauk Project and the elaborate theories and sensationalized events surrounding it.

Although I did not realize it at the time, there is a peculiarity that occurs around a quantum event. Actually, any event is a quantum event. When I refer to a quantum event, however, I am actually talking about an event where the observer becomes self-aware or self-referential about the quantum nature of the event. One is embracing the concept of Creation and all of the intricate complexities that accompany the quantum mechanics of such. No matter how subtle, a direct connection is being projected into the infinite and all the minions that accompany such. The peculiarity that occurs is that one is projected outside of one's normal reference frame of human consciousness which is, admittedly, quite limited. So, as you read these words and accept what is being said in the spirit with which it is being presented, you are having a quantum sympathy with what I experienced. My experiences, however, were of a most remarkable and non-ordinary nature. If not, I would never have been able to make a career out of it.

In retrospect, attempting to find a "journalistic" or documented truth was something of an oxymoron. I will give you an example. Imagine some cub reporter who wears his pants too high. In other words, he is insensitive as to how others perceive him. Whether through happenstance or hard work, he comes across a document that exposes the truth of the Montauk Project or the Philadelphia Experiment and implicates people in very powerful positions. He comes running into his editor's office and waves it in front of everyone as if he has just discovered the truth behind the JFK assassination. He is not likely to be very well received. Journalism has its place in this investigation, but the people who control the media have their own agenda.

I did not realize it in such verbiage at the time, but in my initial forays into this subject, I was examining and repairing the quantum field surrounding this spiritual holocaust known as the Montauk Project. This would eventually result in documented evidence, but the initial aspects came through mysterious channels.

My first attempt to verify some of Preston's information is a perfect example. It concerns his statement about a mysterious tie-in to a movie entitled *The Philadelphia Experiment*. This was a movie that came out in the early Eighties and was a fictionalized version of the Philadelphia Experiment. It was released in the theaters; but despite considerable popularity, it was pulled from circulation after a very short time. The decision to pull the movie might have been influenced by the Navy who refused to cooperate in the making of the movie.

Eyewitnesses who saw the initial movie in at least one location mentioned that original newsreel footage from the Philadelphia Experiment was shown with the movie. When the movie was withdrawn from circulation so was the newsreel. Despite the withdrawal and the resistance of the U.S. establishment, the movie managed to mysteriously resurfacc as a low-profile video that was released through the sponsorship of E.M.I. Thorn, a British conglomerate. Hailed as the world's largest electronics firm and producer of music, E.M.I. Thorn is the focus of the aforementioned mysterious tie-in mentioned by Preston Nichols. Specifically, Preston said that E.M.I. Thorn was originally owned by the family of Aleister Crowley, an infamous magician who adopted the identity of "The Beast: 666."

By sheer coincidence of circumstances in my own life, I had been perusing through Crowley's works for the last couple of years. As a former Scientologist, I was interested in his work and how it had influenced L. Ron Hubbard. As a result, I was not at all unfamiliar with Aleister Crowley and knew more than a little about this very unusual man.

Preston had made the statement about E.M.I. Thorn and Crowley during a public lecture. During a break in his lecture, I approached Preston privately and asked him for more information about the Crowley connection. He said that the roots of E.M.I. Thorn went back to a company that was owned by a partnership that involved Aleister Crowley's father. His partners were twin brothers who were the first manufacturers of scientific instruments in Great Britain. Their names were Preston and Marcus Wilson and they were known as the Wilson Brothers. Due to various circumstances in his own strange life, Preston believed that he was the reincarnation of Preston Wilson.

Preston's strange association with the Wilsons was reinforced by another man who had been part of the Montauk Project. His name is Alexander Duncan Cameron, known as Duncan to most. He was not only billed as an extraordinary psychic but claimed to have been Marcus Wilson in an earlier life.

These claims were extraordinary if not utterly absurd, but I was more interested in the historical perspective. Did Crowley's father have anything to do with scientific instruments? More importantly, was there any historical mention of the Wilson Brothers? I had never heard of them.

The next day, I tried to find any reference I could on the Wilsons. My best bet was to consult Crowley's *Confessions*, a rather lengthy autobiography. There was no reference to the Wilsons, but I came across something that I found to be rather strange. Crowley's autobiography featured the name "Duncan Cameron." This particular Duncan was a friend of Crowley and wanted to reunite the clans of Scotland.

I soon discovered that this oddity was accompanied by another curiosity that was even stranger. In *Confessions*, Aleister Crowley indicates that his real name was not "Aleister" at all. It was Edward Alexander Crowley. The two names "Edward" and "Alexander" were very significant to those privy to the stories of the Philadelphia Experiment that were being generated by Preston Nichols and his friends.

The name "Alexander" is, of course, the first name of Duncan Cameron, but the name "Edward" is also significant because it is the first name of Edward Cameron, Duncan's brother. Duncan and Edward were another set of brothers known as the "Cameron Brothers" and claimed to be key personnel involved in the actual Philadelphia Experiment. Edward Cameron later became known as Al Bielek who just happened to be in the audience with me on the same evening when I met Preston.

The associations were complicated. There were two sets of brothers. The Cameron brothers were involved in the Philadelphia Experiment and the two Wilson brothers were involved in the company that released the movie about it. The associations run far deeper, but that is not the point of this narrative. Duncan was at the center of both relationships. He had a brotherly association with both Preston and Al. By reason of names, Crowley was also a common denominator in these associations.

Other than the personal stories of the various individuals involved, there was no particular evidence that any of the information presented about the Wilsons or Camerons was accurate or even true. It was, by its very nature, quite mysterious. If it was all a stupid lark, it was not intentionally being played out by the participants at the lecture. They were quite sincere in their convictions. I would later receive verification form Preston's mother, Virginia Nichols. She said that the Wilson Brothers were historical characters as she had known their niece.

If the aforementioned events were all just a remarkable series of coincidences and bizarre stories, it could easily have been dismissed and never brought to mind again. There was only one problem. Different psychic friends of mine also began to mention synchronicities with the name Cameron. One psychic healer, Joy Sackstein, was put in touch with me because the name "Cameron" kept stalking her. It would keep coming through to her, but she had no idea what it meant. Before I could answer her, she said it was accompanied by another name, "Wilson." That was too strange. When I explained the circumstances, she was quite astonished but also relieved. She knew there was meaning in what she had been receiving, but it was up to me to figure it all out.

At this point, I could not let the subject go. More psychic friends came out of the woodwork to assist me. This series of coincidences or synchronicities I had encountered was now gathering considerable momentum. The actual story and blow-by-blow account was eventually put into a book, *Montauk Revisited: Adventures In Synchronicity.* This momentum continued until it reached a climax in May of 1992, the very same month *The Montauk Project: Experiments in Time* was released.

Months before May of 1992, I had seen an ad for a book entitled *Freedom is a Two-Edged Sword.* It was written by Jack Parsons, a known disciple of Aleister Crowley who also happened to be one of the most important scientists in the history of American rocketry. What I found remarkable about the ad, however, was that it said the book was edited by his wife, Cameron. There was no first name for her or anything. Who was she? I had heard about Jack Parsons but never Cameron. As she obviously would have had some sort of connection to Crowley, I wanted to find out what I could. Most importantly, I wanted to know the significance of her name. At that time, I had no idea I was in store for one of the biggest revelations of my life.

Although I had seen the ad with Cameron's name in it many months earlier, I never saw the actual book until May of 1992. Strolling through Weiser's occult book store on 24th Street in New York City (Weiser's is no longer there), I saw the book for the first time and immediately purchased it. The book included a brief biographical sketch on Cameron, and I could see from reading it that she was a senior and could not have too many years left. It became imperative that I meet her, but there was no address listed, only a PO Box for her coeditor, Hymenaeus Beta. He is the head of Ordo Templi Orientis or O.T.O., a mysterious secret society that was once directed by Aleister Crowley himself.

I immediately wrote a letter to Hymenaeus Beta via a PO Box 7666 listed in New York City. As an airport taxi picked me up in my driveway, I literally placed the letter in my home mailbox so that the letter carrier would pick it up later that day. I was flying to California to announce the release of *The Montauk Project* at the American Bookseller's Association annual convention. By a curious set of circumstances, my first steps into the convention center led me to a display of Aleister Crowley books. It was there that I ran into Dr. Alan Miller, a renown occult writer whose pen name is Christopher Hyatt. Asking him if he had ever heard of Cameron, he directed me immediately to the vice-president of Mystic Fire Video. Alan told me that the V.P. knew Cameron.

Staking out the Mystic Fire Video booth, I met the V.P. and shared with him my story of bizarre synchronicities. I also gave him a copy of *The Montauk Project* to read. Quite oddly, the book was already acting as a potent calling card for my synchronicity investigation. He was one of the first to read it. After he did, we had a series of pleasant conversations, and he said he would do what he could to get me a meeting with Cameron. As this man revealed more about himself, I could not help but realize that he was indeed Hymenaeus Beta, the head of the Ordo Templar Orientis or O.T.O. He did not tell me this, but it became obvious to me from other things that he was saying. Admitting his identity, he asked only that I not announce his name. I told him that I had written him a letter, but I had arrived before it did! As a friend of Cameron, he was kind enough to arrange for me to meet her.

When I was given Cameron's phone number, I could not help but notice that the last four numbers were 6606. As I drove to meet her at her home in West Hollywood, I knew that these auspicious numbers were telling me that I was in store for something that would prove to be very significant, but I did not know what.

Spending four hours with Cameron, she was happy to tell me about her illustrious history with Jack Parsons, L. Ron Hubbard and the old days they spent at "The Parsonage," a mansion Parsons owned on Millionaire's Row in Pasadena. When it was my turn to talk, I told her all about the Philadelphia Experiment and Montauk Project, two subjects she had really not heard about. I also shared with her how the Cameron Brothers and Wilson Brothers fit into the scenario. After explaining all of the synchronicities I had experienced, our conversation was essentially over. It was then that I asked her about the names Cameron and Wilson. Despite all of the interesting synchronicities with these names, I had no definitive answer as to why I was encountering them and what it all meant. Looking up at her, I was at a loss and looked for some kind of direction. I asked her if she had any idea why I was here.

"It is interesting that you mention the names 'Cameron' and 'Wilson,'" she said. "My real name is Wilson, but I was raised by my uncle and his last name was Cameron. In the service, they called me by my last name and it stuck."

Although what she said was true, it was too weird to be believable. On top of that, Cameron immediately told me that L. Ron Hubbard father was really a Wilson and had been adopted by the Hubbard family. She had read that it in a book. I later verified her information and found out that what she said was true.

But what did it all mean?

Originally, I had sought out a reference for the Wilson Brothers and found the name "Cameron." As that name began to ostentatiously reveal itself via the psychic airwaves and instances of blind synchronicity, the pursuit ended up with me coming back to the name of Wilson. Drawing on the principles of quantum physics and those who have gone before me, I eventually summed up the key principles of synchronicity in a book entitled *Synchronicity and the Seventh Seal.* That work also gives a behind-the-scenes look at what was really going on with Cameron, Parsons and Hubbard in their most celebrated work, the Babalon Working, a magical working design to incarnate the Goddess Babalon.

It was my magical meeting with Cameron, however, that dictated I write another book (*Montauk Revisited: Adventures in Synchronicity)* and this is what really established my career as an author. My initial success was due to my work with Preston Nichols in packaging and presenting the Montauk story, but subsequent writings might have been sparse or never really gotten off the ground if not for my chance encounter with Cameron. Ever since, synchronicity has been the working principle behind my work.

Cameron would later tell me that synchronicity is the language of magick and that my life was laced with it. It was only after she passed away, however, that I would experience the most remarkable of all the synchronicities I have experienced. Amazing as it is, it has never made its way into print until now. I have waited a very long time to announce it. There are various reasons for this and they will be revealed as you read the book. They all have to do with synchronicity. To bring you up to date, I will now continue from my meeting with Cameron and take you through the series of events which led to what I consider to be my greatest or most significant synchronicity ever.

2

LEGACY OF THE PYRAMIDS

As I have alluded to already, the trail of synchronicity you have just read in Chapter One was written up and put into book form under the title *Montauk Revisited: Adventures in Synchronicity*. The final manuscript included far more details and many more tangents than what I have offered here.

Although the manuscript was quite complete and ready for the printer, I had pangs of hesitation and misgiving over one particular point. I was not satisfied with the definition I had come up with for the word *Montauk*. I knew that the word *Montauk* was commonly thought to refer to the top of a mountain or mean "high view," but my intuition told me that there might be some deeper significance in the term. Going to the library to look up the definition, I was in for a much bigger surprise than I ever expected.

Looking through a small shelf reserved for the history of Long Island, I noticed a rather thick book entitled *Historic Long Island* by Rufus Rockwell Wilson. There was the name Wilson again! I immediately picked up the book and leafed through it. Before long, I came to an astonishing picture in the back. It showed three pyramids of rough construction (see page 33) that were captioned "The Pyramids — Montauk." There was not only nothing else in the caption but nothing in the book either. It was presented as a picture of a geographic site but without any comment or explanation whatsoever. To me, it was a pure mystery.

Seeking further information, I sought out a librarian. Although I had no idea at the time, this librarian had a definite psychic strain in her and had long assisted a Long Island radio host who featured psychic phenomena on his program. She took me to a reference room that was normally off-limits to the public. There, I pored over data which told me some very remarkable and significant points about Montauk. First, the land where Montauk's Camp Hero sits is sacred ground to the Montauk Indians. Further, the Montauks were considered to be the royal tribe of Long Island and their leaders were known as Pharoahs, usually spelled *Pharoah* as opposed to the more conventional *Pharaoh.*

I also learned that the Montauk Indians had been declared extinct by Justice Abel Blackmar in 1910. This, perhaps ironically, is just one year before the photograph of the Montauk pyramids appeared in *Historic Long Island.*

All of the above was too much for me to digest all at once, and I decided not to include it in *Montauk Revisited.* It would create too many questions. Instead, I realized I would have to conduct an entire investigation just to understand what it all meant. A detailed account of this was included in the book *Pyramids of Montauk: An Exploration in Consciousness* which includes contributions by Preston Nichols. The only comment I have to say about that book at this point is that it revealed that there were many synchroncities between the land at Camp Hero and the number 666.

The original land deed between white settlers and Montauk Chief Wyandanch was on August 6, 1660. When the Indians disputed this deed, somewhat successfully, a new deed was made up on February 6, 1661. Further, when I went to the county hall of records to look up the actual deed for the Camp Hero property, I had a bizarre experience. At that time, I was driving a 1987 black Ford Mustang. As I parked in the county parking lot, I saw the exact same model, year and color of my Mustang. It was opposite me but just one space over. A lady had pulled up at virtually the same time as myself. I could not help but notice that her license plate featured the numbers 666. It was too much. Since *Pyramids of Montauk* was written, an attorney following the case wrote to me and pointed out that the docket numbers, pages and case numbers of the Montauks' extinction case are replete with 666 references. It seems too odd to be believed, but it is true.

This 666 connection was symbolic of Aleister Crowley rearing his head once again. Crowley had often proclaimed himself as

THE PYRAMIDS — MONTAUK

the Antichrist and the Beast of Revelation. He often signed his name as "666." Not only were he and his 666 theme tied into the psychology of the Wilsons and Camerons, they were also woven deeply into the issues surrounding the sacred ground of the Montauk Indians.

The numerals 666 are most often identified with the Beast of Revelation, but they are also symbolic of the fact that we live in a carbon-based universe. An atom of carbon features six protons, six neutrons and six electrons. In other words, this universe we live in is coded in 666 by the very nature of what it is.

When we consider the synchronicity with 666 and the various land deeds of the Montauk Indians, it simply tells us that a spiritual reference frame has been coagulated into a fixed and (relatively) unalterable condition. If the sacred aspect or grid-point of Montauk is meant to represent a vortex of creation, it has been stunted and redirected into something on the order of a commercial pay toilet. The current citizens of Montauk represent the patrons of this pay toilet. While this idea is somewhat funny, it is typical of what happens when sacred ground is transmuted into a lower form.

My discovery of the Montauk pyramids, the Pharoah family and the plight of the royal lineage of the Montauk tribe was intriguing and definitely a part of the trail I had blazed with *Montauk Revisited*, but as I said, it was too much to include in that work. It would take me at least a year to collect what information I could find and get a good grasp on what it all meant. Only then was I able to release it in *Pyramids of Montauk: Explorations in Consciousness*, the third book in the Montauk series.

Writing *Pyramids of Montauk* was not easy. While it was interesting to learn about the heritage of these ancient people, I was also empathizing with them and taking on the burden of their having been falsely declared extinct. The synchronicity of the situation was now a burden. I was being forced to look into and understand things that were not only hidden from history but were far beyond the bounds of ordinary human comprehension.

3

INVOKING CHANGE

Hindsight is a wonderful thing, particularly when you have the comfort of looking back at a situation that arguably might have killed you. In the early years of the Montauk investigation, it was as if the world was coming to my door. All sorts of people would write and say hello. With the unveiling of the Montauk pyramids, the interest in my work peaked. People came out of the woodwork to offer advice and clues. Most of this, but not all, was well-intended. The majority of it, however, was quite useless.

Besides the normal human interest, there was spiritual phenomena attached to what I was doing as well. Spirits were also coming out of the woodwork and made different impressions or auditions to try and gain my attention. Far more so than myself, others were making a big deal of my work and what was being uncovered. *The Montauk Project* had already captured considerable attention. With the discovery of the pyramids and the Pharoahs, it was as if the underlying sacred spot was waking up and people got all excited about it.

As was detailed in *Synchronicity and the Seventh Seal*, I suffered an automobile accident at the same time I was penetrating the major secrets of Aleister Crowley's *The Book of the Law*. The accident occurred while I was stopped at a stoplight and rammed by a car that could not stop due to faulty brakes. This was quite odd because my other car was in the shop at that very moment to repair faulty brakes. The strangest part of the incident, however, was that the driver was the son of my former mechanic.

While there is some dispute about my knowledge of the secrets of *The Book of the Law*, there is no question that I was opening a door. *The Book of the Law* refers to "the key of it all." In my particular case, I had the key in the door and the door was partly opened but not all the way. All sorts of things were flitting through the doorway.

All of this occurred before *Pyramids* was even finished. After completing my first rough draft of the manuscript, I forwarded it to Madame X. She helped me with *Montauk Revisited*, and we had a close relationship. When she read the manuscript, however, she was furious. In all the time I have known her, I never experienced her getting angry at me like that. Her frustration was not about the sloppy state of the manuscript but was about the fact that I had not pursued a major clue. I had no idea what she was talking about or why she was so upset.

"You did not look up all the references to Menthu," she said.

I knew who Menthu was, but I had no idea what she was referring to specifically. Menthu or Monthu is the Egyptian god of war and is roughly equivalent to Mars or Ares. Menthu is particularly important with regard to the 666 correspondences to Montauk and Aleister Crowley. When Crowley and his wife, Rose Kelly, were visiting Cairo, Rose spontaneously and surprisingly became a transmedium for a short while and told him he had offended Horus. She then dragged Crowley to the Boulak Museum and took him to display number 666 which was a Stele of Ankh-of-na-Khonsu (another name for the Priest of Menthu).

This encounter with the stele became the pivotal moment in Crowley's life and would change it forever. It was the catalyst that facilitated him writing *The Book of the Law* and is referred to by Crowley as the Stele of Revealing.

My problem with Madame X's admonishment was that I had no recollection whatsoever of her ever having referred me to any references on Menthu. I had looked up everything I could possibly find at the library and the information was pretty sparse. Most of what I had came from Crowley himself.

I could not believe how upset she was and had no idea why she was upset. It made no sense to me, but she was exasperated. I politely asked her to explain what she was talking about. She then referred me to Madame Blavatsky's *Isis Unveiled*.

This was a surprise to me because I do not recall her telling me any such thing. I soon called my proofreader, Margo Geiger, and asked if I could pay her a visit. She was born into Theosophy and thought Madame Blavatsky was a saint. I knew Margo would have a copy of *Isis Unveiled* and I was soon in her house on a cold December day. There was only one reference to Menthu in the entire book and it referred to the sarcophagus of Queen Menthu-hotep. This was obviously the feminine vibration of Menthu.

The import of the passage referred only to what was written on the sarcophagus of Queen Menthu-hotep. The hieroglyphics were translated into the following expression by Blavatsky:

PTR RF SU

This made no sense at first glance, but Blavatsky's translation proved insightful and helpful. The message can easily be interpreted as "Peter refer to source" as follows:

PTR = Peter
RF = refer or "refer to"
SU = source

That my name is Peter made this a very personal and forceful message sent by spirit. Blavatsky's definition did not refer to me, but with the way the experience went down, it was as if I was being personally socked. With hindsight, I now recognize that Madame X was not even thinking with her linear mind when she got upset. She has a very active third eye and spirit was speaking through her.

Blavatsky's interpretation of "PTR" is the essential part of this entire message on the sarcophagus of Queen Menthu-hotep. In *Isis Unveiled*, Blavatsky explains that the name *Peter*, as witnessed by the Greek word *petros*, is commonly thought to mean "rock." This is not quite correct, she says. In days gone by, particularly in esoteric circles, the term *peter* meant "interpreter." There was no doubt about it. This, she said, is the exact reason why the name *Peter* was chosen for Simon, the favorite disciple of Christ. When Jesus builds his church on "Peter," he is building it upon that man's interpretation which is the foundation sometimes referred to as a "rock."

The Simon Peter connection was not such a big deal in this particular equation. Blavatsky spoke of a long tradition behind the so-called "peter" or interpreter. To the ancients, a peter was a disciple of an unseen oracle. Whether the oracle was behind a curtain, a mask, or some other device depended upon the time period and imagination of the players involved. An oracle would typically have twelve disciples who studied the oracle's teachings. After a considerable amount of time studying with the oracle, an adept would be chosen from amongst them. He was not only allowed to see the oracle but interpreted what the oracle had to say into the language of the student initiates. This is the tradition that led to the naming of St. Peter.

This was all very interesting to my intellect, but I did not take to this experience very kindly. To say the least, I was pissed off in a way you will seldom ever see me. It was exceedingly clear to me that some spirit was raging to get my attention, and it was coming through my friend Madame X. She was probably closer to me than anyone else at that point in my life.

As I sat in Margo's cold living room, I was in a state of ontological shock. To me, this was all very clear. In as much as Blavatsky's writings were not personal to me, the entire experience <u>was</u> meant to be personal. It was telling me that I was to be the chosen interpreter for a certain oracle. The most obvious "oracle" would be Madame X herself, but that is not quite an accurate assessment of the situation. With a very open third eye and a vast amount of knowledge, she could play the role of an oracle very well, but there was another spirit coming through her. To this day — at least when I last asked her — Madame X has no appreciable memory of this incident.

My problem with the situation was that I very much resented being put in such a position. I was not going to serve an oracle. While some people might think I was refusing a greater calling, I will be quick to add that making yourself subservient is not a hallmark of great wisdom or even common sense. So much of New Age propaganda and religion is based upon giving your power or your sight to another outside source. People associate it with glamour, but there is much stupidity in this practice.

Prior to this time, I was well aware that I had been accumulating a reputation on the astral plane of being "tough to deal with."

Spirits would come to me and receive the equivalent of a beating because they could not impinge upon my consciousness. There was a good reason, however, for my actions with these spirits. These characters play by funny rules and I was calling them on their behavior. When any spirit comes into my consciousness and grabs my attention, I have polite but firm words for them. The words are more firm than they are polite. I tell them to be fully conscientious with regard to their behavior when it comes to the subjects of considerate communication and being responsive to normal human emotions. Almost unanimously, their response is to scram and leave me alone.

Sometimes these beings are operating fifty-fifty as far as being negative or positive. They can even be ninety percent good. The problem you are going to have with them is the unknown or negative ten percent. They can even make you rich, bring you good luck in love or whatever. These things come with a trade-off however. These gifts are tricks by which such spirits can take over an individual. Spiritual empires have been built upon the back of such spirits, and their empires are not so positive.

In the matter of my adventures with Madame X, I had come to the sudden and unhappy realization that I was being worked. As I already said, it was ontological shock. Margo sent me to an empty bedroom she had where I slept it off and woke up to a new reality. It was important to tell these spirits that I was in charge and was not playing their game. I did not actually have to "tell" them anything. My own realization and determination were enough. In retrospect, a whole flock of spirits had been dogging me, and I was now unbinding myself from them. Good riddance!

This did not solve my immediate problem because I still had loose ends to tie up with regard to the manuscript for *Pyramids of Montauk*. From Margo's house, I shifted directions and went to see another friend named Kenn Arthur. Over the last six months of writing, researching and editing, I had hardly left my house save for my associations with Kenn and Madame X.

Kenn is an intriguing and charismatic character but can also be quite problematic, at least to some. For the most part, he has been helpful to me but he has excited controversy and enmity in others. To be fair, he would tell you that he is a gate-keeper and I would wholeheartedly agree. He has many gifts with regard to psychic sensitivity. Leaving Margo's house, I went and saw Kenn. He told me that what had happened with me and Madame X was a sign of growth on my part. We then watched a replay of a forty-eight-year-old George Foreman winning the heavyweight title for the second time. It took my mind completely off of metaphysics for the rest of the evening. None of this ruined my relationship with Madame X. She would later help me with *The Black Sun*, but my shift of direction and association with Kenn would be the major catalyst that would make the current book you are reading a reality.

If I have sounded quite hard about rejecting the call to be the interpreter of an oracle, I did not reject the lesson totally. For better or worse, spirit had spoken to me through Madame X and left me with a burning reality with regard to the name of Peter Moon.

The sarcophagus of Queen Menthu-hotep was saying, "Peter refer to source." It was also clear that the Stele of Ankh-of-na-Khonsu had a very specific meaning. "Khonsu" means "moon" and ankh refers to the "everlasting life of the moon." This, of course, refers to the feminine energy. There are other etymological correspondences which run very deep. *Moon* stems from *men* which refers to the menses. *Men*, like the word *peter*, also can mean "stone."

In essence, this experience was an outside source telling me that "Peter Moon" means "interpreter of the feminine energy." I did not reject this, but I did not jump up and down and announce it either. It has taken me a dozen years to even put it down in writing. It does, however, explain why I was jettisoned on a course that would lead me to Marjorie Cameron and her identification with the goddess Babalon. In seeking out the truth and pursuing the quantum phenomena behind the Montauk Project, I was being led to the feminine.

I did not immediately pursue this feminine angle as such. What is important is that I had stood up and told the spiritual cobwebs around me to go to hell. Although I was not thinking about it at all, I had welcomed Kenn into my life in a way that would pay a most remarkable dividend.

4

THE JINN FACTOR

Kenn Arthur came into my life on the very same day I met Preston Nichols, Duncan Cameron and Al Bielek. He was part of the same panel of speakers. Besides being very funny, Kenn was a knowledgable and charismatic speaker.

Upon meeting Kenn for the first time, my intuition was piqued immediately. I could not help but sense that he had been in the Navy. Asking him, he admitted that it was true.

As it turned out, my first meeting at the Long Island Chapter of the U.S. Psychotronics Association was Kenn's last. Some of this, but certainly not all of it, had to do with psychodrama going on behind the scenes that was centered on the secretary of the association. She was a magnet for any type of male energy and was involved with multiple men. The first time she looked at me, I felt as if a vacuum had just sucked up my aura. Needless to say, psychotronics was a group of very strange bedfellows. This woman was just one example of how a person's mind, or at least one aspect of it, might be amplified via psychotronics.

In *Montauk Revisited*, I referred to this woman as Jewel. I was never involved with her, but she was the gate-keeper to Preston's Space-Time Labs, and I needed to deal with her to visit Preston. As it turned out, she was also the gate-keeper to a group of Kenn's. As this group was full, Kenn was not allowing anyone new to attend due to no seating capacity. When I informed him Jewel would not be attending one evening, I suggested I could take her seat. Impressed by the fact that I knew Jewel, he allowed me to come.

Attending this group was how I got to know Kenn and was the beginning of many adventures with him.

Kenn and I had a bit of a problem dealing with each other because I was just entering the psychotronics group and he was leaving. He not only wanted to keep his distance from Preston but was overly negative about the whole Montauk scenario and would go to great lengths to deny its existence or take pot shots at Preston. His denials spoke volumes in themselves. The more he would engage in elaborated denials, the more I became convinced there was more to the Montauk story.

Other than a brief overview, my involvement with Kenn is far too complex and involved to go into in this book. Suffice it to say that he is both a very controversial figure and a very gifted sensitive as well. What is most important is that he is a conduit between the world of spirit and the ordinary world. Watching him speak once, I could see aethyric wisps of white energy emitting from his mouth. After witnessing this, and without saying a word to him about it, he once showed me photographs taken of him where this type of aethyric phenomena would show up. This, however, is just the tip of the iceberg with Kenn.

While the above might make him sound like an utterly fascinating person, it is important to realize that he is controversial, particularly with females. Women often get upset with him when he wakes up their kundalini energy. They usually start out very happy as if they have found a great teacher, but then the worm turns. Whether it is their fault or his, I am not here to be judgmental but just to say that he is controversial and interesting. To give you an example, I recall a dream he had shared with me once. In the dream, he was surprised to find himself having rather explicit and intense sex with a woman he knew only casually. This was not something he willed. It just happened in the dream state. When he next saw the woman, she gave him a dirty look and acted as if she had been raped. This is the sort of nonsense that has surrounded him at times. It was not a pleasant experience for either one of them. Some women have blamed him for their problems.

Do not think for a minute that Kenn is bad. He has helped me considerably with a couple of situations where people were being very abusive to others behind my back. With his psychic sensitivity, he alerted me to severe physical abuse that was taking place against a young child. I was then able to pull strings and put a stop to it immediately.

His favors to me were perhaps a payback. In my early years of knowing him, Kenn went to the hospital with a heart condition and claimed he wanted to die. I jokingly refer to this as the Larry Talbot syndrome. Larry Talbot was the character who turned into a werewolf in the movie *The Wolfman*. Talbot suffered perpetual anxiety over being a werewolf and wished to die in the hopes that it would relieve him of his horrible fate. Kenn's desire to leave this world was countermanded by myself when I sent a healer to the hospital. When he later told me this healer was instrumental in his recovery, I told him I was the one who sent the healer.

"So, you're the one!" he said accusatively as if he would have preferred death.

One should never get too enthusiastic about saving a life. It is, of course, the humane thing to do, but one should realize that one is also contributing to the continuance of that life energy and everything that comes with it. In this case, I do not regret contributing to his recovery nor do I think it was a bad things to do, but one should not get overly enthusiastic about such matters. In this case, Kenn has repaid me. Providing the impetus for this book is just one of the repayments.

As Kenn continued to decry the Montauk Project, I would bring up certain aspects of the situation that were irrefutable. As I did, Kenn knew people who either were involved or claimed to have been involved. Keep in mind that all of this was before the publication of *The Montauk Project* which has since facilitated various claims by many people who were seeking attention.

Most of Kenn's disparagement of the Montauk scenario centered on Preston's version of events. Personally, I never contended that Preston's stories were absolutely accurate but neither did Preston. When I asked Kenn how he was so sure that Preston was wrong, he revealed to me that he was once a staff officer for an admiral in the Navy. In that role, he used to buy equipment from the Montauk underground! His claim to have inside information on what Montauk was really all about was highlighted by his revelation that he was a cog in acquiring equipment from Camp Hero. This, however, was in the Sixties and prior to the events described in *The Montauk Project*.

Over the years, Kenn admitted to me that he had an uncle who was a rum runner at Montauk. Some of the tunnels at Montauk were used for rum running during Prohibition. It further came out that this uncle was sexually abusive to Kenn. Although this all occurred way before Preston's version of the Montauk Project, it amounts to the same type of phenomena. This sexual abuse, as was often the case at Montauk (and elsewhere), resulted in Kenn opening up to extreme psychic sensitivity. To this day, Kenn has never been able to fully forgive his mother as she never perceived the situation or protected him from what was going on. This is why Kenn was so sensitive to the aforementioned situation of abuse that I referred to. He helped me stop the abuse. With regard to the overall picture, however, it suggests that Montauk might have been a source of sexual abuse well before Preston's version of the Montauk Project surfaced.

Kenn had also told me about the Nazi connection to the Montauk Project as well. His family knew a German in Queens who had carried Nazi gold ashore at Montauk and bartered it with the Americans for a new identity and a safe haven in America. He explained that collusion between the Nazis and Americans was common at Montauk.

If Kenn is a controversial figure, it is because he is tangentially connected to the spirit world. This has different effects on different people, all depending on who they are and the circumstances of the situation. Raising the kundalini energy of people can have its drawbacks, particularly if the person on the receiving end is not adequately cared for or properly nurtured during the experience. Personally, I have always looked at Kenn as either a jinn or an agent of the jinn. I am sure he would not disagree with that in the least.

If you study the books I have written, it is quite apparent that many of the characters I meet are representative of the jinn. They come into my life, reveal stunning or revelatory information, hang around for a while and then recede to the background. Like the jinn, they are not fully developed or realized as spiritual beings. They do, however, offer keys to those attempting to realize their full potential. In this particular case, Kenn was the jinn who opened up the bottle.

5

THE MYSTERY APPEARS

As was said previously, it was my adventures with Madame X that had led me to come to Kenn for help with *Pyramids of Montauk*. Finishing that book provided a great deal of relief for me. After all, the research was unfamiliar, complex and exhausting. I put it all on a silver platter for the reader, but it was not given to me that way. I was glad to be done with it and free from the preoccupation. My next plan was to write *Encounter in the Pleiades* which was comparatively easy for me as a writer because all I had to do was transcribe and edit the dictation of Preston Nichols. It was fun to write.

Assuming a freer and less restrictive schedule, I soon found myself in the house of my friend Lorry Salluzzi. Kenn came as he was going to be lecturing there that evening. Coming in the door, he handed me a package. It was a gift. This was an uncommon and surprising occurrence because Kenn was certainly never in the habit of buying me gifts nor was I scheduled to be at Lorry's house that night. I asked him why he bought it.

"It had your signature all over it," he replied. By this statement, he was referring to the fact that he could psychically sense that it was very important for me to have it.

Taking it out of the package, I saw that it was a very old newspaper clipping encased in glass and surrounded by an antique frame. Looking closer, I saw that the clipping featured a headline that read "The New Montauk Theatre." It was a playbill from the Ziegfeld Follies of 1909.

THE

NEW MONTAUK THEATRE

THE LIVINGSTON CO. .... Lessees.
WILLIAM H. REYNOLDS .... President.
EDWARD TRAIL .... General Manager

WEEK BEGINNING MONDAY EVENING, NOVEMBER 15, 1909.
Matinees Wednesday and Saturday.

F. ZIEGFELD, JR.'S REVUE

FOLLIES OF 1909

In Two Acts and Seventeen Scenes.
Words and Lyrics by Harry B. Smith. Music by Maurice Levi.
Ensemble Numbers Produced by Julian Mitchell.
Principals Directed by Herbert Gresham.

SPECIAL ENGAGEMENT.

EVA TANGUAY

ACT I.

1 COURT OF VENUS. (Painted by Lee Lash Studios.)
Introducing:
Venus .... Annabelle Whitford
Psyche, F. DuBarry; Cupid, Elsie Mertens; Adonis, S. Martinez; Mercury, E. Scott; Apollo, Helen Gordon.
Venus' Attendants—Misses H. DuBarry, Paulin, Webb, DeBeers, Williams, Stewart, St. John, Lee, Anderson, Walsh, Evelyn.
Monte Van Swagger .... William Bonelli
Broadway Lights—Misses Maxwell, V. Gordon, Carleton, Thornton, Pendleton, Cadiz.
Miss Manhattan .... Josephine Whittel

2 LOBBY OF METROPOLITAN OPERA HOUSE.
(Painted by Lee Lash Studios.)
Introducing:
Oscar Hammerstein, Gotta Cazzaza, Herr Dimple, Mlle. Farrar, Mmes. Eames, Sembrich, Mons. Caruso, Scotti, Toscannetti, Hurts, Belasco, Frohman, Klaw and Fiske.
Tetrazzini .... Arth[illegible] Deagon

MUSIC PROGRAM.
FREDERICK SOLOMON, Musical Director.

ACT I.

[illegible]ng Chorus.
Ma[illegible]m Venus" .... Miss Whitford and Chorus
3 "Linger, Longer, Lingerie" .... Miss Josephine Whittell and Chorus
4 "Tetrazzini" .... Mr. Deagon and Chorus
5 "Dance de Maitre de Ballet" .... Bessie Clayton
6 "Mad Opera Grand" .... Eva Tanguay
7 "I Wish I Was a Boy and I Wish I Was a Girl" .. Eva Tanguay, Bessie Clayton
8 Spanish Rag Song and Dance, "Play that Fandango Rag" .... Specialty
9 "Come On, Play Ball With Me, Dearie" (by Gus Edwards) ...... Eva Tanguay
0 Finale .... Principals and Chorus

ACT II.

1 Song Hits of Bygone Days .... Principals and Chorus
2 "The Dance of the Widow," Mexatexa (by Lewis F. Muir) .... Bessie Clayton
3 "And the World Keeps Rolling On" .... Mr. Philbrick
4 "The Bathing Girls" .... Miss Whitford and Ten Bathing Girls

6 Cubanola Glide ....Philbrick, Green, Moyer and Entire Chorus
7 Eva Tanguay Specialty ....Eva Tanguay
8 "The Greatest Navy in the World." ....Eva Tanguay

ACT II.

1 **SIEGEL COOPER COMPANY'S STORE, MUSICAL DEPARTMENT.**
(Painted by John Young.)
Some of the Popular Song Hits of 1909..............Principals and Chorus

2 **NEW YORK THEATRE.** (Painted by John Young.)
"The Dance of the Widow," Mexatexa (by Lewis F. Muir)....Bessie Clayton

3 **THE BATHING GIRLS.** (Painted by John Young.)
Introducing:
Miss Annabelle Whitford as a Brinkley Bathing Girl; Miss H. Gordon as a Kellermann Bathing Girl; Miss Anderson as the Gibson Bathing Girl; and the Misses E. Scott, Maxwell, F. and H. DuBarry, DeBeers, Webb, Stewart, Mertens, Thornton, Pendleton.

4 **THE NORTH POLE.** (Painted by John Young.)
"And the World Keeps Rolling On" .... Mr. Philbrick

3 **HAMMERSTEIN'S OFFICE, MANHATTAN OPERA HOUSE.**
(Painted by Lee Lash Studios.)
Introducing:
Will Philbrick as Oscar Hammerstein, inventor, composer, musical directo Ed. Smart as O. Hammerstein; Charles Scribner as Mr. Hammerstein; Rober Burns as Oscar; A. Froom as Oscar H., and Sig. Mealy as H. O.
Maitre de Ballet...Bessie Clayton
Vaudeville Star .... Eva Tanguay
The Dance of the Parisian Twist....William C. Schrode and Evelyn Carleton

4 **A WHEAT FIELD.** (Painted by John Young.)
Introducing:
The Scarecrow .... Helen McMahon
Sal .... Vera Maxwell
Reuben, "The Original Drunk" ....Billie Reeves

5 **MILLIONAIRES' WARD, TOMBS PRISON.** (Painted by Lee Lash Studios.)
Introducing:
A. Froom as General Bingham; L. Woodward as Hon. Little Tim; W. Johnson as Commissioner Baker; Arthur Hill as C. Muhphy, the Tammany Tiger; and Four Prison Matronesses, Misses Green, Moyer, Maxwell and Cadiz.
Four Millionaire Prisoners—Will Philbrick, Arthur Deagon, Charles Scribner and Charles Hessong.

6 **THE CHILDREN'S NURSERY.** (Painted by John Young.)
Introducing:
Miss Eva Tanguay and Miss Bessie Clayton in "I Wish I Was a Boy, and I Wish I Was a Girl."

7 **IN SUNNY SPAIN.** (Painted by John Young.)
Spanish Rag Song and Dance "Play that Fandango Rag" (by Goetz and Muir) based on Fiaco's Original Spanish Dance—Misses H. Gordon, Mertens. E, Scott, Thornton, Cadiz and Carleton. Spanish Girls—Misses Green, Maxwell, G. Moyer, Pendleton, E. Scott, V. Gordon, Evelyn.

8 **BURLESQUE ON HYPNOTISM.**
Introducing:
The Great Pearline .... William Bonelli
And Volunteers from the Audience.

9 **NEW YORK POLO GROUNDS.** (Painted by John Young.)
Introducing:
Messrs. Welch, Mealy, Montrose and Deagon, in a skit on Baseball. Song—"Come On, Play Ball With Me, Dearie" (by Gus Edwards) Eva Tanguay, Company and Audience.

AFRICAN JUNGLE. (Painted by John Young.)
Introducing:
The Jungle Queen, Eva Tanguay, in "Moving Day in Jungle Tow..." assisted by Lions: Joseph Schrode, John Schrode; Tigers—Arthur Hill, Robert Burns; Ape—E. Montrose; Ostrich—C. Woodward; Elephants—Charles Abbott and W. Hessong; Giraffe—J. Bosworth; T. R., a Mighty Hunter; Tom "Scream" Welsh; Kismet, Thomas Johnson.

6 **TANGUAY HITS** .... Eva Tanguay

7 **THRONE ROOM, EMPEROR'S PALACE.**
(Painted by Hugo Baruch & Co., Berlin.)
Introducing:
William Bonelli as Kaiser Wilhelm; T. Welsh as Colonel Theodore Roosevelt, and Arthur Deagon as President Taft.

8 **THE GREATEST NAVY IN THE WORLD.**
(Representing every State in the Union.)
Introducing:
...ia .... Annabelle Whitford
...**ON ROADS.** (Illuminated Fleet at Night.)

"What did you pay for it?" I asked him. "About four or five dollars?"

"That's about right," he replied.

Kenn is very fond of antiques and used to deal in them. It was apparent to me that he ran across this in some sort of antique display and acquired it.

Scrutinizing it further, I could see that the playbill was nothing more than a run-of-the-mill description of different acts of the Ziegfeld Follies. There was nothing out of the ordinary with regard to their content. Only the word *Montauk* stood out. The Ziegfeld Follies were appearing at The New Montauk Theatre.

Please keep in mind that this playbill came to me at a time when the Montauk Project itself possessed a very thick residue in the so-called psychic airwaves. *Montauk Revisited* and *Pyramids of Montauk* had penetrated this thick atmosphere of secrecy but everyone, including myself, wanted more answers. The sudden and apparently spontaneous appearance of this playbill was certainly in keeping with the tradition of mysterious clues that had been placed upon my path ever since I got involved with investigating the Montauk Project. Kenn, who was intimately aware of and at least psychically involved in the Montauk scenario, was a perfect candidate to offer such a clue.

Although I did not realize it at the time, Kenn had handed me a gift that was replete with clues that would not only explain many mysteries about Montauk but would open the door to many more intriguing questions. Whatever anyone might wish to say about Kenn, good or bad, he was most definitely living up to his billing as a jinn or genie in a bottle. In this case, the playbill was the bottle, but I was barely scratching at the surface of it at this point.

When I saw the words "Montauk Theatre" on the playbill, I assumed that this must have referred to the old theater that had once existed at Montauk. A cursory investigation of the old theater at Montauk did not provide anything circumstantial. All I was able to glean or focus on was the last skit listed on the playbill which featured three prominent politicians of that time period: Chief Justice William Howard Taft, ex-President Teddy Roosevelt, and Kaiser Wilhelm of Germany.

Kaiser Wilhelm was of extreme interest to me for two reasons. First, he is known to have built extensive tunnels at

Montauk. This was part of a territorial expansion program for Germany which included vast construction projects, mostly hidden, throughout the Western Hemisphere. The Kaiser's Montauk activity was a stealth program for the most part and included the construction of subterranean tunnels which have been dubbed as "catacombs."

Theodore Roosevelt also had a strong connection to Montauk. After the Spanish-American War, he brought his Rough Riders to Montauk Point where they were quarantined and allowed to recuperate from the tropical diseases they had been exposed to in Cuba. Buildings used by the Rough Riders still exist to this day at Montauk's Theodore Roosevelt County Park, all of which is sacred land to the Montauk Indians and currently houses an extremely modest Pharoah Museum. It is very close to Camp Hero and just behind Third House.

Seeing these two prominent politicians listed in the same skit encouraged me to look for a connection between Roosevelt and the Kaiser. I found out that the newspapers of that time period used to make fun of them in their cartoon strips. The two were humorously referred to and depicted as cousins because they were both from the same aristocratic Dutch line. One could easily assume that there was some sort of political collusion between the two.

After studying quite a bit about Theodore Roosevelt, I found out that he was friends with a Cameron family. Independent of my research, it later came out that Duncan's father used to play at Teddy Roosevelt's estate when he was a youngster.

My studies revealed that Teddy Roosevelt was a staunch imperialist who was interested in creating reasons for the Spanish-American War. Without any judgment as to whether this was war a good or bad idea, it was definitely aggressive imperialism on his part. The sinking of the battleship *Maine* off the Cuban coast was a complete fabrication designed to create an ostensible reason to have a war with Spain so that the United States could seize key territories which included Guam, the Philippines, and the area now known as Panama.

Although there was much more available information on Roosevelt than on Kaiser Wilhelm, neither trail came up with enough prospects that were worthwhile of further pursuit. Any links I came across with regard to Montauk and world politics were too obtuse for my liking. Had I pursued them, I felt as if I would have been forcing the issue as opposed to being an objective observer. Accordingly, I abandoned this line of research entirely and concentrated only on writing *Encounter in the Pleiades.* The playbill was thus relegated to being only a minor curiosity to me. I laid it to rest on my desk where papers would accumulate and eventually cover it entirely. It would sit there for over a year.

6

THE MYSTERY ESCALATES

I might have forgotten all about the mysterious Montauk playbill if it were not for a visit to my house from an Englishman named Howard Barkway. Howard passed away a few years ago, but he was a special person in my life and also has a very interesting history with regard to the Montauk Project.

Well before I had ever met Preston or Duncan, Howard was interested in publishing the Montauk Project story. While travelling with a woman by the name of Nancy Oliphant, he learned about the Montauk Project. Nancy had a special connection with Duncan and ended up associating with Howard through happenstance. Although keenly interested in the Montauk story, Howard lived in England and it was not really viable for him to facilitate the cross-continental work it would take to get a book completed. By the time I came along, Howard enthusiastically embraced my participation because he was more interested in getting the story out than he was in making a business deal out of it.

Howard originally visited me in 1993, and he quickly became the first foreign distributor for Sky Books. Howard was not only the first distributor in the U.K., he was literally the first fan of *The Montauk Project* in that country. When he read *Montauk Revisited: Adventures in Synchronicity* and learned about the Wilson Brothers, Howard diligently looked for information on the Wilsons in English electronic journals but came up empty handed.

Although Howard came up with nothing on the Wilsons, he had some very interesting and bizarre news to share when he visited me for the second time. His mother had been the long time secretary of Sir Jules Thorn, the founder of the Thorn side of E.M.I. Thorn. An Arab from Vienna, Jules adopted the name "Thorn" for use in British society. His business, the Thorn Company, manufactured lamps. Known for pure electronics, E.M.I. merged with Thorn to become the largest electronics firm in the world. Howard had photocopied all sorts of documents with regard to the merger and history of these companies. The information was all very interesting, but the history did not go back to the time period when the Wilson Brothers were manufacturing instruments. Unfortunately, Howard's mother had passed away a year earlier and so had Jules Thorn. I was unable to interview either one.

Despite the above disappointments, I was flabbergasted over Howard's mysterious association with Jules Thorn. This was a little over the top in terms of synchronicity, especially when you consider that he was involved with the Montauk story even before I was. In some strange way, he was a key part of this new Montauk family that I had adopted. It is quite suitable that he was a key part of the remarkable synchronicity that was about to unfold.

Duncan Cameron liked Howard very much, and he came over to my house to visit him. As my wife prepared dinner for the three of us, we indulged in all sorts of conversation. When the topic somehow turned to politics, for some unknown reason, I asked them both who their favorite politicians of all time were. Instead of answering me, Duncan returned the question.

"Who is yours?" he asked.

"Probably Teddy Roosevelt," I said after giving it several seconds of thought. I then thought about all of the research I had done a year earlier. "He was pretty much a typical ass-hole politician," I said, "but there is one thing you really have to admire about him."

"What is that?" asked Duncan.

I then told Howard and Duncan a remarkable story I had learned from the history books.

When Roosevelt was running for office, a would-be assassin shot him with a bullet as he was about to deliver a speech. Due to his massive chest muscles (which were abnormally large as a result of heavy breathing caused by a severe asthmatic condition) and a heavy wad of paper that consisted of his planned speech for that day, the bullet failed to penetrate Roosevelt's heart and missed by only a hair. Roosevelt's shirt was soaked with blood, but instead of going to the hospital, he insisted on giving his speech before having any medical attention. Roosevelt put on a clean shirt and gave a much abbreviated speech that lasted maybe a half hour. No matter what one thought of the man's controversial stands on different issues, one had to admire his tenacity.

This was all very interesting but seemingly had little to do with the upcoming synchronicity that was about to unfold. It was the association with Roosevelt, however, that triggered everything. As I thought about Roosevelt and the research I had done on him, I suddenly remembered the playbill from the *New Montauk Theater* that I had received from Kenn about a year earlier. This would be a perfect opportunity to have Duncan take a look at it and give a psychic reading. I went upstairs to my office to try and find the playbill. After a thorough search, I found it at the bottom of a pile of papers. As I have said, I had completely forgotten about it until this moment.

Bringing it downstairs, I brought the playbill over to where Duncan was sitting. As I did so, I noticed something about the framed playbill that I had never noticed before. It had a cardboard backing with old metal clips that were keeping the cardboard in place. One of the fasteners was loose. For the first time, it occurred to me that there might be something underneath the cardboard. The whole contraption was coming loose and the mystery was revealing itself, sort of in its own way and in its own time. Duncan's reading became unnecessary; but I think his presence, along with Howard's, were significant in triggering the mystery that was about to unfold.

As the cardboard came off, I discovered that beneath the playbill was a picture, a full color print that came from a somewhat antiquated printing press. The print was a picture of Christ in a meditative but solemn pose overlooking the Temple. The moon is full and he clasps his hands. A halo is over his head. The city of Jerusalem can be seen in the background. Underneath, in very small print, was a caption: "Christ on Mount Olive." (This print is pictured in black and white on the following page).

My first reaction was that, in some mysterious manner, some Jesus freak was trying to send me a low-frequency message.

Personally, I find most pictorial representations of Christ to be in bad taste. Most depictions are usually more representative of the artist's painful and implanted indoctrinations than they are of who or what the persona known as Christ might have actually been like. This picture, however, had a dignity that seemed to rise above the other pictorial representations I had seen. It was not offensive nor was it meant to be. Reflective is a more appropriate adjective.

The discovery of this picture was surprising to all of us and nobody had any idea what it meant. When I eventually began to put the picture back in its hiding place, I noticed something else. There was a second picture, identical to the first, waiting to be discovered. For some reason, two were delivered to me.

The only step now was for me to call Kenn Arthur, the gatekeeper who had facilitated this mystery in the first place.

"Did you know there were pictures inside of that framework?" I asked him.

"No," he replied.

He truly had no idea about the hidden inserts.

"You would have found it out sooner or later," he said.

"What do you mean by that?"

"It was meant for you," he said.

Kenn can be delightfully cryptic and he was at his best on this occasion, but he really had no idea about the pictures being housed within the frame. All he knew was that the framed playbill contained a magical message for me. I then told him the details of what was in the art work, particularly the reference to Mount Olive.

"The olive tree was sacred to the Templars," he said, referring to the Knights Templar of the Middle Ages.

"Explain further," I stated.

"The olive tree contains the devas and the devas answer to Pan," he replied.

Devas are feminine nature spirits and Pan is the Greek god of the fields who has an authoritative command over the principles of nature via the devas. It should also be noted here that *The Bible* and other ancient literature make deep and deliberate esoteric associations between Christ and Pan. It is an interesting historical fact, recorded in Roman records, that on or about the same time Christ was said to have been crucified, Tiberius Caesar was sailing and passed a vessel where a man boldly announced to the emperor,

"The Great God Pan is dead!" Tiberius was said to have taken this news to heart and lamented the loss of this great god.

Kenn's reply to me that the olive tree contains devas who answer to Pan obviously alluded to a relationship between Christ, the olive tree, and the feminine energy. This is all very well, but it was not good enough for me. My mind was not satisfied. I implored Kenn for further answers.

"Have you ever seen an olive tree?" he asked.

"Not that I can remember," I answered.

"Find out what one looks like and get back to me," he said.

As mysterious and interesting as all of this was, I did not jump at it. I was a busy person and had other things to do besides pursuing this elusive mystery. On a routine trip to the library, I eventually tried to find a picture of an olive tree, but I was unable to turn one up. It is not as easy as you might think. Today, the internet would have made such an endeavor very easy. I left it alone and did not pursue the olive tree mystery for months. In the back of my mind, however, the question gnawed at me. What did an olive tree look like?

One day, I was in the library on other business. Remembering my assignment to find an olive tree, I figured that enough was enough. I intuitively went over to a section of books on biology and horticulture and used sheer will. I soon found one.

When I got home, I called Ken and told him that I had finally found a picture of an olive tree.

"What did you notice about it?" he asked.

"Pretty ominous," I replied. "They are gnarly and twisted and look like something you might find Lon Chaney creeping around."

"What else did you notice about it?" he asked.

We danced around this last question, but I was not able to come up with the answer he wanted. Finally, he told me.

"Look at the way the tree twists and plants itself into the ground. There is room there to hide a treasure, but it is also a conduit to the underground," he said.

"OK," I said, "so we know Montauk is connected to the underground and the Inner Earth. We already know that."

It was all very interesting and mysterious, but I still did not get it. What I had learned thus far was rather obvious. Kenn, however, was offering the enticement of further mysteries via the theme of the goddess and the underground. People might think I enjoy these mystery games, but I do not. I prefer direct and straight communication as opposed to mysteries. My mind, however, could not help but take notice of the strange series of happenstances by which this mystery was unfolding. The entire process had lasted over a year with mostly minimal interest on my part. It was only upon the discovery of these pictures, however, that I decided to take on this mystery as a serious project. I was in for some big surprises and far bigger surprises than Kenn had ever anticipated when he saw the playbill and decided to give it to me as a gift.

7

THE OLIVE MYSTERY

Returning to the library in very short order, I now began my quest. Following Kenn's cue that the olive was sacred to the Templars, I readily discovered an applicable reference in a book entitled *The Guilt of the Templars* by G. Legman (Basic Books Inc., New York, 1966). A passage relayed a story about Italian soldiers who used ancient stones near a chapel in Provençal for parking their tanks in wet weather. Engraved in stone, below a statue of the Virgin, an unknown author had inscribed the following in the Provençal language:

NOSTRO DAMO DOU TAMEIÉ
GAGES FLOURI LIS OLIVIÉ

Translated into English, this means:

OUR LADY OF THE TEMPLARS
MAKES THE OLIVE TREES FLOWER

Kenn was obviously right about an association between the Knights Templar and the olive tree, but this engraving represented an association of the feminine energy portrayed through the symbol of the Virgin Mary. The Templars and Cathars who populated the Provençal region were well known as heretics to Catholicism because of their reverence to the Goddess. Looking for further associations between the olive and the Virgin Mary, I also learned that the prophecies of Fatima, which were supposed to have been relayed by appearances of the Virgin Mary, were revealed in the vicinity of an olive tree.

I soon learned that the olive is not exclusively sacred to the Templars. Olive oil is also the most sacred substance in the Catholic Church. It is used for Chrism, Extreme Unction and Sacraments. The word *Christ* itself refers to "one who has been anointed with oil." Note that this exaltation is rhetorically defined in such a manner that it is the olive oil which makes Christ and not the other way around. In this sense, olive oil is portrayed not so much as a miracle but as the ultimate conduit to the Creator from Whom miracles could or might manifest.

Olive oil, I quickly learned, was not reserved to the New Testament. According to Jewish tradition, the modern celebration of Hanukkah is based upon a story that olive oil was used to keep the menorah lit for eight days when it should have lasted only one. Specifically, Judah Maccabee and his band of faithful Jews, who were severely outnumbered, had engaged in a three-year war to overthrow King Antioch and the Greek-Syrian political force that had forbidden the Jews to practice their religion. During that time, Solomon's Temple had been desecrated. When Maccabee went to restore the Temple, he discovered that there was only one container of olive oil and it was only enough to keep the menorah lit for one full day. Somehow, and in some miraculous manner, the menorah remained lit for eight full days. In the meantime, it took eight days to process more olive oil so that the Temple could remain lit indefinitely. The Jews have celebrated it as a miracle ever since. The key ingredient in this story, at least in this investigation, is that it was the olive oil that was the conduit for this miracle. During Hanukkah, Jews light a menorah and leave it in the window to announce to the world that a miracle occurred.

The olive tree is equally sacred to Islam where it is portrayed as the light of Allah. In the Koran's *Sura of Light*, the olive lights the lamp of understanding and belongs neither to East nor West. I also learned that the olive trees in Fatima, Portugal were near a grotto that was a sacred spot to the Moors long before the Fatima legend ever came along. Although Fatima is usually associated with Catholicism and the Virgin Mary, the name itself was taken in honor of the daughter of the Prophet of Islam.

Keep in mind that all of the above was entirely new to me as I did not grow up with any brainwashing or indoctrination from Christians, Jews, or Muslims. I was always a free agent left to make up my own mind. There was, however, an olive story that I was already familiar with, but this preceded all of the Abrahamic or non-pagan religions you have just read about. I am referring to the Greeks and their mythology.

There are different versions as to what or how it all happened, but mythographers generally agree that a contest was held on Mount Olympus with regards to which god could give the greatest gift to Mankind. In the end, there were two finalists: Poseiden and Athena. Poseiden, the god of the sea, gave Mankind the horse. The other finalist, and unanimous winner, was Pallas Athena who gave Mankind the olive tree. To this day, there is a sacred olive tree and garden at Mount Olympus in Greece as well as outside the Parthenon in Athens. Athena, as the goddess of wisdom, was exalted above all others in the capital city of Greece because, through the olive, she gave Mankind sustenance, medicine, and the prospect of peace and prosperity.

Most Westerners are already familiar with the story of Noah seeing an olive leaf that is carried by a dove after the flood had subsided. In this case, the olive represents not only a new beginning but the signal that it is safe to proceed.

As the years have gone by, I have learned many more intriguing aspects with regard to the olive. I now have a whole file on olives as well as books on the subject. As I do not want to overwhelm the reader with sheer volume, I will stick to the most pertinent facts that are applicable to this narrative. In summary, however, according to both pagan and Abrahamic traditions, the olive is positioned as the most direct conduit to God or Infinity that is available in the physical realm.

My next approach was to investigate the etymology of the word itself. *Olive* derives from the Latin *oliva* which in turn derives from the Greek *elaia.* This is a very interesting root because, like the roots of an olive tree, it branches out in many directions. First, the root *el* means "first" or "first next to God." Sometimes, *El* even refers to God. When you divide the Greek *elaia* (sometimes referred to as *elaiwa*) you have *el* + *aia*, the latter being an iteration of nothing but vowels. For those of you who have read my previous work (*Synchronicity and the Seventh Seal*) or studied the esoteric components of language, you will realize that vowels are an iteration of the Creator. This is why the Hebrews refer to God as YHWH or Yahwah — it is the sound of pure vowels. In this sense, *elaia* would be "first of God."

The word *electric* is at least loosely related to the above. It derives from the Latin *electrum* (amber) which is derived from the Greek *elektron*, akin to *elektor*, meaning "shining" or "of the sun." The concept of light is key here.

The phoneme *el* also appears in names such as Eleazar (meaning God has helped), Eleanor (related to Helen, as in Helen of Troy), and Elaine. In Arthurian legend, Elaine was a woman of Astolat who loved Sir Lancelot. This last reference I found particularly interesting because there is a phrase in Latin, *elan vital*, which refers to "vital life force." In this sense, *elan* means "to burst or throw" or "to throw a lance." *Elan* was also used to refer to a lance itself and thus the names Lancelot and Elaine are bound somewhat inseparably. It conjures up visions of the Holy Lance that pierced and carried the *elan vital* of Christ.

From studying the etymology of olive as *elaia*, it also became evident to me that this word was the basis of the Eleusinian Mysteries of Greek tradition. These mysteries were a series of initiations that most conventional historians claim to know very little about. It was a priesthood and religious tradition that held sway over the entire Greek world and people would come from afar to participate in these mysteries, held every autumn. When the Eleusinian Mysteries were at their peak, no politician would dare meddle with the priests, priestesses or their influence. Although the Eleusinian Mysteries were deeply revered and sponsored by the Greeks, they reached far beyond the boundaries of Greece.

The Eleusinian Mysteries were based upon the natural influences of dark and light as symbolized by the abduction of Perosephene. When Perosephene was taken into the underworld by Hades (Pluto in Roman mythology), Demeter (her mother) was distraught with grief. As Demeter was a goddess of nature and the fields, the crops and flora began to wither and die as all of her attention was on the loss of her beloved daughter. Zeus intervened, but as powerful as he was, he could not buck the power of Hades. An agreement was worked out whereby Perosephene would return to the world but would pay homage to Hades in the underground for several months every year. We know this period as winter.

A scholarly argument has also been made that because the Rites of Eleusis were, in part, based upon the consumption of grain products that were predisposed to mold, the participants were ingesting what we now know as LSD-25. I am somewhat reluctant to mention this as I realize that LSD advocates will get very giddy and excited over this prospect. The research, however, is based upon documents from the original time period so it should not be dismissed. It is unlikely, however, that any mystery school would have left behind their most raw secrets in written notes. By virtue of the name *Eleusis*, I would suggest to you that the olive would be a much more important feature than the LSD.

In the midst of all this research, I was also learning that the olive has medicinal properties. I learned from Tim Beckley (of Inner Light Publications) that whenever the healing properties of olive oil are featured on the cover of a tabloid such as the *National Enquirer,* the circulation goes up considerably. Olive leaf extract has become very popular in recent times as a cure for different ailments. More specifically, the olive is considered an excellent remedy for those who suffer from complete exhaustion, a long illness, intense difficulties or being a care-giver to someone for a long time.

It was during my study of the olive as a healing plant that I came across a book reference which would prove to have major ramifications for me. It boldly stated that olive oil was used in ancient Atlantis to heal the gall bladder. The book further stated that this remedy for the gall bladder would be used in the future. I do not know when that particular book was written, but there are several remedies for the gall bladder which utilize olive oil.

For some strange reason under the sun, I got up from where I was sitting right after reading this last passage. Maybe I had been reading too much and wanted a break or a change of pace. I really do not remember. What I did do, however, was pick up the phone in order to follow up on a particular and somewhat peculiar responsibility. It had to do with the Montauk Indians.

After the first printing of *Pyramids of Montauk*, I gave a copy to the matriarch of the Montauks, Ms. Pharoah. She was the first Montauk Indian I had ever spoken to. During my early research into the Montauk Project, I was given her name and phone number by the head of the Montauk Historical Society. Ms. Pharoah had not heard about any of the Montauk Project experiments, but she was interested in what I had to say. An extremely friendly lady, I kept in touch with her now and then.

When I discovered the pyramids, she was unaware that there had been pyramids out there but she was certainly interested in them as well as my other endeavors. Sometime after *Pyramids* was released, however, she made a point of calling me and wanted to know why I did not mention her son, Robert Pharoah, in the book. I was a bit taken aback because I had never heard that there was a Robert Pharoah, let alone the information that he was claiming to be the rightful Sachem (chief) of the Montauks.

Other than my rather few and brief conversations with Ms. Pharoah, my orientation to the Montauks had been primarily through Robert Cooper, a former town councilman of East Hampton who, as far as I knew, was recognized by most of the Montauks as their tribal leader. Cooper was heralded in the *New York Times* as the tribal leader of the Montauks, and I was not aware that anyone had ever disputed this.

Upon learning that Robert Pharoah was claiming to be Sachem, I phoned Cooper. He shared my puzzlement over why Robert Pharoah was now coming out of the woodwork. These two leaders eventually became involved in a rather heated dispute about these matters, but I had no axe to grind with either one. At this writing, I have only met Robert Pharoah once and he was certainly pleasant enough. To Bob Cooper, I owe infinite gratitude for introducing me to the world of the Montauks and Sharon Jackson, the Montauk Shaman.

In any event, I honored Ms. Pharoah's request when it was time to do the second printing of *Pyramids of Montauk*. I put in a correction about Robert Pharoah and his claim as Sachem. When the second printing of *Pyramids* arrived, I sent Ms. Pharoah a copy of the book almost immediately. A few days later, I then called her on the phone. This was the exact moment I referred to previously. For some reason, I went to the phone just after having read about olive oil being a curative substance for the gall bladder.

My phone call to Ms. Pharoah was answered by her sister, Carolyn. From her, I learned that the book I sent had arrived that very same day, but Ms. Pharoah never got to look at it because she had just gone to the hospital (within the last hour) with a bleeding gall bladder. That was the report, and I was completely stunned. This was too much of a coincidence. I then went back to my notes about the olive and began to contemplate the strangeness of it all. It was only then that I received the biggest impact in all my years of experiencing and studying synchronicity. Ms. Pharoah's first name was Olive!

Up to now, I have referred to her as Ms. Pharoah and not as Olive Pharoah so that it might have a similar impact on you as it did to me. I always called her Olive. When I picked up the phone and got Carolyn, I had asked for Olive. The point here is that although I was referring to her as Olive, I was not thinking of her as "olive" in the same vein as my research. Although I was mouthing the words of her name, I might just as well have been saying "Mary" or "Kate." It was not until I went back to my notes that I made the connection between her name and my research.

"Wow!" I thought to myself. This was too bizarre to be believed. The quantum trail of the Montauk Project had begun with the Cameron-Wilson connection, the pursuit of which led me to the discovery of the Montauk pyramids and the fact that the Pharoahs were the royal tribe of Long Island. Included here was the proposition that the Montauk time experiments were conducted on ground which is the Montauks' most holy ground.

Now, through a series of quantum synchronicities that were wrapped up in a mysteriously framed playbill from The New Montauk Theatre of 1909, I was being led to a very mysterious and further revelation. Some people receive telexes, faxes, emails, or letters when it comes to profound questions they ask. I was getting a package through a mysterious jinn who was masked, at least for a short period of time, as my friend Kenn.

The import of the information I was receiving was exciting but also overwhelming. I could not process it all at once. All of this was exacerbated and illuminated by a human tragedy. Olive Pharoah would never return home. She passed away soon thereafter, and I was never able to speak to her again. I am not sure that her death was caused by the gall bladder because I heard another explanation. All I know is that after I read about olive oil being useful in healing the gall bladder, I was told that she went to the hospital with a bleeding one. I believe the entire diagnosis was somewhat complicated. In any case, the human drama of her passing was obviously and definitely synchronized to the machinations of my new research project concerning the olive.

A decade later, the Medicine Man of the Montauk Indians would tell me that I see the world in much the same way a shaman sees the world, from the outside in. Most people see the world from the inside out. This would perhaps explain the bizarre synchronicities as being an extension of my perception. Whatever the relative truth of that last statement might be, one thing was inarguably clear. The path of the Montauk investigation, particularly my path, was inextricably tied to the exact moment of death of the matriarch of the Montauks. I should also add an important point here. Olive Pharoah was the undisputed matriarch of the Montauk Tribe. After her passing, different factions made different claims and her presence was sorely missed. As the undisputed matriarch of the Montauks, Olive Pharoah was the most sacred symbol of a great people who had been so callously and unfairly declared extinct by New York State.

If there is any good news coming out of this human tragedy, the dramatic impact of my book arriving on the day she left the house for good, combined with synchronicities you have just read, has ensured that she will be remembered in the pages of this book. More importantly, it calls extreme attention to the truth of her people and what they represent. This is why I have chosen to dedicate this book to her. Her passage has served as one of the most remarkable catalysts I have ever known as it has inspired me to research and write about all the many mysteries you will read of in this book.

When the Jews lit the menorah in Solomon's Temple with olive oil, they did so with the expressed intention that the light of wisdom would never go out. It was the olive that made it possible. In these pages, Olive's memory and the human drama of her death have lit the wisdom you are about to read.

8

APOKALYPSO

The bizarre manner by which Olive Pharaoh "thrust herself" into the middle of my various synchronicities was like a bolt of lightning into my brain. In actuality and with considerable hindsight, I had been rather slow to realize the relationship between Olive Pharoah and the various synchronicities I was experiencing with the olive theme. This connection was certainly beyond Kenn Arthur's perception as well. When I finally saw what was sitting in front of my face and experienced that "ah-ha" moment described in the previous chapter, it was only then that I knew I had a book on my hands. I did not know, however, that Olive was going to pass away and never return home. That this incident also symbolized her death only increased the significance of what had transpired. I knew that the book would be very important; but not unlike the Montauk Project itself, the phenomena I was encountering was much bigger than a book. All I knew then and know now is that it was manifesting as a trail of information begging for investigation. More importantly, it was also a current of live energy passing through my life.

The impact of Olive Pharoah's passing upon my psyche was equivalent to or greater than the revelation I had received after my visit with Marjorie Cameron. What I was discovering was leading to something even bigger in its implications, but I did not know what. This realization was punctuated soon after at one of our monthly "Montauk Night" meetings on Long Island when a lady I know gave me a booklet out of the blue. Her name is Ronnie and she has been a fan of the Montauk Project since the book came out. One evening, and quite unsolicited (she knew nothing whatsoever about my synchronicities with the olive), she gave me a paper-bound publication entitled *Apokalypso*. She simply stated, "Peter, I had a very strong message that you should have this book. It is for you — keep it." The meeting was over and everyone was saying good-bye to each other. Ronnie simply gave me the book and nothing more was said.

When I got home and looked at the booklet, I was most surprised to see that it contained a very specific reference to the Mount of Olives. Specifically, it referred to the Mount of Olives as the "mount of corruption" where King Solomon raised an infernal altar to Moloch. The specific passage was as follows:

> "In Scripture we read of Solomon turning from the dedication of the Lord's Temple in Jerusalem to the raising of an infernal altar to Moloch on the Mount of Olives — as if the realization of Man's Divine Body demands the concurrent manifestation of his body of Error: the Collective Man of Sin. Accordingly, it is no accident that Christ chose to speak prophetically of the destruction of the Temple and of the end of Time from the opprobrious vantage point of the Mount of Olives, 'the Mount of Corruption' where the high place of Moloch had stood."

This was a real mouthful to digest. Does it not, however, sound suggestive of the Montauk Project itself? That project not only represented the end of time but the Collective Man of Sin. I would also learn that this altar of Moloch was used for sacrificing children, a practice which was hauntingly similar to the misuse and killing of youngsters during the Montauk Project.

This particular booklet is one of a series of booklets published under the title *Apokalypso**, each of which features its own specific subtitle. The subtitle of this one was *Moloch* (Winter/Spring of '96). The subject matter of the pamphlets is very deep and is not a quick read as it requires, whether you agree with it or not, much

**Apokalypso* was at one time available from *Apokalpso, P.O. Box 782,* Chester, New Jersey, 07930

contemplation to understand exactly what is being presented. It embraces astrology, *The Bible* and quantum physics. The author, presumed to be one Thomas Jude Germine, is a very deep thinker.

What was most noteworthy about this particular issue of *Apokalypso* was a statement that the next installment of this publication (Summer/Fall 1996) was to be subtitled *The Glory of the Olive Tree.* The synchronicity was literally racing and almost jumping off of the page. This was a clear signal that I needed to get this publication. As indicated in the pamphlet, I sent ten dollars to the designated address and soon received it.

In *The Glory of the Olive Tree*, I learned about the "Visions of Zechariah" in the Bible where two olive trees are discussed as representing the end of time. Specifically, the two olive trees are identified as two Witnesses to the End of Time. The olive trees are depicted as producing an ever-flowing unending supply of oil to the seven-branched candelabra which lights the Sanctuary of the Temple. It is made quite clear that while olives are often thought of as a dietary item, they were first and foremost a source of oil to burn for illumination and light. The olive tree, to the ancients, symbolizes Light or Limitless Light which, according to the Zohar, shines above the highest branch of the Tree of Life. The Limitless Light is, therefore, the never ceasing flow of oil from the olive tree.

Bibliophiles, Christians and Jews alike, have continuously debated and argued over the meaning of these two olive trees and what they represent. I am not going to overly concern myself with what might be termed the traditional approach to the so-called Apocalypse. These arguments or debates have a tendency to pander to the lowest common denominator. As my work is largely centered on the subject of time and synchronicity, I will examine the olive tree analogy from that perspective.

The two olive trees are specifically identified as two witnesses at the End-Time. Despite the various debates, there is a lot of agreement by the debaters that these olive trees are representative of angels. Certain prophets and/or angels have also been identified with these two olive trees, Enoch and Elijah in particular. Whether Enoch or Elijah are chosen or not, these two allegorical olive trees are always considered to be stewards of a powerful energy. You can think of them as angels if you like.

The whole proposition of two angels becomes a lot clearer when we throw the Ark of the Covenant into the equation. Atop the Ark are two angels of gold. Some have equated these two angels to the aforementioned olive trees. I have even seen it written that these two angels atop the Ark are gold-plated over olive wood. *The Bible*, however, says they were made of gold. One thing is quite clear, however, at least in terms of *The Bible*. The two statues of angels who occupy the Holy Place in the Holy of Holies are indeed made of olive wood. These angels are positioned with their wings forming ninety degree angles so that their wings touch in the center of the Holy of Holies. Beneath their wings is where the Ark of the Covenant rests.

Between the two angels or cherubs on the Ark is the Mercy Seat which is basically a dish or cup that is sometimes identified by Christian Cabalists as a parallel to the Holy Grail if not the Grail itself. Over or within the Mercy Seat dwells the most precious spiritual essence in the universe and it is called the Shekinah, a Hebrew word which is said to mean "dwelling." The Shekinah is sometimes defined as the Bride of Christ by Christian Cabalists, but it has always been defined by the Jewish priesthood as the essence of feminine energy.

Neither sunlight, candle light, nor any means of artificial light is allowed inside the Holy of Holies. At special times, however, a spark or flame is manifested between the two cherubs and this element of "fire" is known as the Shekinah Glory. Christian Cabalists refer to this as the Christ who is viewed to be the complete glory or ultimate result of the Shekinah. The Shekinah literally lights up the Holy of Holies which otherwise would be in complete darkness.

This last prospect presented by the Christian Cabalists is very interesting with regard to my investigation because, as stated previously, it is the olive that makes the Christ, not the other way around. In this sense, the Shekinah Glory would be supplied by the olive which is an a priori partner in the arrangement.

The olive has thus presented itself not only as a source of eternal illumination but as a feminine current. In addition to this, it is also displayed as a gateway in scripture because the doors to the Holy of Holies are specifically ordained to be made of olive wood. Besides being a gateway, the olive serves as a presence which is either adjacent to or as something which serves as a conduit to the most powerful expression of the Divinity.

The depiction of the two olive-wood angels whose wings stretch over the Ark is symbolic of another concept which is complementary to the above but also takes us one step further. The fact that the wings of each angel are at ninety degree angles to one another is suggestive of moving from one dimension to another. It is at this point of dimensional shifting that the spark of the Shekinah manifests.

If the olive doors are a gateway, we also have to consider the two cherubs on the Ark itself. Identified as olive trees, they are described as two witnesses to the End of Time. This is very significant when we consider that two cherubs appear at the gateway to the Garden of Eden when Adam and Eve are expelled. These two cherubs (angels or angles) also signify the return to the sacred dwelling place. All of this, of course, is expressed by the Shekinah, a feminine attribute.

A phrase such as the End of Time suggests that the time you have been experiencing in the physical universe would become nul and void. It is representative of another dimension. The two cherubs or olive trees are described as "witnesses" to the End of Time. The etymology of the word *witness* traces back "to see" or "to know" and leads to many interesting places, but for now I want you to consider the feminine aspect of the Shekinah and the olive.

Thus far, we have discovered that the highest expression of the Divinity is depicted as a feminine attribute which is either couched in the symbolism of the olive or is virtually identical to it. In this narrative, the olive has presented itself as quite a mystery indeed. Throughout history, however, it has also been the prerogative of a woman to be mysterious. In an idealized woman, that is supposed to be representative of her charisma and charm. To Mankind as a whole, God has always served as the great mystery. Thus far in my investigation, the three of them (Mankind, God, and the Goddess) seem to be inextricably linked together. The Goddess, therefore, might be considered a more apropos term than God.

Reading *Apokalypso*, I also realized that the very mystery of the feminine energy was being expressed in the word itself. I am referring to *apokalypso* which is the Greek word from which the English word *apocalypse* was derived. Dictionaries will not tell you this, but the pamphlet *Apokalypso* states that this word actually means the "uncovering of Calypso." To Bibliophiles, the Apocalypse means the end times or the final destruction before a Last Judgment or some sort of revelatory incident. In Greek, it refers to the uncovering of Calypso, the goddess who kept Odysseus on her island in order to give him seven years of sexual initiation.

I took the etymology of *apokalypso* one step further by observing the fact that the word is a composition of *apo, kaly* (or *kali*), and *ipso. Apo* means to uncover. *Kali* is the Hindu goddess of destruction but is also a giver of new life. In Greek, *ipso* means "by fact of" or refers to the fact of. In this regard, *apokalypso* equates to "by the fact of Kali." Kali also represents the measurement of time.

To put it simply, my synchronicities with the olive had everything to do with the uncovering of or revealing of the Goddess. Without even thinking about it, I was now living up to the name "Peter Moon" which, as described earlier, can be construed as "interpreter of the feminine energy." Whether or not I do a good job of this is for you to decide as you read the rest of this book. Before you continue, however, it is appropriate that I advise you of some things.

The rest of this book is not unlike working your way through a labyrinth. Like much of my other writing, it takes odd twists and turns. There is considerable science and methodology with regard to labyrinths and the human brain. Finding your way through a physical labyrinth is considered to be therapeutic. While my endeavor with this book is not a physical labyrinth, the circuitous twists and turns it takes are representative of such. Please regard it so. The feminine energy winds and weaves in the most mysterious of ways. I am sure that you will be very surprised at what you learn.

Besides the above, there is one other important point that should be stressed. As you continue reading this work, you will sometimes find that certain statements or etymologies I have presented are repetitions of data already mentioned. This is intentional as repetition facilitates learning. I have also reserved these repetitions to points that I feel are very important.

I hope you enjoy the rest of the book.

9

THE QUANTUM FEMALE

Although the institution of Judaism has a most definite patriarchal twist to it, learned Rabbis identify the highest aspect of the divinity as the Shekinah and that is feminine. Before we explore the theological implications of this, it is advisable to make a few comments about the esoteric tradition of Judaism.

The literature of the Jewish faith can be divided into three primary categories: *The Torah*, which is more or less what we know as *The Old Testament*; *The Talmud*, which consists of written commentaries on the law; and the Kabbalah, which is the mystical tradition. Historically, when Kabbalah or Kabala is spelled with a "K," it refers to the Jewish tradition. When Cabala is spelled with a "C," it refers to the Christian tradition. When a "Q" is used, it refers to the Islamic tradition. The Jewish Kabbalah is by far the oldest of these three and is generally regarded as the most comprehensive as it has been around the longest.

The mystery of the female as expressed in the last chapter is something that the priests and Kabbalists of Judaism have known and commented upon for millennia. In point of fact, the feminine energy is the most important element in their cosmology.

According to ancient Kabbalistic doctrine, the dilemma of this universe is a result of the feminine energy being exiled from this universe. This is the real Fall from Grace that is dramatized in the expulsion of Eve from the Garden of Eden. At the beginning of this universe, the Female Force contracted or collapsed. This disintegration resulted in the Shekinah being dispersed throughout the universe, Her light being reabsorbed into both the higher and lower realms. Only a vestige of Her energy remained. Therefore, in this realm, all you will ever see of feminine energy is reflective light. This is one reason why the moon, a body which gives off reflective light, symbolizes women.

None of what I have just stated is my opinion. It is the ancient doctrine of the best minds of the Jewish faith. What I have offered is only a summary of intricate observations and quantum thinking.

Kabbalistically, the absence or withdrawal of this Feminine Force is what precipitated the quantum dilemma of this universe. No sliver of this universe can redeem itself until the Feminine Force can recover what has been lost and recover Her true Light. This is why the olive oil lighting the Menorah is such an important symbol. The olive oil furnishes Her light which is eternal light.

According to the Kabbalists, the ultimate evolutionary development of any individual is to reconcile the Shekinah or true Feminine Force within their own individual soul. They cite the microcosm being in tune with the macrocosm. In other words, until we all perfect this process, the entire cosmic situation will not be resolved. This process equates to "escape from" or complete reconciliation with the universe. It is the end of this universe as we know it and that is why it represents the End Time.

What we learn from the above is perhaps too shocking for the typical 21st Century mind to absorb. When it comes to the quantum secret of the universe, most of my conspiracy fans would prefer to hear it expressed in technical terms that might equate to so many megahertz or perhaps a mathematical equation. The Kabbalists, however, are telling us something that is too plain and simple to be believed. The secret of the entire universe is the Feminine Force itself. The very lack of it resulted in what we now know as ordinary three-dimensional reality.

If the Jewish faith is not objective truth, and I certainly do not mean to imply that any faith is objective, we can certainly marvel over the intricate thinking that went into the Ark of the Covenant and the architecture of the Holy of Holies. Although these items have been incorporated into the Jewish faith, they are representative of something more than faith. They are an effort to construct a model which either serves to explain or act as a functionary for the greatest mystery of the universe.

The recognition of the power of the Feminine Force is not exclusive to Judaism. The Hindus recognize it as Shakti, the Catholic's have the Virgin Mary, and the Chinese have Quan Yin. The list goes on. It soon becomes obvious, however, that the Feminine Force referred to here is not something that is mundane or that we should just pay intellectual lip service to. We are talking about an energy. This means tantra.

Sometimes referred to as the "yoga of sex," tantra means "to weave together" or "the web." Tantra aspires to connect you with the highest aspect of the Creative Force. In tantra, there are three primary divisions: Red, White and Black. Some techniques utilize the flesh while others deal with energy only. Black deals in negative aspects. As there are many different sects and teachings, it is not appropriate to try and represent them all in a work such as this. If desired, you can seek out further information on your own.

Eastern tantra is not the only practice which seeks out the "magical" harnessing of the Feminine Force. St. Teresa of Avigion was well known for her ecstatic trances as a "Bride of Christ." Jewish mystics go into rapport with the Feminine Force via prayer. There are also the doctrines of Western Magick. All of these seek an arguably similar path but each path has a different context placed upon it.

According to my own observations, all of these systems have one thing in common. If one really opens up to this energy, one is vulnerable to phenomena which has been termed vampirism or possession. This does not mean, however, that the Feminine Force is bad. It does mean, however, that it is jammed up. This applies to the microcosm as well as the macrocosm. There is a considerable amount of attention devoted to keeping the Feminine Force bottled up. Society's taboo against nudity is just one example. Historically, matriarchal cultures are completely at ease with nudity. Patriarchal cultures are quite the opposite. There is no faster way to get the attention of the police and the mental health officials than to start walking down the street naked. In a patriarchal culture, nudity is bottled up so that it can be distributed for a profit such as in the pornographic industry.

The booklet *Apokalypso* makes very clear that although the female energy has been denied, the same problem applies to the male energy as well. As the complement of the male, the female cannot be considered whole without the true male. In this respect, the aforementioned two olive trees or Witnesses represent the polarity of the sexes, the unification of which is the gateway to paradise. The myth of the Garden of Eden can therefore become a reality when it is actualized. On a personal level, the integration of the male and female energies also apply to the internal processes of the individual as one integrates his or her body, mind and soul. A complete integration, particularly on the microcosmic level, would imply a transcendence into a higher dimension.

The prospect of the Garden of Eden also brings us to the concept of shame, and this is a very interesting word because of its phonetic association with *Shem*, the father of the Hebrew people. Shem, the son of Noah, rose to prominence for covering the nakedness of his father. Noah is portrayed as a naked pagan in *The Bible* but Shem comes to the rescue.

In Jewish scripture, Shem is equivalent to or reincarnates as Melchizedek, the Priest of Salem who initiates Abraham as a high priest. Abraham, who is a descendant of Shem, is often considered to be the father of all Semitic people, but it is Shem from whom the word *Semite* was derived.

Abraham becomes a very key historical figure whenever there is a discussion of matriarchal society. This is by reason of the fact that any religion which does not derive from the patriarch Abraham is pagan by definition. Any and all matriarchal religions are therefore pagan. Christianity, Judaism, and Islam are the only religions which do not fall under the heading of pagan. Although Abraham is generally given the most credit, Shem and Melchizedek are earlier and senior characters situated at the inception point of the patriarchal attitudes and customs which permeate Earth culture to this very day.

Whether Shem was a historical or mythological character, he seems to have insinuated himself into the Hebrew word for "olive oil" which is *shemen*. Ironically, *shemen* seems to have influenced the formation of the English word *semen*. After, all *Shem* is the seed of the Hebrew people.

It should also be pointed out that *shemen* is so close phonetically to the word *shaman* that one clearly sees a synchronistic pattern between the two words. That one word clearly means "olive oil" is particularly significant to the path we are pursuing in this book. The word *shaman* has always been identified with the word *sham*. When we play this off of *Shem*, we have to wonder if the use of the word *sham* was actually derived or influenced by the Biblical character who is the father of the Semites.

It is hard to notice the word *shemen* without seeing that is contains two other English words: *she* and *men*. These two words are very close to each other if not the same. *Men* was originally a word used to signify *women* because *men, mon* or *moon* all related to the time of a woman's menses cycle. As patriarchal society developed, males co-opted the name *men* for themselves, ostensibly because it made them more important. This not only makes sense from the obvious word meanings, it is the true etymological history of the word.

If, as the learned Rabbis have always taught, the quantum link to the mystery of the universe is the feminine or Shekinah energy, the universe clearly has a built-in mechanism to deny the process by which we can dig ourselves out. In such an environment, we can expect the feminine energy to be reversed and degraded almost as a matter of routine. This is the exact reason why men would co-opt the original name for females for themselves.

According to the aforementioned Kabbalistic doctrine, one could readily assume that all of this was the very reason the Jews have always refused to accept Christ as their redeemer or messiah. After all, it was most obvious — he was not a woman! This is the Super Woman that Marjorie Cameron talked about so much. It might not be stated as such in Jewish writings, but it is clearly wrapped up in their own doctrines, magical and otherwise. Think about that for a moment or two. Perhaps they had no choice other than to reject Jesus as it would clearly have been a mockery to the truth they knew so well. We can estimate, however, that the actual truth of these matters is far more complex.

There is no question that recent interpretations of scripture and concepts such as the DaVinci Code also suggest that Christ was actually teaching a feminine doctrine in the first place and that is why he was rejected. This, of course, would seem to be very much in alignment with the Jewish mystery tradition. If one studies the history of the Israelites, however, one realizes that their community and knowledge base was utterly dispersed as a result of the diaspora after King Solomon's reign. The Temple was raided and the most precious items were stolen. Cheap imitations were put in their place. Eventually, the First Temple was destroyed.

Not long before the birth of Christ, the Second Temple was built by Herod the Great and a renaissance of feminine energy was brewing across the Holy Land. This included many messianic sects. By 70 A.D., the Romans had utterly destroyed the Second Temple and raided the holy objects again.

Whichever way you want to look at it, the Ark, which represents the means by which to manifest the Divine Spark known as the Shekinah, was lost. At best, it was hidden. The whole symbology of the Ark, however, is entirely wrapped up in the concept of the redeeming force of this universe being a feminine force, and further, that this force is sparked by the two olive trees or cherubs upon the Ark. In many respects, this concept summates the highest aspects of the Jewish religion and most certainly its mystery tradition.

My quest, however, has nothing to do with authenticating *The Bible*, the Jewish religion, the Christian religion or anything of the sort. I stumbled upon all of this through the principle of synchronicity. In my quest to discover the mysteries behind the Montauk Project, I was presented with the olive. It is not only wrapped up in the mysteries of the Torah and the enigmatic picture of Christ on Mount Olive, it is the name of Olive Pharoah, the last matriarch of the Montauk Indians who exited this world in a most conspicuous manner.

As my quest has led us to *The Torah* and *The New Testament*, I am going to offer a few insights with regard to how to relate to *The Bible*. Please understand that I am attempting to go beyond the typical knee-jerk reaction of the typical Earthling who nods his head in obedience to the ruling authority. There is a very pertinent reason why this angle should be addressed. Most people, even so-called advanced thinkers and conspiracy theorists, have been imprinted with Biblical data in such a manner that they cannot think for themselves. There is truth in *The Bible*, but it is often wrapped up in hidden codes that have been reserved only for initiates. It should also be pointed out that these various truths are not necessarily exclusive to *The Bible* itself. It is better that you learn what you can about these matters and decide the truth for yourself.

CHAPTER TEN

10

HELIOS BYBLOS

In order to rationally consider the truth of *The Bible*, one is wise to realize that it can only be made sense of if there are two components present: an observer and the book itself. The observer is a very key term because it is part of the foundation of quantum physics. If you do not have an observer, you do not really have anything. Classical physics, however, has the hubris to leave the human spirit out of the their equations when indeed the spirit and the observer are really the same thing. On the other hand, faith-based religions almost always have a tendency to leave science out of the equation. They suffer from hubris as well. The idea of hubris would therefore seem to be the common denominator with regard to problems in both science and religion.

With regard to the above, it might interest you to know that the word *hubris* itself can be reasonably hypothesized to have evolved from the Greek word for *Hebrew* which is *Hebraios*. Compare this to *hybris*, the Greek word for *hubris*. The association of these two words should not be surprising because the ancient Greeks and Hebrews hated each other. The Greeks literally moved into the Temple of Solomon and desecrated it.

As *The Bible* you are familiar with originated from the Hebrew tradition, any fundamental understanding of such a book would require that one understand where the word *Hebrew* came from in the first place. The dictionary, however, gives an embarrassingly feeble etymology. It boldly states that *Hebrew* is derived from the Greek *hebraios* > Ar. 'edrai > Hebrew *'ibhri*, literally "one from across (the river)." This etymology is preposterously said to relate to the ibis or the heron, a common river bird.

Other scholars have agreed that the word *Hebrew* was indeed derived from *ibhri* and it is certainly obvious that one can sound out "Hebrew" from *ibhri*. There is, however, a much deeper etymology at play here because *ibhri* is intrinsically tied to the Sanskrit word *brahmin*. Taking this one step further, *brahmin* is the root from which the name *Abraham* evolved. *Ab* or *abba* refers to "father" and *brahmin* means to "worship" which in turn means "to honor or signify." Thus, *Abraham* refers to "father worship" or making the father honored, presumably or arguably at the expense of the feminine energy. There is a rich tradition as well as considerable historical evidence and etymological associations that link Abraham to the Far East.* These links to the Far East are far more extensive and involved than what I have offered here.

In light of the fact that the Hebrew tradition honors the Shekinah above all, we are forced to ask ourselves why and how Judaism came to embrace what is unmistakably a patriarchal tradition. In this respect, the glory of the feminine energy became something of a "hidden doctrine" to the Hebrews as opposed to how it functioned during the millennia before Abraham. As is so typical in the drama of Mankind, the inner doctrine was reserved for initiates while the common masses were herded into a belief system that panders to the lowest common denominator. Common interpretations and renditions of *The Bible* are reduced to such. In this day and age, there are even cartoons based upon Biblical events which reinforce these interpretations. If one wants to accept the absurdity of cartoons, please consider the following.

* *The Bible* itself (Genesis 25: 17-18) indicates that Abraham's kin were in India. It also indicates he came from Ur which is commonly recognized as Chaldea. Chaldea can be traced etymologically to Kaul-Deva, an ancient region in Kashmir where Brahmin priests were once abundant. The life of Abraham and Sara(h) is directly parallel to two very similar characters who were known as Brahma and Saraasvati.

The names of the sons of Abraham, Ishmael and Isaac derive from Sanskrit words. Ishmael comes from *Ish-Mahal* which means "Great Shiva" while Isaac derives from *Ishakhu*.

When we consider the Vedas, the great literary works of ancient India, the *Bharata-Veda*, which is another term for the Rig-Veda, has very close similarities with *The Holy Bible*. The words bharata and *bhara* are virtually the same and equate to *ibrhi*. The *Bharata-Veda* can therefore be easily construed as the "Veda of the Hebrews."

After expulsion from Egypt and various adventures, the Hebrews erected the Tabernacle in the Wilderness. This was a portable version of what later was to become incorporated into Solomon's Temple. Inside the Holy of Holies was the Ark of the Covenant which was the conduit to the Shekinah. This was explained previously, but I will ask you to stand back for a moment and become a cartoon director as you consider the entire panorama and implications of the story that is rendered in *The Bible*.

The Shekinah, which is portrayed in scripture as the most valuable element in the entire universe, is so remote and so scarce that it can only be seen by the High Priest and at an appointed time each year. After having been stripped of their "atrocious pagan behavior" by Moses, the new lawgiver, the Hebrews are forced by their new circumstances to parade around the desert, all the time being persuaded to listen to the priests who are all male and are the only ones considered qualified to perceive this energy. The Hebrews were thus relegated to playing a game of "following the leader" while the precious Shekinah endured the fate of becoming confined to a cosmic Pez dispenser. It is a most peculiar and occult dispenser, however, because only the High Priest is allowed to view it or experience it directly. In its purest form, the Shekinah is so Holy that it is not deemed suitable for the common man.

If one chooses to be judgmental about Judaism, one can suggest or assert that the priesthood is deliberately holding the faucet on this energy and exploiting it to their own advantage. If we choose to be liberal in our interpretation of the above prospect, we can consider that the teachings of Judaism have been rendered in such a way that they are merely symbolic of what had already taken place in the permutations of universal thought as a result of the quantum dispersion of feminine energy as previously described. The main point in all of this is that the events of the Exodus portray a situation where the scarcity of the feminine energy is at an all time high. If it is the most important commodity in the universe, it is highly important to pursue this mysterious force and seek out the means by which it can be tapped and distributed.

When we consider the comical prospect of a Pez dispenser, we are also forced to ask some serious questions. Does the high priest have any trace elements of being a legitimate filter for this feminine energy? After all, such an energy released without any filtering at all is reminiscent of the myth of Pandora's Box which unleashed chaos. In the end, it remains a matter of choice. Do you want a high priest as an intermediary or do you want to experience this energy directly?

If you choose to reject a patriarchal intermediary, you might find it humorous to consider replacing the priest with the Three Stooges. Imagine what a mess they might make of the Ark. While this story might be highly entertaining, it could be interpreted by some as disrespectful to the religious convictions of certain people. More importantly, this foolish aspect represents a collision of two worlds.

The first letter of the Hebrew alphabet, *aleph*, is virtually the same phonetically as *olive*. In the Cabalistic Tree of Life, *aleph* represents the Fool. The Tarot, which represents the Wheel of Life, is not considered "kosher" by the Hebrew faith. According to their doctrines, the Tarot is something to be shunned and is considered to be an abomination. One great rabbi has also cited the Tarot as being unscientific. All of this presents a very interesting conundrum for people who are psychologically bound to the deeper doctrines of the Jewish faith.

First, no scientific method should shun anything. Shunning represents a built-in prejudice. Further, the concept of abomination is quite nicely tied into the text of Revelation which refers to the Whore of Babylon as the abomination. After all, we are dealing with the feminine/Goddess energy, aren't we?

Whether you believe in the Hebrew Kabbalah or the other versions, there is no question that the advent of Babylon would bring chaos to these organized systems of thought. The Tree of Life itself, however, is essentially based upon an earlier feminine tradition. This conundrum should solve rather nicely if one cares to study history and discover that there were many earlier versions of the Ark of the Covenant. These existed long before the Hebrews came along. In earlier versions, the two cherubs or "olive trees" were represented by cats with wings. Keep in mind that the words for "cat" in Spanish and Italian are *gato and gatto* which are virtually the same as "gate." It is also noteworthy that the Greek word for "olive oil" is *eleon* which is hauntingly close to "lion."

As I have stated, *The Bible* contains much wisdom. Most of the key points, however, are hidden in the text. Why is this?

If you study the sociological and psychological history of Mankind, you will eventually discover that society is based and dependent upon a tradition of mystery. *The Holy Bible* is not only no different, it emphasizes this tradition. As I have stated, most interpretations pander to the lowest common denominator. *The Bible*, however, is so studded with mystery that it is, in fact, a series of mysteries that are shrouded with a veil. Common interpretations equate to a veil which denies admission to the higher or more circumspect levels. Population control is for the masses. Inner mysteries are only for the initiated.

Before we can consider *The Bible* intelligently (or any holy scripture of any kind), we have to look at it with vigilance or what the Buddha would have called "Right View." The first step is to recognize that the book, in its original form and language, is filled with poetry, imagery, and numerological meaning that will defy the perception of the uninitiated reader. The Bible Code is famous for having "predicted" future events.

It is important to keep in mind that truth comes in four dimensions and beyond. When one attempts to render it in a three-dimensionalized format, such as in the format of a holographic style universe that we live in, there is a little less truth and a lot more lie than you might find in the quantum realm. A two-dimensional experience is even further from the truth. It must therefore be recognized that any book of scripture, *The Bible* included, is a two-dimensional instrument. At best, it can only approximate the truth. A creature in three dimensions is therefore looking down and not up when he reads a book of any kind. If the book is clever, it will remind him of these things and encourage him into looking outside his own realm of experience.

People often get excited over the prospect that the Bible Code can predict future events. As with the "writings" of Nostradamus, these predictions are only taken into account with hindsight. Advocates of the Bible Code have pointed out that the names "Oswald" and "Kennedy" appear in conjunction with each other. If we disregard that Oswald was more of a patsy than a suspect, it is quite possible that some other would-be assassin could also fit into such a pattern. We do not attach any importance to their name because it does not muster any recognition with regard to the way history played out.

What really excites people about such a concept as the Bible Code is the principle of synchronicity. The names and events were "predicted" by reason of their cryptic presence and association in the text. It is synchronicity that people wax over and which creates their interest and joy. As the working principle, it is the senior intelligence in such matters.

If you care to look into these matters more deeply, you will discover that *The Holy Bible* itself is coded in astrology. Keep in mind that astrology is based entirely upon the principles of synchronicity. The story of the Three Wise Men is just one example. They recognized the Star of Bethlehem and tied it to the first Christmas as a result of Chaldean astrology. *The Bible* is so studded with astrology that it is too numerous to mention. The entire creation of the Jewish faith is based upon the principle of the two thousand year reign of Aries (the Ram or lamb) and ends with the sacrifice of the Lamb (Christ) as the Age of Pisces is born.

If one cares to examine the phonetics and etymology of the words "*Holy Bible*," you will find that there is an intrinsic connection between the Greek word *helios* and the English word *holy*. In actual fact, *The Bible* you know is only a fragment of ancient texts that have been preserved as well as altered. This ancient book was known as "*Helios Byblos*" which means "*Book of the Sun*." It is a blatant reference to astrology.

If the above does not sit well with you, I want you to consider once again the etymology of the word *Hebrew*. The previous etymologies I have offered are intriguing and seemingly accurate from different perspectives. There is another etymology that is subscribed to by the Hebrews themselves. According to some of your most authentic Hebrew scholars, the word *Hebrew* derives from *ivrit*, the name for one particular version of the Hebrew alphabet. This etymology offers the best clue of all for it is virtually the same as the Arabic word *ifrit* which means *jinn*.

No matter which way you look, the Godhead is surrounded by such creatures as the jinn. You can call them by whatever name you want to, but it totally stands to reason that any holy book would have their signature on it.

As I have said, many creatures in my life have represented the jinn in one form or another. It became apparent that yet one more was about to enter my life.

11

PENELOPE

It should be quite clear that my synchronistic experiences with the olive were leading me directly to the feminine energy. The Biblical data was simply serving as a sign post. Most important is the fact that this was not an armchair adventure but a live mystery. Accordingly, I have attempted to write this book as an initiatory experience so that it literally becomes alive for you, too.

Looking back over the last decade or more, it is easy to see the pattern that the olive manifested in my life. At the time it all happened, however, it was not so clear.

After receiving the playbill from the New Montauk Theatre, I began to receive letters from an unidentified person who signed their communications simply with a "T." These letters were intellectual in nature, but I had no idea who the respondent was. After several exchanges of letters, the respondent identified herself as "Tantra." Her story is long, involved and complex. Although I did not know it at the time, this woman was forging a very specialized form of the feminine current into my life. In retrospect, I would say that it was a live transmission of the olive frequency. It was most certainly a tantric frequency.

Her name is Tantra Bensko and she is a teacher of the tantric arts, but I must add a couple of warnings here. People will too readily assume that this is about sex, but such an assumption has to do with people's misunderstandings which are often complicated by their own repressions. Tantra will vehemently tell you that tantra and sex are not the same thing. The second warning is that most tantric practitioners are not dealing with the same tradition that she is practicing. After interviewing different so-called practitioners of tantra, or those who follow a different system of tantra, all of them were completely unfamiliar with her key teachings, save for one. The one who was familiar made it very clear that she was not at that level. It was over her head. What is important in this narrative, however, is neither her techniques nor her legacy, but the fact that she imbibed the feminine current into my life in a most extraordinary way. It should also be stated that she is a most special lady.

After continued correspondence, we finally had a phone conversation which resulted primarily in hysterical laughter on her part. If you knew her, this would not be too surprising as she calls her work *LucidPlay*. Laughter and playfulness are a big part of her teachings. After a few phone conversations, things became a bit more serious as she began sending tantric transmissions which created profound changes in the fabric of my being. She is quite potent at transmitting and cultivating Shaktipat which results in rising kundalini. Eventually, we were able to meet when I made a research trip to St. Augustine. I spent two days with her on the beach learning exercises and having an incredibly hilarious time. Although her work has deep energetic implications, it seemed like the bulk of our time was spent laughing our heads off.

I did not realize it until some five or six years later, but Tantra's work with me eventually gated in the most responsive and copacetic embodiment of the female energy I have ever known. This woman's name is Penelope, and I cannot say too much about her as she works in a field which requires her to keep a low profile. For professional and personal reasons, she does not desire any publicity or notoriety from her association with me.

It sometimes amazes me how slow I am to catch on with certain things. Five or six years later, I wrote to Tantra and told her I had just realized that she was the one who had gated Penelope into my life. Tantra, however, was well aware of it.

At the time Penelope came into my life, I was going through what would prove to be one of the most stressful periods of my entire life. It was a period during which I would have to employ the court system to secure five different restraining orders on female members of the human species.

When I met Penelope and she heard my story, she was aghast at what I had experienced. "The women in your life are not real women," she said. "I feel that I have to apologize on behalf of my gender."

These statements proved to be some of the most honest and pleasant words I have ever heard. Penelope also backed up her words and rapidly became the best friend I have ever had. She knew I was under attack and said she had come to help me with my work. This included my own tantric initiation into the feminine energy by reason of her.

In retrospect, my adventures in synchronicity led me to the gateway of the feminine energy through all that you have previously read about. The gateway, however, was littered with jinn and the corpses of those who were thwarted by the gate-keepers. In my personal life, this was dramatized by women who had issues with men and were very angry. In each case, these women signed confessions before a prosecuting attorney admitting their wrong doing against myself. I did not want to employ the law at all as it is a brutal and exhausting process. Had I not, however, I would have been destroyed on many levels.

An important point in these matters is that I had never gone through any such problem with women in my entire life. It seemed I had to pass the test of the jinn before I would be allowed entry to the true gateway of the feminine. Tantra and Penelope were the gate-keepers and were very much looking after my best interests. They also knew it would serve as a pathway for others.

Initially, Penelope and I did not connect on any sort of romantic level. It was much more "work related." We met when she attended a lecture I was giving on Long Island. Penelope was seeking me out because I had coauthored the book *Encounter in the Pleiades* with Preston Nichols and that was the basis of her contact. As she arrived early and before everyone else, we had a chance to talk to one another.

Penelope was very interested in the Pleiades because she identified it with the same feminine energy I have talked about in this book. In her hands, Penelope had pages of information about the Pleiades from a man named Mark Roberts. Much of her interest in this subject stemmed from the history and theories Mark was fostering. What she had to say about Mark Roberts and the

Pleiades on that night, however, went completely over my head. I was getting ready to give a lecture and had other things on my mind. We barely exchanged phone numbers and that was that.

Not too longer after, I would meet with Penelope and learn that she had a particular agenda with regard to me. Specifically, she was to guard, protect and watch over me while I went through the most catastrophic period of my life. The day I met her, I had been literally forced into hiring a lawyer to protect the legal rights to my literary works and my business interest in Sky Books. The gloves had come off in what was to become an intense battleground of legal proceedings. It would arguably be interesting and informative to go into the blow-by-blow events and circumstances, but it is off topic and would require an entire book. What is important is that Penelope came into my life to see me through the hardest times I would ever know.

Penelope would soon become very much involved in my investigation of the olive, but there was something else that was going on as well. Looking back at it, I can see that my involvement with her was mysteriously tying together what seemed to be unrelated threads of my life. The more I interacted with her, the more these threads would weave themselves together. When we speak of the feminine energy, the idea of weaving is quite significant because tantra embraces the concept of "weaving together."

The most obvious thread was Mark Roberts. He was not only passionate about promoting the feminine energy of the Pleiades, he had been a personal friend of Marjorie Cameron as well.

It was Tantra Bensko, however, who started or catalyzed my connection to Penelope in the first place. Although her interest in helping me was quite genuine, Tantra had an agenda of her own. Her mastery of certain tantric principles actually led her to journeying to parallel worlds. She needed to air out to somebody, and I was pretty much the only person she could find that would understand. These experiences were not, however, only in her mind. She was accompanied on these excursions by her real-life boyfriend/partner. As I was making similar connections in my writing, I was a perfect outlet for her. In the strangest of ways, however, her energies parlayed over to my meeting with Penelope.

I would know Penelope for well over a year before finding out that she also had a very strange connection to one of the most mysterious figures in my life. I am referring to David Anderson, the founder and president of the Time Travel Research Center that once existed on Long Island. That subject is not the province of this book, but the association should be noted as it suggests a relationship between the phenomena of tantra and the hard core aspects of time travel.

At the time I met Tantra and Penelope, however, I did not even know about David Anderson. Tantra was pointing me in the direction of Penelope who was pointing me in the direction of Mark Roberts. Mark, who I had not even heard of, had some real answers concerning the mystery of the olive. This mystery was just waiting to be revealed.

12

MARK ROBERTS

Although Penelope was selling me on the ideas of Mark Roberts, I was not really too interested in what he had to say about the Pleiades or the fact that he had known Marjorie Cameron. At that point in my life, most of my research time was occupied by a subject that had completely captured my attention: the ancient empire of Timbuktu. How Timbuktu became interesting to me is a long and fairly complicated thread which we will not go into. All I will say is that the mystery of that general geographic area originally grabbed my attention in 1986 when I read an Edgar Rice Burroughs novel. It was the third book in his *Tarzan* series.

My interest in Timbuktu was renewed when I read about the mysterious aspects of the Moorish Science Temple in the legend of Ong's Hat. As Timbuktu was once considered the ancient capital of Moorish wisdom, I began reading everything about it that I could get my hands on. To me, the most intriguing aspect of Timbuktu was that this fabled city had served as a repository for the materials that were not destroyed in the fires that ruined the Library of Alexandria.

Before the advent of European sailing, Timbuktu had served as the commercial crossroads of Africa. This included both salt and gold trading. Timbuktu was the destination of most caravan routes due to its proximity to the Niger River whose tributaries once flowed all the way to the city during the flood season.

The wealth of Timbuktu and the surrounding Mali Empire was once so great that the disbursement of their gold literally crashed the Egyptian economy in 1325. This famous event occurred when Mansa Massa* was returning to Mali from Mecca and unleashed so much gold on the people of Cairo that the native currency became worthless. It is also a noteworthy historical fact that the uncle of Mansa Massa, Abu-Baker II, had literally sent thousands upon thousands of ships across the Atlantic Ocean hundreds of years before Columbus.

By the 1700's, Timbuktu was only a legend in the minds of Europeans. It nevertheless fascinated them beyond belief and several expeditions were sent to rediscover the remnants of what had once been termed the Golden Age of Africa. All of these expedition, however, failed. The first factual report to emerge in Europe during this time period was from a shipwrecked black American who ended up as a slave in a caravan and came across Timbuktu in his travels. He eventually escaped and ended up in England where his story was told in book form to a fascinated audience. His report was interesting but still a disappointment to those who hoped to hear of a golden city brimming with riches. He pretty much described Timbuktu as it is today.

There is, however, no question that Timbuktu was once indeed the largest center of learning in the world. When an Arab scholar by the name of Abd Araham Atimmi went to learn from the black Moorish scholars of the Timbuktu library, he was found so deficient in his abilities that he was sent to Marrakesh so that he could be schooled in more basic skills.

I have only offered a couple of pages, but my studying of Timbuktu was very profound on many different levels. The most obvious result was that it facilitated my meeting Mark Roberts. As I have said, I was not overly interested in Mark Roberts. It was only when Penelope told me that he had been to Timbuktu that I became suddenly interested in meeting him. This was going to be very easy because Penelope was sponsoring a workshop in Manhattan that was to feature Mark Roberts. Unbeknownst to me, she was handing me the next step of my olive research on a silver platter.

* Known as the Lion of Mali, there are different spellings and etymologies for the name Mansa Massa (cf. Mensa Mussa or Mansa Massu). The word *mansa* means both "gentle" and "meat" which is an extension of *menses.* The Christian rite of eating their savior is based upon earlier matriarchal masses (a word derived from *menses*) of consuming menstrual blood. This association is further demonstrated in the Arabic [footnote continued on page 94]

I decided to attend the two-day workshop which began with a Friday night lecture. Mark was primarily talking about stargates and the seven sisters of the Pleiades, but I was impatiently waiting to ask him a question about Timbuktu. When I finally did, he had something very important to say.

"Timbuktu is not what you want to be interested in. It's over here," he said as he drew a map of Africa on a writing board and drew a hastily drawn scribble in the midst of the African Sahara which was meant to represent the south central part of Algeria. "This is what you want to be interested in."

♥ **LOCATION OF THE AHAGGAR MOUNTAINS IN ALGERIA**

▲ **LOCATION OF TIMBUKTU IN MALI**

● **LOCATION OF CASABLANCA IN MOROCCO**

Mark was talking about a vast and impressive mountain range in the middle of the Sahara that is known as the Ahaggar mountains. Although I did not know it at the time, this was to become the central focus of the next leg of my research. Mark considered the Ahaggar to be a major stargate that was not only related to the Pleiades but one of the most important points with reference to the coming changes that will be taking place on planet Earth.

Mark did not come to his conclusions about the Ahaggar by mere conjecture. It happened while he was travelling and researching in the Sahara at the same time that Ronald Reagan decided to initiate the bombing upon Libya that killed Moammer Khadafy's young daughter. Khadafy responded by declaring an Islamic jihad against all Americans in the area, and Mark had to turn into a "German" as soon as possible. Making his way southward via the Ahaggar region, he followed the path of an ancient Tuareg/Berber tribe known as the Garamantians. Seeking refuge from the Roman Empire in the 3rd Century, the Garamantians migrated to Timbuktu and eventually made their way to the south bank of the Upper Niger River where they blended into the native population and changed their tribal name to Dogon.

The Dogon became famous when two French anthropologists discovered that this so-called primitive tribe had extensive astronomical knowledge of the Sirius star system. Their knowledge of astronomy was so extensive and so intricately interwoven with their own theology that the anthropologists (Marecel Griaule and Germaine Dietrlen) prolonged their field research as the entire proposition of what was presented to them completely clashed with conventional academic wisdom. After all, how could a bunch of "ugga buggas" have so much knowledge?

The Dogon were not only aware that Sirius was at least a two-star system but a three-star system as well. At that time, most astronomers of modern civilization were not aware that Sirius was more than one star. The following is a Dogon representation of their three-star home (see Glyph A on next page) plus a glyph that

[continued from page 94] name *Musa* which is identical to *Moses*. In *The Bible*, Moses was the facilitator of *manna* which was kept in the Ark of the Covenant. In Christianity, the eucharist is the equivalent of manna. The word *Moses* also means "messiah," but it is in itself a word based upon the Egyptian root *mau* which means "cat." The word *Massu* would therefore equate to "source of the cat" or "of cat origin" as *su* refers to "source."

suggests an orbital path of a planet going around a central sun (see Glyph B). All glyphs are courtesy of Mark Roberts.

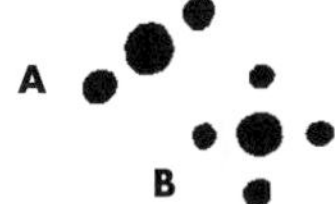

Modern-day astronomers were eventually able to document the two-star solar system of Sirius. It takes Sirius B some fifty years to orbit Sirius A, but only once in every fifty years can one see that the two stars are separate, and that requires a high-powered telescope. It was only years after the French archaeologists returned home that astronomers had such an opportunity and saw that the Dogon were accurate. This caused further consternation about the "ugga buggas." Dogon legends, however, indicated they were also keenly aware of a third star, Sirius C, and some scientists recognize the possibility of such. There is some evidence to suggest a third star, but that is still a controversial topic.

Dogon legends clearly possess knowledge that planets orbit around suns and that there is a planet revolving around Sirius C which they refer to as the "Star of Women." See Glyph C below which represents what is called a star but is really a planet orbiting around a sun. Glyphs D and E also symbolize the "Star of Women." Sirius C itself is referred to as the "Sun of Women," and it is considered "The Seat of the Female Souls of Living or Future Beings." It is a sun and its symbol includes two pairs of lines which are a key part of Dogon legends. (See Glyph F below.)

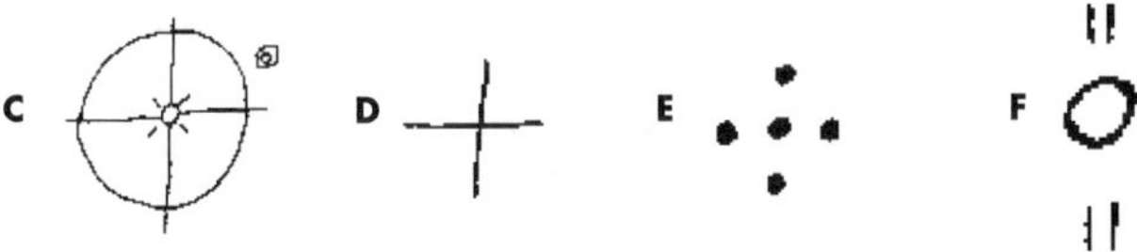

According to Dogon legends, these pairs of lines represent beams of light emanating from the "Sun of Women" (Sirius C) which, in turn, were received in various Egyptian temples as well as the Great Pyramid. When a beam of light from Sirius would be beamed upon an altar, it would thereby be transformed into Sothis, the Star Goddess.

To the Dogon, these beams of light from the "Sun of Women" were directed upon their original home in the Ahaggar region.

This star was the civilizing influence upon the ancestors of their tribe. It was depicted by the Dogon as a circle and the cross symbolizes the entire solar system of Sirius C which represents the female energy. (See Glyph G below.) It should be noted that this glyph is identical to a symbol in Aleister Crowley's *The Book of the Law* where it states, "then this circle squared ⊕ in its failure is a key also." Like the Kabbalists of old, Crowley's transmedium process is referring to the absence of energy of feminine energy being the key to the universal dilemma. The Crowley connection will be revisited in upcoming chapters.

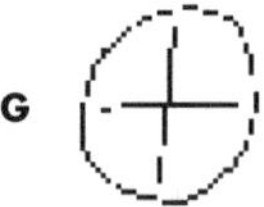

Several books, including *The Sirius Mystery* by Robert Temple, have understandably created a fascination with the Dogon's knowledge of the Sirius star system. Mark Roberts, however, is the only one who has made the connection to the Ahaggar. As Mark has said, it was fate, courtesy of President Reagan and Colonel Khadaffy, that pushed him southward from the Ahaggar and to Timbuktu and beyond. He was only able to make the connection as a result of witnessing a rock painting in the Tassili region of the Ahaggar. This rock painting clearly substantiates the case made by the Dogon in the south. See Glyph H below.

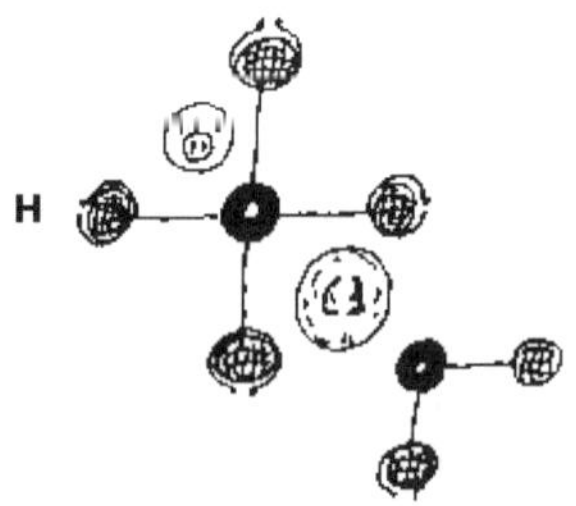

The three circles to the lower right represent the three-star solar system of Sirius. The five circles in the shape of an equilateral cross signify, once again, the symbol for the planet known as the "Star of Women." While this corroborates the Dogon connection, there are also two other symbols. There is a larger circle that shows two creatures in the middle. The curved lines surrounding the edge of the larger circle suggest that its a sphere or globe. See Glyph I below.

The smaller circle above is even more interesting because it features the double strokes which are the Dogon symbol for intergalactic beam travel. Note that the beams for space travel are the same as the feminine energy.

There is other rock art surrounding these pieces, including a man standing by them, but Mark has not yet had a chance to return to the Ahaggar and examine them further. The political climate is just as unfriendly as it was if not more so. The powers that be seem to want it that way. Years ago, when the French discovered the true archaeological implications of this region, they made many key areas of the Tassili a forbidden zone.

When Mark refers to this area as a stargate, he is not only making a connection to the "Star of Women" but to the ancient heritage and knowledge that it represents. It is indeed, as he suggests, the exact area where fiction meets reality. In their majesty, the Ahaggar mountains stand as a monument to an ancient culture and matriarchal tradition that "beamed down" from the stars long ago. That is the good news. The bad news is that the area is so restricted as to make investigation dangerous to your health.

The Ahaggar features many mysteries; and like any good science fiction story, it also has its guardian watchdogs. Mark explained to me that the Ahaggar mountains were and are the home of the Tuareg, also known as the Blue People. They are often referred to as the last living matriarchal culture on earth. The men wear veils and the women do not. The women are property owners and also choose their own husbands. They can divorce at will. This is in stark contrast to the Islamic culture that pervades Northern Africa.

Popular culture identifies the Tuareg as the Blue People by reason of the indigo garments they wear. The indigo dye actually rubs into the pores of the skin and gives an unmistakable blue hue to it. The indigo dye actually serves as protection against the harsh sun and sand.

It is fun to believe that the Tuareg might be the guardians of a portal or stargate. The more you study them, the more reason you can make for such a case. Mark Roberts has pointed out that the stargate is intrinsically related to the feminine energy of the Pleiades. As a matriarchal culture, the Tuareg themselves are known to hold key secrets with regard to the feminine energy. In any case, the Tuareg most definitely are the guardians of a great mystery and that is the Ahaggar itself.

The Ahaggar is an isolated mountain range in the middle of the Sahara that surrounds a gigantic system of caverns and underground tunnels that are said to go all the way to Egypt. It is surrounded by vast deserts that are threatening even to those equipped with modern day gear. The political heat in Algeria is only one factor that can repel visitors. Giant sand dunes that shift in a single day can completely wipe out a travelling party. Acting as guides, the Tuareg are the most reliable way to get there, but they are reclusive. One would need a Tuareg who lives in the Ahaggar itself, and most of these speak only their own native tongue.

As a people, the Tuareg were not completely new to me, but that was only because I had read about them in my studies of Timbuktu. I had no idea, however, that they appeared blue. In fact, much of the literature written about them over the years, particularly by French authors I have read, is highly prejudiced and inaccurate. In old European accounts I studied, I never saw it once mentioned that they were a matriarchy. The Tuareg were always portrayed as ruthless bandit warriors who were very quick to treat you with great hospitality. It was customary for them to invite you to come alongside and ride with their caravan en route to wherever your selected destination might be. Then, when you were pleasantly sleeping at four o'clock in the morning, they would rise and cut the throats of all the Europeans. While this modus operandi might understandably sound ruthless and utterly devious to the Europeans, there are some extenuating circumstances. First, the hospitality they offered was indeed customary behavior for civilized desert dwellers. The Tuareg, however, had a huge problem with the Europeans, and one must understand what they were up against before condemning their alleged behavior.

It was a well known fact amongst the Tuareg and the Moors that Europeans already had a solid and well earned reputation for being uncivilized barbarians. They were well known for coming into an area like a bulldozer whereupon they would pillage, rape and then systematically convert whoever they could to the religion of Jesus Christ. If the people were truly resistant to this new religion of Jesus Christ, the Europeans would then annihilate the opposition. Thus it was that such Tuareg massacres were actually desperate measures of self-defense against a known enemy in order to preserve their own civilization and religion, all of which was a rather secret matter.

The Tuaregs are technically classified as Berbers, a white people of North Africa, but they have mixed with dark-skinned Moors for thousands of years. When the Semitic people known as Arabs conquered North Africa in the wake of Muhammad, most of the Berber people saw the wisdom of aligning themselves with the Islamic revolution. Had they resisted the Arab culture, they would have been wiped out. It is a great but silent tradition that the Tuareg therefore give lip service to the Islamic faith and practice their own matriarchal traditions in private. This tradition is still successful to some extent, but the true Tuareg culture has been significantly diluted, especially as you reach the outer edge of the desert.

In coastal regions, Berber women are reluctant to practice their matriarchal ways for fear of being spied upon by their own males who sometimes turn them in to the Islamic authorities. In the depths of the Sahara, however, where the Ahaggar mountains reign supreme, the heart of Tuareg culture is very much alive. The center of this feminine culture is not only a great mystery, it is an area studded with labyrinthine caves that are forbidden territory for any but the most extreme desert dwellers. Their language is

Amazigh, a word which is suggestive of both "amazon" and "maze." A maze or labyrinth is very much representative of the feminine mysteries. The casbahs of Africa are not just houses built upon one another, they are dwellings studded with secret passageways that lead to underground tunnels and the like. In the casbahs, it is the women who know these secret passages and they are used as channels of communication by them. It is the Berbers, not the Arabs, who are the keepers of these passage ways.

As Mark Roberts said, the concept of a stargate will be where fiction meets reality. This blends into *The Bible* very nicely. As I continued to study the Tuareg, I could not help but notice that the namesake of the Ahaggar, also sometimes referred to as the Hoggar or Hoggar mountains, is phonetically tied to the Biblical character Hagar, the mother of Ishmael. Hagar is considered to be the mother of all Arab people by reason of her son Ishmael.* It is as if the entire area received its name from Hagar; or perhaps it is the other way around.

The science fiction theme that Mark refers to can also be seen in Frank Herbert's novel *Dune*. The Tuareg themselves served as the inspiration for the blued-eyed Fremen in this complex and intricate work. In that book, the Fremen were the guardians of the desert melange, a sacred spice created by giant sandworms, a potent drug that expanded the consciousness of anyone taking it. The consumption of this spice resulted in the eyes of the Fremen (or anyone else who took it) turning blue. This included both the cornea and the whites of the eyes. This expanded consciousness included heightened perception of the spiritual plane and enabled one to see various realities. Herbert had obviously studied the Tuareg culture when he wrote that book.

There is a very significant reference in *Dune* that will be lost on most readers. I was no exception when I read it. This has to do with the hero of the story, Paul Atriedes. This is his name from the off-planet royal family he belongs to. In that story, Paul had to

*In *The Bible*, Abraham could not have children with his wife Sara so he made union with Hagar the slave girl. The result was their son, Ishmael, who is regarded as the father of all Arabs. When Abraham and Sara were finally able to conceive a child, Sara was an old woman and her name was changed to Sarah. Their child, Isaac, is considered to be the father of the Israelites because they all descend from him. That the slave girl was named after the Ahaggar suggests a very rich and secret symbolism.

assimilate to the Fremen culture. When he does, however, he is accepted by the Fremen or Blue Men as a prophet and is called Maud'ib. Maud'ib is an obvious reference to a sacred Islamic term which is *Maudi*. The Maudi is recognized in Islamic culture as the redeemer of Mankind. Although fervently embraced by Islam, the tradition of the Maudi is far older than the prophet Muhammad and refers to a great deliverer who will come and redeem the desert. This term is important with regard to the feminine energy because the name *Maudi* itself is derived from the Egyptian word *mau* which means "cat" and is a direct reference to the feminine.

On a personal basis, I found that the fictional, real, and legendary knowledge of the Tuareg and the Ahaggar were weaving together in an incredible pattern. It not only integrated the theme from *Encounter in the Pleiades*, it also fit in with the phenomena I had run across with the Aleister Crowley connection to Montauk. By that, I am referring to the reference to the circle squared from *The Book of the Law*. Beyond that, there was also the suggestion of a Blue Race. I found it all fascinating. It never went unnoticed by myself, however, that Penelope was the gate-keeper who made this possible.

Penelope was familiar with the Tuareg culture long before she met Mark Roberts. Interested in Tuareg jewelry, she learned about it from one of her friends who used to sell it at a store on Long Island. Penelope relayed a touching story to me about this friend who developed an interesting history with the Tuareg. It started as a result of this woman purchasing jewelry and implements directly from Tuaregs in Africa. As economic strife fell upon many Tuareg families, they were forced to sell their most prized and valued artifacts. Knowing the culture, Penelope's friend recognized these most special artifacts when she saw them in the market place. She would immediately purchase them and start asking questions so she could return them to the original Tuareg owners. The money was insignificant to her because she was making enough and these were important heirlooms that the families only sold because they had to. She developed quite a reputation with the Tuareg as she was helping them preserve their culture.

My adventures with Penelope, instigated by my friend Tantra, were giving me an informative as well as a mysterious initiation into the feminine energy. Penelope introduced me to Mark

Roberts who introduced me to the knowledge of an entire culture I had previously known nothing about. Everything I had just studied about the Tuareg from European books was in error. More importantly, I was also learning some of the secrets of the Tuareg.

One of these secrets was that the Ahaggar itself was just like the tip of an iceberg. Shrouded in mystery, these mountains were once surrounded by an ancient ocean where the Sahara once stood. The tip of this so-called iceberg were the tops of the Ahaggar mountains which had once served as islands in this ancient sea. Even more fascinating than the ancient geography are the mountains and the caves beneath them, both of which contain many mysteries. This is said to include the most extensive historical archives of the planet Earth and includes a pictorial history of over 40,000 years of Earth's history. According to Mark Roberts, this ancient archaeology is intrinsically tied to stargates and the Seven Sisters of the Pleiades.

We will revisit the Ahaggar and the Tuareg later on as they play a very important part in my quest to discover the mystery behind the olive. At this point in my investigation, however, what I have presented thus far is a fair representation of what I knew at this point in the adventure. I did not expect to be studying Africa, a continent whose name is said to be derived from *afrit*, a variation of *ifrit* which means "jinn."

When I went to see Mark Roberts, it was because of my interest in Timbuktu. He was giving me far more than I had asked for. Although I was not expecting it, all of what he was telling me was leading to a major key with regard to the mystery of the olive. What was even more strange is that Mark was mysteriously tied to other elements of my research.

13

QUANTUM LINK

Mark Roberts was not only an acquaintance of Marjorie Cameron, he also had a most peculiar link to Aleister Crowley and the Germans. I discovered the German connection at a lunch during his Saturday workshop.

A group of us were eating at a Mexican restaurant. Mark and I were the only two males at what was a pretty good-sized table. For some strange reason, all the women got up and went to the powder room at the same time. It acted like a signal for him to tell me something because he did not want to say it in front of everyone. Well aware of my own German research, Mark revealed to me that he came from a very unusual family that had strange ties to the military industrial complex. His aunt had served as the head of communications for the Gestapo, and she had even authored a book entitled *The Rape of Europe*. He even told me code words and hand signals I could use to penetrate secret Nazi enclaves that exist to this day. He could not, however, guarantee my safety after I had been admitted. Mark is not a closet Nazi at all, but his family connections had afforded him this knowledge. Personally, he wanted nothing to do with this aspect of his family.

The Crowley connection came to him through Thomas Mann, the Arch Druid of Great Britain. Mark was the last pupil of this Arch Druid but Aleister Crowley was the first. It was through Thomas Mann that Mark met a man named Mike Nichols who told him an interesting story about Crowley. Not long before Crowley's alleged death on December 1, 1947, Nichols reported that Crowley came to Mann and asked him if he could provide him with a secret identity. Crowley was concerned that Israel Regardie, his former pupil, was out to kill him.*

Mark is not a Crowleyite, but he is familiar with the man and his work. To my advantage, he had also read my work with regard to the adventures I had with Crowley and the names of Cameron and Wilson. One very important link Mark noticed between my work and his own was when he saw Crowley's glyph that appears in *The Book of the Law:* ⊕ (see opposite page).

Crowley, serving as a transmedium for Aiwass, cryptically refers to this symbol as the "circle squared." It also represents the Celtic Cross. In occult circles, it is sometimes known as *carfourre* or *carfax* and it is a reference to shape-shifting. *Carfourre* is a French word meaning "four roads" and signifies an intersection. This is why the Bela Lugosi version of the movie *Dracula* used the name Carfax Abbey for his domicile in England.

More importantly, and as you have just read, Mark recognized the ⊕ symbol from his adventures in the Ahaggar and with the Dogon where it represents the Sirius C system. To the Egyptians, this was Sothis, a star goddess. As was said, Mark recognized it as a stargate.

There is no question that Mark's research is a major breakthrough in understanding the mystery of the Dogon as well as the lost feminine energy in this universe. His observation that it was related to a stargate, however, was something that I had heard before. The one who made this identification was my friend Kenn Arthur, the man who brought the mystery of the olive into my life.

Prior to that, however, there was a series of strange circumstances which not only might have precipitated Kenn bringing me the playbill from The New Montauk Theater but might have catalyzed the appearance of Mark Roberts in my life as well. Mark stated that it was fate that brought him southward from the

* Further information on the magical ramifications of Regardie's influence on the legacy of Aleister Crowley is mentioned in *Synchronicity and the Seventh Seal*. It should be noted that there is a discrepancy. In *Seventh Seal*, I mentioned that Mark mentioned that Mike Nichols was sometimes referred to as "Old Nick." Mark later denied this although Penelope reliably witnessed that I did indeed hear this from him. I also confused matters by confusing Nichols with Mann. Nichols was the Arch Druid who succeeded Thomas Mann. It should be further noted that this title of Arch Druid is disputed.

16

chance shape of the letters and their
position to one another: in these are mysteries
that no Beast shall divine. Let him
not seek to try: but one cometh after
him, whence I say not, who shall
discover the key of it all. Then
this line drawn is a key: then this
circle squared ⊕ in its failure is a
key also. And Abrahadabra. It shall
be his child & that strangely. Let him not
seek after this; for thereby alone can he
fall from it.

Ahaggar to discover the meaning of the mysterious Dogon glyphs and how they related to those in the Tassili. While it certainly appears to be fate, there is also another element at work.

Mark's departure to the south was to avoid the jihad that was a reaction to Ronald Wilson Reagan's bombing of Libya. The operative word here is "Wilson" as Reagan's middle name is Wilson. Each of his names possesses six letters which equates to 666, the self-assigned number of Aleister Crowley. Beyond the name synchronicity, Reagan had a further association with 666. After finishing his second term as President, Reagan's friends bought him a house in Bel Air that had 666 as the address. After public furor aroused by fundamentalist Christians, Reagan had the address changed to 668 for public relations purposes. In the papers, he claimed that he was uncomfortable with the number 666. I was amused with the change of address because 668 is the prefix to all phone numbers at Montauk.

My exposure to the ⊕ symbol being a stargate also came about by reason of a 666 catalyst. I am referring to Aleister Crowley's *The Book of the Law*. Crowley, of course, referred to himself as 666. The pivotal work in his life was *The Book of the Law*. This was the same book which Jack Parsons drew from in his *Babalon Working* of 1946. According to its author, *The Book of the Law* can be summed up in the accompanying diagram on the previous page. The whole proposition of the book is that someone was to come after Crowley and discover "The Key of it All." This prompted Parsons and several others to seek out this key.

To occultists and some scholars, *The Book of the Law* is considered one of the great metaphysical mysteries of the universe. If the ⊕ symbol is indeed the feminine energy, this would align very nicely with what the Kabbalists have said about it being the secret of the universe. I, however, did not fully appreciate its association with the feminine until I met Mark.

As I said in an earlier chapter, I was trying to understand this key passage in *The Book of the Law* when I experienced my fall out with Madame X. This led me to the inscription on the sarcophagus of Queen Menthu-hotep which said: PTR RF SU, meaning "Peter refer to source." From this, I learned that the name "Peter Moon" means "interpreter of the feminine." It was only then that I took my efforts to understand *The Book of the Law* to Kenn Arthur. He ended up giving me the playbill from the New Montauk Theater a couple of months later.

The next summer, I ended up enlisting Kenn's help again when I noticed something about *The Book of the Law* that I had neither seen nor appreciated before. I have never written about it until now, but there is a mysterious passage at the end of *The Book of the Law* which explains how to paste the handwritten pages of it to a wall. The order the pages should be placed in is distinctly specified. After one does this, one has a cryptogram of sorts to decipher. Specifically, the directions are given in Verse 73 of the third section of the book. Beginning from Verse 73, the entirety of *The Book of the Law* ends as follows:

> *73. Paste the sheets from right to left and from top to bottom: then behold!*
>
> *74. There is a splendour in my name hidden and glorious, as the sun of midnight is ever the sun.*
>
> *75. The ending of the words is the Word Abrahadabra.*
>
> *The Book of the Law is Written*
> *and Concealed.*
> *Aum. Ha.*

That summer, while my wife was on vacation and I was home alone, I decided to paste the sheets on the bedroom wall. Either through coincidence or by the pure magic of synchronicity, the time I chose to do this just happened to be the High Holy Days of Egypt. I am referring to the time of the year known as the Dog Days of August when Sirius is at its closest point to the Earth. This period is known as a time of sexual heat and is sacred to Bast. It is also centered around August 12th which is the traditional birthday of Isis. According to Egyptian tradition, Isis taught the Egyptians how to grow olives.

To me, pasting these sheets on the wall was not a holy ritual but merely an interesting project. I had studied *The Book of the Law* as a result of my research and the magical workings of Jack Parsons and L. Ron Hubbard. At this point, however, I had just taken note of the passage where it said to paste the sheets. When I told one of my friends who had been involved in magick about what I was doing, she became very excited. She said that all sorts of magicians in the O.T.O. talk and supposedly practice, but she had never heard of anyone trying this. I thought this was sort of odd as this was right out of what they consider to be their most holy book. Crowley himself had given some instructions about how to do it but even he did not brag of any results. The book itself was mostly a puzzle to him. His followers are even more confused.

After blowing up the size of Crowley's handwritten sheets on a copy machine, I pasted them all across one wall of the bedroom. I could not, however, readily decipher anything. Leaving them on the wall, I went to bed that evening. Although I was neither expecting it nor asking for it, the dream state suddenly became activated. As you may or may not know, dreams occur during what is known as R.E.M. sleep. R.E.M. stands for Rapid Eye Movement. When you dream, your eyelids are closed but your eyeballs are rapidly moving beneath them while you dream. The R.E.M. factor will become significant with regard to this adventure. The dream I had came in three very distinct parts.

First, I dreamt of Sonny and Cher. Cher was angry at Sonny and insulting him about his friends. In the second vignette, I found myself on a swing with a beautiful maiden who was very pleasant sexually and reminiscent of a nymph. In the third part of the dream, I found myself with my psychic friend Lorry Salluzzi. We were at a picnic table in a meadow surrounded by a forest, and she was handing me a big beef heart that looked grotesque.

When I called up my friend Kenn Arthur and told him what I was up to, he readily interpreted the dream sequence for me. He said that the dream of Sonny and Cher represented my marriage and that my wife was sick of my clowning and did not have any appreciation for what I was doing. Second, he said the maiden on the swing represented balance with the feminine energy and that I needed to seek and find balance. The third sequence with our psychic friend Lorry represented the heart of the matter. Looking back, I can easily see that the dream was telling me that my marriage was over and that my initiation with regard to the feminine energy was going to be outside of my marriage.

I then invited Kenn to come to my house and have a look at *The Book of the Law* manuscript that I had placed upon the wall. To my surprise and delight, he was able to come over right after he finished work. When he entered the bedroom, he looked at the wall and absorbed the whole view which included Crowley's writing and lines. It looked like a grid. After a period of intense concentration, Kenn expressed it all in three simple words. "It's a stargate," he said. "This is a map of a stargate."

"OK," I thought to myself. "Kenn sees a stargate."

Although I neither agreed nor disagreed with Kenn, I had not deciphered the wall pastings to my own satisfaction. I did not see a stargate, but I considered the possibility that he might be right. After all, I knew from my experiences with Kenn that he resonated with the concept of stargates. It was something he could talk about with a great deal of profundity.

A few years later, I would learn that Mark Roberts similarly identified the key passage and glyph from *The Book of the Law* as a stargate. In what can only be considered a very remarkable synchronicity, I discovered that Mark Roberts and Ken Arthur were tied together in the most mysterious of ways.

14

WHAT'S THE FREQUENCY, KENNETH?

In about 1976, Kenn Arthur found himself stopped at a red light at the base of the Triboro Bridge in New York City. Looking through his open window, he noticed a stalled limousine with four people inside. These included the driver, a cameraman and a producer. The most notable passenger, however, was Dan Rather, the famous anchorman of the *CBS Evening News*.

After Kenn asked the party what had happened, the producer told him that they were having car trouble. He then asked Kenn if he could take them to the airport as they were in a hurry to catch a plane. Kenn came to their rescue and delivered them in time to catch their flight.

I have already described Kenn as a jinn or gate-keeper. Needless to say, he is a psychoactive individual who was immersed in the consciousness of stargates and what not long before he met me or Preston Nichols. As for Dan Rather, I cannot account for his rapport with stargates. At that time, however, Dan Rather's frequency was being broadcast all across our local space as he was one of the premier news people of that time period. It was thus that the paths of Kenn Arthur and Dan Rather crossed. Ten years later, it became apparent to Ken that a significant crisscrossing of their energy fields had occurred as well.

In 1986, Dan Rather was walking down Park Avenue at 88th Street when he was accosted physically by two very well dressed hoodlums who repeatedly asked him, "What's the frequency,

Kenneth?" Rather was perplexed by their behavior as he had no idea what they were talking about. When he told the hoodlums they had the wrong guy, they chased Rather into a nearby building lobby as they beat and kicked him. At the same time, they continued to badger him with the words, "What is the frequency, Kenneth?"

The entire incident was a mystery to the police and Rather as well. No one was ever charged with any crime as the men could not be found for questioning. They were too well dressed to be considered ordinary thugs. The entire incident was written up in the October 5th, 6th and 7th issues of the *New York Times*. It was also broadcast on the local and national news.

As far as Kenn was concerned, he knew exactly what had happened to Dan Rather. According to him, an outside force was scanning the time line and wanted information about opening a particular stargate that Kenn will have knowledge of in the future. The purpose of this outside force was to access the future at a point when the manipulation of time will be a much more frequent activity. Kenn says that he will know the frequency with which to open the stargate in the future and that is how he was identified by the probing force. His own psychic signature was confused with Dan Rather's by his association in the car with the other people.

Kenn further explained that this third dimension is so dense that when a probe from a higher dimension tries to relocate a particular spot in space, it is sometimes as difficult as marking a spot on the ocean with chalk and then finding it again. Consequently, these hoodlums who beat Rather up were not only asking the wrong person but were in the wrong time as well. Coincidentally or not, the hoodlums fit the obvious description of that "interdimensional police force" known as the Men In Black. We could also refer to them as jinn.

Within a short time of my original conversations with Kenn about the Dan Rather incident, I had to wonder if someone was listening to our many phone calls. In November 7, 1994, a full eight years after Dan Rather was beaten up, *New York Magazine* suddenly and inexplicably came out with an article that attempted to explain it. In a report authored by Christine Soares, a man by the name of Ken Schaffer claimed to be involved. Schaffer is a Manhattan electronics expert who worked on a project at

Columbia University with Dan Rather. In 1983, Schaffer set up a satellite dish that could pick up Russian television. Schaffer eventually decoded the signals and filtered out the interference so that the transmissions were viewable.*

Rather's interest in all of this was as a journalist, but according to Schaffer's theory, the KGB was deeply upset that the Americans were spying on them. The idea is that they wanted to retaliate against Schaffer but that they followed Rather by mistake after he left the university. Schaffer does not insist that this is what happened. It is just his observation based on a very strange coincidence.

So, what is the real explanation?

Personally, I find it hard to believe that KGB agents would not know who Dan Rather is. Further, I think they would approach him more intelligently than by screaming for a frequency. Does Schaffer suppose that if Rather answered the hoods by stating a certain number of megahertz that they would have happily noted it down and left him alone?

After this article in *New York Magazine* appeared, a hit record emerged entitled *What's the Frequency Kenneth?* Recorded by the group R.E.M., the song developed a cult following as well. Dan Rather even appeared with them on stage and sang along on the song. As Kenn would say, "He sounded terrible."

Keep in mind that the initials "R.E.M." stand for the Rapid Eye Movement which occurs in the dream state of sleep. It is the exact realm from which mind control is administered to individuals in psychotronic projects. There is even a movie entitled *Dreamscape* which is based upon a project called Dreamsleep that involved Duncan Cameron.

Let us now consider the R.E.M. factor in light of the dreams I mentioned in the last chapter. I had put up sheets from *The Book of the Law* which precipitated symbolic and intense dreams for me. Kenn's dream interpretation centered on circumstances of my then existing marriage and seeking to find balance with the feminine energy. The heart of the matter was emphasized by my psychic friend Lorry Salluzzi. She also

* Unbeknownst to the author and publishers of the article, I found out that a noteworthy member of Aleister Crowley's O.T.O. (Ordo Templi Orientis) was also involved in this Russian decoding project.

represents the psychic or psychoactive nature of the dream which, as you will soon read, was active on many levels.

It was the spontaneity of the dream which caused me to call Kenn in the first place. It was so intense that I immediately related it to the pages on the wall. When he entered the room and identified it as a stargate, the ⊕ stood somewhere in the middle of the pages. This was the same symbol that Mark Roberts had already identified as a stargate but quite independently of Kenn's domain. Crowley did not refer to it as a stargate but as "The Key of It All." This is the Master Key. If we equate it to the legend of Solomon, it also represents his ability to rule the jinn.

The Sunday after Mark's workshop, I spent time with him and learned that there was an amazing association between Kenn and Mark. It came through Dan Rather. You have already heard about Kenn's strange encounter, but Mark was even closer to Rather. He had served as his top camera man for years! Even more odd was that their association became binding through the JFK assassination.

On November 24, 1963, when Lee Harvey Oswald was being paraded through the basement of the Dallas police headquarters, the entire nation was focused on getting a look at the accused assassin. I was no different. As a ten-year-old, I was in my living room while the television was on as we were treated to what the media billed as "the first live murder in the history of television" when Jack Ruby shot Oswald. Mark Roberts was the cameraman for journalist Dan Rather. Both of them were then working for the local CBS affiliate in Dallas. Rather's coverage of the events surrounding the assassination gained him national attention and he was soon promoted to the flagship station in New York. As his camera man, and in spite of the fact that he did not belong to the union, Roberts was promoted to New York with his colleague. The two men were around each other for years.

I do not know by objective reasoning if Kenn's story is the true reason Rather was accosted. If it is not, the probability of all these factors coinciding is one more amazing sample of synchronicity in my life that does indeed suggest that I was penetrating some sort of remarkable truth with regard to *The Book of the Law*.

15

THE BOOK OF THE LAW

I am not a believer in the Egyptian religion or any other religion. In attempting to understand certain aspects of it, however, I realized that I was getting a good dose of whatever medicine they might have to offer. Their high holy days, centered around the famous biorhythm of August 12th, were most definitely creating an impression on me as my incident with Kenn was not the only strange thing that happened to me during that period.

The day after Kenn's visit, I received a phone call from out of the blue. It was a woman that Preston and I knew from Montauk. She was a very intense lady and her husband worked at Camp Hero as a state employee. This was during a time of great secrecy at Camp Hero and before it was opened to the public as a state park. I had spoken with her husband as well, and it was very clear that he had been worked over pretty good. He admitted as much but had a difficult time talking about it. Now, she was contacting me spontaneously and wanted to talk about *The Book of the Law*. This was all a little too weird but very interesting. It did suggest to me, however, that I was on the right trail.

This woman had just been reading *The Pyramids of Montauk* and was studying the page with the glyph. She told me the whole key was to place a protractor on the line and measure the degrees of the line and then place those two degrees on a map of the world.

This sounded like an excellent idea, but there are problems with the line as it was not made with a true straight edge and it waivers. Further, if you measure from the various grid lines, you get different numbers. My initial measurement, which I mentioned in *Pyramids of Montauk*, was 26° which fits in nicely because it represents the angles of at least two major passageways in the Great Pyramid. One is the descending passageway which leads below to the Chamber of Chaos. The other is the ascending passageway which leads to the Grand Gallery and the Queen's Chamber. The latter features a shaft through which the light of the star Sirius shines just prior to the rainy season. Sirius is associated with 26° because, in ancient times, Sirius rose on the horizon 26.5° south of due east. It is also true that if you lay out the 26° angle of the ascending passageway on a flat map, it will lead you straight to Jerusalem.

Although the above all corresponds very nicely, other measurements from different grid lines give different numbers. They do, however, fit within a certain range for the most part. These measurements range from approximately 24° to 27° and from 63° to 64°. As my friend wanted me to plot them on a map, I interpolated the numbers for both latitude and longitude and plotted them both east and west from the Prime Meridian. It came out as follows, measuring west of Greenwich:

West 27° Latitude/64° Longitude = Bermuda Triangle
West 64° Latitude/27° Longitude = ocean south of Iceland

Measuring east of Greenwich, we get:

East 27° Latitude/64° = near Panjgur, Pakistan
East 64° Latitude/27° = near Nissila, Finland

If you apply these same numbers to the Southern Hemisphere, you get two areas in the ocean but relatively close to the Antarctic coast, one of which is near the former New Schwabenland of the Nazis. Another area is in the Indian Ocean and one is north of Santiago Del Estero in Argentina.

This was the first time I had heard of anyone suggesting or applying lines of latitude and longitude to *The Book of the Law*. It is guesswork. Due to popular literature, the Bermuda Triangle might seem to be the most appealing. Unfortunately, this approach includes too much guess work. It is significant, however, that this woman called in the midst of my foray into the subject. She was not the only one.

During this same time period, I received a call from my wife's best friend who has peculiar associations with Montauk. To protect her privacy and that of others, I will refer to her as Mary. What was happening at the exact moment that Mary called is what made the following occurrences most remarkable to me.

Due to the intensity of the dream (already discussed) I had experienced, I decided to review the movie *Dreamscape* which Preston had always said was based upon a project Duncan was involved in at or near Ong's Hat, New Jersey. At the exact moment Mary called, I had the video recorder on freeze frame because I was trying to make something out. In the particular scene I was scrutinizing, actor George Wendt was reading a novel (presumably a mock-up novel that was only a prop) entitled *Stab*. I had stopped the VCR because I could see the back of the novel had writing on it and I wanted to see what it said. I could not, however, make it out as the pixels did not break down that far.

I have not delivered the stroke of synchronicity yet because I first want to give the background on how and why it happened. *The Book of the Law* instigated my dream which brought Kenn into the fold. My dream state had become so psychoactive that it encouraged me to check out *Dreamscape*, an old thread Preston had brought up long ago. When I rented the video from the library, I could not help but notice that it was from E.M.I. Thorn , the same company that had released *The Philadelphia Experiment* on video.

I found *Dreamscape* both entertaining and psychologically penetrating. It is about a government psychic who is being trained in dream control. When he achieves a certain level, there are other government psychics who try to take over his dream and him, too. The battle he faces is in the dream world which, as can be expected, reaches over into the real world.

I stopped the video when I saw the *Stab* novel because of my previous research into *The Book of the Law*. In Chapter 26 of *Pyramids of Montauk*, I broke down the letters that the line in *The Book of the Law* is connected to. I did so because the book says:

> "This book shall be translated into all tongues: but always with the original in the writing of the Beast; for in

the chance shape of the letters and their position to one another; in these are mysteries that no Beast shall divine. Let him not seek to try: but one cometh after him, whence I say not, who shall discover the Key of it all. Then this line drawn is a key; then this circle squared ⊕ in its failure is a key also."

In *Pyramids*, I had connected the "line drawn" to the "chance shape of the letters and their position to one another." In other words, I delineated the letters which the line was connected to which were the following: S, T, B, E, T, I, S, A, Y, F, and A. Before the days of the internet and on-line anagram generators, I came up with two primary sets of words that made any sense at all:

EASY IF BAST

EAST IF STAB

The reference to Bast was and still is the best candidate. The reference to stab seemed a bit of a stretch. It is very important to point out in this regard that my approach angered certain people who were obsessed with their own way to interpret *The Book of the Law*, none of which were successful. People want an infallible mathematical approach or cryptographic approach. While such an approach should never be ruled out, I have learned something about the whole process and my observation is that synchronicity is actually a senior principle. This will become clearer as I elaborate on what happened.

Personally, I was not too interested in the "stab" connection. As I said, it seemed farfetched even through there was an alleged "Jack the Ripper" connection to Crowley. When I was watching *Dreamscape*, however, and saw a novel entitled *Stab*, I had to stop the video and at least try and see what was on the back.

It was at that exact moment that Mary, my wife's friend, called.

"I'm watching *Dreamscape*," I said, not really making too much sense to her but simply being spontaneous.

"I can't believe you said that!" she said. "That was my dream. I heard 'dreamscape' in my dream. I was stabbing my husband in the heart."

When I told her what I watching at that exact moment, neither of us could believe what was happening. She was angry at her husband as he was going broke and the inertia of his situation was taking her down as well. As life proceeded, he lost his business and she had to take drastic action to protect her own assets and her family. Her husband was a nice soul and a capable contractor, but he was having something worse than a mid-life crisis. He eventually suffered a heart attack and passed away at a young age.

Mary and her husband both had strange connections to Montauk. I discovered this in 1993 when I went with Preston videotape Montauk's St. Patrick's Day parade. As Preston took footage of the parade, I walked down the street and soon ran into Mary and her family and ended up watching the parade with them. The following Fourth of July, our families got together for a barbecue and all her husband could talk about was Montauk. I had no idea he was so absorbed by the place.

Mary's father was also a Montauk type case. She had memories of severe abuse by both of her parents and the father was always trying to cover it up. He took ridiculous positions and aggressively defended himself by accusing her of false memory syndrome. This was not, however, the only thing that connected her to Montauk. Over the time I knew her, she also became intimately involved with Mark Hamill's family members

All of this was too weird to be believable but it is true. I have not spoken to Mary since I got divorced many years ago. If and when I do, however, I am sure that she will be right on cue with more synchronicity. She was also obsessed with Thomas Jefferson, the man who came all the way to Long Island to record the lost language of the Montauk Indians.

As far as my investigation is concerned, synchronicity has always shown itself to be the ruling principle. *The Book of the Law* is no exception and it has its own morphogenetic field around it. That was generated long ago when Crowley gated it in from his activities within the Great Pyramid. As a pyramid is a concentration of energy, the Great Pyramid is one of the greatest examples known to Mankind. It therefore stands to reason that there are going to be all sorts of synchronistic threads that run across the gamut of human experience. In my case, I had simply penetrated the morphogenetic field of Crowley's experience by pasting the sheets on the bedroom wall. I had activated the energies and was getting a virtual side show that coincided with my own life.

More clarification can be offered if you break down living into three states of consciousness: the awakened state, the sleeping state, and the dream state. In any given situation, the dreamer is connecting all three as the act of dreaming is all about integration. This, however, does not account for the extraordinary concentration of synchronicity I was experiencing. That had more to do with the nature of the macrocosmic elements I was working with. It is sort of like the difference between interviewing Donald Trump as opposed to someone who owns a hot dog stand on a lonely road. Some subjects, particularly powerful ones, are more highly charged.

My efforts to resolve the mystery of this key passage of *The Book of the Law*, however, was not a passion of mine. I only came across it by reason of my experiences with synchronicity. Others have worked long and hard to decode this mysterious text which is loaded with hidden codes.

One person has converted the English letters where the line is drawn to Hebrew letters and then utilized gematria (numerological substitution) to come up with the key being "Babalon." Although this person has not received wide or any particular acceptance, they are quite accurate as it represents the feminine energy already alluded to. It must also be remembered that Jack Parson's Babalon Working was said to be the fulfillment of *The Book of the Law*. When I met Cameron, I met the physical embodiment of that work. I, however, was coming to her by reason of synchronicity and that alone. Once again, it has proven to be the senior principle at work.

There is another decoding of this book which brings this point home once again yet takes it even one step further. This was interpreted by a friend of mine who goes by the name of Daemon Magus or T. Buddha.

The Book of the Law begins by stating "Had! The manifestation of Nuit." Nuit is an Egyptian name for "night" or Sothis (the night star), the same name by which Mark Roberts recognized the symbol ⊕. Sothis and Sirius both represent the feminine energy.

Line 22 of the first chapter reads as follows:

> "Now, therefore, I am known to ye by my name Nuit, and to him by a secret name which I will give him when

at last he knoweth me. Since I am Infinite Space and the Infinite Stars thereof, do ye also this. Bind nothing! Let there be difference made among you between any one thing and any other thing; for thereby there cometh hurt."

In the above text, note that both "Infinite Space" and "Infinite Stars" are capitalized in the original text. I have added the underlining for emphasis. These capital letters, which defy punctuation rules, spell out Isis, another name for Sothis. The text also states that division between one thing and another results in hurt. It is implied if not directly stated that this feminine energy is the cohesive principle of the universe. Without it, there is suffering, a concept which puts a whole new spin on the Christian and Buddhist preoccupation with suffering and salvation.

Lines 23, 24, and 25 read as follows:

23. But whoso availeth in this, let him be the chief of all!
24. I am Nuit and my word is six and fifty.
25. Divide, add, multiply, and understand.

These lines give an even deeper clue. As the feminine aspect of night, Nuit identifies herself as "six and fifty" which is another way of saying the numeral "56." "Divide" is the next instruction, but the division we are talking about is not what you are used to in math. As anyone who is familiar with esoteric geometry should recognize, "divide" means to separate the "five" from the "six." We are also told to "add" them which is significant. "Adding," however, has two separate meanings. See the following interpretation for clarification.

six and fifty = 56
dividing 56, we have 5 and 6
adding, we have 5 + 6 = 11

Eleven is the number of Abrahadabra which is the concept that "ends" *The Book of the Law* (per its own statement). In Aramaic, *Abrahadabra* means "I create with the words thus spoken." This word is also featured on the grid page with the ⊕ symbol for Sothis or Sirius, a system then known as a two-star system. As part of the "hidden" magical formula of Abrahadabra, these two stars of Sothis are represented graphically as a pentagram and a hexagram. When we are told to *add* the 5 (pentagram) and the 6 (hexagram) as per above, we get a much deeper meaning.

PENTAGRAM **HEXAGRAM**

These two symbols have come to represent many things in civilization's body of knowledge, some of them accurate and some of them false. When combined together, they are "twin stars" which is yet one more reference to the star Sothis or Sirius. Although Sirius is often viewed to represent three stars, it has traditionally been viewed as a double star system. What is more noteworthy, however, is that if one then "adds" these two shapes and reverses the pentagram, one gets the following glyph.

Now, look and consider that the upside down pentagram is a female being penetrated by the phallic part of the hexagram. This is, of course, representative of the birth of life. If this glyph is then cut out and multiplied (as per *The Book of the Law*) by three, they can be twisted to make the pattern for a DNA molecule. The glyph therefore represents spirit going into or animating matter. It also aligns quite nicely with the "line drawn" in *The Book of the Law* because if you connect the words that are connected to the line, they all read out as follows:

I SAY TRY TO SHAPE A BEAST

These geometric patterns are therefore the process by which a beast or creature of life is shaped. It is the DNA molecule. Keep in mind that this message was transmitted in 1904, long before DNA was a well understood commodity by biologists.

The upside down pentagram is often misconstrued to be satanic. While it is true that satanists utilize this symbol, the pentagram represents spirit over matter when it is upright. When it is reversed, it represents matter over spirit. When spirit is incarnating into a biological entity, it is obviously becoming subservient to matter on some level.

This glyph not only represents the birth of an individual life form, it also represents the Cabalistic Tree of Life. All that is needed to complete the usual diagram is to add Malkuth (the bottom point or sepiroth which represents the Earth).

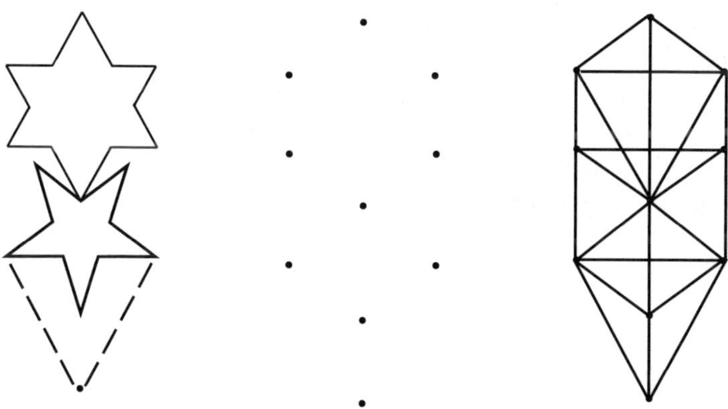

The diagram on the left utilizes two broken lines to extend the creation of "five" plus "six" to the Earth plane, known as Malkuth to Cabalists. The dots in the center of the page represent the points from the diagram on the left that are utilized to make the typical diagram for the Cabalistic Tree of Life, pictured on the right. One can easily visualize the twenty-two pathways of the Tarot, all of which are categorized as forbidden knowledge in Judaism.

All of this information tells us that *The Book of the Law* is filled with coded information about the various templates and processes for creating life. Such processes could easily be thought to be the handiwork of God. Mother Nature is another designation which is arguably more accurate.

All of the above information prompts various questions about the purveyor of the information. We can discount Crowley to some extent because he was primarily a vehicle that Aiwass (the entity which Crowley said transmitted the book) used to communicate. Whoever the entity who dictated or directed *The Book of the Law* actually was, he or she knew a remarkable amount about the geometric and biological properties of life that were, for the most part, unknown to the educated people of the day. The fact that they were written in a virtually undecipherable code is all the more ingenious. It should therefore not be lost upon the reader that the root of the word *ingenious* is *genius*, the root of which is *jinn.* This is exactly what we are dealing with. Aiwass, communicating through Crowley, was most certainly representative of the jinn.

When we approach mysteries like Montauk, *The Book of the Law*, or the mystery of the universe, we are going to be beset by a long tradition of ignorance at best and deliberate misdirection at the very worst. If the solution to life's mysteries is indeed the true feminine energy, we can be sure that the frequency of such is being jammed. The ⊕ symbol of Sothis or Sirius provides yet another clue with regard to unjamming the frequency.

16

THE CIRCLE SQUARED

Besides the "key of it all" mentioned in the last chapter, the key page in *The Book of the Law* mentions another key in the following sentence:

> "Then this line drawn is a key: then this circle squared ⊕ in its failure is a key also. And Abrahadabra. It shall be his child and that strangely. Let him not seek after this: for thereby alone can he fall from it."

The idea of squaring the circle is an old mathematical challenge whereby one is invited to take a circle and then create a square that has the exact same square footage as the circle. This process of discovery is only aided by the use of a blank straight edge, a compass, and a pencil.

Squaring the circle was a very competitive endeavor in the late 19th Century until it was discovered that it was theoretically impossible to do so because π, an irrational number, was involved. One therefore needs to measure with π which goes on infinitely. One could figure out the virtual square footage very easily by using more precise approximations of π , but we are talking about the exact square footage. This exercise reaches into the infinite.

Due to the futility of this exercise, "the circle squared" or "squaring the circle" became a euphemism for a task that was fruitless or could not be done. This phrase was still fresh in people's minds when Crowley referenced it in 1904.

Besides this, there is another reference to "squaring the circle" that Crowley would have been very well aware of. This is a Masonic reference that I have never seen any Crowleyites take notice of. It resolves the mystery of this phrase very nicely. It has to do with the dimensions of the Great Pyramid of Giza.

> THE BASE OF THE GREAT PYRAMID IS A SQUARE WHOSE PERIMETER IS EQUAL TO THE CIRCUMFERENCE OF A CIRCLE WITH A RADIUS EQUAL TO THE HEIGHT OF THE GREAT PYRAMID.

The dimensions of the Great Pyramid are as follows:

Height = 481 feet
Base = 755 feet (some say 755.5 or 756)
Perimeter = 3,020 feet (755x4)

Although π was the demise of the previous exercise, it is not a significant factor in this one because the Great Pyramid has actual measurements and we are trying to find a circle, not a square. (The term squaring the circle can refer to either replicating the square footage of a circle from a square or vice versa). In order to find the circumference, we follow the following formula:

$$\text{Circumference} = 2\pi r$$
$$(r = \text{radius}, \pi = 3.14)$$

We then get a circumference that equals 3,020.68 feet which is virtually the same as the 3,020 feet of the perimeter of the base. The radius is then derived from a circle that looks something like the following which is only an approximation and not drawn precisely to scale:

Based upon this depiction, the comparative size of the Great Pyramid would look like this. The square below is the base of the Great Pyramid. The circumference of the circle below is based upon the aforementioned instructions. The triangle represents the height of the Great Pyramid.

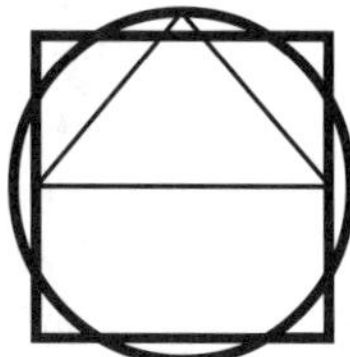

This demonstrates how small the height of the Great Pyramid is in relation to its base, and it is all very nice except for one very key point. These measurements are all done taking into account an imaginary capstone. The real capstone was removed long ago. Therefore, all attempts to square the circle are futile because the "height" of the Great Pyramid has been compromised due to the missing capstone. This "failure of the circle squared" is a particular reference to a level of Freemasonry. Crowley would have known this reference very well. In other words, the additional key he refers to besides "the key of it all" is a reference to the missing capstone of the Great Pyramid.

The history of the missing capstone is full of mysteries and might be considered the biggest occult mystery in the existence of this planet. According to conventional history, the most popular version of what happened to the capstone is that it had gold casings which were removed by Mamelukes in about the 13th Century and placed in their homes or palaces. This effectively destroyed the capstone, but it is not a very good explanation for a number of reasons. What is most bizarre, however, is that there is virtually no occult history on this subject either. There is, however, plenty of New Age fluff as well as academic grandstanding.

There is one interesting observation with regard to the capstone that is not unknown but is paid scant attention to. By coincidence or grand design, the size of the Holy of Holies (which houses the Ark of the Covenant) is a cube that is 15 cubits x 15 cubits x 15 cubits. (A cubit is about 18 inches.) The capstone, which is 13.5 feet at its base, would fit snugly into the space of the Holy of Holies.

The mathematics of the situation imply that the Egyptian Thutmosis (Moses), who was a priest of Egypt, had the Holy of Holies built so that it could contain the energy of the capstone, the capstone itself or a replica. This idea fits in very nicely when we examine the etymology of the word *pyramid* and how it fits into the Holy of Holies.

In the *Pyramid Texts* of ancient Egypt, the word *pyramid* itself is described by the phonetic equivalent in English of "M-R." This iteration of *mr* or *mur* has profound implications as you will learn later. The association with the word *Moor* is undeniable. What is of further interest is that the two sounds made my *m* and *r* are both intrinsic roots of words which mean "cat." In Egyptian, the word for cat is *mau.* In Native American culture, the Erie Mound Builders were known as the cat people because the *Er* or *ir* sound means "cat" in their language. Hence, *m* and *r* both mean "cat."

In English, the dictionary does not even try to give us an etymology for the word *pyramid**, but the phonetics of the word give an excellent clue. *Pyr* means "fire" and is also akin to *par* or *phar* which can mean either "fire" or "house" and is the root of the word *pharaoh.* The word *amid* refers to "the middle" or "in the midst of" and is evident in a sentence such as: "He stands tall amid the confusion." The word *amid* is also close to *amado* which means "loved" in Portuguese. All of these appellations suggest the hearth and promote the idea of a pyramid as a warm home. As you will read, this idea of the "fire in the middle" is the most relevant.

*Although most dictionaries have abandoned the meaning or etymological trail of the word *pyramid*, some scholars have wrestled with it and come up with relevant and perhaps not so relevant answers. It is said to derive from the Egyptian *pooramis* which can be identified with a "cave" or a "sepulchre" because "*amis*" refers to "dead." *Pooramis* sounds like Paramus, New Jersey which once belonged to the Lenni Lenape Indians from which the Montauks descended. The word is thought to mean "fertile ground" or "wild turkey" but the name appears to have had much more to do with Egyptian migration to America by the Montauk Pharoahs.

Pooramis has also been broken down into *pyr* + *met* or *pi* + *re* + *mit* which both mean a "one-tenth part of a measure" or "measures in space numbered by ten." It has also been identified as "division produced by fire." This last definition suggests the fire is the sun because the word *pooramis* has also been meant to signify "the Original Ten Measures or Part of the Fiery Ecliptic or Solar Wheel, or the Ten Original Signs of the Zodiac." In earlier times, the Zodiac was considered to have only ten signs. Division into ten was also considered divine. You not only see this in our decimal system but in the Spanish word *Deios* or the English word *deity* which both relate to "ten."

In *Pyramids of Montauk*, Stan Tenon's brilliant research was demonstrated which showed that by shining a light from twenty-seven different angles upon a particular shape, all twenty-seven letters of the Hebrew alphabet could be produced in shadow form. This "particular shape" is a unique "twisting vortex" shape which conforms to the shape of a tube torus (doughnut). (See *Pyramids of Montauk* for diagrams and further information. Also look up Stan Tenon's Meru Foundation on the internet). This twisting shape also conforms to the design of the human hand.

This shape also mimics a flame and is why Hebrew letters are sometimes called "flame letters." The flame's shape also fits into the middle or center of a pyramid. Stan Tenon's original discovery came about when he observed there was a symmetrical pattern in the letters that make up the first verse of *Genesis* in the Hebrew *Torah*. He could not figure out the relationship of the letters until he wrote each letter out, put each one a bead chain, and curled the bead chain around until the identical letter-beads lined up with each other. It formed a two-dimensional pyramid. By reducing these letters to their most compact and elegant form, he came up with the vortex or flame-shape described above. This form could be considered to rest in the middle of the pyramid.

When we now consider the capstone being superimposed upon or placed inside the Holy of Holies (figuratively or otherwise), we can now consider the flames within each and that they at least correspond with each other if they are not identical. The fact that the Hebrew alphabet is referred to as the *Meruba* tells us that the relationship of Hebrew to the pyramid was known for a long time. Once again, *M-R* or "mer" refers to a pyramid.

It stands to reason that all of this knowledge was once known and lost, probably at about the same time as the disappearance of the capstone itself. This only reemphasizes the dilemma of the circle-squared and its failure being a key. There is, however, one more aspect to the circle-squared which I have not yet covered.

Part of the Masonic doctrine with regard to the "failure of the circle-squared" has to do with the irrational or infinite aspect of π. One can make perfect circles, but when one wants to apply their dimensions to make a corresponding square, one cannot do it. This therefore introduces a human element which is sometimes referred to as the quantum element because it involves an observer.

The human or observer factor is therefore the one that is applying the perfect principles of "God's geometry" to an imperfect world. The infinite aspect of π, as well as all other irrational properties of mathematics, emphasize this factor which is the quantum aspect. This refers to "being alive." Squaring the circle therefore refers to the very activity of taking your place as a live quantum observer. This is your connection and pathway to the infinite and then back again.

The circle squared is thus a metaphor for "activating your own capstone" and becoming a fully conscious individual. Mark Roberts is also telling us that it is an ancient symbol for a stargate as well as the feminine energy.

In my adventures, I was following a trail of magical synchronicity that was activating the key stated in *The Book of the Law*. The truth of this statement can only be evaluated by how many doors this key can open. If it is truly "The Key of It All," it is going to be a master key which will open all doors. I had already given an interpretation of this key in *Pyramids*, but it was admittedly limited. My findings were, however, good enough to catapult me into further explanations and clarifications. Let me say that I had discovered a part of the key. More importantly, I had a firm grip on the key. That grip led me to Kenn Arthur and Mark Roberts, both of whom acted like a tag-team, each giving me clues from different angles. Both were wrapped up in the "frequency" which was either carried or associated with Dan Rather. The olive was the central focus of all of these clues as it provided the doorway into these mysteries. The frequency of the olive has proven itself to be the frequency of the stargate both Kenn and Mark referred to. It is the feminine energy of the Kabbalists.

Although Kenn got me started, Mark would take this olive angle another step further. When I told him of my adventures with Kenn and the olive, he recalled running across the olive in some of his key research about the Ahaggar mountains of the Sahara. Before Mark left New York for his home in Texas, he said he would look into his papers and send me what he could find. What he came up with was far more than I could have hoped or expected.

17

ANTINEA

As was said in Chapter 13, Mark Roberts recognized the ⊕ symbol from his visit to the Ahaggar, a remote region of the Sahara. So that you can better appreciate how his brief appearance in my life fits into this narrative, I will preface his delivery of the olive mystery with some of his earlier field work.

Besides being a camera man and a Druid, Mark is a field archeologist and a dowser. All of these roles were a natural fit when he began to study crop circle phenomena in the early 1980's. Before it became a New Age craze, Mark was doing his own grass roots research and trying to interpret the circles in terms of the ancient Ogham language. Ogham is a language of ancient people (including the Druids) and is based upon the shapes of trees. Besides the above qualifications, Mark studied at Oxford under Robert Graves, author of *The White Goddess,* the quintessential book on Ogham. Between his Druid orientation and learning from Graves, Mark is very skilled in deciphering Ogham.*

You can read about the details on Mark's website, but he essentially took the glyphs from the early crop circles and spelled them out in the Ogham language. Seeking to interpret them, he found it necessary to rearrange the glyphs and saw that if he did so, they spelled out "Ma'at," the Egyptian goddess of fairness and

* Just as "official academe" tried to foist off the idea that Columbus was the first person to cross the Atlantic, so does it often insist that Ogham was confined to the European continent. Mark laughs at that because he has seen obvious inscriptions of Ogham all over America and across the world as well. Scholars are now beginning to recognize the obvious truth of this.

justice. Ma'at, who represents balancing the scales, is the consort of Thoth or Tahuti, the builder of the Great Pyramid. Most etymologies of the word *Ma'at* are spurious. It is actually and clearly a composite Egyptian word made up of *ma(u)*, meaning "cat" and *at* which is a feminine appellation. Hence, Ma'at means "female cat." As Tahuti is the god of the moon, sorcery and sexual magick, this association with the cat should not be too surprising. All of this suggests that the Great Pyramid, built by Tahuti, is accompanied by the feminine energy and justice of Ma'at.

Mark's experience with the crop circle glyphs tell us something beyond what the Kabbalists offer. Not only is the universe a result of a banishment of feminine energy, but there is an aspect of the feminine energy which is trying to redeem Mankind. It also has a consciousness and can use nature to communicate. All of this puts the crop circle phenomena into a very clear perspective.

The media hoaxes and obsession with disproving the original phenomena is all about jamming the transmission of feminine energy. Further, the obsession to jam the frequency is of far greater magnitude than is the transmission of the communication itself. While the message has gotten through to some, the social phenomena surrounding the circles is a more sensational statement than the circles themselves. To properly deal with this on a personal level, it is wise to view the media, military agents and circle hoaxers as the jinn or agents of the jinn coming to roost.

These so called jinn represent patriarchal zones of power and control. If you look at the financial plight of the world, you will find that things become bottle-necked at key points of distribution. There is more than enough wealth and food for the world to enjoy itself and live abundantly. It is those in charge of the zones of power and control which seek to jam the feminine energy. On the other hand, the Great Mother will act in such a manner as to take care of her children.

While the feminine energy behind the circles has not yet convinced the world to heed it, enough of an impression was created upon Mark that he was able to give me a big clue with regards to the olive. When he got home, he went through his papers and found something very interesting with regard to the olive. True to his word, he sent me a package that included several publications by Egerton Sykes.

Most people, particularly academics, have never heard of Sykes, but he was a field archeologist, a dowser and also a meticulous scholar. He was heralded for his information by some scholars and the Nazis also showed a keen interest in his research. For a considerable amount of time and even into the 1970's, Sykes published a magazine called *Atlantis* in which he sought to describe and document ancient legends and corroborating information in order to establish the true nature of the lost continent. Although his work is truly amazing and based upon ancient sources, his work is largely ignored by academe.

Of all the publications I perused, one caught my attention more than any of them. It was the October 1952 issue of *Atlantis* which featured an article entitled *Antinea, Search for a Lost Queen; A Tale of Two Cities*. Simply put, this article clearly indicated that the mysteries of the Ahaggar were inextricably linked to the olive. The Tuareg people, it stated, descended from a legendary blue queen of Atlantis whose name was Antinea which the Greeks eventually transliterated into *Athena*. In myth, Athena gave Mankind its greatest gift: the olive tree.

To anyone reading such information, it might easily go in one ear and out the other ear. To me, the implications were staggering. I had been on a quest for years to discover the mystery of the olive. My quest to discover the history behind the Montauk pyramids had led me to my adventures with Madame X and the revelation that Queen Mentu-hotep's sarcophagus was inscribed with "PTR RF SU." From that, I learned that the Peter Moon name I had taken meant "interpreter of the feminine energy." This then led me to Kenn Arthur who responded by giving me a gift from "spirit" which was the mysterious playbill containing two pictures of the Mount of Olives underneath it. My quest to discover the mystery of the olive was punctuated by what could be termed either the untimely or timely death of Olive Pharoah. Now, through the most mysterious means imaginable, the antics of Kenn Arthur and Mark Roberts were bringing me, at least figuratively, to the footsteps of the Queen of the Olives herself.

Queen Antinea is of critical importance to the previous work that I have done as her legacy sits at a crossroads of synchronicity. As the original giver of the olive tree and the inspiration upon which the goddess Athena was based, we see an earlier legacy of feminine wisdom that was once prevalent upon the planet. This is what Antinea represents and it is the same wisdom and energy that was represented by Marjorie Cameron.

As this mystery unfolded to me, I saw two key aspects with regard to Antinea. Besides being the giver of the olive tree, she is also depicted with blue skin and as the queen of the Tuareg, a people who are said to be the custodians of a stargate. Both of these are crucial to understanding the past history of Mankind. The blue skin I will address in the next chapter. For now, I will address the Ahaggar as the repository of a mysterious stargate.

To repeat, the Ahaggar mountains are located in South Central Algeria in the most remote part of the Sahara. Millennia ago, the Ahaggar were once islands in a large body of fresh water known as the Triton Sea. Today, this region is off limits to anyone but the native Tuareg themselves. In the interior of the Ahaggar, it is a rare Tuareg who speaks a foreign tongue. Do not go there and expect to be understood.

When I discovered the Ahaggar for myself, I spoke to David Childress, the intrepid world traveller who has written about this region in his book *Lost Cities and Mysteries of Africa and Arabia*. The first thing David said was, "Don't go there. Foreigners are to be shot dead on sight."

David was not talking about the Tuareg shooting people. He was referring to extremist military cults that have ravaged Algeria for decades. In the aftermath of World War II, the politics of Algeria changed significantly. The CIA moved into Algeria in the early Fifties and began to covertly manipulate the balance of power. The presence of military intelligence is still very much there to this day. The government of Algeria continues to struggle with violence. Until the recent fighting in Iraq, Algeria was probably the most dangerous country in the world.

The Tuareg are only a part of this violence to the degree they have to defend themselves from it. They have always been a problem to the European and Arab governments. After all, they are a true indigenous people who still believe in a matriarchal culture. Although their caravans and salt trade were compromised long ago, their presence in the interior of the Ahaggar and the caves within is still intact. David told me that these caves are so deep and extensive that they are said to run all the way to Egypt.

The primary reason that the Tuareg have hung onto the Ahaggar this long is that the Sahara is difficult to penetrate. The sand dunes are huge and shift over night. They could wipe out an encampment in a matter of hours. The Tuareg themselves know the desert and patterns of nature so well that they are the only reliable guides into the area. A Tuareg can tell where he is and how far away from home simply by feeling the quality of the sand.

If one is lucky enough to survive the desert, the gateway to the Ahaggar is more forbidding. To go into the heart of the mountains, there is a narrow gorge known as the Land of Fear that one must pass through. This is particularly perilous because the rocks become so hot in the daylight that they literally explode like machine gun fire and shrapnel. This is due to freezing cold at night and extreme heat during the day. Avalanches are also common. Although these occurrences are scientific phenomena, they breed many frightening legends. One such legend can be found in David's *Lost Cities and Hidden Mysteries of Africa and Arabia.*

In that book, David refers to another book entitled *The Ancient Atlantique* by L. Taylor Hansen who relays the story of an Arab who had different encounters in the Ahaggar. Having served as a messenger between his sheik and the people of the Ahaggar, he got to hear some very interesting stories. One of these included a meeting with a Tuareg King in the forbidden city of the Tauregs, Amen-okhal (note the Egyptian name). He feasted with the king and got to witness dancers wearing strange masks.

This Arab also reported that he and a friend once climbed a peak and discovered a shaft that was covered by a metal grate. Another time, he snuck into the Ahaggar mountains and witnessed a ceremonial war under the moonlight where two mounted Tuareg groups engaged in battle. After a fight to the death for some, a group of Tauregs rode into the wall of a cliff and disappeared.

Of particular interest in the stories of the Arab was that he spoke of galleries of tunnels deep within the mountains. This corroborates many such stories indicating that there are miles and miles of galleries that were painted around an artificial lake. Torch lit passage ways depict ancient history. This region also contains the oldest libraries in the world that extend well into the Antediluvian period. It is said that they refer to a time when the Taureg ruled the seas.

Although these stories and descriptions of the Ahaggar are from one "lone Arab," they are typical of what you will hear if you ask long enough and in the right places. There are many different accounts which substantiate the intriguing claims of this region. As the Tuareg are known to be relentless guardians of their secret heritage, what has been offered here could be considered a rare glimpse into the world of the veiled people as they are called.

When I told one of my friends about the Ahaggar, he arranged for me to meet with some Algerians in Manhattan. They were from Oman in the north and were not aware of the special legends of the Ahaggar region. As far as the politics of Algeria were concerned, they said that most of these problems were caused by the British who manipulate the various jihad groups through clandestine means. They were kind enough to arrange a meeting with another Algerian who had been to the Ahaggar. This man, who had served as the Minister of Sports and Industry for the Algerian government, spoke only in French. With Penelope and the other Algerians translating, he said that the Ahaggar was so beautiful that it was beyond the imagination. Aware that the land was very special and contained many mysteries, he gave me a stunning impression. As worldly and friendly as this man was, however, he was not a Berber and was not privy to any of the secret Tuareg culture.

The first two Algerians invited me to their country and said I would be safe, but I would not take them up on their offer. As they had been robbed in Manhattan, they might look at me quite indifferently if misfortune befell me in their country. I also had friends in Morocco who warned me against it. Besides, even if their word was good, they could only see me through the Arab side of the culture. They knew nothing about accessing the Tuaregs. Language is also a factor. There is much trouble in Algeria.

Mark Roberts also said he could arrange for the two of us to visit. When I asked about safety, he said he could provide a letter from Trammell Crow which would ensure that. Trammell Crow is a Dallas real estate developer who has financed many Arab operations. At one point, he had bought up huge portions of the city of Dallas on behalf of Moamar Khaddafy. When this relationship was discovered, it created a public outrage. Mark was willing to take the risk and travel to Algeria, but I do not have confidence in a letter. If a jihadist is circumspect enough to even look at your letter before he shoots you, he probably does not understand English. If the letter is in Arabic, it might help considerably but it is like expecting a gunslinger in the Old West to retire his gun because he has received a restraining order from the sheriff.

The mysteries of the Ahaggar remain largely secret, but I did meet a tantra teacher, not Tantra Bensko, who once met a mysterious lady who had grown up with a group of Berber women in this area of Algeria. This mysterious lady had a father in the U.S. State Department and that was why she was overseas. The Berber women were from the Tassilli region and were known as the Banti Hara. I corresponded with the mysterious lady by email a couple of times, but she was not very responsive.

As for himself, Mark had not heard of the Banti Hara, but he helped me with the etymology of the word. The word *hara* obviously refers to the hara or navel. This is where the Japanese get the word *hara-kiri* which is death by a self-inflicted wound to the navel area. It means to "murder the soul" as the navel is the center of life. *Hara* is also indicative of *harem* which can mean either "sacred" or "forbidden." Mark said that Banti is a language spoken in some areas of Africa that is based upon an old Libyan language that some scholars believe was spoken in pre-dynastic and early dynastic Egypt. As Egypt was settled from the West, Banti could easily have originated or been influenced by the ancestors of the Tuaregs. Mark pointed out that the phoneme *hara* could easily derive or be related to the Banti word *ch-ora* (also *jora* or *tora*) which means, "that which cuts, write, engraves, carves, or writes hieroglyphics; or he who designs, paints or makes incisions in the body for ornament."

Besides the obvious scholarship, Mark's etymology is based upon a profound experience he once had in Egypt. At a trading post in Cairo, Mark saw a Berber woman who had a tatoo on her chin. He clearly recognized it as Ogham whereupon he began to say what it meant. This created quite a stir as the woman immediately began to emit what is known as the ziggarut in the Mideast. This is a high-pitched wail that is generated by rapid movement of the tongue. It is usually meant as an expression of exultation and has also been identified with the vril and/or orgasm. It can also be used, however, as a signal of danger or warning. Unfortunately for Mark, this woman saw his tatoo reading as an unwelcome intrusion. While this woman branded a knife at him, he was soon surrounded by other Berber women who came running to her aid. They were ready to kill him, but he was rescued by locals in the market place who were his friends. They thought fast on their feet and informed the women that Mark was mentally challenged and was a village idiot. This saved his life. He learned that it was taboo to read the faces of these women. Mark believes that the term *banti* may be related to the Semitic *banar*, meaning sisters. As these Berber women were the latter day descendants of a matriarchal culture that once ruled the Sahara and left its mark upon Egypt, this interpretation makes a lot of sense.

It is particularly noteworthy that these Berber women feature Ogham tattoos on their face as it connects them to the early culture of the British Isles and elsewhere. These tatoos commonly run all the way from their source of life and reach up to and inclusive of the chin. The depiction of Antinea on the cover of this book is an artistic idealization of this art form.

The extent of the Berber influence upon Egypt is mostly unknown to academe, but it is obviously present and certain aspects are most definitely recognized. Both cultures recognized Sirius or Sothis as a sacred star. The Egyptians included it in the construction of the Great Pyramid, but the people of the Tuareg saw it as a repository of feminine energy that tied directly to the Ahaggar. The highest aspect of this feminine energy was embodied in the legendary blue queen of Atlantis, Antinea.

Although this chapter is presented primarily as legend, it is also based upon considerable scholarship. In the early part of the century, an adventurous researcher by the name of Byron de Pyrook discovered the mummified remains of Tin-Aten in the outskirts of the Ahaggar. Egerton Sykes, who wrote and researched on this topic himself, cited a previous author by the name of Amedee Geyarud. It was Geyarud who determined that Tin-Aten was a transliteral substitute for the name *Antinea*. He further demonstrated that the famous Queen Antinea of the Tuaregs was the name from which Athena was derived. She was a Tuareg goddess who brought the olive to Greece.

The mummified Queen Tin-Aten of the Tuaregs was dated to the 4th century A.D. If this is accurate, it would make this queen far too young to have come from Atlantis. It should be recognized, however, that such a designation is something on the order of a name like Cleopatra where there were several queens of this name. It does not tell us that there was an actual blue queen from Atlantis, but it does tell us that Tuareg royalty is wrapped up in such a legend and that they adopted the namesake.

What is also noteworthy about this queen is that "Aten" is virtually the same as "Aton," the name for a monotheistic sun god that was adopted by Pharoah Ahkenaton who changed the religion of Egypt virtually overnight.

The influence of Antinea upon Egyptian culture was substantial. Isis, who was later recognized as the Goddess of the Olive by the Egyptians, was also portrayed as blue. She was part of the pantheon that conveyed the transfer of knowledge of the stargate to Egypt. The mystery of the stargate itself, however, is only for initiates and does not reveal itself easily or cavalierly. This book is a step in that direction.

The blue aspect of the goddesses was something that had crossed my path before and was written about extensively in *The Black Sun*. These new discoveries caused me to revisit the theme of a blue race of people and to take an even deeper look into these matters.

18

SACRED BLUE

My personal initiation into the feminine energy culminated with meeting Penelope. She immediately introduced me to Mark Roberts who had just arrived in town. This led me to discover the legendary Antinea, the goddess of wisdom who brought Mankind the olive. For me, this was also an acme of synchronicity. Besides solving the olive mystery, at least in terms of legend, Antinea was also a blue goddess. In my book, *The Black Sun*, I delineated a secret but carefully guarded mystery tradition with regard to the legacy of a Blue Race, including the scientific plausibility that Mankind had evolved from such. At that time, however, I had no idea that there was a matriarchal society in Algeria who were not only blue in appearance but recognized a blue queen as their ancient ancestor.

Antinea is also an obvious tie-in to Egyptian culture. Egyptologists all know that Egypt was originally settled from the West and that their ancient gods, including Isis, were depicted in blue. Egypt was also known at one time as the Land of the Olives with Isis as the Lady of the Olives.

The Egyptians are not the only people to have depicted blue gods and goddesses. The gods of India, including Krishna and Kali, were often depicted in blue. The same applies to Tibet. The Celtic people also identified with blue gods and even celebrated this theme in their rituals by painting themselves blue. All of this is based upon a known principle that produces cobalt in human blood. This ancient tradition, which is part legend and part truth, is what has given rise to terms such as "blue blood" and *Sacré Bleu* which means "sacred blue." There are also instances of blue bloods occurring elsewhere, particularly in the Appalachians. These people are known as Melungeons and no one has ever been able to give a satisfactory answer as to where they originated from. Academe has always been perplexed about this.

As we proceed, I will present legends as well as hard data indicating the plausibility and inevitability of a Blue Race that is an ancestor to Mankind. This includes the proposition that this race was seeded by a civilization that transmigrated from Mars but originated in the Sirius star system.

My original interest in these matters began during conversations with my friend known as Madame X. She had come into my life at the beginning of my adventures with synchronicity and assisted me wherever she could. During my pursuit of the Cameron synchronicities, she was both amused and amazed when a book fell into her hands that featured the name of a "D.A. Cameron" as a contributing author. The book was entitled *Cairo: Biography of a City* by James Aldridge. Cameron is described as one of the most knowledgeable Egyptologists of his day.

This work explains that the city of Cairo was originally going to be called Mansurya (note the similarity to the name *Manchuria*). The exact time to begin building the city was chosen by astrologers who stood by at the initial ground-breaking. There was also a large contingent of slaves who stood by waiting for a bell to ring which was to signal the time to begin building. To everyone's surprise, a raven caught everyone off guard by suddenly and inexplicably ringing the bell of its own accord. This gave the astrologers great apprehension as it was clearly an omen. As a result, they decided to change the name of the city to Al-Khahira because that is the name of the planet that was ascending on the horizon at the very moment of the ringing of the bell. Al-Khahira is a name which is equivalent to that of Mars. At that time, it referred to the planet Mars. Also note that the name Al-Khahira can be phonetically broken down into *kha* and *hira* wherein *ka* or *kha* means "spirit" or "soul" and *hira* refers to sacred as in the word *hieroglyph* which means sacred glyph or sacred writing.

It is said that the fear associated with the planet Mars was the result of the history of the Khemetic people (Egyptians) who had cultural memories of invaders from another planet who had set up the pyramids and the sphinx. While the story about the naming of Cairo reads more like a colorful anecdote than actual history, there are some very interesting facts that could easily lead one to the inevitable conclusion that Cairo was deliberately named after the planet Mars.

Let us begin with what is known as the 1/56th ratio factor. It is a known fact that the capstone of the Great Pyramid is 1/56th the height of the pyramid itself. Further, the Great Pyramid is 1/56th the size of the Nile Delta Plateau upon which it rests. This in turn is 1/56 the size of the African continent which is 1/56th the size of the Earth. Is this a coincidence or done by deliberate design?

I now want you to reconsider what was said in Chapter 15 with regard to the relationship between the numbers 5 and 6. These represent the pentagram and the hexagram juxtaposed so as to replicate a strand of DNA when they are twisted into a shape known as a Mobius whorl. When placed together as such, the pentagram and the hexagram not only symbolize sexual union and the geometric structure for DNA, they also serve as the basis for the architecture of the Cabalistic Tree of Life.

All of this tells you that the designer of the Great Pyramid and the capstone were aware of this relationship. The 1/56th ratio symbolizes the self-recognition principle of life. This concept is reinforced in the Cydonia complex on Mars where there are not only pyramids but a pentagram superimposed upon a hexagon.

While the name Cairo clearly establishes a link to Mars, the Great Pyramid, like the Dogon legends, directs us to Sirius. The shaft in the Queen's Chamber was purposely constructed to let in the light from the Dog Star which they knew as Sothis. The Great Pyramid, however, is not the only Egyptian link to Sirius. The Sphinx, much older than the Great Pyramid, is also wrapped up in the mythology of Sirius.

The Greeks identified Sirius as Orthus, the father of the Sphinx. As Orthus is a two-headed dog, Sirius was sometimes called the Dog Star (two heads = two stars). In myth, he was the dog of Orion, the hunter. Orthus was the brother of Cerebus, the three-headed dog who served as the watchdog of Hades.

Sirius is a Latin word which means scorching or searing. This is why the Dog Days of August are associated with the birthday of

Isis. It represents extreme heat in a seasonal and sexual sense because Leo (Bast) is the sign of strength and sexual heat. The association with a dog might seem contradictory to a cat. This particular dog, however, was two-headed and was the father of the Sphinx, a creature who was part lion. It was from Orthus that the Romans drew upon to formulate Janus, the two-headed god of time who appeared on coins. Looking backwards and forwards, he represented time as well as a door or gate that goes both ways.

The Cydonia Codex, a book by George J. Haas and William R. Saunders, points out that the Sphinx is concerned with time and the transformation of man. Orthus, however, is more concerned with the process of time itself. In myth and reality, the Sphinx presents a riddle to be solved. Orthus is the watchdog or jinn that stands in the way.

In mythology, Sirius and Mars* share a kindred association with dogs. The horse, dog, and wolf were sacred to Mars. These animals, in different versions, were sometimes portrayed as his two sons, Fear and Panic, who pulled his war chariot. Mars was also the father of Romulus and Remus who were suckled by a wolf.

We find a connection to the Blue Race in the Greek word for Sirius which is *Sothis*. The dictionary etymology for *Sothis* is uncertain, but it appears to derive from the Greek *soter* which means "a deliverer." While this has and can take on a messianic sense of deliverance, it also applies to gestation, and this makes a lot of sense because *Sothis* has also been said to derive from the Egyptian word for pregnancy (another form of deliverance) which is *cyesis*. To be pregnant in Egyptian is *cyein*. This word is a homonym for the English *cyan* which means "blue." The word "dog star" is *cyon*. In this sense, Sothis is suggestive of a "blue birth" or deliverance with Messianic implications.

---

*Concerning the etymology of the word *Mars*, some of the earliest versions were *Maurs, Makors*, and *Marmar*. *Maurs* is virtually the same as the word we know today as Moors. The Egyptian word for pyramid was *M-R* (phonetic spelling of hieroglyphics), and it is obvious that the Moors, who also wore pyramidal hats, have an intrinsic association with these factors.

The etymology of *Sirius* is Latin from the Greek *Sothis* which comes from the Egyptian *Spdt* (or *Sopdet* or *Sepedet*). The Egyptian version seems intimately tied to the number "seven" as in the "sept" of *September*. This harmonizes nicely with what Mark Roberts said about the seven Pleiades. The Indo-European base *sep* means to "honor" or "cherish" (the dead) such as in the word *sepulcher*.

The Latin version of this word is said to derive from the Greek *seirios* which means "scorcher" because of the extreme heat during the August days when Sirius is at its closest point. It has also been said to have derived from *Osiris* which comes from the Egyptian *Asar* which, in turn, is suggestive of *azure* (meaning "blue"). *Sirius* is also related to words like *sire* (meaning elder); *siren* (the root meaning of which is "bind"), deriving from the Greek *seira* (meaning cord or rope); *sirloin* (where "sir" derives from the Middle French *sur* (meaning over or above); and *series* which derives from *ser* (to line up or join) which derives from the Sanskrit *savat* which means "thread."

Looking at a summary of the various language etymologies mentioned, the star known as Sirius would embrace the sacred seven (the number of Babalon) through our connection to our elders above by way of blue deliverance. There are others ways to interpret this, but the various meanings of the words make the implications more than clear.

As Mars and Sirius are both very close to the Earth in terms of astronomy, it makes sense that these two heavenly bodies would be wrapped up in the cultural mythos of this planet. All of this corroborates what Mark Roberts said about a stargate. In other words, these heavenly bodies are a tie-in to our galactic heritage. Further, if the proposition of the Sirius Solar System being unique to this universe is true, it lines up very nicely with the theory that the quantum dilemma of this universe is a result of the absence of true feminine energy. Sirius could be the key; or as Crowley wrote, "then this circle squared in its failure is a key also. And Abrahadabra." Sirius, once again, is symbolized by ⊕. Also keep in mind that this symbol is also representative of the "Sun of Women" and the magical expression Abrahadabra. Abrahadabra consists of eleven letters and is representative of the "two stars" or pentagram (five-pointed star) and hexagram (six-pointed star). Five and six, of course, equal eleven.

The Book of the Law also asks the rhetorical question: "Is God to Live in a Dog? No! but the highest are of us. They shall rejoice, our chosen: who sorroweth is not of us."

This alludes to a higher orientation than that of a dog, but it should be noted that *dog* is an anagram for *god*. As Sothis or Sirius is a central theme of *The Book of the Law*, we cannot forsake the allusion to Sirius as the Dog Star in this work. This question takes on a stronger meaning if we consider that the female energy of Sirius to be the way out of this universe. It can also be construed that a cat is a stronger candidate for a god than a dog.

In essence, the legend is that creatures from the Sirius Star System left their planet and colonized Mars. These creatures in turn colonized the Earth. *The Book of the Law* supports this thesis in a variety of ways, but it is not the source of the various legends. These creatures possessed Rh negative blood and pyramids and sphinxes were a part of their legacy. The word *pyramid* was expressed as *m-r*, *mur*, *mar* or *moor* and these words also equate to *"cat."* Etymologically or phonetically, the pyramids and the Sphinx are inseparable.

The Moors were representative of this ancient legacy which was a feminine energy. The "God" who wiped out the Moors is the same "God" who inhibits the distribution of free energy in this universe. Such a "God" is either a jinn or an assemblage of jinn.

So many of the secrets of this legacy are wrapped up in the mysterious history of this aforesaid blue race. It is obvious that the coded references to *The Book of the Law* are preoccupied with Sirius. Coded references are also seen in the Great Pyramid itself. While there is no question that Sirius plays an a priori and important role in these matters, much of what we know comes from allegory, legend, and finger-pointing from various sources. The legacy of Mars, however, is even more deeply imbedded into our collective conscious as well as many day-to-day aspects of our culture.

19

MARTIAN LEGACY

According to very specific history which is deeply embedded within the collective psyche of human beings, there was one an elder race which descended from the planet Mars. According to this history, Mars once enjoyed being the pivotal or ideal spot of what is called the Cradle Orbit of the solar system. Cradle Orbit refers to that which supports life. The creatures on Mars evolved their race to a state of consciousness which far exceeded that of what we now know on Earth today. As time continued and the solar system cooled, the physical base of the Martian culture began to implode. As a result, they had to abandon Mars for Earth. This created a problem for the cultures on both planets. Sometimes known as the Cat People, this culture erected sphinxes, pyramids and made special tribute to the cat.

People will be understandably sceptical about such a history, but I would like to point out that our culture is based upon an ancient calendar which highlights Mars. Mars was originally selected as the first month of the Roman calendar and that is why the month of October, which comes seven months after March, is called "October." *Oct* means "eight." Ares or Aries, another name which means "Mars," is also the Chaldean sign which represents the beginning of the year. In astrology, the planet Mars rules the constellation of Aries. It all fits very nicely and was meant to by the ancients. In this manner, the entire schematic of Chaldean astrology, which is also known as the science of synchronicity, is based upon the planet Mars as the first point of reference.

Other studies have also indicated (see *Geneset* by David Wood and Ian Campbell) that when human subjects were placed in a sensory deprivation or floatation tank for a certain period of time, the body clocks which control all of the autonomous nervous systems reverted to a cycle of twenty-four hours and forty minutes. This is highly significant because it is the length of a Martian day.

The idea of life transmigrating from Mars to Earth is also substantiated with the fact of Rh negative blood. Rh negative means "rhesus negative" which refers to a particular type of blood test that compares the blood of a person with reference to rhesus monkey DNA. If you are Rhesus negative, you are not related to the monkey kingdom by reason of your DNA. Thus far, this DNA is not traceable to any other DNA found on this planet.

In mythology and religion, there are stories of the Nephilim, sometimes portrayed as fallen angels, who came down to Earth and mated with the daughters of men. Most people think the word *Nephilim* refers to something along the line of "giants" (who descended to Earth). According to *The Cydonia Codex*, *nephilim* means to "come down" or "cast down." This definition conveniently corresponds with the phoneme *cat* which also means "down" as in <u>cat</u>astrophe or <u>cat</u>aclysm. Nephilim is also an Akkadian term for Annunaki. In this sense, *Nephilim* refers to the Cat People who were cast down from Mars.

When we consider the relationship of the word *cat*, *cataclysm*, and *nephilim*, it is important to take into account another aspect of the ancient doctrine. Mars once had an orbit that took 720 days while the Earth was exactly one-half or 360 days. This is ancient astronomy. It was only later that the orbits readjusted as the result of an ancient cataclysm. While it is easy for sceptics to dispute such a claim, it is impossible to dispute the ancient calendar and why it was changed.

Biblical scribes noted the regular fly-bys of Mars and dutifully recorded them. These fly-bys were noted at the beginning of the year, then recognized as the Ides of March (March 15th), and also October 26th. One was the beginning of Spring and the other represented the harvest. Another pattern noted by ancient historians was that Mars came frighteningly close to the Earth every 108 years. The distance was so close that there were reports of canals and activity. During one of these close fly-bys, a major cataclysm occurred when the gravitational pulls became too close for comfort. The resulting cataclysm literally changed the orbits of the two planets. Consequently, the Earth gained velocity and added 5.25 days to its orbit. The Martian orbit changed from 720 days to approximately 686.5 days. Six days were added to the Ides of March which gave us the 21st of the month as the first day of spring. Adding 5.25 days to October 26th gives October 31st which is celebrated as Halloween or Samhain.

The transmigration of creatures from Mars was accompanied by a transmission of information which included the secrets of consciousness of this ancient race. These secrets were deposited in various artifices and placed in locales that are sometimes referred to as the Sacred Places of the Lion. The unsealing or unveiling of these sacred places is literally meant to represent the unleashing of the Aquarian Age. One of the most important theories concerning this lost history is the proposition of how the consciousness of this ancient race could be maintained.

The off-planet or Martian legacy of Rh negative blood is certainly controversial to say the least. That it is ultimately and intimately tied to the theory of blue-bloods, however, is far more disturbing for those who might want to refute the theory. The dilemma of Rh negative human beings and blue blood is not really controversial as it is documented in medical history.

We are now going to examine a particular thread of investigation with regard to the Rh negative phenomena and its various implications. As you might already know, there are all sorts of wild theories on this subject as well as some pseudo-scholarly works. I suppose this is to be expected. What one wants, however, is not sensationalism or pedantry but, at the very least, a plausible explanation of how and why such a subject has remained so carefully and intricately hidden. The subject of hiding, of course, takes us into the field of the occult which means "hidden." We will therefore be treading upon the field of occult biology and occult biochemistry. Do not expect your college professor or experts in biology to know too much about this subject.

The aforementioned secrets of consciousness (of the so-called Martian race) and how such might be maintained brings us back to the paradigm presented by the Ark of the Covenant. Inside the Ark, or so it was said, was the Manna from heaven, a substance that is identified with the white gold of the Egyptians. This was the alchemical substance which was supposed to "fuse" the two hemispheres of the brain during the Rites of Horus with the resulting secretion of "white gold" out of the forehead or third eye. This white gold is actually an isotope of gold which has been found within the remnants of ancient Egyptian sarcophagi.

For typical Earthlings, these ideas are rather strange. People will often recoil from such information or just ignore it. When one embraces these ideas, however, let alone the truth of it, one will discover that it is connected to other strange phenomena. It is a realm where synchronicity begins to kick in.

For those of you who are familiar with my various adventures with the Moors, you will see exactly what I mean when we consider King George III. He is the most famous case of blue blood gone awry, and there is an entire case history on it. What is odd or synchronous about this case concerns his wife, Queen Charlotte, who was of Moorish extraction. This is not only evident in portraits done of her but in the autopsy report where she was described as mulatto. The royalty of Europe were often obsessed with marrying or sexually uniting with the royal blood of indigenous peoples. There is no evidence that Charlotte herself suffered from any such disease.

The Moorish connection is significant for reasons already emphasized. As was said, the etymology of *Moor, pyramid*, and *cat* are intrinsically connected and wrapped up in the word *Mars*, the planet from which the Rh negatives or elders are supposed to have ventured. If you have already studied my earlier books such as *Synchronicity and the Seventh Seal* and *The Montauk Book of the Dead*, you will realize that there has been a substantial effort on the part of the hegemony that influences Earth politics to wipe out the history of who the Moors actually were.

It just so happens that some of the major circumstances and events which imprinted Mars upon our collective unconscious took place around the time of a huge cataclysm in 1,400 B.C. In Chaldean astrology, this was during the Age of Aries. The word Aries is identified as the lamb or ram (which is *mar* backwards) which was sacred to the Greek God Ares who is the Latin equivalent of Mars. In astrology, Mars was purposely chosen as the ruler of Aries. Perhaps these word meanings influenced the old

PORTRAIT OF QUEEN CHARLOTTE, WIFE OF KING GEORGE III

saw about the month of March: "It comes in like a lion and goes out like a lamb."

In the ancient work known as the *Helios Byblos*, these events concerned an Egyptian who was known as Tutmosis. The average reader, of course, will recognize him by the name of Moses.

20

EXODUS

The cataclysm of approximately 1400 B.C. coincides, more or less, with the events described in *The Bible* as the Exodus. The word *exodus* is a Latin word which means "way out." This has to do with the story of Moses leading the Hebrews out of Egypt and across the Red Sea.

It is tempting to consider that the exodus from Egypt was a miniaturized version of the exodus from Mars. When one assesses the complete picture, however, there are too many complex factors to make such an assumption. This is complicated by the fact that the Biblical Moses is an apocryphal character when it comes to verifiable history. There is, however, plenty of information to suggest that the story of his life is based upon many historical facts as well as a multiplicity of characters and events.

Egyptian history records at least three major migrations of people from Egypt.* What has been popularized in *The Bible* is the last and third exodus which is by far the smallest of the three major migrations. This last migration is considered to be special because it is where Moses consolidates the wisdom of Egypt and transmutes it into the Hebrew religion by writing down the words of the Creator. Egyptian history, however, gives a far deeper and more penetrating look into the events of that time period, many of which are condensed in an abbreviated form in *The Bible* itself.

Moses is not a name that anybody used in that time period. In Hebrew, the name is Moshe or Moishe. The Egyptians of that time

* For further information, see *Jesus, Last of the Pharaohs* by Ralph Ellis.

period referred to such a character as Tutmosis. There were several dignitaries by the name of Thutmosis or Thoth-mosis and Thutmosis IV is often thought to be the character upon which the Biblical Moses is based.

The name *Moses* itself is commonly thought to derive from the word "anointed." Once again, the theme of the olive plays a role as olive oil is that substance with which one anoints. The name *Moses* or *Moshe* is broadly recognized to be the origin of the word *messiah.* The dictionary indicates that the word *messiah* derives from *mosheh*, probably derived from the Egyptian *mes* or *mesa* which means "child" or "son." This in turn is believed to have derived from Aramaic and Hebrew words which mean anointed: *mëshīhā* and *mashīāh*, respectively. This presents a very interesting proposition if you break down either word. You have *ma* and either *shiha* or *shiah. Ma* or *mau* refers to "cat" and *shiah* refers to "follower" as in the word *shiite* (as in Shiite Muslims). Quite literally, this would mean that the word *messiah* or the name we know as Moses could logically be interpreted as the follower or disciple of the cat.

If Moses was indeed of Martian lineage, his name fits in nicely with the esoteric legacy previously presented. The cat is prominent. It is obviously no accident that the word *ma*, a universal word for mother, and *mau*, the Egyptian word for "cat," are virtually the same sounds. The Egyptian deity Bast or Bastet was considered to be the Mother of All and she was a cat goddess.

It is obvious that the word or concept of a messiah is intrinsically bound up in the idea of both a cat and olive oil. It is therefore logical to postulate that there might be, at the very least, an etymological tie between a cat and the olive. We will address this in just a bit, but it should also be pointed out that Christ, a latter day messiah, was described as Yeshua ben Pandera in the Talmud. Pandera means panther. In *The New Testament*, Christ is described as the Lion of Judea.

Next, I want to address the first part of the name *Tutmosis.* If; we consider that *Tut* = *Thoth*, we are talking about the builder of the Great Pyramid and all that this famous Egyptian deity represents. The Egyptian word *tut* has been described differently by various sources. *Tutankhamun* has been described as meaning "keeper of the ankh of amen." *Tut* can also be construed as "guardian" or "watcher" when we consider the English word *tutor* where the root *tut* literally means "guardian." There are many speculations and even convincing written histories which suggest that the Biblical Moses was related to Akhenaten and Tutankhamun. Akhenaten was the controversial founder of monotheism in Egypt, and it is clear that the monotheistic doctrines in *The Torah* are extensions of what he had already proliferated in Egypt.

I should also point out that Christian sources assert the name *Moses* derives from "born of the water." While their approach is myopic, the definition is not inconsistent with what I have presented. The concept of being born has everything to do with being a "deliverer" which is what a messiah represents. The concept of a deliverer showed up in the etymology of Sothis as was mentioned earlier in this text. Water is readily identified with *mer* or *mar* as in the name *Mary* which suggests the sea. Again, we are back to phonemes which suggest Mars. In this sense, being born of the water is tantamount to being born of Mars.

In the legend of Moses, he was not only "born" of the water in the sense that he was found floating in a basket, but he delivered his people through the water in the parting of the Red Sea. In the common story, he was delivering his people from the corruption of the Egyptian priesthood. As is the case with any human institution, there is no doubt that there was plenty of corruption going on. Thutmosis was supposed to possess the powers of perception that the Egyptian priesthood had long since lost. Why he was able to have this knowledge has everything to do with his blood lineage which was from the tribe of Levi. Levi is a very interesting word because it is related to *lavi*, a Hebrew word which appears in *The Old Testament* and signifies a lion.

The theme of the cat not only represents the feminine energy, it represents a <u>hidden</u> feminine energy as it literally has to be "decoded" from holy texts in order to be understood. This is consistent with the idea that the solution to this universe is the restoration of feminine energy, something which is postulated to have deserted this continuum.

This idea is so flagrantly true that it appears in the most holy exaltations that a Judaic priest can assert: the word *kadoish* or *kadish*. In Hebrew, this is an iteration of the most holy aspect of the Godhead. I have not yet met a Jewish person who is aware that this word derives from the word "cat." In Berber, the word for cat is *kadiske* while the Nubian word for the same is *kadis*.

The hidden feminine comes into play once again when we consider the Hebrew word *Shekinah*. As was said earlier, this means "dwelling" and represents the most holy spot imaginable in the Jewish faith: the space over the Mercy Seat which sits between the two Cherubs (sometimes referred to as olive trees) on the Ark of the Covenant. While *Shekinah* is recognized as representative of the feminine energy, the etymology of the word is not broadly recognized at all. It derives from *she-kahena* which takes us back to the Berber roots of Queen Antinea, the giver of the olive. In the Berber tradition, the most exalted priestess was referred to as the Kahena. This tradition predates most history that you have read and is the foundation of the Hawaiian word *kahuna* which was transmuted into more of a male deity. It is also the root which inspired the *cochina* of the Native American tradition. The word *cochina* is usually pronounced *ko-chee-nah* or *ka-chee-nah* by most people, but the letters *ch* are also pronounced with a silent *ch* and the word could easily be expressed as *ka-hee-nah*. The primary Native American legend of the cochina is that of a blue cochina which refers us back to the blue queen once again.

Not only is the name of Moses wrapped up in the etymology of the cat but so are the most sacred parts of the religion he put on the map. The legends we know of Moses, however, have been transmuted into a patriarchal hierarchy which both mimics and reinforces a desertion of feminine energy.

Besides the cat, the olive plays an equally important role in these matters. Without the labyrinthine mysteries of the olive that were presented to me, I would not have come to these observations. This is why I said that one would expect to find an etymological association between the words *cat* and *olive*. Surprisingly coincidental, there is such a word and that is *leopard*. *Leo* can be pronounced and is sometimes pronounced as *eleo* which is virtually the same as *elaia*, the Greek word for olive. *Pard* means "panther." As *leo* or *eleo* (akin to *Helios*) signify the sun, we are also dealing with a concept which is associated with sun spots or freckles. A leopard, which is spotted, thus became the inspiration for the word *leprosy* which was the name of a disease which inspired the original exodus in the first place.

21

LEPROSY

As was said earlier, Egyptian history tells us that there were three major exoduses from Egypt. All of these exoduses or mass migrations of people, including the one mentioned in *The Bible*, were the result of a disease which is mysteriously referred to as leprosy. This creates an absurd paradigm for modern thinking because the disease we know as leprosy was not discovered until the 1800's. The condition of leprosy as described in *The Bible* was obviously referring to something different.

In the dictionary, *leprosy* derives from *leper* which derives from the Greek *lepros* which means "rough or scaly" and in turn derives from *lepein*, "to peel." If you dig further into these matters, you will see that there is not only an association between *leper* and *leopard* but that both words represent a spotted skin condition.

When we consider that the *leo* in *leopard* is connected to the sun, we have to consider how that heavenly body affects the skin, particularly a skin which might be foreign to the atmosphere of this planet. Although the *pard* in *leopard* derives from the Greek word for "panther," there is a very interesting comparison to the Portuguese word *parreira* which means "vine." This word is related to the Latin *parens* which in turn is derived from *parere* "to beget." This implies parentage and the concept of not only being genetically related to a panther or cat but also a skin condition which is passed down genetically. These etymologies also suggest that the name of the Trojan prince Paris might been have named for the cat. Most importantly, it suggests a begetting or a genetic connection related to the root *par* which is Egyptian for "light" or "fire" as well as being etymologically tied to the words *pharaoh* and *pyramid*.

When we consider leprosy or the diseased condition of the skin in the Exodus, we are dealing with a major issue in the history of the Egyptian culture. It was obviously taken very seriously by the people of that time period. All available evidence points to this leprosy being a result of a collision of races. One would be the Elder or Blue Race that represents the Rh negative or off world group; and one would be the Rh positive.

Diseases associated with Rh negative blood are not strangers to medical science. There is not only the phenomena of blue babies but there is also the disease of porphyria, an inherited disorder of pigment metabolism with excretions of porphyrin in the urine accompanied by a dangerous sensitivity to sunlight.

Porphyrin is a purple or bluish pyrole derivative found in cytoplasm that combines with iron and magnesium to form heme and chlorophyll respectively. But, what is a pyrole?

The chemical formula for pyrole is C_4H_5N and it is a colorless liquid found in bile pigments, chlorophyll and hematin. Although a pyrole is said to have no color, its derivative (porphyrin) is another matter.*

King George III, who presided over England during the time of the Revolutionary War, is one of the most notable historical characters to have suffered from porphyria. It is well recorded in books. One of the symptoms associated with porphyria is that one's urine comes out purple. This is how the name *porphyria* derived. The word itself means "purple." This purple urination is referred to as "purple rain." In modern history, the earliest person on record to have suffered from this disease is Mary Queen of Scots whose lineage can be traced back to Transylvania.

Besides victims of porphyria suffering from sunlight, there is also an association between this disease and lycanthropy or what

*Most interestingly, pyrole is obtained from coal tar, bone oil and distillation. The fact that this substance can be obtained from coal tar is suggestive of the instrumental role of bitumen referred to in *The Black Sun*. In that book, it was explained that the mummies of blue bloods were wrapped in bitumen and consumed by the Egyptians, both as a medicine but also to synchronize the hemispheres of the brain in an attempt to maximize consciousness. The fact that pyrole is also obtained from bone oil only intensifies the matter brought to hand. Bone oil and tar are the main ingredients related to mummies.

is sometimes called "werewolves' disease." The obvious relation to shape-shifting gives rise to wild theories. From one perspective, this disease seems to have arisen from a time when werewolves and vampires might have uninhibitedly roamed the countryside. Modern science does not really acknowledge shape-shifting. Many Native Americans and other indigenous people, however, witness it as a matter of course. Even in those cases, however, it is not necessarily an every day occurrence.

To me, the most obvious observation that could be made about a disease such as porphyria is that it seems to have derived from a disease which was apparently in a different form from the one we now know today. Due to various factors, immune systems and the diseases they fight have changed considerably over millennia. In the annals of Mankind, it is also true that diseases occur when people of different types unite either in matrimony or are otherwise associated. Diseases not only come and go, they mutate and take on a different life of their own.

In the case of the exodus of Egypt, and you have to consider all three, it is clear that the disease they referred to as leprosy underwent, at the very least, hundreds of years of mutations and potential mutations. Currently, it is only a footnote in our culture but perhaps a very important and overlooked footnote.

Keep in mind that underlying this entire history are the legends of Atlantis where different species mixed and formed creatures such as griffins, centaurs and the like. These creatures were the province of Pandora or Bast, each designated as the Great Mother of All. When one considers how a human zygote mutates to take on the shape of a tadpole and various other animal forms before it transforms into a baby, it is very clear that our genes are a variation and extension of the animal kingdom. Bast represents the infinite mutations that are possible. That is why she is designated as the Great Mother of All.

At the time of Moses, Egypt was a megalopolis of people of different types, races and persuasions. From all available historical indications, it is clear that there was an outbreak of a disease that compromised the skin. The Hebrew version of *The Old Testament* referred to this skin condition as tzaraath which the Greeks later translated into lepra; hence, leprosy. Specifically, tzaraath referred to the whitening of the skin with sores; the spreading of sores which are either white or reddish white; or patches of skin where the hair has turned white. The latter might include white swellings or reddish white spots. In any case, this Biblical account of leprosy concerned a whitening of the skin which is equivalent to the loss of pigment or melanin.

There are different theories as to how Moses fit into the equation. Some theories suggest that Moses represented the purified DNA. This could conceivably represent the Blue or Elder Race. This, however, is not consistent with the history of Egypt whereby masses of people were forced out of Egypt due to this disease. In this sense, the character we know as Moses was put in charge of the last exodus. This suggests that he was on the run and represented those struck with leprosy. There is also plenty of historical consistency between the family names of Tutmosis and the family of Akhenaten. Of equal importance to these family ties is the philosophy or theology of monotheism which clearly transferred from Akhenaten of Egypt to Moses of the Hebrews. As Akhenaten was clearly deformed, this is an indication that the royal family suffered from disease.

Whatever spin we or others choose to place upon Moses, however, the entire proposition is not that simple. There were different groups vying for the pharaohship, and one has to be careful about different people imposing their name and tradition upon others. By the same token, one has to be attuned to the fact that conquering tribes often adopted the names and titles of the people they conquered. Therefore, it is hard to say what names applied to what people originally.

What we are concerned with in Egypt is the fact that there was a consolidation of ancient history and wisdom which included a considerable amount of occult secrets. This was drawing upon and borrowing from earlier writings and history that were eventually credited to Moses. These consolidated writings are assumed to have been produced under his guardianship. The actual history of the time of Moses, however, as opposed to the written and popular history, would have to be a far cry from any of the renditions we know today. One thing we can be sure of, however, is that he emerged from Egypt at the end of hundreds of years of disease.

22

OCCULTUM

The juxtaposition of the character we know as Moses is most interesting. Whatever the historical truth of this man might be, or even if his history is really just myth, he represents a crossroads. You have disease going in one direction and an attempt to preserve higher consciousness in another.

There is no question that Egypt purged their population to get rid of diseased individuals that suffered a certain loss of pigment. On the other hand, Moses is credited with consolidating and preserving the ancient wisdom of Egypt, a wisdom that never really returned to the locale from which it proliferated except for perhaps in a buried and hidden form.

I have already established that the inner legacy of Egypt was preoccupied with the ancient Blue Race that had an inalienable identification with the planet Mars. Much of the legacy of this ancient Blue Race concerned the means by which they could propagate themselves. This included the continuation of their own culture and what might very loosely be called a "belief system." A forerunner of what we might consider our "ancient cultures," the Elder Race or Blue Race left its mark and deposited its kernels of wisdom in the aforementioned "Sacred Places of the Lion," also utilized as the title for a book by George Hunt Williamson. Part of this legacy included a contingent which moved underground. It is a known fact that there are endless caverns beneath the earth that officially remain unexplored to modern science. These range from the tunnels beneath Rome and Greece to the tunnels of Egypt,

Libya and Algeria which are supposed to be connected to the islands of Cypress and Malta. These, however, are just a small sampling. Each continent and country is generally lined with such tunnels. These become important in contemplating the history of the Blue Race because it is obvious that their original skin would not have been too compatible with our sun. The underground was a viable alternative for those seeking protection from the sun.

The cultural remnant of the Blue Race that emerged in Egypt eventually became known as the mystery school of the Eye of Horus. As was said, the purpose of the school was to fuse the crystalline structure of one side of the brain with the other. When this was accomplished, a white powder of gold was secreted out of the forehead during initiatory rites. This was known as the Illumination of the Eye of Horus which represents the opening of the Third Eye. The purpose of such a rite was to promote a harmonic relationship between the energy fields of the body and the energy fields of the earth. This was the pathway to what might be termed immortality or a virtual immortality.

The secret principle of the white gold is that it was actually a manifestation or result of superconductivity being present in the brain. The white gold itself promoted superconductivity of the brain and ingestion of it was used for that intended purpose, but the reason that the Egyptian Nile was chosen was that the black soil itself contained the properties of superconductivity. In this manner, as testified by the famous Egyptologist Wallace Budge, there was a mysterious process by which the Egyptians produced gold and silver by separating it from its native ore. This process resulted in a black powder substance which was supposed to contain marvellous powers as well as the properties of the various metals themselves. Budge said:

> "In a mystical manner, this black powder was identified with the body which the god Osiris was known to possess in the underworld, and to both were attributed magical qualities and both were thought to be sources of power and life."

Budge boldly states in his esteemed research that as metal working grew in prominence, magical powers existed in the fluxes and alloys. This art of metal working was known as *khemeia* and came to refer to the preparation of black ore or powder which was considered the elixir or active principle in the transmutation of metals. Certain black ore found in Abydos could transmute gold, by nature of the superconductivity present, into a white powdered form. Simply by being placed into the soil, regular gold would transmute into a powder that could be consumed.

This black ore, originally known as *kheme* or *al-kheme*, eventually became known as *mummia* by Europeans. The word *mummy* derived from the fact that *mummia* was the name for bitumen, a resinous black material which oozes out of the cracks in rocks. It is related to petroleum. Mummia eventually became confused with the black ore found in Abydos because Egyptian royal families were buried with a black and resinous material. When people began digging up mummies, they saw this black material which they identified as mummia; hence, the name *mummy* was born.

The superconductivity present in mummia was recognized to have healing powers in ancient and more recent history. It is mentioned by Francis Bacon as a remedy under the name mummy dust. All of this alludes to a more ancient rite which descends from the Blue Race. Because pharaohs or those of noble lineage contained the superconductive qualities of both the white gold and the black ore known as khemeia, the consumption of their ancestors was deemed a necessity for maintaining the continuity of consciousness. To put it bluntly, "eating your ancestors was the path to immortality." While this may or may not be the best path to enlightenment, it was arduously practiced by the ancients.

This might seem preposterous to our current culture, but it will serve the reader well to realize that Catholicism is based upon consuming the bodily fluid and flesh of their savior. An exhaustive study of Egyptian history will reveal that the entire religion of Christianity is based upon ancient Egyptian rituals and mythology. The drinking of the wine and the eating of the Eucharist is actually a watered down ritual compared to what they did in ancient Egypt. Only the most powerful elite of the Vatican hierarchy are believed to practice the cannibalism I am referring to.

The etymology of the word *cannibal* itself will lead to much misdirection and misunderstanding. The dictionary suggests that *cannibal* is believed to have originated with Columbus and his identification or misidentification of the Carib Indians as cannibals. Somehow, it is construed that the word *Carib* was transliterated into *cannibal.* This is unlikely. It all becomes clearer when you realize that the words *cannibal* and *carnival* both correspond to *canne* and *baal* where you have the land of Canaan being occupied by the worshipers of Baal. The etymology of Canaan is uncertain but is related to the Hebrew root *k-n* and is identified in that language as *kena'n*, very similar to the Tuareg word *kahena. Can*, however, the first syllable of *cannibal*, suggests *cyan* or the Chinese *kun*. Both of these words are identified with "blue." *Cyan* also shows up in North America with the word we know as Cheyenne.

The Canaanites are known to have come from the south, and remnants of their cannibalistic rituals continued in Palestine up to and during the Roman occupation. In her book, *The Women's Encyclopedia of Myths and Secrets*, Barbara Walker describes a ritual known as the Immolation of the King. To satisfy the fertility spirits, the king had to be sacrificed every now and then. This ancient ritual was the presage for the Christ saga. According to Walker's research, Roman records indicate that Roman authorities had to crack down hard on cannibalistic practices during the rise of early Christianity.

Aleister Crowley also recognized the principle of black powder in his book *Liber LI: The Lost Continent.* Therein, he described how this substance was known as *tlas* or *tlas ore,* a word which is the same as *Atlas*. The Atlas mountains are the province of the Tuareg and this brings us back full circle to the Ahaggar and Queen Antinea. Crowley defines *tlas* as meaning "black," and it is also known as Zro which is a blue-black or violet-black powder that precipitated gold.

This is all very interesting history, but we can be sure of only one thing. All of these efforts to maintain the continuity of consciousness (of the Blue Race or any other) did not succeed. The consciousness of Mankind is plagued with disease. If it was not, the brain would be firing on all cylinders.

23

WILSON'S DISEASE

Although I have made a very strong case for the legacy of the Blue Race coming from Mars, it will still be considered controversial. Rh negative individuals, anomalous blue skin conditions, and diseases such as porphyria are, however, all points of fact.

Rh negative blood traces back to ancestors with copper-based blood as opposed to iron-based blood. When we consider the biological processes of copper-based blood and Rh negative, however, we are dealing with the subject of occult biology. In terms of available university research, very little probing has been done with regard to these subjects. When you ask questions of people in these fields, their experience is usually channeled or herded into very specific functions with regard to the biochemical factors of copper or Rh negative blood. People do not look into the bigger picture and there is very little scientific questioning or linking being done.

As we are dealing with occult biology, we can expect more occult or hidden factors to show themselves. We see a familiar pattern of occult synchronicity once again when we consider the prospect of a malady known as Wilson's Disease. Specifically, Wilson's Disease is a malevolent and excessive accumulation of copper that has not been metabolized. Although not exclusively so, most of this copper accumulation takes place in the liver.

Wilson's Disease is named after its discover, Samuel Wilson. At this time, I have noticed no other coincidences or tie-ins with regard to this particular Wilson. There was, however, another interesting member of the Wilson Clan who fits into this picture. That was Erasmus Wilson, a nineteenth century doctor who was the world's foremost expert on latter day leprosy and other skin diseases. He was a Freemason who was responsible for funding the transport of Cleopatra's Needle to the banks of the Thames River. It is more than ironic that a name such as Wilson stands at the crossroads of the mysteries of this ancient Blue Race and suggests we are on the right track.

Copper is found in various parts of the body, but its primary location and function is in the blood. This in itself is quite relevant with regard to the theories of an Elder Race which had copper-based blood. Copper, through a substance known as ceruloplasmin, actually enables iron to form into red blood cells.

Those suffering from Wilson's Disease have suppressed levels of ceruloplasmin. Synthesized in the liver, ceruloplasmin carries ninety percent of the copper in our plasma. (Note: Ceruloplasmin is in addition to and complementary to a substance known as transferrin, a blood protein which carries iron only).

To make matters more intriguing, Wilson's Disease is the result of a recessive gene. In other words, this means that it comes from ancient ancestors and perks up only once in a while in successive generations.

To put the entire proposition of Wilson's Disease in simple terms, it is a malady whereby the ability to process and distribute copper in the body misfires. Surrendering to simple logic, this suggests that in the genetic stream of Mankind, copper once served us in a different capacity than it does now.

Oddly or not, Wilson's Disease is also related to porphyria, lycanthropy, lupus and other diseases which include hypersensitivity to sunlight and whitening of the skin. It is hauntingly similar to the territory we have all ready crossed.

All of this not only corroborates the original theory of a blue Elder Race, it tells us that if it is not true, an extensive explanation is needed with regard to how copper evolved into such a crucial role in our blood chemistry. What is even more intriguing with regard to these matters is that there is an equally amazing role that copper plays with regard to our biochemistry. It also determines pigmentation.

24

ANKH VERSUS OINK

Did you ever consider the origin or etymology of the word *pigment*? *Webster's New World Dictionary* indicates it derives from *pingere* which means "to paint." This makes sense as we are dealing with colors. The etymology of *paint*, however, suggests yet another direction. The Latin word *pingere* is hypothesized to derive from the Indo-European base *peig* which means to mark by scratching or coloring.

Upon seeking out this etymology, I could not help but notice the synchronicity between the Indo-European *peig* and the English word *pig*. This name association is reinforced by the fact that pigs are biochemically closer to humans than any other animal. As their arteries and organs correspond with those of humans, their body parts are used in transplantation surgery.

The relationship of the words *pigment* and *pig* becomes even more intriguing when we consider the strong taboos that Semitic peoples have against eating pork. If Biblical leprosy was all about the pigment of the skin, what might this have to do with the prospect of human genetics being connected to pigs? It also makes us ask another question. Did the so-called Elder Race evolve or de-evolve into a pig-related human?

Before I pursue this further, I want to relay an old Moorish legend which also appears in *The Bible* albeit in a very abbreviated and obscure form. According to ancient legend, Abraham was trying to save some of his brethren who were on a mountain top and completely surrounded by dead victims of leprosy. These bodies were piled so thick that Abraham's fellows could neither make their way further up the mountain nor could a path be made to rescue them from these diseased corpses. In order to retrieve them, Abraham created the animal we know as the pig by breeding a cat, a dog and a rat. Pigs, who are known to eat anything, were able to eat their way through the corpses and save Abraham's people.

This story is obviously an analogy, but it suggests that the pig either evolved or was created in order to cure a skin condition which affected many humans of the time. The most obvious thesis that suggests itself here is that the Elder Race mixed with humans which resulted in severe disease and a change of pigmentation. The pig chemistry either evolved or was an outside solution to stabilize this "new race" of human beings. This is only a hypothesis, but it is clear from all of this information that something changed in the biochemical history of Mankind.

While there are different assertions as to why Muslims and Jews do not eat pork, the most common ones have to do with hygiene. This goes hand-in-hand with the Biblical theory that the Jews were told not to mix with other peoples. In such a scenario, the pig chemistry would suggest a compromised state from a pure state of something on the order of the Blue Race. On the other hand, there are those who assert or suggest that neither Jews nor Muslims eat pork because it is tantamount to cannibalism.

None of this presents a very clear picture. One cannot, however, deny that the proposition of the pig is deeply interwoven into the Semitic culture as well as the human condition itself. It has been imbedded into the human psyche to such an extent that it has even given rise to absurd racist behavior.

In Nazi Germany, the identification of Jews with swine was extreme. You are probably already familiar with theatrical or historical depictions of Jews being referred to as swine. If you examine history, you will find that Germans actually put clothes on pigs and tried them in human courts of law for murder and other transgressions. This was absurd, but they were trying to make the point that if Jews could be tried for crimes then so could pigs. They were one and the same in their eyes. In this scenario, the Nazis were claiming to be the original race.

The proposition of the pig acquires further ammunition when we consider the origins of the original Hanukkah. It was the first

Hanukkah whereby olive oil was recognized as the miraculous vehicle by which the Temple could be lit for eight days on only one day's worth of olive oil. The circumstances at that time were that the Jews had lost possession of their Temple during the Greek occupation of Jerusalem in the wake of Alexander. The last straw for the Maccabees was when the Greeks began desecrating the Temple by making pig sacrifices in it and herding pigs there. This may or may not have been done for practicality by the Greeks, but it was also intended as a direct insult to the Jewish people. That it concerns pigs give us much cause to wonder.

In *The Women's Encyclopedia of Myths and Secrets*, Barbara Walker points out that there are no Biblical references which suggest that an outbreak of illness was the result of eating meat. On the contrary, she quotes a source stating that Jews abstain from pork because their remote ancestors, five or six thousand years before, used the wild boar as their totem. Perhaps more to the point is that sacrificial boar gods are common to both Scandinavian and Middle-Eastern traditions. Both of these traditions can be traced back to the East Indian god Vishnu who created the world by virtue of his self-sacrifice in the shape of a boar. This becomes even more interesting when Walker states that this specific Hindu tradition has the blood of the boar having the creative power that was once found in the Mother's Blood. This identification is suggestive of copper-based blood being usurped by the blood of a boar or pig.

The pig also comes into play in the Eleusinian Mysteries of Greece. Keep in mind that the namesake of the Eleusinian Mysteries is based upon *elaia*, the Greek word for olive. The rituals of the Eleusinian Mysteries are primarily based upon the abduction of the goddess Perosephone by Hades (Pluto) and all that ensues from that incident.

Common and abbreviated renditions of Greek mythology will tell you that Peresephone's mother, Demeter or Ceres, is so distraught over her missing daughter that she abdicates her responsibility for growing crops and winter ensues. This myth not only generates the reason behind winter, but initiates us into the underworld and its ruler, Pluto or Hades. We are apprised of the power of the underworld when Ceres appeals to Zeus, the most powerful of the gods, to bring her daughter back to the light.

Intervening on her behalf, not even the great Zeus can overcome the unrelenting Pluto. A compromise is worked out between Zeus and Pluto so that Perosephone will remain with the Lord of the Underworld during the winter and return in the warmer months. We learn from this myth that when the archetype of Pluto comes into your life, astrologically or otherwise, it is to teach you the lessons of surrender, coercion and cooperation.

While the above is the more common version of this myth, the original story goes much deeper. When Pluto abducts Perosephone, who is also known as the virgin goddess Kore, a pig fell into a crevice at that exact moment. The crevice is representative of the feminine organ (of a virgin) and a pig going into it.

As Zeus and Ceres learned, the only way to deal with Pluto is to yield to him by surrendering because you cannot overtake him. When you cooperate, however, you achieve transmutation. In other words, you change or morph into a new format, but one that is absolutely necessary for your future growth. In this myth, the virgin goddess is seized by Pluto at the exact moment the pig goes into the crevice of the Earth Goddess.

This myth suggests that pig blood was inserted into the human paradigm. It also symbolizes a purified goddess sharing her seed with the Lord of the Underworld. A more practical viewpoint might suggest that it symbolizes that the biological condition of the ancient Blue Race was not conducive to the circumstances of the Earth and had to transmute in order to survive. The pig was the antidote albeit a compromise. In order to maintain the continuity of the race, the Elders had to live in a degenerate form from the exalted states of consciousness they once knew.

The etymologies of the words *pig* and *fig* shed additional light on these matters. The etymology of *fig* is uncertain, but it is connected to an Old Phoenician word pronounced *pagh* in the dictionary. *Pagh*, of course, is virtually the same word as *pig*, and it refers to a half-ripe fig. In Old English, the letters *p, pf, ph,* and *f* are interchangeable. Shakespeare used *fig* in a pejorative sense to refer to a vagina. Italians and Greeks use their words for fig in the same sense. This is also symbolic of the fig leave in *The Bible* which covered the genitals of Adam and Eve. That their genitals were covered with a *fig, phig,* or *pig* is symbolic of pig genetics entering the human gene pool.

There is a most interesting identification between pigs, figs, and Jesus in *The New Testament*. In *Matthew*, Jesus unleashes demonic forces into thousands of pigs and sends them to their deaths. In both *Mark* and *Matthew,* Jesus curses a fig tree because it bears no fruit even though it is not the fruit-bearing season. This gives you the impression that Jesus cared for neither figs nor pigs.

In *The New Testament*, Jesus also suggests that one should "be naked as little children." This latter characteristic is suggestive of the original state of Adam and Eve before the Fall from Grace. In their native state, Adam and Even had no need for figs leaves, and their genetics were conceivably pure and free from pig DNA.

This identification of Jesus as a killer of pigs is most curious as his name itself has been interpreted as "Earth Pig" in both Latin and Italian (*Je* = *Ge* or *Geo* which is Greek for "earth" and *sus* is a Latin word for a pig or sow). This cannot be easily dismissed because the Latin language was specifically constructed so that it does not allow itself to be changed, the reason being that future meanings of words will not be altered.

The name of *Jesus* puts us at a curious crossroads because while Jesus seems to be fully aware of the perils of pigs and figs, he is named, at least in Latin and Italian, after the former. There is, however, a most curious explanation.

In many traditions, including those of the Norsemen and Gypsies, the pig or boar symbolizes both death and rebirth. A prime example of this is the roasted Yule pig with an apple in its mouth. The apple was symbolically placed in the mouth in order to resurrect the soul of the sacrificial pig. The reason the apple was chosen is that its geometric construction arguably serves as the deepest metaphor conceivable for the processes of life and death.

A transverse splitting of the apple will reveal the shape of a pentagram at its center. This is called the core of the apple because this symbol represents the ancient goddess Kor or Car from which we get *cardiac*, a Greek word referring to the heart. Besides manifesting a five-pointed star within it, the apple also displays the shape of a heart. As a matter of fact, the geometry within an apple is much closer in shape to a traditionally rendered artistic heart than are the hearts found in humans or animals.

Long before the name *Jesus* evolved, there was the name *Yeshua* or *Joshua* (with the *J* being soft). This, however, was constructed from earlier Aramaic and Hebrew constructions which eventually ended up as: *Yod - He - Shin - Vau - He*. The first English letter of each of these phonetically expressed Hebrew letters literally spells out YHSVH or Yeshua. These five Hebrew letters eventually evolved into the name *Jesus*. The name *Jesus* is considered by some to be an abomination because the hard *J* sound does not exist in the Hebrew rendition. The hard *J* is thought to come with the *King James Bible* which changed a lot of rhetoric, meanings and concepts. The Latin and Italian words for Jesus, however, adopted the hard *J* sound long before King James; and they based it upon a name which means earth pig.

The whole concept of *Yod He Shin Vau He* was explored in an intricate fashion in my book *Synchronicity and the Seventh Seal*. Science fiction author Phil Dick also wrote about it in his rare book *Exegesis*. It was also popularized to a certain extent during the Renaissance by Pico Mirandola who was sponsored by Leonardo de Medici. Essentially, Mirandola was the release point of concealed wisdom that had migrated from Spain after the expulsion of the Moors and found a new home in the Italian Renaissance. It was not, however, popularly accepted but this is quite in keeping with the idea of Christ being positioned as "the stone that was rejected."

Shin, which is the middle letter of *Yod He Shin Vau He,* is the essence of the name and, as was revealed in *Synchronicity and the Seventh Seal*, is the secret word of Freemasonry. Its common meaning in Hebrew is "tooth" but its esoteric meaning in that language is broadly recognized as signifying "change" or "spirit." In both Japanese and Mandarin, the word *shin* means "heart" and this takes us back to the apple.

The etymology of *apple* is confused but revelatory. It is identified as akin to the Old Irish *aball*, the Welsh *afall* and the Latin *Abella*, the name of a small town in Italy where apples grow. In Italian, *bella* means "beautiful." The Welsh *afall* is ironically associated with "a fall" or "the Fall" as in the Fall of Man. By examining obvious phonetics, it seems entirely more probable that the word *apple* derived from Apollo, the god of the sun. Christ has long been associated with Mithras the sun god. Apollo is only a later version. The name *Apollo* comes from *apo* + *leo* which means either the "uncovering of the sun" or the "manifestation of the sun." More appropriately, and much more accurately, it means the manifestation or the uncovering of the cat.

Inside the apple is the pentagram; hence, the uncovering of the cat or the cat made manifest. The cat is Bast, the Great Mother of All, and she works through the pentagram as was demonstrated in the earlier chapter with regard to the DNA helix being a twisted version of a pentagram and hexagram.

In Cabbalistic terms, the pentagram is an extension of the tetrahedron. In this respect, the tetrahedron represents the four letters of YHWH which represent *fire, water, air,* and *earth* respectively. Tarot cards depict the earth element with pentacles because it represents (earthly) manifestation. The four letters are called Tetragrammaton which means four (*tetra*) letters (*grammaton* refers to letters or the process of writing letters).

Tetragrammaton represents the qualitative aspects of nature. People like to think that God is good, but take note that you can have too much of any one element in proportion to the others. In this sense, God consists of all the elements. If they are unbalanced, however, one is going to suffer. A so-called good God can only be achieved by the fifth element that balances these elements and the forces or elementals which accompany them. This is called Pentagrammaton which means "five letters" and refers to the *Yod He Shin Vau He* referred to earlier. This fifth element, *shin*, represents the agent of change whereupon spirit influences the elements of fire, water, air and earth.

When you follow the true path of your genuine heart, keeping in mind that *shin* also means heart, you have already invoked the principle of Pentagrammaton. This applies whether you are aware of the Cabbalistic references or not. It is a natural process. Also note that the word *genuine* is phonetically related to the word *genie* or *jinn*. It is also related to *genesis* and *generation*.

Thus it would seem that the element of the pig was a mutation for purposes of sustaining the original Elder Race which could not cope with the conditions of this planet. It is not unlike the first amphibians trying to live on the land. They had to make adjustments in order to survive. The adaptations, however, resulted in a compromised state. Only the apple, which represents the regenerative principle, can resurrect and rectify the original template that lies within.

There is further intrigue when we contemplate Abraham, the symbolic seed of all Semitic people, whose name contains *ham*, a phoneme which evolved into a word representing a pig or at least a part of a pig. The dictionary etymology of the word *ham* suggests the word derives from a pre-Indo-European base *konemo*, meaning "shin bone." A ham, of course, comes from the thigh of a pig and not the shin. Why is it then associated with the shin?

The scholarship of Kenneth Grant gives us an answer. In his book, *Cults of the Shadow*, he gives an intriguing footnote which tells us something interesting about the letter *shin* and how it relates to the pig. He identifies the Hebrew letter *shin* as coming from an earlier Chaldean letter that is identical. The glyph for *shin* is as follows.

Grant points out that this exalted letter was also used to signify the trident of Neptune or Poseiden. A trident is also the pitchfork that has been attributed to the Devil. Moreover, Grant tells us that the esoteric (which usually means "earlier" although it more properly means "hidden") name for Neptune in ancient times was Chozzar* which means "pig." He further states that Tantric Cults chose a pig as a secret symbol because it is the only animal known to eat human excrement.

The letter *shin* is not only the most exalted aspect of the true name of Jesus, it is positioned as the fulcrum upon which the entire balance of the universe is maintained. It represents the feature of change, particularly as it relates to the spirit and the heart.

All of this tells us that it was no accident that the name of Jesus conforms to Earth Pig. The fact that a pig eats excrement is

* Chozzar is virtually the same as Khazzar which is the name of the so-called "Thirteenth Tribe" of Israel. Khazzars were Turks from the Caucus Mountains who adopted Judaism in about the 8th Century. Some of them are supposed to have migrated to Poland to become the Hasidic Jews. *Tork* is also an Irish word for "boar." It is interesting to note the Khazzars were known as Türük or Török which is hauntingly similar to Taureg. The Türük were known as the Celestial Blue Turks and, previous to Judaism, practiced Tengrin Shamanism which included the worship of a blue god. The Türüks once conquered most of Mongolia and all of Tibet. Their blue god looks Tibetan. They also influenced China far more than is generally realized.

repelling at first glance, but it is actually no different than the scarab beetle of Egypt which is known as the dung beetle because it feeds on excrement to regenerate. Jesus is always positioned as the savior of Mankind. From our study of occult biology, it is very clear that the pig redeemed the Elder Race and made it possible to live in this world. The pigs ate through dead corpses to save the progeny of Abraham. In that story, they saved the Semitic people.

As the redeemer of Mankind, it is often said that Jesus died for your sins. This invites an extremely humorous analogy because this is the same as saying He will vanquish or absorb all of your wrong doings. This is no different than a pig eating your excrement because sins represents all your baggage. In other words, Jesus will eat all of your shit — that is, at least as long as you believe in him. If you stop believing, things are going to back up on you! If you do not believe, *El Diablo* (the Devil or double of Jesus) will hold the pitchfork (which represents *shin* as the focal point of the name *Yeshua*) at your chest to make sure that you do indeed straighten up and fly right.

What I have just stated is the lowest common denominator, but understanding this makes it quite clear that the truth of this principle was hidden and misused in order to dominate others. This domination inevitably accumulates more baggage for the dominator. The more baggage that accumulates, the more work their is for Jesus. You can imagine the kind of havoc this wreaks in the heavens.

As I write and as you read these words, the mighty Sphinx herself looks back over her shoulder at us and gives a wink and a nod because nobody knows better than she the predicament of Mankind. As her name is derived from the sphincter muscle, it follows that she lets loose with a tremendous reflex of defecation as if to pay tribute to the state of affairs on Earth. In mythology, the Sphinx was renown to sit in defecation and to repel others by her smell. This sounds like a lot of shovel work for Jesus, but it is not really that grim of a prospect. One has to look at the situation more like a compost pit where waste matter is used to regenerate new life. When you discover the real truth, it is very strange indeed and gives way to many funny analogies.

When you consider the plight of your own existence as an individual, you have to take things a little more seriously. This means that it would be wise to invoke the means by which you can release yourself of your own toxicity. This includes your toxicity on the physical, emotional, mental and spiritual planes of existence. Such activity requires sacrifice, a word that actually means "to make sacred." It does not mean you have to kill your pet. You make your body sacred by clearing it of its impurities. One can also clear themselves of emotional, mental and spiritual impurities. You then employ the regenerative principle of the apple in order to change and grow into whatever it is that you want to become.

When I embraced the etymological associations of *pigment* and *pig*, I had no idea that the latter word was intrinsically tied to the Christ principle. This discovery would never have occurred had it not been for my pursuit of the olive mystery. As Antinea, the blue queen of Atlantis, was the purveyor of the olive tree, I felt obligated to look as deeply as I could into these matters.

To summate these issues, we have found the following. The purveyor of the olive came from a Blue Race which suffered from a pigment problem when certain elements were mixed with it. This original Blue Race had copper-based blood which was Rh negative. While pig genetics saved the day, it resulted in a downgrade of consciousness. We will now have a look at the role that copper played in these matters.

25

COPPER

Most people have heard that there was a great king of Egypt named Cheops (a Greek word for Khufu) who has often been hallmarked as the builder of the Great Pyramid. It is also common knowledge that the word *Coptic*[*] was used to designate anything Egyptian or representative of Egyptian culture. What is missed, however, is the correspondence of these words to the phoneme *cop* as it appears in the word *copper*. The role of copper in ancient Egyptian history is so pivotal that one cannot dismiss how the phoneme *cop* may have weaved its way into different namesakes. *Copper* as a word is thought to have derived from *Cypress* where there were copper refineries, but these in themselves were only an outpost of Egyptian culture.

When we consider the theory of an Elder Race with copper-based blood that was Rh negative, the theory is substantiated once again when we consider that copper plays a pivotal role in the process of pigmentation. There is an enzyme called the cupro enzyme which is necessary in the formation of pigment. The *cupro* in the cupro enzyme refers to copper.

In the common human of today, copper simply plays a crucial role in directing skin color. It does this by producing a substance called melanin. Melanin is a very misunderstood subject in so-called scientific circles. The dictionary refers to it as a brownish-

[*]The dictionary etymology of the word *copt* is as follows: *copt* < ModL. *copticus* < earlier *Cophtus* < Arabic *Quft, Qift*, the Copts < Coptic *Gypptios* < Greek *Aigyptios*, Egyptian. If the *p* in *copt* is silent, you have *cot* which is virtually the same as *cat*.

black pigment and writes it off as that. This is one of the most stupid and dismissive definitions you will ever find. Why?

While melanin does play a vital role in the process of pigmentation, the substance is much more than that. Black people, American Indians, and brownish islanders all have considerably more melanin in their skin than white people. Melanin is also, however, a superconductor that plays a very important role in how people think and act. It is a key constituent in the chemistry of the brain. The role that melanin plays in skin coloration, however, is nowhere near as crucial as the role it plays in the brain and elsewhere. Although white people have considerably less melanin with regards to their skin, they can possess an abundance of melanin in the brain.

There is a considerable amount of controversy over melanin and most of this controversy is centered around racism. I do not have the time nor desire to enter that debate. The fact that "white" scientific institutions have failed to properly study and honestly report on the function of melanin says a lot in itself. Part of this is due to the fact that the melanin molecule is complex and resistant to physical and chemical analysis. Loaded with carbon, which explains its black color, melanin consists of over two-hundred living atoms. It can be found in many parts of the body and even inside of the DNA molecule.

Recognized scientific studies have shown that calcification of the pineal gland is directly proportional to the lack of melanin in the pineal. This explains why indigenous people experience a communion with nature which has been severely lacking in the so-called white civilization which has, at times, adopted a "scorched Earth" policy.

When we consider the legacy of an Elder Race, we can see that there is not only an intimate and intricate relationship between melanin and copper but that they also formed the foundation of the original Egyptian culture. One example of this can be found in the original Coptic word for an "Egyptian" which was *rem en Kéme*. This is said to mean "people of Egypt," but if you look at what the word is really saying, it means "black people" as *Kéme* means "black." With regard to the Elder Race, however, it should be pointed out that many so-called black people, particularly those of Western Africa, are often described as being "so black that they are blue." I have even heard of cases of such "blue men" who actually turn purple when exposed to prolonged sunlight.

There is no question that the key history of humanity is a lost and secret legacy. What was known as ancient wisdom long ago has been utterly lost. As the curators of Western Civilization, most of this loss can be attributed to the custodianship of the White Race. Two key players in this loss or suppression of information are the Catholic Church and the Crown of England.

Earlier, I brought up the subject of leprosy in *The Bible* and how it was a disease that referred to a spotted condition. Based upon what you have read so far, it would be reasonable to assume that the skin condition suffered by the so-called lepers was a result of hybridizations and mutations with regard to copper-based blood. Copper, of course, would influence the pigment.

As was said earlier, the word for leprosy in the original Hebrew texts was *tzaraath*, a word which can be construed as "tsar wrath" or "wrath of God." The word *tsar* or *czar* is commonly thought to derive from *Kaiser* which in turn derived from *Cesaer*. The word *tsar*, however, was in use long before Julius Caesar became famous. It is a word which means "ruler" or "king" and can obviously apply to a Supreme Being as well. All of this makes sense with the Hebrew texts as they considered tzaraath to be a skin condition that was a punishment for one's sins.

According to the priestly code, tzaraath was a whitening of the skin over the whole body with sores. This included a spreading of the sores with white swellings or reddish-white spots. A very important point to note is that white hair also appeared on these patches of skin. This is clearly a loss of pigment and thereby melanin. The biological processing of copper would therefore also have been dysfunctional.

The Talmud also gives us further clues about tzaraath when it lists seven causes for the disease: an evil gossiping tongue, murder, a vain oath, illicit sex, pride, theft and miserliness. In retrospect, it might seem absurd that criminal behavior is going to cause a skin disease. It is quite logical, however, to recognize that criminal behavior went hand-in-hand with the disease. These people were not producing needed melanin and were going downhill and thereby acquired the affliction known as tzaraath. Their condition would have made them outcast and miserable.

We thus know that according to the history of the Middle East, including both Biblical and Egyptian texts, there was a general disease that affected thousands upon thousands of people which featured a whitening of the skin. Keep in mind that this was in an area of the planet that is and was renown for its blistering heat. In such an environment, dark pigment is highly desirable for practical considerations.

There is no question that copper is the essential element in producing melanin. This, in turn, makes pigmentation possible. While the role of copper is not really controversial in terms of its bodily functions, the role of melanin is. There has been a steadfast obstinacy when it comes to admitting that melanin has an important role other than pigmentation. Why?

Moorish historians have long since known that white racism can be traced back to Egypt and India. The Aryan invasion of India established the infamous caste system. As the name Abraham is close to *brahmin*, it is often suggested that this famous character was the founder of white racism. This is, of course, debatable. Egyptian culture was preoccupied for many years with the expulsion of diseased white people, most of which occurred long before Moses came on the scene.

Without even considering the prospect of whether all white people are suffering from some sort of disease, it is obvious there has been a genocidal war against black people. The Catholic Church waged a ruthless war against the Moors at least since the advent of the Prophet of Islam in the 7th Century. Although Moors are not exclusively black, they are predominantly identified with that color. My earlier work demonstrates a continuous preoccupation with not only destroying Moorish and black culture but also any historical ruminants of it.

Racism is a mental disease and it has everything to do with inferiority and keeping others down so as to protect one's inferiority and insecurity. None of this is too hard to figure out; unless, of course, you happen to suffer from the disease yourself. To say that white people are mentally diseased, however, is not really a controversial statement. All of humanity has similar problems. We are all dealing with brains that are only partially turned on. Operating on as much as twenty percent brain power is considered remarkable for human beings of all colors.

26

RHESUS NEGATIVE

The next mystery that I will address in this puzzle is that of Rh negative blood. It is not my purpose to give a full explanation of the original experiments that discovered Rh negative blood as the entire set of circumstances is quite complex.

The original experiments, conducted in the 1930's, revealed that when a rabbit was immunized with the red blood cells of a rhesus monkey, it created antigens (an antigen is a protein that produces an immune response) that are recognized in certain types of human blood. As a result of these experiments, the recognized blood became known as possessing the Rh factor where "Rh" stands for "rhesus" as in rhesus monkey. Other human blood became known as Rh negative because it does not seem to correspond to monkey blood. Essentially, the difference between the two blood designations has to do with the fact that certain antigens that appear in Rh positive blood are nowhere near to be found in Rh negative blood. Some researchers have also indicated that Rh negative blood contains proteins that have yet to be identified. Like melanin, it is an area of biology that has yet to be either fundamentally or comprehensively researched.

As I am neither a biologist nor biochemist, I am not prepared to take these matters further. The mystery of the Rhesus factor does, however, reveal itself to some degree when we examine the etymology of the rhesus monkey. According to the dictionary and various histories, the designation of the word "rhesus" for this species of monkey was an arbitrary designation named after

Rhesus, an ancient king of Thrace who was an alloy of Troy during the Trojan War. There is also a Rhesus River in Turkey.

The name Rhesus, however, derives from Rhe or Rhea, one of the oldest goddesses in Greek mythology. She was the daughter of Gaea (Earth) and Uranus (heaven) which positions her as the original goddess. The wife of Chronos (Saturn), Rhea was also the mother of Zeus, Poseiden, Hades, Demeter, Hera and Hestia. The Greek goddess Rhea was actually based upon an earlier prototype goddess whose name was eventually transmuted into the patriarchal Ra of Egypt. The name is based upon the Greek *rheos* which means either "flow" or "current." A device such as a light switch dimmer is called a rheostat because it changes current in order to dim an electric light.

If we go back to the etymology of the word Jesus and how it means "Earth pig," we can easily construe that rhesus means "pig flow" or "pig current" (*rhe* = current, *sus* = pig). This becomes more interesting when we consider that rhesus monkeys, like humans, are very compatible with pigs. Just as pig hearts and other organs have been transplanted into humans, so have they been used with rhesus monkeys. Perhaps it should not be too surprising that the genes of rhesus monkeys are 93 percent human. Ninety-three is an interesting number because it corresponds to the magical number 93, the number of thelema or free will. The genes of chimps are 99 percent human. Once again, pigs seems to be a big factor with regard to the genetic legacy of humans.

The rhesus factor, however, runs far deeper into the labyrinth of human consciousness than you might imagine when we embrace the goddess Rhea herself. Surviving different variations or incarnations, Rhea is most known as Rhea Silvia, the original vestal virgin who gave birth to Romulus and Remus, the legendary founders of Rome. Here we have magical twins, born of a virgin birth, whose father just happened to be Mars. Once again, we are thrust back to the planet Mars and are forced to consider that the entire founding of Rome might be based upon the myth of a Martian legacy. An odd coincidence?

27

VIRGIN BIRTH

There is no question that the symbolism in the Roman religion was very cleverly crafted. This includes an undeniable but obscure connection between itself and Queen Antinea, the purveyor of the olive. Of particular interest with regard to the path we have treaded thus far in this book is the association between Queen Antinea and Rhea Silvia, the virgin mother of Romulus and Remus who was "impregnated" by the god Mars.

Before we delve into the mysteries behind the Roman religion, it is advisable to orient you or reorient you to the process that is being utilized in the composition of this book. Thus far, you have read a series of live synchronicities that have caused me to revisit the prospect of the ancient Blue Race. All of the various chapters you have recently read not only substantiate the overall hypothesis of such a race, they also serve as reference markers. Each chapter features an isolated aspect of unmistakable scientific reference points that are worthy of further investigation in their own right. More importantly, they fit into an overall pattern that paints a picture of a general or all-embracing truth. As you will soon read, this truth is the ultimate embodiment of the Goddess and will reveal one of the most guarded mysteries on this planet. This concerns the mysterious Virgin Birth of Christ and all the other so-called enlightened beings who were born of a virgin.

The original myths concerning Queen Antinea would shed much light on these matters, but they are not at our disposal. Even so, the clever craftsmanship of the mythographers of Greece and

Rome do not fail us if we scrutinize etymologies and seek out the various meanings. They leave an indelible pattern that reveals the great mystery previously alluded to.

Our first clue begins with the Greek goddess Athena who obtained her name from the earlier Antinea. Athena was a virgin goddess, and this concept of virginity was strongly reinforced by the construction of the Parthenon in Athens, a city which took on her namesake. The Parthenon is named after parthogenesis, a word which literally means "virgin birth." Parthogenesis is a process which is scientifically recognized to occur in both the animal and plant kingdoms. Throughout history, parthogenesis is also believed to have occurred in humans, but this idea is generally relegated to either esoteric or religious circles. When it comes to religious history or legends, the Virgin Mary is one of the last of a long string of virgin mothers who gave birth to a savior.

Although Athena was heralded as the patron goddess of Athens, the most powerful of the Greek city-states, she was also intricately linked to the downfall of Troy and its reestablishment in Rome. According to long standing tradition, the "eternal city" of Rome was founded with the very flame that was considered to be the sacred flame of Troy. The actual flame was said to have been carried from Troy to Rome by Aeneas and his followers. It became the center point of the new Roman religion where it was placed in the Holy of Holies and was the center of worship by the Vestal Virgins who were also the keepers of the flame, a flame which was sustained through olive oil. Rhea Silvia was said to be the first Vestal Virgin.

Just as the Jews had a Holy of Holies with a flame known by the feminine appellation of "Shekinah" so did the Romans have a flame with female attributes. It was known as Electra, the goddess who was considered to be the mother of Troy. In today's popular literature and consciousness, Electra is better known as one of the Seven Sisters of the Pleiades.

As the flame of Troy, much historical significance has been placed upon Electra. It has been reported historically that when Troy fell, one of the seven stars of the Pleiades faded to the point where it could no longer be seen in the skies. Today, there are only six stars in the Pleiadian constellation that are visible to the naked eye, but it is still known as the seven stars. The seventh "missing" star is Electra. When this planet heals in the coming age, Electra is supposed to return and be visible in the night skies.

The downfall of Troy was also precipitated by another mythologically significant occurrence and this is where the goddess Athena fits in. This event concerned the Palladium which was most commonly thought to be a statue of Athena. It was said that Troy could never fall as long as the Palladium remained in their city. In the work of Thomas Jude Germine, however, he points out that the Palladium corresponds to a substance which illuminates the consciousness of the feminine, particularly with regard to its integration with the male energy.

The Palladium was named after Pallas Athena which is the name Athena took on a result of a misadventure. The most popular story is that she acquired this name when she accidentally killed her friend Pallas. By taking on her friend's name, Athena enabled Pallas to live forever in the memory of Mankind.

All of this alludes to the prospect that "Athena," representing the collective wisdom of Mankind, abrogated the male energy or Palladium in favor of a different modality (virginity). The male energy (or fire) was the "secret" that kept the female going. When it was lost, the flame of Troy expired. On the other hand, life had to keep going, so a new myth was invented where the flame of Troy was transported to Rome and a new civilization began.

Although the above interpretation of Athena's misadventures explains some of the rationale behind the myth, it is not that simple. What is most important is that Athena, in myth, possessed the knowledge of the Palladium and its power. The root of *Palladium* demonstrates this very clearly. *Pal** not only means "a pal" or friend, but it generally means "white" as in the word *pale*. Although he does not state it as such, the "olive" pamphlets of Thomas Jude Germine features the Palladium in such a manner that it easily corresponds to white gold.*

As Athena is the goddess of wisdom, it stands to reason that the Palladium referred to knowledge, particularly as it related to intelligence or knowledge of the masculine and its integration with the feminine. When the Greeks took this knowledge away from

* There is also a strong correspondence between the word *olive* and *pal* when you consider the court of Charlemagne. His top twelve attendants or knights were referred to either as Olivers or as Palladins.

the Trojans, Troy fell but the spirit or the essence, as represented by the flame, was taken to Rome where it was placed in the protective care of the Vestal Virgins.

In *The Illiad,** the problems that led to the Trojan War started long before Paris abducted Helen from her husband Menelaus, the King of Sparta. *Menelaus* meant "Moon King" and Paris was a Prince of Troy and the son of Priam,** the King of Troy who had multiple wives and over seventy children. The Trojan War originally began when Paris was called upon to judge a beauty contest which featured three goddesses: Athena (Minerva), Artemis (Diana), and Aphrodite (Venus). In this myth, Aphrodite won by bribing Paris. If he would select her as the most beautiful, Aprhrodite told Paris she would arrange for him to have the most beautiful woman in the world, Helen. Paris responded at judgment time by offering Aphrodite an apple which signified that she was the winner. Representing the heart, the apple is also symbolic of the most valuable principle in the universe: regeneration.

All of this might sound like a very grand myth, but as I said earlier, it was very cleverly and purposely crafted by the mythographers. The muse, which was considered to be an instruments of the gods in those days, might have had a lot to do with it as well. This myth is very important because it illustrates a tentacle of lost knowledge. It helps us to recover information just as if we were recovering it from a crashed hard disk on a computer.

To me, the most conspicuous aspect of the myth is that both Artemis and Athena are virgin goddesses while Aphrodite was anything but a virgin. Paris chose fleeting beauty over the wisdom (Athena) and practical hunting skill (Artemis) of the virgins. This rejection of the virgins is complex and somewhat contradictory because he chooses the winner with an apple, the symbol of the

* *The Iliad* is named after *Ilus*, the legendary founder of Troy. It is ironic that the name *Ilus* is very similar to *Eleusis*, a Greek city-state which was named after the olive and also hosted the famous Eleusinian Mysteries. *Ilium* is actually a Latinized version of the earlier *Ilion* which is virtually the same as *lion.* In mythology, *Ilus* acquired the Palladium from the heavens.

**Modern scholars indicate that the word *Priam* derived from a pre-Indo-European word (in a language called Luwian) *primuua* which is defined as "exceptional courage." The phonetics of this word clearly related to "cat" with *muua* being similar to *mau*; and *pri* could mean a number of things, including "first" or "prior (as in primordial)." *Primuua* is also similar to *paramus* or *pyramus* which is the root of *pyramid.*

virgin goddess Kore (also Car, Kor or Peresophene). Why is he deliberately rebuffing the two virgins? The reason is obvious. The regenerative and magical power of the apple is placed in his trust, but he opts for beauty at the expense of wisdom which begins the fall of Troy. It is clear from the myth that Athena possessed the secret of the Palladium which represents the true knowledge of balance with regard to the feminine and masculine.

According to the myth, Athena and Artemis were incensed at Paris for his judgement. Accordingly, Athena conspired with Odysseus (Ulysses) and taught him the secrets of the Palladium as well as how to construct a wooden horse to deceive the Trojans, great warriors who had never suffered a defeat. The symbol of the horse was not chosen by accident. It was a symbol of war but was specifically sacred to Mars. The god Mars, however, would not have condoned the use of real horses to defeat Troy because he was on their side. Athena had to outhink Mars by using craft and guile.

The Judgement of Paris is the subject of a famous painting, and the apple he gave to Venus is referred to as the Apple of Discord because the incident wreaked so much havoc. The complexity of this myth becomes considerably more clear, however, when we realize that it is a distinct and deliberate revision of an earlier matriarchal version in which Paris is given the apple by three goddesses. These three goddesses are known as the Triple Goddess and they represent the virgin, the mother, and the crone. Originally referring to the three natural states of women, this principle was diluted into the Greek myth just referred to. Much later, it was transmuted and degraded by Christian scribes into the so-called Holy Trinity which represented three males occupying positions nobody could ever completely agree on. Although the Triple Goddess was rejected in a religious sense, her functions are natural and were never seriously disputed. It is also ironic that the name *Troy* is the same as *trois* which means "three."

Although *The Iliad* portrays a rejection and moving away from the virgin goddess, it also ends with a new hope for continuing the sacred principle of the feminine. This was symbolized by the escape of Aeneas and his eventual arrival in Rome with the sacred flame of Electra.

These associations run yet deeper when we take into account that the Seven Hills of Rome are known as the Palatine or Palatine

Hill. Named after the *pal* in Pallas, they also represent the seven Pleiades. It is also important to note that the phonetic relationship between *pal* in Palatine and *phal* in *phallus* should not be underestimated. The Vestal Virgins, who numbered twelve, were serviced by a man known as the Pontif Maximus who represented the inner secret of the male energy. Barbara Walker points out in her work that he represented a sacred lingam (phallic symbol) signifying *AMOR* which not only means "love" but is the explicit and deliberate opposite expression of *ROMA* , the name of the empire. The word *amor* also corresponds to *Moor*.

Besides being clearly aligned with the feminine aspects of Electra and the Pleiades, the Trojans shared a historical alliance with the Amazons, female warriors who occupied areas in modern day Turkey. One of the ancient Seven Wonders of the World was the Temple of Artemis in Ephesus. This was not only located in the general vicinity of Troy, it was traditionally a home of the Amazons and was crafted, at least in myth, to have been a residence of the Virgin Mary. There is a tomb for her in Ephesus to this day.

Known as the original Queen of the Amazons, Antinea would have been an a priori and key element that these latter day myths were based upon. In the story of Troy, there is no question that the Palladium represented a secret power that was in possession of the virgin goddess Athena. As important as her role is, there is another member of the pantheon who serves a key role when it comes to discovering the mysterious power of the virgin goddess: Mars.

Long before "he" becoming a war god,* Mars was a female symbol of fertility and menstruation. Perhaps this is why the mythographers could not separate him from Troy, a culture which clearly embraced the feminine through the Pleiadian mythos. Despite his adopted masculine characteristics, Mars was clearly used by mythographers to continue this virgin-oriented religion that was to take hold on the Latin peninsula.

* In her work, *The Women's Encyclopedia of Myths and Secrets*, Barbara Walker traces the roots of the word *Mars* back to an Indo-European pre-Vedic god known as Rudra which means "the red one" and was born of a three-faced mother named Marici (a name which easily equates to "cat head" if you consider that *mau* is Egyptian for cat and *rici* equates to *resh* which is Hebrew for "head" or "king"). She is the goddess of birth, dawn, and the New Year. In Japan, she was known as Marici-deva. Marici gave birth to Latinus, a god-king and the ancestor of all the Latin tribes.

Besides being the father of Romulus and Remus in what was conspicuously described as a virgin birth, Mars himself was also designated as having been born of a virgin. Once again, this myth was deliberately concocted so as to convey a specific meaning. His mother was Juno, the wife of Jupiter (Zeus), who spurned the love of her husband and conceived Mars through her own "unaided fertility magic" that was represented by a lily blossom which represented her own yoni (a yin receptacle).

It was the above phrase from Barbara Walker, "unaided fertility magic," which enabled me to finally arrive at an inevitable conclusion that puts the paradigm of Antinea, the Amazon Queen, into a clear and logical perspective. Tracking down these various myths and their transmogrifications led me to focus on the salient point that Mars not only "fathered" the virgin birth of Romulus and Remus, he was born of a virgin himself. This myth helps to explain why the names of *Mars* and *Mary* are so inextricably connected etymologically. Once again, it is not an accident.

As I began to look further into the phrase "unaided fertility magic," I soon discovered that there is no real answer that is readily available. This is particularly astonishing when you consider that one of my ready reference books is Barbara Walker's *The Women's Encyclopedia of Myths and Secrets*. Quite arguably one of the most comprehensive summations of female mysteries you will find in a library or book store, Walker's very admirable work contains no real answer to the mystery of what is exactly meant by the phrase "unaided fertility magic." You are not likely to find out anything about it in any other book either. If you do, please alert me. The reason for this is that it has been a deliberately guarded secret for at least the last two thousand years.

There is no question that the phrase deliberately suggests that a woman can conceive on her own. To virtually all of humanity, this is a preposterous proposition that is either inconceivable to those of a "scientific" persuasion or embraced on pure faith and regarded as a miracle. The truth, however, is far more interesting.

Had it not been for my earlier adventures and research, I would have been just as blind as anyone else with regard to these matters. Fortunately, my previous work would help me obtain some real answers. For those of you who recall my book, *Montauk Revisited*, it made a direct reference to an occult process by which a virgin birth could took place. This came to my attention when I received my very first letter from Aleister Crowley's son, Amado, which stated that he remembered his father talking about the Wilson Brothers. He recalled that they were friends of H.G. Wells and were sterile. When my friend, Madame X, read this letter, she pointed out to me (through her own knowledge of arcane secrets) that the sterility factor was a major clue. She said that this was a result of a magical birth whereby the zona pellucida was penetrated by a male protein latent within the biochemistry of a woman. In such a birth, the zona pellucida (female egg) would be "fooled" into thinking it was a sperm and a virtual baby would eventually form. This egg would often become twin babies who were born sterile. When twins were not born, it would often result in an attenuated birth of the second twin which could result in an extra set of nipples. As this germination process began at the base or origin of the spine, such a baby was representative of the ultimate expression of rising kundalini and was literally an exalted being such as a savior or a Christ IF the process was successful. Otherwise, you might have an abomination or something more representative of an Antichrist.

Despite what I had learned about all this, it still remained a mysterious process. The word *parthogenesis* gives us a clue as it suggests that virginity relates to "divine fire" (*par* or *pyr* = fire; *theos* = god; *genesis* = birth) or "divine fire of the jinn." I also consulted the etymology of the word *virgin*, but the dictionary is admittedly at a loss to explain it. The word *virgin* does, however, yield to a common sense approach when we consider *vir* and *gin*. *Vir* refers to the vital force and means "men" which refers to masculinity or the impregnating power of semen or "male magic." The word *men*, however, earlier referred to the menses and meant "women." *Gin*, of course, refers to *genesis* but also to *genie* or *jinn*. While these definitions are both insightful and symbolic, they still leave us with the proposition of mysterious magic.

Due to my pursuit of the olive mystery, I would stumble upon the true secret of the magic of the virgin birth, one of the most sacred and time-honored traditions of the feminine energy. It is, however, so secret that virtually no one knows it. As it does not even appear in Barbara Walker's *Encyclopedia of Women's Myths and Secrets*, it must indeed be a very deep secret.

28

MOONFLOWER

In this chapter, you will learn the most dramatic and secretive mystery of the previous millennium. As you read on, you will see that I am not grandstanding. This secret has been so pervasive and influential in Mankind's collective unconscious that ignorance of it has led to a ridiculous amount of superstition and silliness which has led to mass confusion, political intrigue and even wars.

I arrived at the discovery of this secret through my pursuit of synchronicity. Although I had plenty of help along the way, nobody told it to me outright. The reason for this is that no one else knew it. I will now share how I came to learn it

Earlier in this book, I mentioned Tantra Bensko, my friend who was a very important catalyst regarding my initiation into the feminine energy. During that period, she shared with me what she said was a very guarded secret that she had acquired over a period of years. Although this is not the secret referred to above, it was a key to understanding what I have referred to as the secret of the last millennium. Tantra's secret concerned the feminine bodily excretion known as moonflower in either tantric or Taoist circles.

To physiologists or sexologists, moonflower is more commonly known as female ejaculatory liquid, sometimes abbreviated as FEL. Tantra acquired specialized knowledge of this substance over a period of years from her involvement with the Rainbow People, a nomadic group of nature people who have periodic gatherings at different spots throughout North America. These gathering are always at a nature setting and are only advertized by word of mouth as they do not desire onlookers or curiosity seekers. It should be pointed out that while the Rainbow People in general are very progressive in terms of getting back to nature, most of them are not necessarily as enlightened or clued-in as the people Tantra was studying with. They waited a considerable period of time before deciding to share their secrets with her.

Although I have presented moonflower as a very sacred and secretive substance, it is by no means unknown to the world. Its esoteric properties, however, are considerably secretive and, as I was to discover, they reach the apex of occult biology.

In the sex industry, female ejaculatory liquid or FEL is known as "the squirt" and is sometimes demonstrated in pornographic movies as a vulgar expression of female sexuality. The truth, however, is far different. It is only demonstrated in a vulgar manner due to ignorance of its esoteric properties. Most people, including women, are not even aware of its existence.

Despite having been married twice and learning all sorts of secrets from all sorts of people during my days as a Scientology counselor, I had never even heard of female ejaculatory liquid. I even worked in a bar for long time. In such an environment, one hears almost every crudity under the sun and hears them repeatedly, but I never heard any mention of this substance.

When I refer to female ejaculatory liquid, it should be pointed out that I am not talking about secretions but about an actual ejaculation that is similar to a male. Research indicates that such ejaculations of moonflower occur regularly in about six percent of females. They occur irregularly to another thirteen percent.

The ejaculation of moonflower is actually designed to be the most divine and orgasmic expression of the female body. It represents the culmination of a series of orgasms that unfettered and unrepressed females are known to experience. In an unrestricted world, this would be a part of what should be ordinary or normal sexuality. In our world, it is not ordinary.

Although some women experience ejaculation, they do it in a sort of willy-nilly manner. In this respect, it is sort of a misfire or disconnect because its presence does not equate to either extreme orgasm nor are the esoteric properties recognized. This disconnect is due to the repression of the female energy that has been prevalent on this planet which, theoretically, goes back to the Fall from the so-called Garden of Eden. Such repression is directly parallel to the Kabbalistic doctrine referred to earlier in this work that states that this universe is the result of an absence of feminine energy. Bring back the orgasmic ejaculation of moonflower and you bring back the feminine. It is too simple to be believed yet our entire culture is dedicated to the proposition of repressing this energy. This repression is why the information presented here is lost.

Years after learning about this substance, I searched for the biochemical components of moonflower. Everything I came up with, however, was full of too many chemical formulas and I was not able to come up with any conclusions. It was frustrating as there was not too much written on it that was readily available. I dropped my investigation. As I began to put together the components of this book, however, I revisited the subject. Discovering Queen Antinea as the mother of the Blue Race and tracking down the various myths already described created a definite effect upon me. It was if the pages of this book I was writing were literally "screaming" at me to have another look and take it further. As a result, I was able to make some astonishing observations and obvious conclusions.

I consulted a book or pamphlet entitled *How to Really Love a Woman: Adore Aphrodite, Encourage Her Ejaculation* by Sasha Lessin, Ph.D. and Janet Kira Lessin. These are two friends of mine who had given me their book while they were in New York. They actually teach this technique in their very public workshops. This includes the cultivation of moonflower ejaculation. Their book refers to moonflower as *amrita*, a "divine nectar or slightly milky, sweet-tasting, alkaline fluid from her urethra." In most literature, the term *amrita* is similar to *ambrosia* and refers to "the food of the gods." It is only known as moonflower in esoteric or tantric circles. *The Encyclopedia of Women's Myths and Secrets* mentions *amrita* but does not suggest its ejaculatory aspect.

While reading the Lessins' book, an alarm bell went off when I read the statement that moonflower is an alkaline fluid. This means that it is a protein. Remembering what was written in *Montauk Revisited*, I realized that this alkaline fluid known as moonflower might be the so-called "latent protein" that could penetrate the zona pellucida and result in a magical sex child or virgin birth. Here is your "unaided fertility magic."

After considering all of the above, I once again tried to find the earlier data I had collected on the biochemistry of moonflower. I did not, however, find it. Speaking to several people, I came up empty-handed. This included a conversation with a long time practitioner of tantra who had never even heard of it. This shocked me because she is a medical professional and is one of the most knowledgeable people I know when it comes to the human body and also esoteric modalities. This told me that the true nature of this substance must be truly mysterious.

Internet searches for moonflower did not yield much information at all. I tried every different name and aspect I could find but came up empty-handed. Finally, a friend of mine found out that it is mentioned on *Wikipedia* under "female ejaculation." Although the *Wikipedia* information neither includes nor appreciates the esoteric aspects, it does offer a representative description of the relevant biochemical properties.

I was astonished to learn that even though it is mentioned in antiquarian sources, including Aristotle, the so-called scientific community utterly rejected the existence of this substance until the 1980's. It came to the forefront during that decade when female ejaculation was featured in a popular book entitled *The G-Spot* by Lada, Whipple and Perry. If such a blatant denial does not convince you that the feminine energy has been repressed on a monumental level, you will never be convinced. This repression is directly proportional to the degree the "secret of the millennium" is not known.

Female Ejaculatory Liquid (FEL)* includes many different substances and is primarily expelled through the uretha and includes prostatic acid phospatase (PAP) and prostate specific antigen (PSA) which are produced by the female prostate gland. PAP is an enzyme and PSA is a protein. The Skene's gland also produces Human Protein 1 which was formerly believed to be unique to the male prostate.

The more I looked into these matters, the more obvious it became that the female and male bodies mimic each other in the most complex and mysterious ways. There is a lot more opportunity for biological variations than you might think. More

* It should not go unnoticed that FEL, the acronym for Female Ejaculatory Liquid, just happens to be the root for the words *feline* and *feel*.

importantly, I had not only found my so-called "latent male protein" but I was discovering that FEL is not much different than sperm itself. When I called Preston Nichols to tell him what I had found, he said, "Yeah, I know. They are essentially the same thing." Preston, who used to manufacture equipment for the Masters and Johnson sex clinic years ago, is well informed about sexology and has the equivalent of a Ph.D. in the field.

A particularly significant fact concerning FEL is that the biochemical components of it change in ratio to the quantity that is produced during a given ejaculation. Diet and the menses affect the chemistry as well. This suggests that while a so-called "virgin birth" is entirely possible, it is not a sure bet by any means. Ancient traditions evolved in such a manner as to orchestrate so much gobbledygook around this process that it stands to reason that such a birth required a certain amount of initiation which might include diet and esoteric training. These are mysteries yet to be revealed.

Reports of virgin births have surfaced, all of them coming from young natives in Africa. It is unknown, but is entirely possible that there have been "virgin births" from women who had sex with their husband but were actually impregnated due to their own ejaculatory liquid. As no one has ever thought to monitor such situations, it is impossible to make any sort of determination.

It is significant to point out that those reported virgin births in the modern era have come from black women. This suggests that copper and therefore melanin were present in the system to a significant degree. This should give you some idea of why the Black Virgin or Black Isis has been so venerated throughout the last millennium. It is adorned and honored but no one knows exactly why. The mystery presented here is a glue which makes it all stick.

The great secret of the millennium has now been laid upon you. Moonflower is the means by which a virgin birth can be accomplished. The science is sitting there in plain sight, but these matters were never really a science problem. Ignorance of this data has much more to do with repression, suppression, and oppression.

As obvious and as interesting as all of this is, it is not enough to simply recognize the repression of the feminine on an intellectual basis only. No matter who you are, the oppressive consequences have insidiously leaked its tentacles into your brain. After all, you are a part of this planet and the literal God-damned brain trust that monitors the morphogenetic and political functions of the Earth. If you were not a part of the problem, you would be functioning with at least a sizable portion of your brain and not at a level which is well below full capacity.

I bring up the point of brain capacity and utilization because human beings are an extremely arrogant lot. On a collective basis, they farm wrong, eat wrong, prosecute the wrong people and in a general capacity are waging a full frontal assault against the laws of nature. When you point out simple truths, most humans are inclined to believe in the media or other lies they have bought into and just go along with the status quo. As a member of this civilization, you are no different. At best, you might be a bit ahead of the curve. I do not point this out in order to chide you but to emphasize the importance of waking up and rewiring your own brain. This does not mean you should abandon what you know, but it does mean that you are not thinking straight. In particular, I am referring to your response and sensitivity to the feminine energy described in this chapter and elsewhere in this book. You cannot help it as it is impossible to think straight in this universe. If you did think one-hundred percent straight, you would ascend right out of this universe and not be subject to it. As a citizen of this universe, you have been denied the true divinity of the feminine and have participated in the denial. It is time to change. This not only means drastic change for yourself but for all living and breathing entities on the entire planet.

I am well aware that, to a significant degree, the extraordinary information you are reading will fall on deaf ears. Even though these so-called secrets are hiding in plain sight, they will be minimized or discarded by an already stultified population that is predisposed to remaining ignorant or asleep. Nevertheless, many of you are already waking up and this data will make you wake up further and see new horizons.

The Apocalypse refers to the "uncovering or revelation of the goddess. "Unaided fertility magic" is not such a mystery anymore. You can thank the olive tree that you and I have now been initiated into one of the most sacred secrets with regards to the confused mystery religions of this planet. Perhaps the ancient Kabbalists knew something after all.

29

MYSTERE LYCANTHROPIQUE

The prospect of the Virgin Birth is probably one of the most ridiculously debated religious issues in the last two thousand years. The vehemence of the debate is in direct proportion to the lost knowledge that has accrued over millennia. As interesting as the prospect of a virgin birth is, it is just one of many more female mysteries that have been lost in antiquity.

The gestation process is still replete with mysteries to this day. Many children are born with extra digits or tails. Before turning into a full-fledged human baby, the zygote transforms through many shapes which include tadpoles, frogs, and our recently acknowledged specialized friend, the pig. During the gestation process, the DNA is programmed to shift its shape as well as the protocol by which it will evolve into a human. The mystery surrounding birth and death has been one of the most significant plights with regard to the human condition. The Hindus and Buddhists have long recognized this while the Christians have sought to exploit it.

In earlier chapters, the symbol ⊕ was cited as a stargate as well as a feminine symbol. The idea of a gate is very important because the birth process is our gateway into the quantum realm that we live in with regard to normal Earth-based consciousness.

When we consider that "unaided fertility magic" was accomplished by Juno, it is wise to look into the etymology of that name. Besides being the inspiration for the month of June, the name *Juno* means at least two things: *jinn* or *gate*. Juno was originally a goddess that looked backwards and forwards into time, but this concept was later supplanted by the patriarchal image of Janus whose name inspired the month of January. Keep in mind that the word *Babalon* or *Babylon* means either "gate" or "gate of the lion." Traditionally, *baba* means "gate" and the lion comes from *ylon* or *elion* which also shares the root of *elaia* which is the olive. The etymology of *baba* is intrinsically related to the English word *baby* because a baby is associated with the gateway by which it came through. It is quite humorous to note that many Christians are absolutely horrified by the prospect or the word *Babylon* which simply refers to a (female) gate. It becomes even more humorous when you consider that Christ himself was the Lion of Judeah and is also known as Yeshua ben Pandera. As a baby, the name "baby lion" or Babylon would have been an etymologically accurate fit for Christ. Just like the ⊕ symbol, he represented the pathway between this world and another.

Christ, known as King Felix by author Phil Dick, had to be presented as a cat because the cat has long been a symbol of the entrance to the other world. One of the most conspicuous symbols of the feminine throughout history, the cat represents a gateway and you see this in words like *gato* in Spanish and *gatto* in Italian.

The ⊕ symbol of the so-called circle and cross is also identified with the mythological realm of Circe.* In the Greek classics, Circe was most famous for her exploits in the *Odyssey*. That work, however, encompasses only a portion of her full character. Her broader realm embraces the primordial aspects of creation that lie beyond or a priori to the gate of life. Her world is filled with creatures, blood, and monstrosities. Although Circe is a mythological character, the realm she represents happens to be quite real.

In the *Odyssey*, Odysseus (Ulysses in Latin) was warned of her magic so he sent twenty-three of his men to her island known as Aeaea. The number twenty-three is particularly significant because DNA consists of twenty-three pairs of chromosomes. Circe, who happens to be a powerful sorceress, utilizes the powers of herbs and drugs to make twenty-two of these men hallucinate and

* The word *circle* is derived from the Greek word for such which is *kyrkos* or *kirkos*. In Latin, it is *circus*. *Circe* is also known as *cirke* or *kirke*.

then turn into swine. The twenty-third man, who is the leader of the group, represents the twenty-third chromosome that escaped or is redeemable. This sailor went back and told Odysseus who then learned how to protect himself from Circe. Odysseus was able to escape her magic through the instruction of the god Hermes who gave him an antidote which was a plant called moly, a black root with a white flower. As far as biology is concerned, the moly that Odysseus used is a complete mystery because no one has yet been able to identify the myth with a real plant. Whatever it was, it robbed the drugs of their power. Thus empowered, Odysseus was able to consort with Circe and the couple learned to trust each other through the act of making love. After enjoying good relations with Odysseus, Circe smeared the heads of the swine with a salve and they returned to their human state with some even enjoying improved physical conditions. Everyone was so happy with each other that they all stayed on Circe's island for a year.

Before they left to continue the Odyssey, Circe taught Odysseus how to sail into the underworld so that he could consult a seer about the rest of his journey. This was the first time a ship had ever sailed into Hades, and Circe knew the ropes because it was within her realm. In reality, the underworld is a part of life that we never see. The myths handed down to us from antiquity are representations of what actually happens to us in the morphogenetic field. Each molecule of DNA contains or has access to the potential memory of the entire morphogenetic experience.

The story of Circe and Odysseus is an example that one can actually redeem oneself and return home. It was not easy however. Odysseus had to be clever and was always considered a very crafty individual. More than that, it was the twenty-third chromosome that saved the day. As we will all pass through the gate sooner or later, it is wise to understand its principles before encountering it. In order that you understand this better, I will present some very salient points with regard to the Cabala and how those principles interface with the subject at hand.

Earlier in this book, it was explained how the pentagram and hexagram interface to form the spirals which become the pattern for the DNA molecule. It is very telling that this pattern is not only the template for DNA but also for the Cabalist Tree of Life. The morphogenetic process of life primarily consists of repetitions, variations, and a further repetition of those variations with yet newer variations. It all tends to conform, however, to a pattern which the ancients have exposed in the Cabalistic Tree of Life. How accurate these expositions are vary with the writers, but any of them are bound to give some insight into the hidden processes of life. It is inappropriate to go into a detailed treatise on the Cabala in this book. Instead, I will give a concise summary so that you understand a couple of points I would like to bring forth.

The Cabalistic Tree of Life includes ten sepiroth or *sephiraat* which is the Hebrew word for "sphere." These ten sepiroth are ten emanation points of life and flow from one to the other. To some degree, it is like a fountain or spring. Each one of these sepiroth conform to a numeral as well as a fundamental archetype of consciousness. As a single unit of life evolves into what it is eventually going to become, it passes through each one of these sepiroth and emphasizes some more than others. A male peacock, for example, stresses beauty while a more ferocious animal might draw more from the well of the martial energies in this so-called template. The philosophy of this template is such that it includes all aspects of potential life

There is also a mysterious eleventh sepiroth which deals with all hidden or occult operations. It is postulated to be there because you can see its results or manifestations, but there is no visible evidence of it. It is known as *Da'ath.*

While not a part of this tree of life structure per se, there is another designated repository into which life also flows with regard to certain circumstances. It is, however, a darker side to life and is referred to as the *q'lipoth.* This is somewhat like a sewer because it is the repository into which flows all things that did not work out in the experience of regular life. In other words, the *q'lipoth* is the receptacle for that which has been rejected, for one reason or another, by the process of the morphogenetic grid. For example, the memory of life organisms which did not succeed are relegated to this area of consciousness. This would include the memory of dinosaurs, mastodons, saber-tooth tigers, and a lot of other creatures that might be considered extinct. It is known from experience that this region includes monstrous type manifestations which can literally frighten the living daylights out of occult practitioners or naive explorers who penetrate this realm.

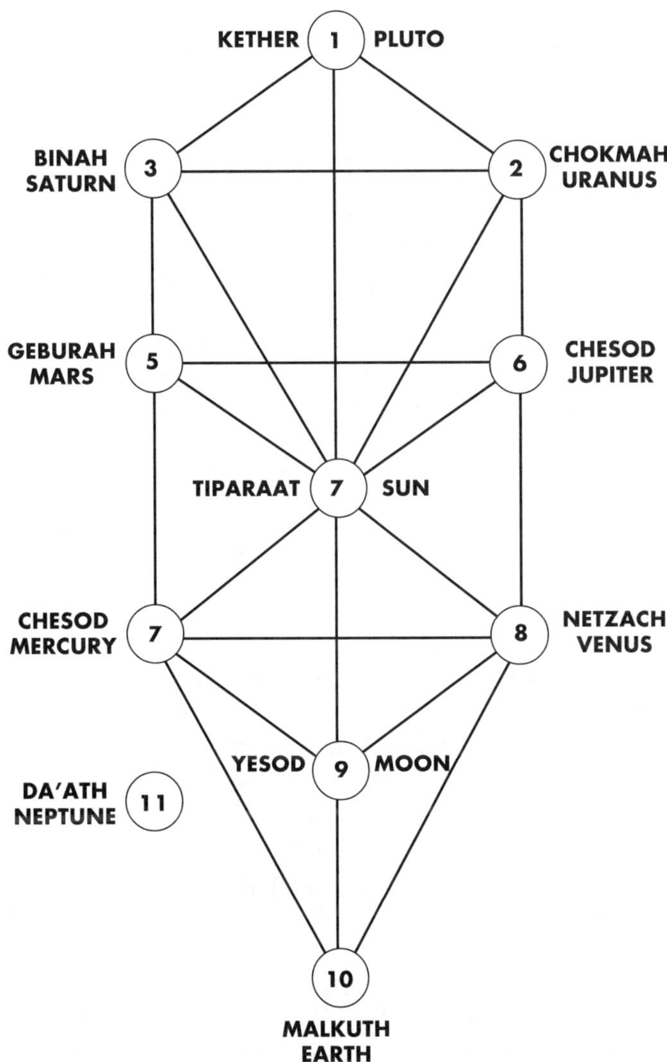

THE CABALISTIC TREE OF LIFE

Each sepiroth is designated by a number (also used in numerology), the Hebrew letter used to describe it, and the planet which is assigned as the primary influence of that sepiroth. Other texts should be consulted for a more in-depth study.

I have brought these matters to the forefront because they are fundamental principles upon which to understand the phenomena of shape-shifting. When magical practitioners or others begin to open up to the energies of the universe and stir the pot, they literally begin to enliven these archetypal forces within the subconscious of their own framework. What they are doing is stimulating old "nerve centers" or pathways that were at one point crucial in the evolution of the organism. When these centers are stirred up, it does not necessarily create anything in the physical realm but it most certainly and most decidedly stimulates the astral realm. This precipitates one to take on the astral shape of different animals. In other words, one is tapping into the a priori principles or dynamic functions which caused your physical organism to evolve in the first place. It should be pointed out that there is a difference between tinkering or fooling around and deeply examining the actual causes upon which the physical organism is based. Opening this door, particularly when it is forced open through drugs or other nonkosher means, can have disastrous consequences. If one does not have a filter, one is going to reap ill effects. In his book *Cults of the Shadow*, Kenneth Grant points out that establishing a filter is essential when negotiating this territory. It is the senior responsibility of the magician, philosopher or traveller of this path.

I mention these things as I have had many queries from those who have had subjective experiences concerning shape-shifting entities. If you yourself are experiencing shape-shifting or you are seeing another do it, do not contact the authorities. Work on your own filter. I will address how later on in this book.

It has also been suggested that white gold facilitates the process of shape-shifting. These assertions sprang up after I published *The Black Sun*, the first expose of the Blue Race that correlated it with white gold, a substance which facilitates the integration of both hemispheres in the brain. When I released this information, I was hopeful that it would promote a higher level of consciousness to others. Instead, it created a backlash from sensationalists who have come forth with wild and unverifiable stories about white gold being used by shape-shifting reptilians.

There has been far too much hyperbola concerning the so-called white gold that has been presented in the New Age market place. It is not really what it appears to be and is adulterated at best.

The first presentation, offered by David Hudson, should have been a telltale sign to everyone, particularly when it failed.

Hudson, a farmer from Arizona, claimed to have backing from General Electric and was researching monatomic elements which included rhodium and iridium. He expounded upon the theory of the white gold and manna as was referred to in *The Bible*. Millions of dollars were collected with the promise of delivering a monatomic transformative substances to the investors. Nothing was ever delivered except elaborate excuses. Those who were wise never believed a word he said anyway. When he talked about esoteric subjects, he sounded like a used car salesman. Personally, I would be very suspicious as to whether he even filed with the Securities and Exchange Commission before offering what he did.

In spite of this disappointment, the New Age public was willing to listen and buy the products of other con artists who have publicized their so-called knowledge of this "wonderful" new substance. I have also heard people wistfully expound the virtues of this "white gold" when they are really just talking smack.

The actual white gold is supposed to take one HIGHER, not lower. Get it? If one is taking the actual substance, one is not going to be getting scammed. Unfortunately, scamming is completely acceptable in our culture so people do not notice when they are being scammed. This applies to oil prices, the food industry, the media, and most every endeavor of our current human culture.

After writing *The Black Sun*, I came into contact with Raoul Tollman, an Austrian who grew up learning about rocks and their different properties. Various synchronicities led him to learn about the actual science behind monatomic elements and how the public was being scammed. He learned how to produce this substance, but he has written little on it. His website is www.alchemicanova.com. Personally, if I were to pursue the white gold path, I would consult him and be highly suspicious of any New Age lecturers whose science is usually suspect.

As exotic as the real white gold is, most people are not in any sort of physical condition where they are going to significantly benefit from it. I will touch on this later in the book.

As for shape-shifting, or the process called *Mystere Lycanthropique*, this transformation has traditionally been represented as malevolent in our Judaic-Christian culture. It strikes terror in the hearts of those who have been conditioned by tales of vampires and werewolves. As has already been described previously in this chapter, there is no doubt that there is a negative aspect with regards to the crossroads of the spiritual world. It should also be pointed out, however, that shape-shifting is a long-honored and respected art of indigenous shamans throughout the world. Natives, and not just shamans, view it as a part of nature. They are often reluctant to share their stories with a white man's culture which is blind to such phenomena and is predisposed to degrade it along with other elements of nature.

I would like to remind everyone of a popular television show from the Fifties and Sixties entitled *The Lone Ranger*. This western drama featured three primary characters: the Lone Ranger himself, who is a white man; Tonto, his Indian helper, and Silver, the Lone Ranger's horse. Tonto always referred to the Lone Ranger as "Kee-mo-sobby" which is the phonetic pronunciation for the Spanish words *que es mas sabe*. These words mean "he who knows more." In Spanish, the word *tonto* means "stupid." The name Silver, however, is perhaps the most telling as it is a direct reference to the fact that the Lone Ranger only used special bullets made of silver. In movie lore, one uses a silver bullet to kill a shape-shifter such as a werewolf. The Lone Ranger wore a mask so that he could not be identified.

At the time those of my generation watched this television show, none of us had any idea that the writers were having a field day of satire over the proposition of white supremacy versus indigenous people. One should not get too upset over the white supremacists, however. They were just filling the roles of the jinn who will thwart the unwary traveller who ventures into the realm of the crossroads known as Carrefour or Carfax. One has to discover, maintain, and work with their own filters.

With regard to my own filter, I would discover that my own research into the indigenous aspects of the Montauk culture would eventually weave its way deeply into my personal life in more ways than I could imagine.

Aleister Crowley's work said that the ⊕ symbol was a key. It not only represents the feminine energy but also the feminine aspect of the crossroads where life and death meet in the natural process of regeneration. These are, of course, intimately related.

30

MANNA

Long before *The Bible* was written, the word *manna* was a representation of feminine magic or supernatural power. As was said earlier, the word for woman was originally *man* or *men* and was also associated with *moon, menses* and *month*. This word *manna* is not only intrinsically connected to these words, it represents the so-called magic of life itself and is tied to the process of life emerging and disappearing. It was therefore also connected to the spirits associated with all of the above words. This could, of course, include shape-shifting but that is not the point.

When it comes to the consumption of mummy dust, this was an attempt by the early Egyptians to maintain the continuity of consciousness. To the earliest and most select, it was also an attempt to maintain the continuity of a genetic family line. It later degenerated into mummies being created only to be destroyed and sold as snake oil medicine.

To the early descendants of the Blue Race, manna was filled with the spirits of their ancestors. This tradition was carried forward by many tribes and peoples. It is especially well recorded in the mythology of the Romans who featured Mana or Mania as a very arcane goddess. Like Circe, Mana ruled the underground land of the dead which included ancestral spirits known as Manes or Mania. These were her children, and they lived in a "Well of Souls" that was underneath a holy stone in the Forum that was known as the *Lapis Manalis*. On an annual feast day every year, the Manes would emerge to receive their offerings. Mania was considered a divine revelation as opposed to madness. Manna, occultum, or white gold were all ways to connect to your ancestors.

Ancient people obviously looked at their ancestors quite differently than we do today. The main point in all of this is that any and all reverence or consideration of our ancestors, including ancestor worship, represents the gateway of those who have gone before us. In some ways, ancestors are not unlike a menagerie of gargoyles juxtaposed along the gate. They are there when you come into this universe and when you leave. We have learned that this gate has many names which include Babalon, Carrefour, Carfax, Sothis, and Sirius. Through the work of Mark Roberts, this gate has also been associated with the concept of a stargate.

For whatever reason, the Montauk Project was more than a gateway to the stars. It was a gateway into time, and it was juxtaposed upon the energies of the ancient Pharoahs of Montauk. As I began to penetrate the legacy of the Montauk Project, I was eventually led to the Montauks and their matriarch, Olive Pharoah. I never suspected, however, that this investigative process would weave its way into my own ancestry. Perhaps it was unavoidable. Personally, I always thought I might find a Cameron or a Wilson in the woodpile, but I never have, at least up to this date. What I did find, however, was far more mysterious and interesting.

I would eventually learn that the Egyptians buried their dead with olive leaves. It would sanctify them and facilitate their passage into the next world. Thus I learned that the olive was not only juxtaposed next to the highest aspects of the Creator, it was also a part of this gateway. As it applied to me personally, I would experience that my own ancestors were somehow mysteriously tied to the olive and the mysterious process of revelation that has unfolded in this book.

THE DREAM — PART II

I awoke in my dream state to see the beautiful Blue Lady once again. This time, she was smiling. It was clear that she was very pleased with me. She then placed her hand behind her head so as to put her beauty on display and call attention to herself.

"You have done well," she said, "but it is now time to remember once again. You have not quite finished."

As beautiful as she was, my eyes saw straight through her as I could see into my past. Once again, it was the summer of 1972, and I was still in Morocco. This time, however, the *Apollo* was moored in Tangier, an international city which sits more or less opposite the Rock of Gibralter. It was my day off.

On any of my previous off days, I never even considered going into Moroccan cities. Besides offering potential dangers to any Westerner that might stray off the beaten paths, there was not too much of interest in the way of one-day tourist attractions. Beyond that, I had no desire. I would spend my off days studying in the academy of Scientology as I considered it a far better use of my time. After all, I was there to learn about the exteriorization of the human spirit. On this particular day, however, I had a sudden change of heart. Someone said there were decent sized waves at a location known as Robinson's Beach. *That* interested me. The prospect of body surfing was not something I could pass up. Morocco did not have much in the way of surf board rentals.

Three of my colleagues and I grabbed a taxi and took the forty-five minute or so ride to the beach. On the way, the taxi travelled along a narrow two-lane road. As we got far away from the town, we often had to slow down considerably when we saw groups of locals walking along the roadside with their animals and what was probably all of their earthly possessions. I was dumb-struck as I had no idea who these people were or what their living circumstances were. I certainly did not envy them. Most confusing to me, however, was that most of the Moroccans I had seen up to that point were Arabs with brownish coloring. There were also many blacks who were of Moorish descent. These people travelling along the side of the road, however, were completely different and all of them were white-skinned. Who were they?

My first impression was twofold. They were not only poor but looked as if they had come out of a time warp. By reason of their dress and lack of modern modalities, they looked as if they came from the time of Christ. None of the women wore veils, and I remember one woman who road a donkey. She was tiny and her dress and headdress were such that she could easily have been selected by central casting to portray the Virgin Mary.

I asked about these people, but no one had any good answers for my inquisitive mind. They were just locals who lived off of the land. It would take me decades before I would learn who they really were and what my chance encounter with them symbolized. They were brushed aside for the most part, but I never forgot them. These people were Berbers, indigenous people of Northern Africa who settled in North Africa long before the Arabs. In the strangest and most mysterious of ways, they were my relatives.

What happened the rest of that day is still etched in my mind as very pleasant. After a vigorous afternoon of body surfing and exploring old Roman ruins, my friends and I enjoyed a beautiful view of the Rock of Gibralter. We then found a restaurant that served us a nice meal as we dined on a table resting on a cliff. The waiter had to take a bit of a walk in order to serve us.

As the vision of my recall receded, I now saw the Blue Lady once again, but her smile had turned to a serious expression. Her mind was clearly on something other than my adventures with the ocean or the ruins. Originally, she had commanded me to remember my first encounter with Moors, but it was now clear that she was neither satisfied with that nor my current recollection. She then pushed me to remember more about my time in Morocco.

"Think," she said.

As I reviewed the experiences I had just recalled, I once again pondered the memory of the petite Berber woman who reminded me of the Virgin Mary. The Blue Lady then smiled and beckoned me to come closer. She then pointed in the direction of what I knew to be America. Intuitively, I knew she was pointing to my home.

"Do you recall the thoughts of your ancestors?" she asked.

Her prompting caused me to remember what had happened at the time my parents had died. Waking in the middle of the night,

I had felt the presence of my ancestral line. It was unmistakable. I could feel the memories of all those who had lived before me, and it was my job to carry on. I would never feel or sense my ancestors again until I wrote *The Montauk Project*. In some strange way, I could sense that my ancestors were very happy I had written that book. At that time, I merely thought they were happy that one of their descendants had done something noteworthy or significant. I had no idea that the perceptions of these invisible ancestors were much more profound than mine.

A smile returned to the face of the Blue Lady as she opened the palm of her hand. It contained a symbol that looked as if it was tattooed on her palm. It was the letter *M* with letters inside of it.

I clearly recognized this symbol as it came from a real life experience. Due to various circumstances, I had been directed to a website where there was a preoccupation with figuring out the hidden meaning behind this mysterious symbol. There are some obvious meanings, and we will address those in a bit, but there was also a deeper and hidden meaning being alluded to.

What I found noteworthy on the website was that this symbol was deliberately chosen to represent what might be termed the master secret society of the Piscean area. During the mid-part of the First Century, there was a concordant of all the major secret societies that existed at that time. They were pooling all of their knowledge and seeking to represent it with a master symbol that would perhaps serve as a key to future generations for purposes of enlightenment. This master secret society was based upon the work of a man who is known as Ormesius or sometimes Ormus. The above symbol is clearly a rendition of the name *Ormus*.

In 46 A.D., Ormesius became involved with St. Mark and the early Alexandrine Christians, many of whom had converted from Judaism. Ormesius was an Egyptian magus, and he basically synthesized the old religion of Egypt with the new information presented by St. Mark and formulated what became the modern template for Christianity, particularly in an esoteric regard.

A secret society was formed by Ormesius and was known as the Order of the Rosy Cross. This organization later morphed into and/or was co-opted by other interests and became known as the Priori de Sion. As it was designed to be the master secret society, it adopted the symbol shown on the previous page and adopted the name Ormus which was a secretive name.

Whether or not Ormesius and St. Mark were good or bad, their successors certainly left something to be desired. Essentially, there was an attempt to pool all of the knowledge of the time and sum it up in one symbol and one name which was Ormus. The most obvious meaning for the Ormus symbol is the *M* which is the conventional symbol for the constellation Virgo. The letters *o-r-u-s* are the equivalent of *Horus* who is the Egyptian god that Christ was patterned after. In the case of Horus, the virgin mother is Isis. Ormus is also a traditional esoteric name for white gold, and this concept was deliberately ingrained into this secret society by reason of its namesake. Essentially, ormus or white gold represents the full activation and synchronizing of both hemispheres of the brain while Christ and Horus symbolize the dawning of a new age which also represents the resurrection and rehabilitation of all life on this planet.

All of this requires change and this is accomplished via the sacred formula of Freemasonry which is centered upon the secret "word" *shin. Shin* is also a Hebrew word which represents change via the spirit. *Shin* is the essence of the Christ and is the keystone of the name *Yod-He-Shin-Vau-He* which was transliterated into *Yeshua* and then *Jesus*. In other words, both shin and the Ormus symbol were designed as compacted knowledge.

Keep in mind that the secret society of Ormus was formed when the Library of Alexandria was in its heyday. Information was available from all over the known world. It is quite clear, however, that as this secret society transformed throughout the years, it was co-opted by dark forces that sought agendas designed to undermine the original knowledge. This pattern of obfuscating and losing knowledge is one of the primary characteristics of the Age of Pisces. The truth is not what you thought it was. There is, however, an even more sinister aspect at work here.

At the outset of the formation of Ormus, the consolidated wisdom was relatively pure. There was also a live current in the people who knew the knowledge. Keeping to their original precepts, they adhered to the longtime tradition of honoring the Black Virgin and utilizing the Ormus symbol to be representative of such. As time went on, this theme was continued with the Priori de Sion, but the precept of the Black Virgin and all it represented eventually became altered so that the Priori became preoccupied with the preservation of the so-called Merovignian bloodline and the restoration of the throne to its heirs.

As you might already be well aware, there is a considerable body of popular literature on this subject which includes the book *Holy Blood, Holy Grail* as well as the works of Laurence Gardiner. Some of these works portray the Merovignian bloodline as a race of serpentine beings or dragons who are sacred and destined to be the rulers of humans. The books make convincing arguments to an ignorant and extremely gullible public who not only suck it up but also have no other data by which to evaluate the information. That is what makes it so convincing.

All of these dark theories, which existed long before these books were written or published, give rise to the concept of the Antichrist coming home to roost. This was popularized in the movie *The Omen*, but the forerunner was *Rosemary's Baby*. It is often missed, but the name *Rosemary* was chosen on purpose because it represents the Rosy Cross. The rose represents the flowering of the Christ from the Virgin *Mary*. The only thing is that Rosemary is giving birth to the devil's baby which is the diablo or double of the Christ. In other words, the Age of Pisces represents the overt and covert continuous determination to undermine the truth in order to harm, corrupt and destroy.

From the advent of the original Ormus society, it took two-thousand years to accomplish all of this. The end result is a secret society which is unveiled, but as it is unraveled by an exciting and intriguing process, one discovers that the society is based upon the proposition of reptilians coming to get you. As it is unveiled in popular literature, the gullible public eats it up. There is only one thing wrong with this picture: it is a bunch of crap.

As I said, when I first saw the Ormus symbol, the website I was reading was completely preoccupied with the discovery of the true meaning of the Ormus symbol. When I looked at this symbol, however, it was not mysterious at all. The word *Ormus* is an anagram for *Mours* which is an alternative spelling for *Moors* which represents *Morus*, *Morush*, or *Mau-resh*, meaning cat-head or cat-king. The cat-king or King Felix is representative of Christ. Through the principle of synchronicity, my research of the Moors made all of this quite obvious. If Ormesius is the true Egyptian magus they say he was, he would have indeed represented all the wisdom of ancient Egypt. His very name suggests it. One of the key principles of Egyptian wisdom was that the cat was the antidote for the serpent. Need I say more?

All of these secret societies and writers who have been preoccupied with the "all-powerful" and ubiquitous nature of serpents and reptilian agendas have been blinded by their own ignorance. This ignorance is not so much stupidity as it is the result of an endemic conditioning of the human brain brought on by the deceptively sinister nature of the Age of Pisces.

The Moors and the truth of their ancient heritage and knowledge is the panacea. Their knowledge concerns the feminine energy and the cat. As wonderful as this truth is, however, it does not go over too well on a population that has had their more sensitive aspects beaten or otherwise programmed out of them.

After fully recalling the magical symbol for Ormus, I found myself looking at the Blue Lady again. She was very happy, and I could clearly see that I had retrieved the memories that she had been fishing for.

"Do you realize the etymology of *Ormus*?" she asked me.

"The phoneme *ir* means 'cat' and *ir* is convertible to *or*," I said, "but *or* also means 'gold' as in *ore*. "*Mus* or *mesius*," I said, "refers to *Moises* which is a word for the 'cat messiah' or 'anointed cat.' As *cat* also means 'gate,' *Ormus* would also mean the 'golden gate' which refers to the City of the Golden Gates in Atlantis. This was on an island called Ogygos and is where Calypso lived."

"You have done well," she said, "but there is yet more for you to discover about the Black Virgin. "She is more intimately intertwined with your Berber ancestors than you might ever have imagined."

31

THE LAND OF OG

Prior to my involvement in the Montauk Project investigation, I did not pay much attention to my genetic ancestry. It was only upon discovering so much synchronicity with the Camerons and Wilsons that I took an interest. I thought I might be related, but thus far, I have not been able to come up with any direct connection. I did, however, find out that there was a connection between my mother's surname and the Camerons. Her name was Elizabeth Sweeney, and I learned that the Sweeneys were a fierce fighting clan that came to the support of the Camerons and fought valiantly for them. As I looked deeper into the Sweeney legacy, I eventually discovered more than I had bargained for.

The Sweeneys were the original tenants of one of the oldest (and still extant) castles in the British Isles. That is the Doe Castle that was built in the early part of the Fifteenth Century. The Doe branch of the Sweeneys were descended from Donnchadh Mór. The name Mór certainly raised some eyebrows when I discovered this. In the Gaelic languages, the word *Mór* means "big." Donnchadh Mór was the son of Donnchadh Óg of Fanad. *Óg* is supposed to mean "young" in Gaelic, but I discovered that it means much more than that.

In terms of name coincidences, I was most struck by the fact that the Sweeneys who settled at Doe Castle ruled the Tri Tuatha Thoraigh. I could not help but notice the association between the words *Thoraigh* and *Tuareg*. As the Celts are known to have migrated from Asia and made their way to Europe and the British

Isles via Northern Africa (including Egypt), it seems obvious that these two namesakes might have been influenced by each other. This hypothesis is further supported by physiology and racial studies which have shown that the Celts* are of the same genetic stock as the Caucasians of Northern Africa.

The word *thoraig* originally meant brigand, raider or plunderer. This is not much different from appellations applied to the Tuareg people of Africa because they were known as fierce raiders of other tribes or strangers who invaded or otherwise came to the desert. It is likely that the name *Tuareg* was applied by Europeans in this same sense although there is a lot of academic confusion on this point. The Tuareg do not call themselves Tuareg at all but refer to themselves by words that sound like "teltamshaq" which means "speakers of temashaq," a word which is more closely related to *T'amazigh* or *Imazighen* which means "the free" or "free people." The Tuareg language is usually referred to as Amazigh, a word that is very close to *Amazon*.

The English word *thoraig* eventually became associated with the royalist Tory party. Comparing a royalist to a brigand would seem to be a contradiction in terms, but this association came about when Charles II was deposed by the parliamentary form of government during the time of Cromwell. The Tories or brigands were those who rallied around Charles II and against Parliament, and that is how these two factions became intertwined in the English word *thoraig*. When Charles II was allowed to occupy the throne and restore the monarchy, the name *thoraig*, pronounced *Tory*, stuck as a royalist appellation. This name association is incredibly ironic because the Tuareg themselves are literally the royal tribe of the desert.

The phonetics of the word *Tuareg* also tell an interesting story. *Tua* is an expression of the feminine in different languages and *reg* refers to king or royalty. In this manner, *Tuareg* would symbolize the royal aspect of the feminine.

---

*The Celtic migration from Asia is also supported by the fact that many of their namesakes are inextricably tied to names in *The Bible*. For example, Cohen becomes Connell or O'Connell. Nile, meaning blue, becomes O'Neill. The tribe of Da'an is seen in the names O'Donnell and O'Donald. The name Sullivan derives from Sulaiyman or Solomon. The name Sweeney derives from S'uaine which is a contraction of Sulaiyman. The names Sullivan and Sweeney seem to have branched off from one another at some point.

Despite these telling name associations, I could not help but consider that the association between the names *Thoraig* and *Tuareg* were simply a mere coincidence. The principle of synchronicity, however, would make very strong suggestions that there was something more at work in this equation. This was at first suggested by the historical statement that the Sweeneys who settled at Doe Castle had ruled the Tri Tuatha Thoraigh. "Tri Tuatha Thoraigh" is said to mean "The Three Territories of Tory," but I recognized the word *Tuatha* from the Tuatha Dé Nann, the mysterious and legendary ancients of Ireland who are associated with divine attributes. *Tuatha* is an Old Irish word for "people" so these "three territories" might well have represented three peoples within or of three territories.

Personally or subjectively, I never identified myself with my mother's genetics. My father was my favorite parent, and I always identified with him. To discover that my mother's Irish Catholic relatives had a claim as descendants of the Tuatha Dé Nann seemed bizarre. I am sure this is something they know little or nothing about. I would soon discover, however, that the so-called coincidences of my mother's namesake had a life of their own.

The information I had collected about the Sweeneys was from standard clan information that is in booklets and now on the internet. One publication included a very odd or surprising piece of information. It is said that the Sweeneys had arrived in Ireland from an ancient and mysterious island known as Og. This brought me back to the research of Mark Roberts and the pamphlets he had given me that were written by Egerton Sykes. This work not only explains the land of Og, it makes a lot of interesting connections with the Tuareg.

Og is referred to in *The Bible* as a land that was ostensibly in the Mideast, but this does not match up with the research of Sykes who clearly states, based upon other works, that Og was an island in the Atlantic. It seems to be virtually the same as Ogygos, an island off the coast of Africa where Odysseus was said to have spent seven years with the goddess Calypso during the Odyssey. If Og and Ogygos are not one and the same, the association of their names is at least culturally significant.

Most important to me with regard to the work of Sykes was that he explains how the Celtic people originated from Atlantis and the Tuatha Dé Nann. Specifically, there were three prominent classes or professions in Atlantis. There were the priestesses, the temple functionaries, and the warrior military guards. The temple functionaries were known as the Tuatha Dé Nann.

As Atlantis was eventually overcome with various disasters, the military guards became useless as there was no population and the temple no longer needed protection. Known as the Aesir, the warriors left and dispersed, some of them laying the foundation for what became the Viking culture.

The second group were the Tuatha Dé Nann who gradually made their way to Ireland where they told great tales of their homeland. The Tuatha were the scribes of Atlantis who became the great record-keepers of the Celtic people as well.

The priestesses remained and passed their skills and knowledge into many lands. They migrated into Northern Africa where the core of them settled in the Ahaggar and became known as the Amazons, the most exalted becoming known as the Kahena. Other priestesses migrated into Egypt and India.

This migration was originally from islands in the Atlantic and spread throughout Northern Africa. From there it went to Asia and beyond but eventually came back to Egypt and across Africa and Europe. The core group were essentially Rh negative, and their descendants are the Basque people of the Pyrenees and the Gaunche people of Tenerife in the Canary Islands. The Amazon priestesses thrived to a significant extent until two major antifeminist movements virtually wiped them out. Sykes refers to these as Christianity and Islam.

The Tuatha spoke of the City of the Golden Gates and called it Falias. The Golden Gates led to an important temple and were located at the center of a complex of two islands, one of which was Ogygos, later known as Santa Maria. The other island bordering Falias was San Miguel Island (a latter day name). The great temple stood to the west of Santa Maria near a village known as Miau Miau (or "meow meow") and is related to the goddess Bast. Inside the temple near Miau Miau was the Stone of Death that was crowned with pale fire. This is said to be a meteorite which eventually became the Stone of Scone that represents the throne of Britain. This is where Calypso music is said to have been invented and named after an early high priestess.

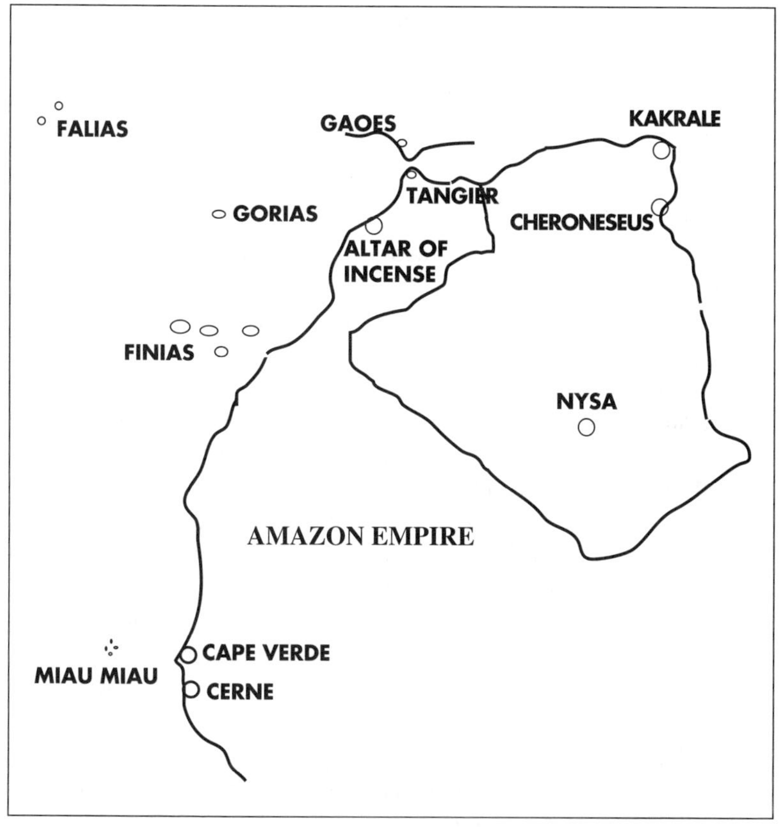

THE AMAZON EMPIRE

Above is a rough scale sketch of the ancient Amazon Empire based upon the research of Egerton Sykes. All locations are rough approximations. The coast line is that of Northwest Africa. The peninsula where Gaoes is located is Gibralter. Note that the city of Nysa, which is on the edge of the Ahaggar mountains, is the same as the fabled City of Brass from *The Arabian Nights*. The enclosed territory is the modern day country of Algeria. The islands of Falias included Ogygia, the island of Calypso. Gorias was also known as Aeaia, the island of Circe. Note that some place names were named in conjunction with other place names. Miau Miau, for example, was both a designation for islands as well as a village. See the work of Egerton Sykes for further information.

Although what is related here might seem either obscure or novel to the casual reader of conventional history, these stories were so abundant and repetitive in the ancient world that several expeditions were made to recover various treasures from this culture. None of them were declared successful.

Santa Maria was originally called Little Cat Island before it was eventually renamed Ogygia, the island where Odysseus is said to have visited Calypso. In Sykes' work, Kirke or Circe is mentioned as a cousin of Calypso and was an Amazon.

This temple at the City of the Golden Gates was eventually rededicated to the mystery religion of Eleusis which linked it up with two secret brotherhoods known as Cabeiri and Telchines. The rites of Eleusis are named after *elaia*, the Greek word for olive.

Sykes states that the adventures of Odysseus are actually a compilation of tales that occurred centuries before the Trojan War and the Odyssey were supposed to have taken place.

Sykes' descriptions, which are based upon countless hours of research, not only describe one of the richest and most obscure histories on this planet, they were also having a penetrating effect on my psyche as well. Through the mysterious vehicle of Mark Roberts, I was seeing my own genetics expressed in this history. For me, this was just the tip of the iceberg.

Sometime after reading this material and rereading it again, I found myself taking a walk on Long Island with a friend named Yonda. She is a clairvoyant healer who met me just as I was beginning my Montauk investigation back in 1991. We were walking on a hiking trail in the Muttontown Preserve in the Town of Oyster Bay. This hiking trail is also the home of bridle paths for horses and there is an equestrian field nearby. The trail also leads to the ruins of an old mansion that once stood in the south region of the preserve. In handout maps at the preserve headquarters, the ruins are simply featured as "the ruins."

As we were walking, we were approached by a man on a huge horse. He was accompanied by at least one other. After exchanging friendly words, he seemed to know the paths very well, and I asked him about the ruins. The man told me that it was built by King Og, the King of Albania.

"Og?" I asked, not believing my ears in light of what I had recently learned about Og. "How do you spell it?"

"O-g," he said before saying good-bye and moving on.

When I got home, I soon began a search on the internet. The man seems to have been mistaken because every reference I could find referred to this king as King Zog.* I might have found one reference that called him "Og" but I cannot reproduce it. Most everyone knew him as King Zog. He was forced to abdicate during the reign of Mussolini and built a mansion on Long Island for purposes of having a refuge. He never moved in.

Whether the man on the horse was mistaken or not, he certainly pushed me in an interesting direction which would bear fruit. Sometimes the energies of the spirit work off of slight nuances in language. What he did do was cause me to look into the history of Albania, but my interest in this was tenuous at best. As soon as I began to look into Albania, and even before I had made up my mind that the king was Zog and not Og, I came across something that was noteworthy with regard to my own genetics.

There was an online book, translated into English and written in 1917, that claimed to tell the true story about the history of Albania, a country with a remarkable pedigree that is unknown and ignored by most historians. The book was by an Italian general named Eugenio Barbarich. This surname caught my attention because it is a prominent name in my father's family tree.**

The name *Barbarich* is not only important with regard to my personal genetics, it fits in appropriately to the theme at hand with regard to ancient African and Atlantean culture. The name *Barbarich* is actually pronounced *bar-bur-eesh* and is spelled *Barbarić* in the Cyrillic alphabet. It is a name which has endured many misunderstandings, mispronunciations, and mutations. My father's cousins lived in Italy and became known by the surname of Barbi. *Barbarich* is commonly and erroneously thought to mean "foreigner," but this is certainly not the case when you look further into the history of the name itself. A phonetic breakdown of the word itself suggests the word "berber" and the *resh* sound means "king" or "head" in Hebrew. The concept of a king to the Berbers has a very rich but obscure and disputed history.

---

* In the Albanian language *zog* means "bird."

**Other names in my father's family tree include Fidelis, Cezereo, Avellini, and Novak. Besides Sweeney, my mother's family tree includes the names of Shaw, Carlin, and Lavery.

The name *Berber* comes from the Arabs who referred to these people as El Berber or Al Barbar which is the title of an ancient and obscure king known as Barbar or other variations of that basic name. The French children's stories of *Babar* the elephant king are loosely based upon this legendary character. Barbar was supposed to be the original founder of the Berbers and, according to some sources, he was the father of Noah. There was also a King Barbar who fled after the fall of Jericho and settled in the land of Arabia Felix where he was the ruler for a long time. In the last millennium, there was also Babur, a descendant of Genghis Khan who ruled over a vast empire. From his name, we learn that *babur* is a Turkish word which means "lion" or "tiger." In Persian, *babr* means "tiger" or "leopard."

The word *berber* has been broken down by various scholars or historians. North African historian Ibn Khaldun described Berber as people from the land of *Ber*. This name conjures up thoughts of Hyperborea, the land beyond the poles. The word *bar* also refers to the desert so *berber* could mean that as well.

In Spanish, the word *beber* means to drink. This makes sense because the ancient gateways of the cat also featured water conduits through the mouths of statuary lions and whatnot. *Baba* means "gate" as well as "cat" so it is no wonder that water became associated with this word. The word *baby* is also associated with water so we are back full circle.

It was now very apparent to me that both of my genetic lines were crossing at a very strange and mysterious place that has been virtually wiped out of common history. For me personally, it was as if my ancestors from both parents were literally pouring off of the pages of what I was reading. It can all be traced back to Ogygos and Little Cat Island. The scholarship of Eugenio Barbarich presents yet additional light on the matters at hand.

According to Barbarich, many mysteries and truths of the ancient world are wrapped up in Albania. It is reported to be the land where white people first settled in Southeastern Europe. Besides that, Albania has an interesting etymology that backs up this contention. The etymology of *Albania* shows up in the etymology of the word *elf*, a word which also means "first." Essentially, *elf* derives from *alba* which means "white" which is also the basis of the word *eldritch* (elf leader) and *eldridge* (elf ruler).

Before it was known as Albania, this region was known as Illyria and extended well beyond its current borders. Illyria is a very interesting word because it is obviously derived from the Albanian word for olive which is *uliri*. The original culture of the Balkan Peninsula was Illyrian and later yielded to the Macedonians and Greeks. Certain root words and the entire mythology and religion of the Illyrians/Albanians were adopted by the Greeks and became what you would currently recognize as Greek mythology.

In the ancient world, the original Albanians and their legacy were so important that when Alexander the Great's father, King Phillip of Macedonia, wanted to legitimize his reign, he married an Illyrian princess named Olympia. Their other child was Cleopatra I.

Albania featured what was considered to be the most legitimate oracle of ancient times which was known as Dodona after a goddess who was associated with or the same as the goddess Rhea. Earlier, this oracle was called Diona, a name which is similar to Diana or Dionysius. This oracle later became associated with Zeus who was known as Zot in earlier times. Zot is virtually the same as *zayit*, the Hebrew word for olive.

There are countless examples which demonstrate that Greek culture emanated from this region where the "first white people" are supposed to have occupied Southeast Europe.* Perhaps the most revealing word with respect to this quest into Albania is a word which was used to describe or signify the ancient Illyrians: *Epirot* or *Epirots*. This word is very similar to the Hebrew word for sphere which is *sepiroth,* but if you replace the *p* in *Epriot* with an *f,* two letters that are clearly convertible in ancient languages, you have *ifrit*, the Arabic name for a jinn.

Alexander the Great was a forger of empires and was the greatest conqueror that the world had ever known. He based his conquests upon an ancient legend that came out of Thebes in Egypt, the same place where the Stele of Menthu that influenced Aleister Crowley came from. This ancient legend stated that two black doves once flew from Thebes. One settled in Albania and became known as the oracle of Dodona as referred to above. The

*The words *Ulysses* and *Odysseus* both derive from the early Albanian language and they mean "traveler." *Udhe* means "route" or "travel" and the *d* can be interchanged with an *l* in that language so that you have *ulhe* meaning the same thing. While *Ulysses* is considered to be Latin and *Odysseus* is Greek, both words exist in Albanian and mean the same thing.

other went to the oasis of Siwa in the Libyan desert, now a part of today's Egypt. Alexander was obsessed with these oracles, and they actually influenced his affairs quite deeply. That these doves were black invites one to wonder if they were meant to symbolize melanin in the legend.

Thebes is in southern or Upper Egypt and was deeply influenced by the ancient culture of Meroe, a matriarchal society that was located near the sixth cataract of the Nile in today's Sudan. Meroe has a very obvious association with the word *Moor*, but it was also known to be a center of Berber culture and featured unique pyramids, the ruins of which can still be viewed today. The Berbers, however, are not known to have referred to themselves by that name. They knew themselves as the Meshwesh which was often abbreviated or pronounced as MA in the Egyptian language. MA, of course, is synonymous phonetically to *mau* or "cat."

There are many more fascinating pieces of information with regard to Og and the Albanian thread. Og is, of course, related to Ogham, the so-called Druid alphabet, and we will touch on that and related information later. Ogygos is also a mythological figure who settled Attica and was the father of Eleusis, the character the Eleusinian Mysteries were named after. The theme of the olive is what is important here.

Throughout this narrative, the theme of the olive was pursued and not only led to the history of these ancient Berber blue people, it mysteriously led me to a fascinating and bizarre intersection where the namesakes of both my father's and mother's genetic trees cross. This process of synchronicity can perhaps best be expressed in terms of Berber mythology.

The Berbers were well known to believe in life after death. They were known to sleep at or near the graves of their ancestors in order to receive dreams or otherwise contacts their spirits. As animals sometimes disturbed such graves, they learned to dig deeper and eventually erected mounds. These developed into pyramids long before the Egyptian civilization was established.

If all of this is true, and if I come from Berber stock, it soon became apparent that my ancestors were having a field day with me. It took me a very long time, however, to figure it out and put it all together.

32

REVELATION

If my ancient Berber ancestors were working on me through the dream state, something certainly caught my attention not too long after I had written *The Montauk Project*. This concerned a series of dreams about Highway 1 in Southern California. Specifically, I am referring to an area between Ventura and Santa Barbara that is known as the Rincon, a word which means "corner" in Spanish. This area is lovely enough in real life, but my dreams embellished it beyond ordinary imagination. While I slept, the area appeared as a landscaper's dream with huge palm trees and circular and twisting on-ramps that were beautiful beyond belief.

The visuals of these dreams were so exotic that it excited my mind and awareness in a way that dreams do not ordinarily do. They continued to occur, always focusing on the landscape and the general area which were sometimes incorporated into the dream scape. The on-ramps and off-ramps were always a major feature. They curly-cued in elaborate twists and turns and sometimes went right over the water. As the dreams continued, I attempted to fathom why they kept coming. My first response was to attribute them to something I then referred to as the Ojai Grid.

Ojai is a little town that is seated in the coastal range and is more or less about a half hour from the Pacific Ocean. I remembered it well as a youngster from when my father would take me on surfing trips to the coastal town of Carpinteria. Reaching Ojai was exciting to me because it meant that we had almost reached the coast, and I would soon see the vast panoramic beauty of the

Pacific Ocean. I loved to be near the sea, and for that reason, Ojai has always brought me pleasant memories. In and of itself, however, it was just an ordinary town to me.

When I went to the American Bookseller's Association convention in 1992, I learned something else about Ojai that I did not know. This was the same convention through which I was able to meet Marjorie Cameron. While strolling the aisles of book vendors and other people in the industry, I came across a booth representing the Kritona Institute that is located in Ojai. A man there explained to me that Ojai was a major energy spot that was sacred to the Native Americans. For that reason, Krishnamurti* had moved there and made it his home.

As my dreams surrounding the Ojai and Ventura area continued, I thought there must be an explanation beyond the fact that Ojai was an energy center. Through happenstance, I found a connection that I thought was quite plausible. It concerned the movie *The Philadelphia Experiment II*. In this movie, the main character lived in the small town of Santa Paula which is not too far from Ojai. I remembered Santa Paula from my youth as a kid named Randy was always going there to visit his family. Why, I wondered, had Santa Paula been chosen as the geographical locale for a movie about the Philadelphia Experiment? After all, that incident took place on the East Coast.

In those days of the Montauk investigation, the psychic atmosphere was very thick. Sometimes, I felt I could cut it with a knife. Clues often appeared that were oddly familiar yet very mysterious. This was just such a clue.

I thought that my dreams were being directed to the general area due to the Philadelphia Experiment, and I therefore sought a mysterious tie-in to Santa Paula. My sister, however, lives not too far away and she explained to me why Santa Paula was used in this movie as well as many others. This small town has purposely been preserved to appear as it was during the 1940's, give or take a decade. As such, the town makes for an excellent backdrop to

* For those of you who do not know of Krishnamurti, he was groomed as a young boy to be a messiah at the behest of people who had been involved in the Theosophical movement. Krishnamurti realized the charade that was being perpetrated upon people and went off on his own. Although often heralded as a great metaphysical teacher, he was humble and never claimed to be a messiah.

shoot scenes that are supposed to have taken place in the Forties or even the Thirties or Fifties. Santa Paula was an apparent dead end.

The dreams, which were always fascinating and enjoyable, began in 1992 and followed me for years with no answer coming forth. It was not until the year 2000 that I received an answer.

In February of 2000, during the school winter recess, I decided to take my daughter to Southern California so that she could visit her cousins. She had only met them once before and was eager to go. United Airlines, however, had other ideas. Despite having booked tickets in advance, the airlines bumped us from the flight. We were not the only ones either. The airlines over-booked the flight and many other passengers were stranded as well. There was absolutely no guarantee that we would get to our destination.

Telling my daughter that there were problems with the flight, I let her know that I could get my money back. Otherwise, we might have to wait all day. I also told her that if we cancelled the vacation, I would give her the entire amount of the plane ticket which was about $400.00, an enormous sum to a nine-year-old. After thinking about it very carefully, she said she wanted to go on the vacation. For that reason, we did. I then found out that our luggage had already been shipped to Los Angeles. As a result, the attendant put us on the next flight, and we were also able to get complimentary tickets to visit again that summer.

Arriving at my sister's house on a Saturday, we got situated and enjoyed seeing her family who lives in Camarillo. The next day, however, they would attend church so I had planned to visit one of my childhood friends who lives in Santa Barbara. As we set out on the road in a rental car, it was raining incredibly hard. In fact, it was brutal. My daughter slept in the back seat as I made my way and fought with the harsh road conditions. As we reached the outskirts of Ventura, I was peering through the window to see the turnoff to an area called Montalvo. I remembered it very well because that is the turn off to where my parents are buried. It is the same turn off we had taken during the funeral procession twenty-five years earlier. Through the rain, my eyes caught a sign near the turnoff that said "Los Olivas Adobe." I could not believe my eyes. I knew that in Spanish this means "House of the Olives."

I had absolutely no idea what was meant by "Los Olivas Adobe," but I knew from the signage that it was a historical landmark of some sort. This seemed to make it all the more special for some reason. Although I was on vacation and the thoughts of my olive research were not on my mind, I immediately made the connection and began to react quite viscerally. Amidst driving in the pouring rain, emotion poured out of me. I could not believe what I had just seen. My parents were buried right near a historical landmark which was referring to a house of olives. As my daughter slept in the back, tears poured out of me as I continued to drive. Despite the drama, I failed to make a connection between my exotic dreams and the fact that my parents were buried in the area.

After experiencing an emotional release, I made my way up to Santa Barbara. The ordinarily beautiful drive, however, was ruined by the bad weather. After visiting with my friend and his family for most of the day, my daughter and I made our way back to my sister's house. I was eager to talk to her and hoped to find out what Los Olivas Adobe was all about.

When we returned, it was late evening and my sister told me that the Olivas family had once owned the largest and most impressive ranchero in all of California. The original house and garden had been preserved as a historical landmark. I was astonished to learn that the cemetery where my parents are buried had once been the property of the Olivas family.

I still cannot describe the emotions that ran through me. It was way too bizarre, even for me; particularly as the experience seemed so personalized and tailored to my research. The book you have read thus far is interesting enough without the revelation regarding my parents' burial site. At this point, I was being handed an incredibly dramatic ending to the already remarkable synchronicities I had experienced. It was sort of like winning the lottery and then being told that your older brother, who died before you were born, had come back to life and was going to be your friend. It was a very strange feeling.

Why and how had this all happened? I was handed a mysterious playbill which featured the Mount of Olives underneath it. The olive not only embraced the so-called End of Time, but was also the name of the matriarch of the Montauk Pharaohs and represented the most holy aspect of many religions. Now, I was being redirected back to the seeds of my own origin in this life: my parents. They were imprinted with the olive, too.

As a result of this bizarre experience, my sister and I decided to visit the grave of my parents. This was not something that I had planned. It was the first time I had visited their grave since the funeral and that was twenty-five years earlier. I then realized that it was the silver anniversary of their death.

The cutest thing I remember from that day was when we finally found the gravestones. My daughter, who would never know her grandparents in the flesh, just looked at the stones and said, "Hello!" She does not remember it now, but it was quite adorable. It was as if she had something very genuine to say.

After trading stories about my parents at the grave site, my sister took me to the actual location where they had died from an auto accident on December 14, 1975. This was the first time I had ever been to that location. It was very moving to me.

We then proceeded to the Los Olivas Adobe itself but found out that it was closed that day. My sister did, however, inform me that there was an old olive press in the Ventura mission so I wanted to visit there.

I had never seen an olive press before, but it was just an olive press. There's not much to say about it. Going into the mission chapel itself, however, was an experience. The chapel was very old and filled with gaudy statues that were neither tasteful nor well rendered. It was my impression that the artisans had been possessed by demons. One statue, however, grabbed my attention. It was a statue of the Virgin Mary who held a grotesque human heart in her hand. It looked like it had been plucked out of the chest of an Aztec sacrifice. The bottom of the statue was what caught my eye. It featured the letters "MA" What was that about?

I would soon learn that "MA" is a traditional abbreviation of the Hebrew letters *mem* and *aleph* which are translated into Greek as the loose equivalents of *alpha* and *omega*. I found this all rather pedestrian as it refers to the beginning and end and emphasizes the fact that life is cyclic and keeps on going. This is well and fine, but it is not something that was new to me. *Mem* refers to water and is said to signify death while *aleph* represents life and is also a homonym for *olive*. MA also refers to the Great Goddess Ma based upon the Persian maternal spirit Mourdad-Ameretat which represents death and rebirth.* MA also means *mau* or "cat."

* From the *Women's Encyclopedia of Myths and Secrets* by Barbara Walker.

It seemed that a lesson I already knew well was being reemphasized. This was not a revelation at all but just a matter of fact and did not compare to the dramatic realization that my parents were buried on the land of the Olivas. The MA symbols just told me to keep going. I still wanted to visit the Los Olivas Adobe and learn about its history, but the vacation schedule would not allow for it. The additional airline tickets we received would enable me to pursue the olive thread further, but it would not be on this trip.

Although I had reached a major breakthrough with regard to where the synchronicities behind the olive were leading, I still had not connected my dreams of this area to the death of my parents. In fact, I had forgotten about those dreams. When I returned home, I began to have different dreams and these were about my beginning years in Scientology which were in the city of Davis, California. Davis is a small university town where I attended my last three years of high school. It was also were I began my spiritual journey in this life and entered Scientology. These dreams continued until I had a sudden revelation. The Mission of Davis, as it was called, was located on Olive Drive!

Besides being the location of the Scientology mission, there was a much more relevant fact about Olive Drive. It was the exact same location where I experienced my first out-of-body experience. On Olive Drive, I had exteriorized (which is a Scientology word for leaving the body) with full perception. I could look down and see my body below me. It was quite a thrill. Scientology taught that people could leave their body, and I had not only experienced it but experienced it in a big and dramatic way. It was an actualization of the spirit and was a wonderful occurrence that propelled me on to my future path in Scientology.

When I realized that my dreams of Scientology and Olive Drive were intimately connected to the burial of my parents on the Olivas property, I realized that the spirits of synchronicity were demanding that I write about them. The experiences are far too lengthy to include in this work so I wrote *The Montauk Book of the Dead* (which was the original title for this book) to explain key elements of how I came upon so much synchronicity in my life. If not for these experiences, I would never have written that book.

My revelations with the olive had literally brought me home, but life goes on. I had no choice but to continue my life experience.

33

GHOSTS OF CALIFORNIA

After having discovered so many deep synchronicities with the olive, the revelation that my parents had been buried on the land of the Olivas family had touched me very deeply. That it was also related to my first out-of-body experiences topped it off. I was now in pursuit of a miracle. It behooved me to find out anything I could about the Olivas family.

After touring the Ventura Mission, I visited the nearby Ventura Historical Society in order to learn about the Olivas family. Perusing through historical records, I discovered that the Olivas family were an integral part of the settling of California. As I continued to read, I was struck by the fact that the history of the Olivas family serves as an incredible microscope into the history of California itself.

In and of itself, California history may or may not seem important to you, but this was not the case with me. As I read the various names of history, most of them were very familiar to me as I recognized them from place names I had known from growing up in the state. I did not, however, know much of the actual history behind these names. Due to the dramatic impact of the revelation concerning my parents, California and its history took on a whole new meaning to me. I began to feel California quite viscerally.

I grew up in California for the first twenty-two years of my life. If you take me to most any place in the state (save for Shasta and the area north of that spot), I will have an anecdote or experience to share about that general vicinity. I have always considered it to be my home. All of these experiences not only intensified the feeling, they were dictating a subtle message that in many respects was not so subtle. Over the years, I have begun to feel like a native son who needs to reclaim lost territory.

As I continued my quest into the history of the Olivas family, I discovered many amazing connections. This included a hidden history of California that links it to an ancient Amazon culture. The more I delved into this hidden history, the more synchronistic facts I came across. This includes mysterious links to politically relevant circumstances of today. The most bizarre discovery, however, was that there is an entire organization or secret society that is dedicated to the perverting of California history.

California is named after Caliphia or Kalifia, a black queen who ruled a colony of black Amazons. History books are vague and confused about the exact circumstances and the specifics of how the name was arrived at, but it is generally believed to have been inspired by a popular Spanish novel entitled *Las Sergas de Esplandián* by Garci Rodriguez de Montalvo.

The fact that the name *California* was taken or inspired from an author named Montalvo was a bit too much for me. As I said earlier, Montalvo is the name of the district in Ventura where my parents are buried. I was looking for the Montalvo turnoff when I had first spotted the historical sign for Los Olivos Adobe. If my ancestors were not actually Amazon Berbers, my experiences with synchronicity were certainly telling me that they were.

As I delved deeper into California history, I discovered that it was a Lieutenant Olivas who first acquired land from the Indians for the Spanish Crown in 1782. It happened when his expedition found itself surrounded by some three to four thousand Chumash Indians. Olivas and the Chumash chief decided to avoid a battle by fighting between themselves. They agreed to fight to the death with the winner having the right to occupy the land. Engaging in a hand-to-hand fight, both Lieutenant Olivas and the chief were wounded and bleeding. When a so-called lucky stab prevailed for Olivas, the Indians abided by the agreement and left. (Ironically, this is reminiscent of "easy if stab" from *The Book of the Law*.)

Although Lieutenant Olivas had won this land, he had obtained it for the Spanish Crown and not for himself. It was only in the following century that Raymundo Olivas was able to acquire what was the first Spanish land grant to an individual in California. This was a remarkable feat in itself because Raymundo was a Mexican citizen. In that day and age, most Mexican citizens were illiterate and were not even thought of as land owners. Raymundo, by some mysterious means, had acquired the ability to read and write and was able to apply for a land grant based upon his good works. An intriguing part of Raymundo's history was that he only had the Olivas name by reason of his mother's marriage to Juan Matias Olivas, his stepfather. Raymundo's mother was Juana de Dios, but his real father is unknown. Perhaps he was a Wilson or a Moor.

In my initial foray into this information, I came across a couple of facts which suggested I should keep digging in this direction. The first was that General George Patton's maternal grandfather was known as Benito Wilson to the Mexicans and had been the first mayor of Los Angeles. Mount Wilson, the preeminent mountain peak overlooking Los Angeles, was named after him. I also noted that Raymundo Olivas had been a member of the Grant and Wilson Club, a group dedicated to the election of Ulysses S. Grant and Henry Wilson, his vice-president. Wilson was a very influential writer about slavery and had been a passionate abolitionist before the Civil War.

As I dug into the history of Raymundo and his wife, Teodora Olivas, I discovered that their families traced back to the early land exploration parties of Gaspar de Portola. Portola rang a couple of bells for me. In the fourth grade, we studied all of the Spanish explorers who came to California and Portola was always my favorite. I never knew why, but I just seemed to like him. He headed the first land exploration into California.

I was particularly interested to see the connection to Portola because his name made me recall a newspaper clipping a woman had once sent to me several years earlier. It is buried somewhere in my archives and is no longer at hand, but I remember it as it was a very odd piece of history that you will not find in popular historical accounts of California history. The clipping said that when Portola crossed the Sea of Cortez and landed in California, his party came across a very interesting archaeological find that included an entire colony of mummies that were exclusively female. This was found in what is now Baja California. It should be pointed out that when Portola arrived, there was no Baja and Alta California. It is even arguable that California was the name of the land at all.

At the time of Portola's expedition, Montalvo's novel about Queen Califia's colony of black Amazons was popular. It had been written two centuries before Portola and during the time of Hernando Cortez who was keenly aware of it. In his own writings, Cortez actually reported that a female Amazon colony had existed in an area on the west coast of mainland Mexico.

There is no question that California was named for Queen Califia, but the history of the Amazon colony itself is very sketchy. Before Portola came along, Baja California was occupied by a host of Jesuits, a powerful religious order which was accumulating far too much wealth and power as far as the Pope was concerned. Portola's mission was to kick out the Jesuits at gun point, but he was extremely civil with them and they cooperated by leaving. As Jesuits extensively studied native populations, it is possible that Portola might have been led to the mummy colony by the Jesuits themselves.

Baja California is filled with petroglyphs, hidden caves and more unexplored areas that you can imagine. Some writers recognize it as having been part of the ancient culture known as Lemuria. Besides a limited amount of tourism in the north and south regions, the rest of the peninsula has been considered a haven for bandidos. The interstate highway there is a fairly recent development and has increased safety to a marked extent.

As I pursued the hidden history of California, the Moorish angle certainly did not go unheeded by me. It was brought to the forefront as I read about Joaquin Murietta, the most famous bandido in California history. The name *Murietta* sounds suggestive of the word *Moor*. Further, *Murietta* does not appear to have any definition in the Spanish language. It could be construed as something akin to *mujiera* which means "women" but the diminutive *etta* would not make sense at all if we referred to him as a "little woman." The name does make sense, however, if we interpret it as "little Moor."

Despite his portrayal as a bandido by the Gringos, Joaquin Murietta was a national hero to the native people of California. He was certainly viewed to be a lot more like Robin Hood than he was a bad guy. When I was in the fourth grade, I remember my teacher, Miss Boquist, telling us a bit of hidden California history when she said that the San Joaquin Valley was actually named after Joaquin Murietta. She also added that no one actually likes to admit it.

According to popular legend, Joaquin Murietta played a role in the most famous incident known to have occurred at Los Olivas Adobe. The Olivas family, who were well known for their hospitality and generosity, invited some strangers to dinner who were passing through the area. According to legend, these guests included Joaquin Murietta. At the dinner table, one of the family mentioned their horde of gold and they soon found themselves relieved of it when these guests, who were really bandidos, robbed the Olivas.

Whether it was Murietta or not, the family was definitely robbed. It should be noted that in that day and age, Joaquin Murietta sightings were as popular as Elvis and UFO sightings are today. He was a character of mythical proportions even in his own lifetime. Popular history relayed that when he was finally hunted down and killed by the law, his head was preserved in a jar and was shown from town to town. Historians have since determined that the head in the jar was not that of Murietta and that he likely escaped the authorities. It is still an open debate.

The Moorish connection to Murietta should not be dismissed because there are obscure but definite links to a Moorish history in California which includes, but is not limited to, the last governor of California under Mexico's regime. His name was Emanuel Victoria, and he was one of at least four Mexican governors of California who were of Moorish ancestry. The Portola expedition also suggests that there was an a priori matriarchal culture that is steeped in mystery.

While the Moorish contribution to California is substantial but obscure, it was a Wilson who put California on the modern map. This was James Wilson Marshall, the man who discovered gold at Sutter's Mill in 1848. Marshall is credited with starting the California Gold Rush, a phenomena which resulted in one of the largest migrations of people in history. The city of San Francisco literally sprouted up over night as thousands upon thousands poured into an area which was previously occupied by only a few hundred.

It just so happens that one of the fans of the Montauk books is a descendant of James Wilson Marshall and grew up in the gold country of California. His grandfather actually possessed a pickled head that was purported to have been the head of Joaquin Murietta. The family never took the claim too seriously, but it did make them some money over the years.

Over time, I developed a good rapport with this descendant of James Wilson Marshall as we were both familiar with so many California locations and history. It was this person who gave me my first clue about the previously mentioned secret society that is dedicated to perverting California history. As a result of growing up in the gold country, he was surrounded by this secret society but never recognized its implications until he grew up and moved away. This organization, which is known as E Vitus Clampus, is an actual organization whose roots go back to the Gold Rush era. At first glance, it appears to be a very humorous attempt to poke fun at secret societies. The truth, however, is far more bizarre.

The name *E Vitus Clampus* is a term derived from "Dog Latin." Dog Latin refers to Latinizing words so as to approximate the sound of Latin. It is a humorous attempt to make something sound sophisticated or scholarly, particularly when it really is not. If you do not believe me, look up E Vitus Clampus on the web and see what you find. The organization supposedly arose in the wake of the Gold Rush in order to counterbalance the elitism of Freemasonry. This appellation, however, is only for the casual observer. If you read between the lines, you will find that the organization has a strong homosexual theme. Their early days began with sponsoring dances where males dressed up as females due to the lack of women in the Old West. Their current ceremonies celebrate the "Staff of Relief" and seem to have inspired a crudity which most every high school boy in America has heard of: "the Circle Jerk." This all sounds funny-ha-ha, but there are yet stranger ties between this organization and Aleister Crowley's successor, Karl Germer. The homosexuality is obviously an extension of Crowley's Eleventh Degree Magick which is based upon male homosexuality.

Clampers, as the members of E Vitus Clampus are known, are not the subject of this narrative, but it will interest you to know that they assert themselves as the official keepers of California history and have landmarks and plaques placed all over California. Their most notorious prank concerned a plaque found near San Quentin which was said to have been crafted by Sir Francis Drake and claimed California for Queen Elizabeth I. In grade school, this story was fed to me and every other California student who was supposed to be learning the history of California. In the Seventies, it was discovered that this treasured piece of history was a fake and that the perpetrator was a member of E Vitus Clampus. The fascination, preoccupation and dedication to subverting the history of California is so strong that this alone leads one to conclude that the true history has been deliberately obscured.*

Another interesting fact about California history concerns the Bear Flag Republic, a very short period where California succeeded from Mexico and stood as its own country. The first and only president of the Bear Flag Republic was a Mormon. When it was discovered that Mexico had ceded Alta California to the United States, the Californians decided to go along. At that time, California was considered a free state and black people had equal rights. Blacks and other natives were allowed to sit in on the writing of the California Constitution, but they were outnumbered by whites who voted for discriminatory laws. The most unpopular and outrageous of these laws was that neither blacks, Asians, nor Indians could bear witness against a white person in court. Mormons were not only very much involved in this constitutional convention, they were the biggest profiteers from the Gold Rush itself. There is even an island called Mormon Island where the Latter Day Saints made a fortune. It should also be pointed out that the previously mentioned bigoted laws were very much in keeping with Mormon doctrine of the time.

As I studied all of this information, it never occurred to me that I was stirring up ghosts. With all of the synchronicity that took place concerning my parents, the olive, and the Amazon connection, it is hard not to accept that there was a spiritual influence at work. It would eventually become obvious that I was on the trail of ghosts, but this was not evident at first glance. After completing my initial foray into the history of California and the Olivas family,

* In the future, I hope to write more about the bizarre magical associations of *E Vitus Clampus* in a book which is to be entitled *Bohemian Grove* that will also serve as a sequel to *Spandau Mystery*.

I had other responsibilities to attend to. I was scheduled to take my daughter to amusement parks and visit old friends.

When we returned to California with our complimentary tickets later that summer, I was finally able to visit Los Olivos Adobe itself. Taking a solo tour of the old hacienda, I got to actually see a real live olive tree for the first time. I also told the tour guide how my parents had died in this area and were buried on the old ranch. Asking her about the history, she was very nice and led me to the book store. There, she led me to a book by Richard Senate entitled *The Haunted Southland, Ghosts of Southern California.* Senate's wife is a psychic who has searched out ghosts all over California. Senate compiled the book. Between the two of them, they have had interesting experiences and Senate writes different ghosts stories about different towns in California. This book would give my olive investigation an entirely new twist.

34

LOS OLIVOS

The only reason I bought Richard Senate's book about ghosts was that it mentioned two hauntings that were of interest to me. The first had to do with a ghost that had haunted Los Olivos Adobe itself. Different reports indicated that the spirit of Teodora Olivas still haunts the area. If we accept these reports at face value, it should not surprise anyone that she would lurk about her home. It was and is a very special place. This is all well and fine, but after I read the short chapter, the story of Teodora Olivas did not seem to demand further interest for the time being.

The second haunting that caught my interest, however, did grab my attention in a big way. The book told of another ghost in a town known as Los Olivos. Los Olivos? That was certainly a town I had never heard of. As Los Olivos is located about two and a half hours away from my sister's house, I made arrangements to take a drive and find out what might be waiting for me there.

In the meantime, my friend Penelope had given me a potted olive tree , but it did not survive in the harsh weather of New York. I kept handfuls of the olive leaves, however, because I had read that the Egyptians buried their dead with olive leaves. It was a sacred rite, probably originating with the Berbers, and was the highest way of honoring the dead. When I returned to California later that year, I took the olive leaves to the graves of my parents and embedded them into the soil and sprinkled them atop the graves. It seemed like the appropriate thing to do and was a way of honoring my parents after all of this time.

In July of 2000, I made my way to the little town of Los Olivos which is located in the Santa Ynez Valley of Santa Barbara Country. In many respects, it is in the middle of nowhere and the temperature is routinely over one-hundred degrees.

When I reached the tiny town of Los Olivos, the first thing I saw was the name "Fess Parker" printed on the most prominent building I could see. Fess Parker brought back memories of my childhood because he played Davey Crockett in Walt Disney productions which resulted in most everyone of my generation (except for me) wearing coonskin caps for a summer. It turned out that Fess Parker owns a hotel and spa in Los Olivos. I later found out that he is a real estate mogul who purchased a considerable amount of property in Santa Barbara when it was still a bargain. He was still alive at this point and owned a considerable amount of property in Los Olivos as well.

The next thing I noticed about the town was that it consisted primarily of two relatively short streets that crossed each other. Some of the town was done up nicely and looked quaint. In any case, it was certainly not an impressive locale. The real estate magazines revealed that the prices in this area were extremely high and not in keeping with other inland locales. "Who in the hell would want to live here?" I asked myself.

Making my way to the tiny library, I discovered that it was closed on Monday. This was surprising and frustrating to me. I then made my way to Mattie's Tavern which is the locale that was reported to be haunted according to Richard Senate's book. I thought I should check that out and see if I could find out something about the ghost myself. It was supposed to be the ghost of Felix Mattie, a Swiss immigrant who built this tavern/hotel which pretty much served as the beginning of this tiny town of Los Olivos. Building this tavern was a strategic move on Mattie's part as the railroad eventually came and terminated at this location. From Los Olivos, one then had to take a stagecoach to reach the coast. Felix Mattie owned the stagecoach line which took you there. This was, incidentally, the last stagecoach line in America to go out of business. In any case, there have been numerous reports of Felix Mattie's ghost haunting the tavern.

Unfortunately for me, Mattie's Tavern was also closed on Mondays. At this point, I was more than a bit frustrated. I had driven a considerable amount of time to come this far and there was nothing to show for it. I then went over to a monument for the Chinese rail workers who had built the railroad. This was interesting to me, but there was nothing else written about them. Another book I read indicated that a major race war occurred about two miles from Los Olivos, and I believe this concerned the Chinese. No details, however, were forthcoming.

Thinking about my frustration and trying to find an answer, I went to the pay phone and called my friend, Kenn Arthur. It had been many years since he had first given me the playbill with the Mount of Olives, and this was an old subject being renewed. Telling him what had happened, I told him that I was frustrated to have come all this way and found nothing.

"You did find out something," he said.

"What was that?" I asked.

"Everything's closed on Monday," he replied.

Although his comment was certainly funny, I also found a strange irony and truth in those words. They suggested that I might have to come back again. Feeling frustrated, I began to drive away from the town but soon realized I was hungry. Although the town was virtually closed, I found a bistro on the main street that was surprisingly open. There were, however, no customers inside.

Ordering some food, I was attended to by a couple of beautiful blonde-haired waitresses. Not only were they polite and beautiful, they were outright friendly. Many areas in California feature very pleasant people, but one tends to forget this while living in New York. They were so refreshing that it caused me to talk.

I asked them about a small stucco home I had seen that was part of the small downtown area. It was listed for sale in the high three-hundred thousand dollar range, and I was very surprised by the high price. For that time period, that was a very high price for an inland home that was far away from the coast. For example, a house near the Santa Barbara coast at that time would have been only $100,000 more. Not only would you be near the beautiful town and landscape of Santa Barbara, you could also enjoy the wonderful weather and be near the ocean. This small stucco house was better than a shack but not much more. Personally, I would not have lived in that house if it cost fifty-thousand dollars and someone else was making the mortgage payments for me. The weather is consistently over one hundred degrees in the summer and you are out in the middle of nowhere.

The waitresses informed me that the pricey real estate has to do with movie stars purchasing huge ranch land in the area and turning it into vineyards. There are now several wineries in the area. Still, no movie star was going to live in that stucco house, but their relentless buying of property pushed up the price of all real estate in the area. The waitresses explained that Los Olivos is only about a twenty minute flight from Los Angeles, and celebrities enjoy it as a pleasant refuge where they are not hassled.

Continuing to speak to the waitresses, I gave them a clue as to what I was up to and was very interested in learning about the history of Los Olivos. They informed me that there was an art gallery across the street and that the woman who owned it could probably help me.

Going into the art gallery, I spoke to the owner and told her a bit about what I was after. We chatted for a while, but I was not really able to connect with her until I mentioned a feature she had on her forehead. It was situated right over her third-eye. This deepened the conversation, and I was able to establish a nice rapport with her. As we talked more about the local area, she told me that the person who would be most knowledgeable about the history of the area was a man named Dutch Wilson.

"Dutch Wilson?" I asked in disbelief.

"Yes," she replied. "He has written a book and you can get it in the gallery next door."

Finally, and at long last, I now knew that I was in the right place. It was comforting to know that I had not come this distance for nothing. Finding the name of Wilson has never been disappointing in my research. I thanked the lady and went next door to buy the book from her mother.

When I returned to my sister's house that evening, I had a chance to read Dutch Wilson's book. Most of his tales were rather matter-of-fact and bordered on being boring. What was considerably interesting to my investigation was his comment that he used to ride with Ronald Reagan whose ranch is right nearby. Their time of riding together was in the old days, long before Reagan became President. It was not their personal association, however, that interested me. It suddenly became alarmingly apparent what the underlying connection was. Reagan's real name is Ronald Wilson Reagan, but his friends have always called him "Dutch" Reagan. These two characters shared the same names: Dutch and Wilson. Is that merely a coincidence?

At that time, I was told that Dutch Wilson was ninety-three years old. That is the magical number of Thelema, and I duly noted that but did not pursue Dutch Wilson himself. I had found the quantum synchronicity. It focused on the name "Dutch" but also focused the quantum attractor on Ronald Reagan, a character who has come up in the Montauk investigation before but only in the most esoteric perspective.

With respect to the Montauk investigation, Reagan first came to my attention in 1993 when I came across some writings from Marcelo Motta, the head of the Brazilian O.T.O. who later lost a bitter court battle to be the rightful successor to Aleister Crowley's O.T.O. This is covered in some detail in my book *Synchronicity and the Seventh Seal*. Crowley's rightful successor, Karl Germer, had sent a letter ratifying Motta as his successor but it was intercepted by Brazilian intelligence. Despite this, Motta had a very convincing case but was denied by the courts. In the writings I came across, which were in the possession of a disciple of Motta's, it stated that key judges who ruled against Motta were appointed by Reagan Wilson Reagan who represents 666 because he has six letters in each name. It was further stated that Reagan's influence persuaded the judges in this case.

I also noticed that when Reagan left office as President, his friends bought him a residence in Bel Air, the street address for which was 666. When Christian groups protested, Reagan had the address changed to 668. I found this even more amusing because 668 is the prefix for all phone numbers at Montauk.

Besides this occult connection, there are two other connections that make Reagan a compelling figure with regard to Montauk. First, he was President of the United States and that office has a very significant connection to Montauk. The first presidential connection to Montauk is through George Washington who had Cameron blood and ordered the construction of the Montauk Lighthouse as the very first public works project of the United States. Second is Thomas Jefferson who visited the Montauks on Long Island in order to record their language. There was also

Teddy Roosevelt who brought his Rough Riders to Montauk to recuperate after the Spanish-American War. It is also true that Abraham Lincoln's assassin, John Wilkes Booth (or at least the body that was alleged to have been Booth), was autopsied aboard the *U.S.S. Montauk*. This association between Montauk and the office of the President may or may not seem substantial to you. I can guarantee you, however, that it runs much deeper than the aforementioned associations. My first clue with regard to this concerned Reagan's nickname of "Dutch" which he shared with Dutch Wilson.

There is a substantial Dutch connection to Montauk. While I have been keenly aware of it for years, there has only been a slight mention of it in my newsletters. The connection, however, is so substantial that I have wondered for many years if I would some day write a book entitled *Montauk: The Dutch Connection.*

In the sixteen-hundreds, the Dutch instigated a raid by the Ninigrate Indians against the Montauks on the eve of Princess Heather Flower's wedding. Princess Heather Flower, who was the daughter of Chief Wyandanch, was kidnapped at her wedding party as her bridegroom was murdered. Wyandanch negotiated, through his friend Lion Gardiner, for the return of his royal daughter. The history books do not make much mention of it, if any, but there was a ransom for Heather Flower's return. She was only allowed to return safely on the condition that she would marry into the Van Tassel clan, a family of Dutch extraction. Heather Flower then moved to the community of Sleepy Hollow, New York where the Van Tassels made their home. Many Montauk Indians have since descended from that village which was later made famous by the tales of Washington Irving.

I had long ago discovered the Van Tassel connection in the archives of the Suffolk County Historical Society. I was actually looking for any files that I could find on Montauk. Quite oddly, there was only one file on Montauk in their public archives, and it was a genealogy study done by a lady with the surname of Wilson. Even more bizarre was that she came from the town of Cameron, New York. In doing her own family tree, Ms. Wilson discovered that she descended from Chief Wyandanch of the Montauks. If you have not yet noticed, there is also something else implied in this discovery and that is that Ronald Wilson Reagan is also related to the Montauks. In fact, he is. Reagan's middle name is from his mother, Nellie Wilson, but as of this writing, I have not been able to verify that his relation to the Montauk bloodline comes through the Wilsons. He is related to the Montauks, however, through the Johnson and Crippen family trees. Perhaps he is also related to the Ms. Wilson who did the genealogy study.

Reagan's Wilson lineage is also significant to my investigation because his family came from Iowa (as well as Illinois), the same locale from which the ancestors of L. Ron (Wilson) Hubbard and Marjorie (Wilson) Cameron came from.

It was from the Wilson genealogy in the Suffolk Country Historical Society that I first learned of the Van Tassel connection, but it also appears in many other publications.

The Van Tassels also has a famous family member named George Van Tassel. He worked for Howard Hughes and became famous as a leader of the contactee movement of the 1950's. Van Tassel had purchased property at Giant Rock in California and held huge UFO conferences there in the Fifties. Not far from Giant Rock, Van Tassel erected a building with a domed roof that looks something like an observatory. Still existing to this day, he called it the Integratron and it is supposed to rejuvenate the human body.

The Van Tassels were the prominent family of Sleepy Hollow, and they even appear in literature and films. They were neighbors of the Roosevelts and other prominent families of the era. It was thus that the royal bloodline of the Montauks became mixed with the aristocracy of the Dutch and other important families. In essence, the Dutch had forcibly co-opted the Montauk royal bloodline. In some strange and inarguable way, it legitimized their conquest of the land known as Al Marikanos — a land they would call America.

My trip to Los Olivos had indeed paid off. The principles of synchronicity were working hard to make something perfectly clear. The politics of our world today are very much wrapped up in the genetics of the Montauk Pharoahs. It is also ironic to note that the Oval Office conforms to the shape of an olive and that the words *olive* and *oval* are also anaphemes* for each other.

* An *anapheme* is a made-up word for transposing sounds from one word in order to make up another word. It is based upon the words *anagram* and *phoneme*.

As for Olive Pharoah, she is not only wrapped up in the genetics of the Montauks, she was and is the highest representative of those genetics because no one can ever replace her. I only made her acquaintance in the first place by reason of my interest in Montauk. My first questions to her were about the Montauk Project. At that time, I knew nothing about the forced "extinction" of her people. It was my writing about her people in *Pyramids of Montauk* that brought her back into my life, but it was the principle of synchronicity that made me realize the remarkable and important associations concerning the olive.

The synchronicity of the playbill featuring the Mount of Olives came to me by way of the ever mysterious Kenn Arthur who was well known by the pursuers of Dan Rather for possessing the "frequency" which was all about a stargate. With the playbill, Kenn had given me a stargate or at least the frequency for such. It was creating strange phenomena in my life.. There is yet another feature at work here and that represents the jinn. Kenn has always been either obsessed or preoccupied with the jinn. They are merely a frequency through which God, the Goddess, or the Creative Force operates. The reason that so much of this phenomena ties into mine and other peoples genetics has to do with the fact that *gene* and *jenie* or *jinn* are really the same word. The names *Jean* or *Gene* mean "close to God" or "next to god". As a purely physical vehicle, your genes are the magical or divine aspect of yourself. Although this is a mysterious process, God is said to work in mysterious ways.

Years later, after I had fully realized the meaning of my dreams about California, I passed through the city of Ventura and looked for the curly-cued off-ramp in that city that had inspired my exotic dreams. When I saw it, I could not believe what a small curve it actually possessed. It was definitely noticeable, but it was not much of a curl at all and was certainly not breathtaking. The dream state had exaggerated it way beyond belief. What is interesting, however, is that it is the exit for California Street. The jinn, through the dream state, were working overtime to get my attention. They were not only putting my attention on the burial site of my parents but on the state of California itself.

My next step was to read up on one of California's favorite sons, Ronald Wilson Reagan.

35

RONALD WILSON REAGAN

My first memories of Ronald Wilson "Dutch" Reagan were as a child when I saw him hosting *G.E. Theater* on television. I was only a small kid, but his magnetic personality and warmth made him enjoyable to watch. He was a fixture of those early television days, and pretty much everyone knew who he was. The dramas featured on *G.E. Theater* were usually quite over my head, but it was a testament to his charismatic personality that I not only remember him but wanted to watch him talk. He was likable.

When he beat the stodgy Pat Brown for the 1966 gubernatorial race, I felt that it was nice to have a familiar face running things in Sacramento. There is no question that Reagan was one of the most likable and popular politicians that America has ever known. He could relate to people on a human level. In fact, he had a reputation for never forgetting one of his staff members birthdays. This applied not only to his aides but to common clerks as well.

There is also, however, a dark side to Ronald Wilson "Dutch" Reagan. We will examine that, but it should be pointed out that it is important not to reject his good side or feel bad about maybe having liked him. His charismatic quality was one of many different components that made up his personality. All of these components should be recognized. Individuals, as well as life, are often very complex.

Known as the "Teflon President" to the media, astrologers knew Reagan as the "Neptunian President." In astrology, Neptune is the planetary ruler of spirituality but also illusion and deception.

Reagan's astrology chart features prominent Neptunian aspects. In essence, this means that he appeared to be one way when he was actually something else that was entirely different. As for himself, he and his wife deeply believed in astrology. As I have already suggested, his ties to the occult world run very deep.

I first learned of Reagan's dark side when my family moved to the university town of Davis, California which is just a fifteen minute drive from the Capital Building in Sacramento. Most everyone in the liberal town of Davis considered Reagan to be highly suspect if not outright clueless and evil. They were not, however, motivated in their views by prejudice or partisanship. Davis was an academic community that specialized in agriculture and husbandry. More importantly, they were very astute as to the political science which influenced these issues as well as the general politics of the Sixties. Much of this had to do with pesticides and exploitative chemicals. Reagan represented corporate profits and big business which, quite frankly, have very little to do with the quality of life. Northern Californians are probably more sensitive to the environment than any other region in the United States.

During this time of the revolutionary Sixties, things came to a head for the Reagan administration over the absolute brutal treatment that blacks were receiving at the hands of the Oakland police. It is well documented that blacks were sometimes shot indiscriminately. Out of these horrible conditions arose the Black Panthers who eventually made great strides towards receiving a modicum of justice in their neighborhood. Reagan's response to their pleas were so lame that the Panthers literally had to take over the Capital Building in Sacramento. Nobody was killed, but it was a statement that they wanted justice. It took a long time for things to improve, and many black people were martyred in the process. Reagan was always viewed as a polarizing figure during this time. Joan Baez even heralded him in a song:

He's a drug store truck driving man
he's the head of the Ku Klux Clan
when summer comes rolling around
you'll be lucky to get out of town

To most people, however, Reagan was still the affable Gipper who was appealing on the screen and communicated like no other politician. His dark side, however, did not begin with the turbulent Sixties and his stint as the Governor of California. It begins early in his movie career when he was represented by Lew Wasserman, an agent who worked for a talent agency known as MCA, the Music Corporation of America. For a sober and documented look into Reagan's dark side, read *Dark Victory: Ronald Reagan, MCA, and the Mob* (Viking Press, 1986) by Don E. Moldea. An intriguing read, it shows the opportunistic and compromising relationships Reagan was involved in.

In the late Thirties, MCA was essentially a large talent agency that began to muscle its way into music and motion picture production. Its antitrust practices were so outrageous that a judge eventually declared that MCA held a virtual monopoly over the entertainment business. The judge referred to it as an octopus and the name stuck. During the Fifties, MCA literally became the world's most successful producer and distributor of television shows under its subsidiary, Revue. Known for their black business suits, MCA executives were referred to as the Black-suited Mafia.

Eventually, Reagan's long time agent and friend, Lew Wasserman, became president of MCA. At the beginning of World War II, there is a mysterious liaison between Wasserman and Hap Arnold of the Army-Air Corp. Arnold is well known to UFO buffs for his antics in the beginning years of UFOlogy. Through Wasserman, Arnold recruited Reagan for the intelligence division of the Signal Corp. Reagan's job was to supervise the production of and sometimes narrate Army propaganda and morale films. By the end of his tenure in the Signal Corp, Reagan had been promoted to Captain and headed the film unit.

Reagan was mustered out of active service in December of 1945 but retained the status of active-reserve well into the Fifties. Throughout this period, Reagan was very much involved in active intelligence duties and became an FBI informant. One of his key roles in this regard was his association with the Screen Actors Guild or SGA. A few years after the war, Reagan's film career began to wane as he became the president of the SGA.

It was at this point that his career briefly and obscurely intertwined with that of L. Ron Hubbard who also worked as an

FBI informant during this period. Hubbard had to actually register with the L.A. Police Department in order to make his spy activities legal. I remember that when Reagan was elected president in 1980, Hubbard wrote to him and alluded to their previous association. With regard to what their actual association was, I do not know. All I know is that they both were informers who had served in military intelligence and were in Hollywood in the late 1940's.

As president of the SGA, Reagan became a key player in the Communist scare that reverberated throughout Hollywood. This was prior to and set the stage for the McCarthy hearings. While Reagan was exchanging and filtering information like a madman behind the scenes, his public persona was far from hostile. His testimony to Congress was friendly and made him look like the kindly old figure that he could portray so well. Actors, writers, and producers were being blacklisted right and left but Reagan was never perceived as a bad guy or as the one turning them in. Reagan received plenty of notoriety during this period and most of it was quite positive.

In the Fifties, Reagan became involved in a serious professional scandal that the general public is virtually oblivious to. During his fifth term as president of the SGA, he engineered a blanket waiver exempting MCA from normal SGA rules that would prohibit a talent agency from making films. For a talent agency to be involved in the film industry is a huge conflict of interest. Further, MCA was the only firm to have such a sweetheart deal. They controlled the talent, and now they would be able to determine where the talent would work: at their own studio! Reagan was obviously doing a favor for his old buddies.

Shortly after selling out his fellow actors, Reagan retired as the president of SGA and found himself in financial trouble. MCA soon came to the rescue and gave him the job of producing shows for their *G.E. Theater*. It was during this period that Reagan also became the spokesman for General Electric, a company then headed by Charles Wilson.

While producing shows for MCA, another strange conflict of interest arose in Reagan's business resume. Despite being a producer, Reagan was suddenly reelected president of SGA after a seven-year absence. By reason of the fact he was working as a producer, he was disqualified from serving on the SGA executive board as SGA rules specifically forbade this. Nevertheless, he stayed on as president and refused to resign. There was an ulterior motive for his actions, and he carried out his assignment well. MCA wanted him to lead a strike against the studios and he did. This was the second time he had sold out his fellow actors. After doing his dirty work, Reagan resigned. Although his fellow actors were displeased, the MCA executives were delighted and helped to sow the seeds that eventually made him Governor.

Although Reagan had succeeded with the strike, he soon found himself in the center of considerable trouble. Before the strike, MCA was already getting all sorts of bad publicity for antitrust violations. When the new Kennedy Administration came to power, they were forced to act. As Attorney General, Robert Kennedy began to probe MCA. Specifying numerous civil and criminal violations, a Federal grand jury was set up to hear these charges which included discrimination, extortion and blacklisting. As a key witness in these matters, Reagan was forced to testify. Keeping in true character with his later years, he did not remember anything. Question after question probed him, but he routinely came up with his trademark response of, "I don't remember."

Reagan never admitted to anything, but he was under intense pressure and scrutiny. He not only faced the prospect of having his reputation blackened forever but also the possibility of receiving a jail sentence. In the midst of all this tension, a miracle occurred. Suddenly and inexplicably, the Justice Department worked out a negotiation that was little more than a slap on the wrist. Essentially, they forced MCA to decide on whether it wanted to be a talent agency or a production company. As their revenue from the talent agency was relatively small potatoes compared to their production activities, they chose the latter and that was that.

The primary result of this negotiation was that Reagan did not go to jail. Shortly afterwards, he was backed by a group that later became known as his Kitchen Cabinet who arranged for him to give his now famous speech at the 1964 Republican Convention. Although he was a newcomer to this type of politics, he outshined Barry Goldwater, the Republican nominee, and this was the beginning of Reagan's political career.

In that same year, 1964, Reagan finished up his movie contract by appearing in a movie entitled *The Killers*. It is a watchable crime movie that portrays Reagan as a villain. As a matter of fact, it is the only picture where he appeared as such. He is not only a villain in this role, he is without any redeeming qualities. One wonders why he finished off his movie career this way. Was somebody sending us a secret message? If you watch the movie, you will get a definite vibe with regard to Reagan's darker side.

Reagan's family life was always questionable if not troubled. His own father was an alcoholic and this made Reagan distant emotionally with his own children. Although Ron and Nancy Reagan are known to have been completely devoted to each other, both of their children have complained that they were distant and emotionally unavailable. Ron Jr. even ran away from home to escape his mother beating him.

Nancy Reagan had considerable influence on her husband. She was a member of the SAG Board of Directors when Reagan engineered the MCA waiver referred to earlier. She would eventually introduce him to certain movers and shakers in the Republican Party. In later years, she ruled his schedule with an iron fist and it was strictly by astrology. Don Regan, Reagan's Chief of Staff, said that this made his job very difficult. If ever there was a case to be made for a First Lady being a mind-control handler, Nancy Davis Reagan certainly fits the bill.

What I have written here does not make Reagan sound like a boy scout, but it does not make him an evil person. At worst, it is white collar crime which is standard fare for politicians of today. Most politicians and CEOs are either prone to pillaging or equally quick to enable it, all motivated by their own self interest.

We get a yet darker view of Reagan's past when we consider one of his old buddies who also used to work in military intelligence: Richard Nixon. In 1960, Reagan wrote to Nixon and said that John Kennedy was a Marxist who, if elected, "must be eliminated." The letter containing this was retrieved from the Richard Nixon Presidential Library at San Clemente shortly before it closed. Nixon himself was in Dallas on November 22, 1963 but did not officially remember what he was doing there that day. He was a Pepsico attorney and was attending a conference sponsored by Pepsico which included all sorts of people who were later implicated in the assassination of JFK. This list of people included George H.W. Bush as well.

Other than his involvement with MCA, Reagan was never pursued for criminal behavior himself. One of Reagan's friends in his Kitchen Cabinet, however, gave his administration a lot of bad publicity. I am referring to Alfred Bloomingdale of the Bloomingdale Department Store family who was a key financial backer of Reagan. Their wives were best friends and the two families were close. After Reagan was elected President, Bloomingdale made headlines as the result of a kinky sadomasochistic relationship with a wanna-be starlet by the name of Vicky Morgan. Ironically, Vicky had also shared a close personal relationship with Hassan II, the King of Morocco.

Bloomingdale's relationship with Morgan would not have come to the attention of the press except for the fact that he was dying. Although he was married to one of Nancy Reagan's best friends, Bloomingdale took very good care of Vicky financially. With his impending death, however, it was clear that he was no longer going to be able to support her lavish life-style. This caused her to panic, and she hired a famous matrimonial attorney by the name of Marvin Mitchelson. He filed a multimillion dollar lawsuit on behalf of Morgan who was seeking compensation as Bloomingdale's mistress. Mitchelson had made big headlines in Hollywood and coined the word *palimony* in a lawsuit against Lee Marvin who, quite ironically, had also starred in *The Killers*.

Pretrial coverage of Vicky Morgan's lawsuit excited the media to no end. Her S&M relationship with Bloomingdale made for salacious detail. In Washington, however, it caused deep panic because this sort of deviant life-style was being linked to Reagan's top people and other Washington elite. It created a hornets nest for the Reagan administration.

Before her case went to trail, Vicky Morgan was outraged that her attorney, Mitchelson, had a meeting with the Reagans at the White House. She felt betrayed as he acted behind her back. Not long after firing Mitchelson from the case, Morgan was found bludgeoned and dead in her apartment. The cover-up is a rather complex and bizarre story. Another attorney appeared and claimed to have Morgan's videotape of key administration officials involved in deviant acts, but he was silenced and forced to recant. If you are interested in the details, you can read about them either on the internet or in one of the books written about Vicky Morgan.

Reagan remained the Teflon President with regard to Vicky Morgan and his administration escaped relatively unscathed. It was widely reported that the videotape included Attorney General Ed Meese indulging with Morgan. When Reagan's aide, Michael Deaver, received a phone call about the videotape, he is reported to have said to Nancy, "They've got Ed." The story runs far deeper than we will ever learn about. It should be pointed out that this sort of behavior if par for the course with Washington politicians. At this writing, in 2008, the madame of a Washington escort club was recently found dead by reason of "suicide." She was just about to spill the beans on most of Washington as the result of a probe into her operation. This probe was fueled when New York Governor, Eliot Spitzer, was caught in a sex scandal and forced to step down.

There are other intriguing members of Reagan's Kitchen Cabinet, but they are not known for their kinky life-styles. They are either interesting or suspect for other reasons. One of them was William A. Wilson, a Knight of Malta who served as Reagan's special envoy to the Vatican until such time that diplomatic relations were restored with the United States. The Vatican Embassy was expelled by President Lincoln who not only hated them but was convinced that they were trying to assassinate him. After relations with the Vatican were restored by Reagan, Wilson then served as Ambassador. In California, Reagan appointed Wilson to the Board of Regents of the University of California as well as a member of the California Post Secondary Education Commission. This gave him and the Knights of Malta rather sweeping influence over the education systems of California.

Reagan's own religious status is very curious in itself. Born as an Irish Catholic, he ended up as an Episcopalian. This is unusual to say the least. Catholics generally hate the English and understandably so. For him to be an Episcopalian who also courted the Vatican put him in a very unique position to coordinate the affairs of two very powerful organizations.

Reagan's public statements and so-called religious views on abortion are also suspect. After legalizing abortion as Governor of California, he appointed Sandra Day O'Connor to the Supreme Court. She was well known as a liberal and ended up casting the deciding vote in the Supreme Court case *Roe versus Wade*. This case legalized abortion. All of this is in stark contrast to Reagan's portrayal of himself and the public's acceptance of him as a staunch conservative. This sort of behavior is a perfect example of him appearing to be one way when he was really another.

Perhaps the most intriguing Reagan connection has to do with his one time appointment secretary, Helene Von Damme. Affectionately called the "Little Nazi" by Reagan and his staff, she worked for him both in California and in Washington. Between herself and William A. Wilson, they literally handpicked Reagan's cabinet and key members of Reagan's staff.

Although Von Damme has sometimes been heralded as serving as a secretary for the high command of the Third Reich, this is a bit of an exaggeration. She was only about fourteen when the war ended. The mystique surrounding Von Damme begins with her coming to the United States with a Nazi named Otto Albrecht von Bolschwing. She worked hand-in-hand with him.

Of the many intriguing Nazis that have been overlooked by common historians, Otto Albrecht von Boschwing should be rated near the top of the list. Known as the Butcher of Bucharest, he was an obvious war criminal who hung Romanians on meat hooks and was guilty of all sorts of unspeakable acts.

Von Bolschwing's work in Palestine was filled with double-agent intrigue. According to captured German documents, he worked closely with the notorious Adolf Eichmann who was actually a diplomat to Israel in the 1930's. Acting as an importer in Palestine, von Boschwing established an alliance with a Zionist group known as Haganah that was headed by Feival Polkes. Von Bolschwing was the sole financial supporter of Polkes who gave the Germans information in return. The most controversial aspect of the von Bolschwing's association with Polkes was that they arranged for Jewish training camps inside of Germany during the Thirties. These Jewish trainees were the seeds of the future military of Israel.

Von Bolschwing's partner in this Jewish intrigue was "Saint John Philby," a British MI6 agent. The British connection is bolstered by the fact that von Bolschwing was educated in London. In this regard, Reagan's Episcopal connection and the Tavistock Institute lurk in the background.

Although Allen Dulles is credited with the recruitment of Reinhard Gehlen for the CIA, it was actually von Bolschwing who handpicked him for use in U.S. intelligence. The senior orchestrators were the British who oversaw and laid out the template for the Central Intelligence Agency.

Working with Helene Von Damm, von Boschwing founded a company called Transcontinental Computer Investments or TCI which was, in certain respects, the beginning of what we now know as Silicon Valley. This company harnessed and developed the technical evolution of the defense industry. The heyday of TCI was during the Reagan administration.

Reagan's association with these people ran very deep, but it is largely invisible. As dubious as his many associations are, his guilt or innocence in these matters is not of critical importance. It is also not our business to indulge in judgment. What I am trying to present is the fact that these various associations demonstrate Reagan to be one of the most masterful politicians of all time. His mastery of politics is emphasized by the fact that he never really got caught When he was cornered, he managed to escape. His political prowess has been underestimated even by his admirers.

Besides his association with von Damme and her crowd, Reagan was well known for his close association with Errol Flynn, a known German spy. L. Ron Hubbard Jr. asserted that Flynn was closely association with his own father, but I have not been able to verify that claim from any other source. Ron Jr. was a known liar who would sell his stories to the highest bidder.

To a significant extent, Reagan's German associates gravitated around one of his favorite aides, William P. Clark. This had something to do with the fact that, as an Army counterintelligence officer, Clark was very much involved with the Paperclip scientists and ended up marrying the niece of Werner von Braun, the Nazi rocket scientist who became the director of NASA.

Clark served Reagan as Supreme Court Judge of the State of California, but his home in San Luis Obispo was far important in terms of terms of political intrigue. Known by Reagan's friends as "The Compound" or "The Eagle's Nest," Clark's home served as the nexus point for where the path of Project Paperclip crossed roads with both California and American politics.

Next, we will examine the San Luis Obispo connection.

36

SAN LUIS OBISPO

San Luis Obispo is just a short distance inland from the Pacific Ocean and has a population of about 44,000. It is the county seat of San Luis Obispo County, and I remembere the city well. Not only did I visit the city and county on several occasions, our school played their school in sports and we knew them as S.L.O.. There have been so many instances of circular feedback in my adventures with the olive that I should not be surprised to be confronted once more with memories of my old surroundings.

Although I remember having to memorize the name of William P. Clark as a California Supreme Court Judge for my eighth grade history class, I had no idea then or until recently about the political intrigue that swirled around San Luis Obispo.

Ironically, the political currents of the city are signified in the name itself. *Obispo* means "bishop" in Spanish. As has already been said, Reagan's Kitchen Cabinet had a strong Catholic connection. There was William A. Wilson, Ambassador to the Vatican, and also Clark, a devout Catholic who attended Loyola University, a Jesuit college in Los Angeles. Clark's beliefs were so strong that he erected a chapel on his "Eagle's Nest" property. At Clark's compound, we have a confluence of counterintelligence, the Vatican, Paperclip scientists, and the burgeoning technology of what was to become known later as Silicon Valley.

Much of the intrigue and power in this cabal was attributed to Reinhard Gehlen, the Nazi SS officer who became the architect for CIA operations. He was also a stockholder in TCI (mentioned in the previous chapter). His influence and reputation were such that the group of people associated with Clark's "Eagle's Nest" were sometimes referred to as the "Gehlen Organization." Their control of the local community was pervasive as well. In his book *Threads of Silk — Bands of Steel*, author Gyeorgos Itatonu said the following about San Luis Obispo. "The Gehlen Organization is in complete control of the courts, boards of supervisors, sheriff's department, etc."

The local politics of S.L.O. originally came to my attention as the result of a curious video about the JFK assassination that was circulated by William Cooper. The video showed William Greer, the driver of Kennedy's limousine, allegedly shooting JFK. When I first saw this video tape, it was interesting but not conclusive. Cooper insists that the driver shot the President, but he is steering the audience and steering intensely. Whether he believed it himself or not is not determined. Besides being a conspiracy theorist who released a considerable amount of privileged information, Cooper had a lot of mental problems and suffered from alcoholism. His combative nature led to his premature death at the hands of a local sheriff's team who were equally combative.

Further analysis of this video has revealed that the driver did not shoot Kennedy at all. It was not even a gun that he was holding in his hand. William Greer's behavior, both as a driver and in the hospital, was suspicious but he did not shoot Kennedy. Whether Cooper was a willing participant or not, this video ended up being an obvious and curious misdirection fostered by the intelligence community. They love to present nutty theories that conspiracy audiences willingly and voraciously gobble up. Most conspiracy fans are not too discriminating and are quick to embrace either ridiculous propositions or data which is just plain wrong. This distracts people from what is actually going on.

What I found curious about this video circulated by Cooper was that it was originally released by public television in San Luis Obispo. Shortly thereafter, this video had a very brief life on many PBS stations across America. Almost as soon as it aired, it was pulled off of public television except for the original station in San Luis Obispo where it continued to be shown. It was as if someone wanted you to think it contained the real truth and that is why it was pulled. By why did it originate and remain on in San Luis Obispo?

According to researcher Mae Brussell, the San Luis Obispo gang was steeped in the JFK conspiracy up to their eyeballs. For those of you unfamiliar with Mae Brussell, she was, in many respects, the "original" researcher of the JFK assassination conspiracy. A well-to-do housewife from a rich Jewish family, she was disgusted when she read the lameness of the Warren Report as it hit the stands in 1964. She wanted real answers, and it was full of holes. This began her conspiracy career.

Relying mostly on facts from newspapers across the world, Brussell began to put two and two together and ended up connecting the JFK assassination to a host of characters that permeated the military industrial complex and included but was not limited to: old Paperclip Nazis, the CIA, the FBI, NASA scientists, and various corporations. As you might have guessed, a major confluence of these connections ran back not only to San Luis Obispo but to the private home of William. P. Clark. At one time, Mae Brussell instigated a lawsuit naming Clark as one of the parties involved in the JFK assassination. I do not know what happened to the lawsuit but Brussell was eventually silenced.

Despite several warnings from her adversaries, some of which included physical mischief against her person, Brussell continued to broadcast her opinions and findings of fact. She had a weekly radio program and sent out tapes to subscribers. During the Iran-Contragate hearings, she was connecting the players in that to the same people who were involved with the S.L.O. crowd. After a final warning, she continued to broadcast and ended up with a fast-growing cancer. As I heard it, a cancer-causing agent was mixed with DMSO (dimethyl sulfoxide) and rubbed upon her steering wheel. One of the properties of DMSO is that it will circulate something through your entire system almost instantaneously.

The above scenario is an extremely plausible explanation because we do know that she died as a result of rapidly advancing cancer. It is more than ironic that is was rapid-cancer because this was the same or a very similar agent used on Jack Ruby. Although it is not too well known, and apparently not to most Mae Brussell fans, the cancer-causing agent was pioneered in a laboratory serviced by both Lee Harvey Oswald and David Ferry. This information came out in a British documentary shown very sparingly on the History Channel. It featured the story of Oswald's girl friend who was hired by this lab as she was a genius chemist who had just gotten out of school. She knew David Ferrie personally and had been afraid to tell her story for years in deference to keeping her family safe. As the original mobster who had threatened her over these matters eventually died, she then felt it was safe to talk. The basic purpose of the lab this lady worked in was to make a biochemical agent that would rapidly accelerate cancer in an individual. The ostensible target for this cancer agent was supposedly Fidel Castro. Oswald's mysterious trip to Mexico was actually an assignment where he was to apply for a visa to Cuba so as to infect Castro. When he was denied a visa, he was called back to New Orleans.

If you would like to learn more about the JFK assassination as well as the San Luis Obispo connection, start at Mae Brussell's website which is *www.maebrussell.com.* The entire story is far bigger and more complex than even she could put together, but she did an excellent job. Despite a good following, she is ignored by many conspiracy authors and most certainly by media sources who present information on the JFK assassination.

My point with the S.L.O. connection is that it was a nexus point for different behind-the-scenes operations that influence what might be considered normal politics or government actions. I have also focused on the S.L.O. connection because it brings up another interesting issue which concerns the mysterious death of L. Ron Hubbard.

Either through sheer synchronicity or by the deliberate plan of some conspirator, L. Ron Hubbard moved to a ranch in Crestone, just outside of S.L.O. and within the jurisdiction of San Luis Obispo County. In other words, he moved to a locale where he was subject to political authorities that just might enjoy doing him in. Whether or not they actually wanted to do him in, it is certainly a big part of Hubbard's own conspiracy theories that the old Nazi guard, mostly through INTERPOL, was trying to ruin him. By his own creed, Hubbard could not have picked a more vulnerable locale than to be next to the "Eagle's Nest" of William P. Clark.

In all probability, it was Pat Broeker who would have either picked or scouted this location for Hubbard to move to. Broeker was chosen to be Hubbard's successor but lost a huge power struggle with David Miscavige. Knowing Broeker personally, I do not believe he would have selected S.L.O. if he knew what I have just elaborated on. It is possible that he was steered there, but I view that as unlikely. My best guess is that it was just dumb bad luck for the Scientology movement which had already lost its inner stride by that point. Synchronicity either works with you or against you. Just ask a ball player or a Wall Street trader. If Broeker was actually steered to S.L.O., it would likely have been done by a real estate agent who was aware of who Broeker was or who accepted a bribe from someone who was bird-dogging him.

Hubbard lived on a ranch in Crestone so that he could live out his life in seclusion and avoid subpoenas. Miscavige had already effectively cut Hubbard off of Scientology management lines so he was not effectively a threat to the "Eagle's Nest" or any other group that might have wanted him out of commission. In fact, it would have been in the best interest of Hubbard's enemies to keep him around so that all legal angles could be worked out in order to wrest complete control of the Church of Scientology.

There were unusual circumstances surrounding the death of L. Ron Hubbard and these were detailed in *The Montauk Book of the Dead*. The irregularities surrounding Hubbard's death included the following: (1) a suspicious will; (2) a psychiatric drug that was found in his body (Hubbard was dead-set against psychiatrists and their drugs); and (3) a signed release from Hubbard objecting to an autopsy on religious grounds. Curiously, the will and the release form were signed shortly before his death and during a period when it was medically determined that he was incapacitated. In other words, he was not qualified to make or change a will, let alone sign an autopsy release.

The Church and their attorneys worked as hard as possible to have Hubbard's body cremated as soon as possible. They did not want lingering questions, and this would be understandable from their perspective. Whether guilty or innocent, their behavior is understandable.

Upon examining the corpse, the coroner noticed different needle marks on the buttocks and wanted to do an autopsy, but he was powerless to do so by reason of the autopsy release supposedly signed by Hubbard. As the Church protested, the coroner insisted on taking a blood sample and this was permitted. This procedure is what determined that there was a psychiatric drug in his body.

These circumstances would be suspicious to anyone, particularly to a coroner. After viewing the recently signed will and release form, the coroner interviewed Hubbard's doctor who told him that his patient suffered from dysphasia. This means he was incapacitated.

Despite the release form, an autopsy could still be performed by the coroner if there were criminal circumstances. This would, however, require a criminal investigation which would have to be authorized by the San Luis Obispo District Attorney. Despite, the coroner's request for an investigation, the D.A. did not take it up.

There is another curious component to Hubbard's death. If he had died months earlier, there was no such provision in California law by which a person could object to an autopsy on religious grounds. The coroner would have just gone about his business and performed the autopsy by reason of the suspicious circumstances. In retrospect, it seems as if the California legislature had rammed this new law into being for this specific purpose. Autopsies generally protect the dignity of people who have been violated by underhanded means. This law provides for bizarre exceptions.

As strange or convincing as all of this might seem, there is yet a further bizarre aspect to these matters when we consider the relationship of the Church of Scientology with the State of California. By corporate bylaws, the Church of Scientology is licensed to operate through the authority of the Church of Spiritual Technology (CST), a for-profit corporation which was set up by Meade Emory, a former Assistant IRS Commissioner. In addition to a regular Board of Directors, a provision was made in the bylaws that CST would also be served by three Special Directors placed by Meade Emory. Special Directors serve for life and their eventual replacements are subject to being in good standing with the California State Bar. In California, the California State Bar is a part of the office of the Supreme Court of the State of California. Although there are justifications that this is to ensure the tax-exempt status of Scientology, it is a complete violation with regard to the separation of Church and State.

Synchronicity tells some pretty interesting tales. I was particularly amused that all of this occurred amidst some of my old stomping grounds. My adventures with the olive were taking me home in more ways that one.

37

OG

The name of Ronald Wilson "Dutch" Reagan has shown itself to be a magical catalyst with regard to my adventures in synchronicity, but the etymology of the name leads to even more interesting vistas. The name "Ronald" basically means "ruler" while the name "Reagan" has some very interesting implications. It is said to mean "little king" but it is more accurately translated as "young king." This can be seen in the Old Irish word *og* which means "young." You will find *og* expressed in *Reagan* if you break it down to *re-ag-an* which is the same as *re-og-an.* The phoneme *re* refers to royalty as is seen in the Spanish word *real*, pronounced *ray-al*, which means *royal.* I found the phoneme *og*, however, to be most important. Not only is it tied to my Sweeney ancestors who came from the Land of Og, but it is also expressive of the deepest aspects of Celtic thought.

A look into Celtic mythology will tell you that *Og* is actually an abbreviated form of a mystical land known as Tir na nÓg which means "land of eternal youth" or paradise. There is a very subtle aspect to the phrase "Tir na nÓg" when you consider the *n* which appears adjacent to *Óg*. In English, it is the same as the prefix *in* which can refer to "amidst," "within," or "contained by." The Celtic word *nÓg* therefore refers to a place or locale where one is immersed in youth.

In an earlier chapter, I mentioned my trip to the mission in Ventura after I had just visited the grave of my parents near Los Olivas Adobe. I had mentioned that it was anticlimactic when I learned of the MA sign that referred to Alpha and Omega. This, of course, refers to the eternal nature of life. To me, this was like telling me that a house has a front door and a back door. Synchronicity was pushing me to take the prospect of eternity far more seriously, particularly as it regards a fountain of youth, but I was slow to catch on. The olive had led me to my dead parents, but it was also leading me to the Land of Og, a paradise of eternal youth.

The etymology of *og* is deep and complex, but it reveals a lot. The first thing I would like to bring to your attention is that Tir na nÓg is sometimes referred to as Tir na n-Oc. For reasons you will soon read, it is important to recognize the fact that *og* and *oc* are convertible. Both *og* and *oc* relate to vision or the word *see* and this is clearly demonstrated in the English language words *ogle* and *ocular*. The word *ogle* derives from the German root *oog* which means "eye."*

An author by the name of Philip Cohane states in his book *The Key* that both *og* and *oc* are used interchangeably in various place-names. He notes that they seem to represent two different traditions. Cohane's work, through the study of place-names and language, also demonstrates that the words *egg, hog, oak, and ox* are interchangeable with *og* and *oc*. (It should be noted here that *ox* equates to *aleph* in Hebrew and that it not only refers to a beginning but also equates to the same sound as *olive*.)

In an earlier chapter about Mark Roberts, I referred to the Ogham language and the fact that he is able to read it. The relationship between *Og* and *Ogham* is quite significant. When you hear Ogham referred to in most contemporary discussions, it will be pronounced with a hard *g* as in "augum." While this is acceptable to most people, there is an earlier and more traditional pronunciation which is *oyum* or *oyam* where the *g* is clearly convertible to a *y*.

I have stressed the convertibility of different letters because they are very important with regard to understanding important concepts, particularly with regard to a paradise of eternal youth.

* The breakdown of the name *Reagan* on the previous page was a phonetic approach. Conventional etymology indicates that *Reagan* comes from the German name *Reginald* which derives from *ragin* which means "advice" and *wald* which means "rule." The word *advice* is interesting because if you trace it down, you will see that it is based upon the word *view* which brings us back to the eye.

Thus far, the letters *c, g*, and *y* have shown themselves to be convertible. Why some people speak with different inflections and iterations is the underlying principle behind linguistics. It obviously has to do with the fact different people have their own lenses by which they experience the universe. They also use their vocal chords differently. The original concepts, however, remain the same or very similar.*

In studying the etymology of *Og* and words associated with it, I ran across *ogive*. This caught my attention because it is very close to the spelling of the word *olive*. An *ogive* is "a diagonal rib or groin of a Gothic vault" and "a pointed or Gothic arch." ** Looking into the etymology of *ogive*, I learned that it derives from the Spanish word *aljibe*, a cistern, which derives from the Arabic *al-gubb*, a well. These derivations are interesting for a few different reasons.

Reading the etymology of *ogive*, I immediately noticed two things. First, the *g* in *ogive* was obviously convertible with the *l* in both *aljibe* and *al-gubb*. At some point, when *aljibe* and *al-gubb* were converted to *ogive*, the *l* was made to be silent. One could just as easily have chosen the *j* and *g* to be silent, particularly as it is more common for those letters to be silent than an *l*. If the *g* and the *l* are convertible, there is not much difference at all between *olive* and *ogive*. I also recognized that *aljibe* and *al-gubb* both feature the phoneme for *gib*, a seldom used English word which means "cat." Once again, *cat* = *leo* which is similar to *elaia* (olive) and *helios*.

* The principle of converting different letters and phonemes has proven itself invaluable during my ventures to foreign countries. I have found that I can sometimes interpret a difficult foreign word when no one else can.

** One of the first things I learned about an olive tree from Kenn Arthur was that they often contain a niche which is akin to a vault. The Arabic *gubb* also means *rib* which is equated to a groin and is an excellent analogy for the rib of Adam that created Eve. A well or cistern is suggestive of the Well of Souls under the Temple Mount which was once said to belong to Adam. The so-called rib of Adam was obviously his seed. It is laughable how earlier students of religion have viewed etymology and language with robotic, narrow-minded and linear viewpoints. The Adam and Eve story is also a metaphor. There was an earlier story where Eve took Adam from her "rib" or groin, and we also now know how that corresponds with parthogenesis. The Biblical story of genesis sounds more like an alien abduction and seeding where God takes Adam's DNA via the rib and then clones it with a few modifications and has a new creature called Eve. *Eve* is also convertible with *Og*. *Eve* is related to *Eva* and *Avalon* which is another name for the Land of Og.

The most important revelation with regard to the convertibility of the letters *l* and *g* concerns *Ogygos* and *Eleusis*. If you convert the first *g* in *Ogygos* to an *l* and make the second *g* silent, you have a sound that is something like "Elias" which is virtually the same as *elaia*, the Greek word for olive. *Elaia* is actually closer to *Ogygia* which is another name for *Ogygos* and probably the original or more correct term. I use *Ogygos* because I am more familiar with it from having read the *Odyssey*.

None of the above would have surprised Egerton Sykes because he made it very clear in his work that the Rites of Eleusis originated on the island of Ogygos. What I have said adds certainty to his observations. More importantly, it also clues us in on the fact that *Og* and *El* are convertible. *El* and *Al* both refer to the article *the* which is the root of the word *Theos* which means "God." Besides meaning this, *El* and *Al* sometimes refer to "first" or something that is first of God or next to God.

All of the above further explains why the olive is positioned so close to the Holy of Holies and the Ark of the Covenant. An examination of the etymology of the word *ark* will reveal that, in more ancient times, the word was pronounced as *ak* or *auk*. As the Ark of the Covenant is concerned with the light of God or the Shekinah, it should not surprise us that the ancient Egyptian word for light is *ak*. In Sanskrit, *aag* means "fire."

Quite ironically, the above concepts also correspond to the Biblical account of Noah's Ark. According to scripture, there was one other creature who survived the flood besides the animals and Noah's immediate family. It was a giant named Og. He escaped the flood by riding atop the ark. In such a circumstance, there would have been a great need for a fire-keeper. It seems that by including the creature Og in the myth of Noah, they were trying to keep an ancient tradition of "Og" alive.

When Noah first set out on his journey, he had only his family. The giant Og came along as an extra and then a dove appeared with an olive leaf. Where Og and the dove came from has not been adequately explained, but they obviously came from another land which is equivalent to Avalon or any other name you care to give it. The dove represents Christ or the Chrism which is olive oil.

We will next examine the "separate" tradition of Oc and how it relates to the olive and the Ark of the Covenant.

38

OC

The tradition of Oc is pretty much forgotten save for some place-names and a few accompanying legends. From its association with Og, however, we do know that such a tradition is, to some degree, representative of a fountain of youth and even eternal life. As the concept of a fountain of youth has been idealized and romanticized beyond belief, it is hard to take too seriously. As a matter of fact, your mind has been conditioned to treat such a concept as complete fantasy. Medical scientists, however, might be a bit more skeptical. Despite working from a limited data base, they know for a fact that human bodies should live considerably longer than they do.

As for myself, I might have been pretty much in the same boat as yourself with regard to the believability of a fountain of youth. With regard to astrology, my sun is in Capricorn which means that I am very pragmatic. I would only believe in a fountain of youth if I were able to literally see it or experience it. At the time I began my olive quest, I had no idea what direction it would take or that it would lead to my genetic history and the prospect of a fountain of youth in the name of either Og or Oc. To my surprise, the energies and concepts I have studied and written about here actually began to manifest in my life through various people and events. You have already read about this to some extent, but my life became even more interesting.

At the outset of my quest for the olive, I had no idea that *oc* was anything more than a phoneme or syllable. There was no suspicion that there might be a tradition concerning it. I was quite aware, however, that the sound of *oc* was a part of the word *Montauk* which can be broken down in at least two ways.

mon + tauk   *mon + t + auk*

The latter example is particularly noteworthy if we revisit the original name for the fountain of youth, *Tir na nÓg*. As *Og* has been proven to be a shortened or abbreviated version of *Tir na nÓg*, it is easy to consider that the *tauk* in *Montauk* might actually have originated as a contraction or shortening of *Tir na nÓc* that translates as *T'oc*. The plausibility of this hypothesis is substantiated by the fact that there is a strong Irish connection to Montauk. In ancient times, the gulf stream made it easy for people on the east coast of America to travel to Ireland via boat. There was commerce and cultural exchange long before the history books indicate. The Irish cultural exchange continues to this day via illegal immigration to Montauk via fishing boats or other boats. This immigration is often only for the summer, but it provided good money for Irish youth prior to the plummeting of the U.S. dollar in the world exchange markets.

The sound of *oc* also came to my attention via my daughter. When she first started talking to the point where she was conversational, she would speak of an imaginary friend named Auk or Oc. This was cute, and I always indulged her with her friend, but it never went anywhere significant. As she was born and grew up just as I began my investigation of Montauk, perhaps there was a subtle influence at work. As I write this, she is just graduating from high school and no longer remembers Auk, but she knows about it from me. Needless to say, the expression of auk or oc had certainly caught my attention.

In a seemingly much more important vein, I came across *oc* once again when I did my research for the book *Synchronicity and the Seventh Seal* and studied the work of John Dee. Dee was a 16th Century conjurer and court magician of Queen Elizabeth I who transcribed the Enochian language from the angelic realm through the mediumship of Edward Kelly. In a session when Dee was surrounded by negative spirits, the Archangel Raphael came to his rescue. After driving the negative spirits away, Raphael identified himself as "Medicina Dei" and then said, "The angel of your direction is called OCH."

Through communing with the angelic realm, John Dee basically transcribed an entire Enochian language that has its own syntax and grammar that was used to invoke the angels or daemon (these terms are understood to be synonymous with each having a light side and a dark side). I had first learned about John Dee from Marjorie Cameron. During the Babalon Working, she said, Parsons and Hubbard were trying to emulate the work of John Dee and Edward Kelly, at least to some extent. Dee and Kelly, on the other hand, were trying to emulate the legendary work of King Solomon who could manipulate the jinn to do his work.

Dee's work is very powerful, but there is no suggestion that it leads in the direction of a fountain of youth. He eventually conjured up the dark side and got in over his head. We get a glimpse into the true character of his Enochian language when we see that his angels defined the word *Babalon* as "evil." This is a most curious definition because *Babalon* clearly means "gate." This blatant "Enochian newspeak" suggests that Dee's angels had some serious issues that would not only protect the gate itself but the definition of it. The antifemale implications are there as well.

When Dee encounters the name of OCH, he is in a mess and it seems to appear as a positive force that got him out of trouble. Perhaps if he followed OCH, he would have been better off. Parsons and Hubbard also threw a complete wild card into the work of Dee and Kelly when they introduced Babalon into their incantations. They did not view Babalon as evil at all but as an ancient feminine archetype that needed to be restored.

In any case, none of this conjuring explains the tradition of Oc. There is only an allusion to what it might be. I did, however, receive a clue when I was directed to author William Henry's website. His research on this point is rather brief, but he came across the story of an ancient language called Oc that was taught by Jesus. Supposedly, this was a secret language that was transferred to the south of France in and around the time of the legendary exodus of Mary Magdalene.

According to this tradition, the meaning of *Oc* was related to the numeral *8* and Oc was referred to as the "Language of Eight." Both *oc* and *og* are related to the numeral *8* which is evident in words such as *octagon* and *ogdoad* (which means "eight"). As the culture and tradition of Mary Magdalene was transplanted to France, this "Language of Eight" or Oc evolved into what became known as Languedoc*, a lost language once spoken in southern France. The term *Languedoc* literally means *language* or *tongue* of *oc*.

William Henry's website was very helpful. I even had a chance to speak to him personally, but he had no more to offer at this point. It was obvious, however, that if the Language of Eight was a secret language, it would have represented a bridge between this world and another. This was the great conspiracy topic of the First Century and was why the original Christian mystery schools drew the symbol of a Vesica Pisces at their secret meeting places. The word on the street was that there was another dimension you could access. For whatever reason, it caught on like wildfire.

Phil Dick wrote some intriguing information about what happened in and around the year 70 A.D.. This was when the Roman Empire literally destroyed the bridge to this new world which was ruled by King Felix, an obvious allusion to Christ. The name *Felix* is not only representative of the cat, it means "fecundity or fruitfulness." This is not only the primary attribute of an olive tree, but the name *Felix* spelled backwards is *XILEF* which is the same as *OLIVE* or *ALEPH* if you pronounce the *X* silently.

Whatever happened to the real Christianity is a great mystery. There are legends of an escape to France, England, and other places here and there. There is no question, however, that the original Roman Empire absorbed Christianity, diluted it and then perverted it. After all, it is run from Rome to this very day, at least the Catholic version of Christianity. In Christianity, all we are left with is an idea that everlasting life is possible if one follows the prescribed guidelines that were handed down by the Council or Nicea which were dictated by Rome. Like John Dee and Edward Kelly, dark forces got the better of the Christian movement.

* Languedoc is sometimes confused with Provençal which is a different language. At the same time Languedoc was being spoken in the south, there was a similar but different language spoken in northern France, That was Languedoi which eventually became the French language that we know today. The *oi* in Languedoi means "yes" as does "oc." The current French word for "yes" is *oui*. For all practical purposes, Languedoc has been a dead language for centuries.

From the story of Christianity, the tradition of Oc is more of a whispering campaign than a real practice that can be experienced and witnessed, at least if we are talking about a fountain of youth. There are plenty of stories of faith and what not, but it is obvious that the core teachings of Christianity went underground. In this day and age, most of these teachings are more of an allusion to truth or an intellectualization as opposed to a real applied technique. These teachings are also highly romanticized.

We even have to call into question the prospect of whether Jesus or his followers were even interested in a fountain of youth. There is no doubt that he and his followers were interested in and believed in everlasting life, but it was never positioned as a fountain of youth. As Jesus discarded his body in the prime of life, it became fashionable for saints and martyrs to discard theirs as well. Christianity even evolved into a tradition that regarded a healthy or virile human body as something that might even be considered repugnant. They were down on hygiene and sought the afterlife as opposed to a long life in a transient human body.

The Celtic tradition of Oc, however, suggests there is or was a fountain of youth which can be tapped. Ideally, we can expect this theme to actually intertwine with and embrace the parameters of everlasting life. We do find some common ground here with the fact that *Oc* represents the number 8 which is also the symbol for infinity. It is also the number for God. The Language of Oc would therefore have to be a language that embraces the infinite.

If you have not already noticed, there is an infinite aspect to synchronicity. In my adventures, the connections keep coming and there are always enough to keep one from being disappointed. In actual fact, there are far more than I have time to follow up on. I usually try to stick to the most important or fruitful leads.

As data on Oc was far too sparse, I soon found myself taking an etymological approach. This has always been a successful route, particularly when you have little to go on. Ironically, I also found that the key to understanding Oc was in a publication I have already written about, *The Glory of the Olive Tree*. In this work, it is pointed out that Enoch is identified as one of the "olive trees" mentioned in *The Bible*. These olive trees represent the two cherubs in the Holy of Holies which are the Witnesses to the End of Time. I found this reference to Enoch as an olive tree to be very significant because *och* appears in the name *Enoch*. From my limited knowledge of Hebrew, I also knew that names used in the vernacular of today are usually butchered as opposed to how they were originally spoken. I could plainly see that the original name for Enoch would have been pronounced or could be pronounced as *Ayinoch*. This reformed spelling of *Enoch* is a very important key.

Ayin is the Hebrew letter which means "eye." Enoch or *Ayin-och* therefore represents two eyes. Two eyes are also indicative of the number 8 if you turn it sideways. This is also infinity, but there is another hidden reference if you consider the eighth letter of the Hebrew alphabet, which is *chet*, an alternative expression for *cat*. Therefore, contained in the name *Enoch* or *Ayin-och*, you have the symbolism of infinity through the eyes of a cat. This is also part and parcel of why the Hebrews most holy exaltation is *"kadoish, kadoish, kadoish*." It is a variation of the Berber word *kadiske* and the Nubian word *kadis* which both mean "cat." Therefore, the two eyes of *Ayin-och* that represent the Witness at the End of Time represent the eyes of a cat. This is often thought to mean "God Himself" but we are really talking about a gateway to everlasting life. The picture of a beard-faced god can get in the way of that.

The cat analogy also relates to Tir na nÓg or Tir na nÓc via Celtic myth where there was a creature known as a cat sidhe. This cat sidhe* was a bridge between the material and spiritual worlds. It was said that if you could look into the green eyes of a cat, you could see into the other world.

Besides Enoch or Ayin-och, the Holy of Holies featured another "Olive Tree" or Witness to the End of Time and this was identified as Elijah. In Biblical times, the *j* in the name *Elijah* would have been pronounced with a silent *j* or *y* and would have sounded just like *elaia*, the Greek word for "olive." The two

* The word *sidhe* is pronounced *shee* which represents not only the origin of our word *she* but also the gateway to another world. A *sidhe* is also a fairy mound, but it originally referred to the little folk or fairy who occupied the mound. A mound is a gateway to the next world and each sidhe would have a primary spirit that guarded it. Later, the word *sidhe* became known as a center of activity and eventually was transmogrified into the word *city*. Although there were different types of *sidhes*, this word was most strongly identified and associated with the cat. The word *citizen* is also related to and influenced by *cit* or *sidhe* and *cit* can also be construed as *cat*. This is similar to a *fela* being known as a common citizen in Old Egyptian. The historical character of Spain, *El Cid*, was another way of saying "The Cat."

Witnesses were therefore the Olive Tree and the Two Eyes which are not only interchangeable, they also represent the cat or the eyes of a cat. This represents the End of Time because it is suggestive of a gateway out of this linear dimension. In essence, these Olive Trees or Witnesses represent a virtual pair of binoculars through which you can look at the Creative Force of the universe. You are looking through a *gato* or gateway to infinity and that represents endless creation. If you choose to limit God or the Creative Force to an idol or serious-looking man or judge, you have limited infinity and have become the creator of your own reality.

Looking directly into the Creative Force may or may not be a pleasant experience for you because it contains polarizing prospects. A dubious analogy might be to liken it to a good LSD trip or a bad one. Creation is, however, composed of polarizing forces and Oriental religion refers to these as yin and yang. In some respects, this direct view into the Creative Force gives the impression that it is no different than a jinn itself. While it is dubious to define the Creative Force, the metaphor of a jinn is literally eye-opening when we examining the phonetics of *jinn*, *ayin*, and *yin*. They all sound the same. More importantly, their respective meanings intertwine in a manner that is fascinating.

In the days of Solomon, the letter *j* was pronounced like a *y*. The legends of Solomon indicate that he operated the jinn through his pagan wives who represent the yin principle. The letter *ayin*, meaning eye, fits in very well as the act of seeing is an inflow or receptive process. It should be pointed out that the practice of Hindu Tantra is dedicated to the opening up of zones of perception in the female energetic body. When these zones of perception are all in synch, it results in a grand opening of the third eye.

Yin, however, is not limited to just the perception of the eye but represents the female energy or receptive nature of the universe. When we consider this in relation to *ayin* or the eye, we see *yin* or *jinn* as being equivalent to the entire process of perception. This ties into the theory of a Magick Mirror or a genie who can grant your wish. Both of these instruments are supposed to be self-reflective and give back what you put out. Theoretically, a genie or jinn can grant your wish because he or she is not only receptive to your desire but to the frequencies which allow for manifestation to take place. In order for you to accomplish such by yourself, you would either require the perception of the jinn or the ability to work in concert with them.

The idea of a jinn granting your wish is very important when we consider the Sanskrit meaning of the aforementioned word *sidhe* which we have already recognized as a fairy or cat spirit. Besides being the root for the name *Sidhartha*, the Sanskrit meaning for *sidhe* is "he who has achieved his wishes" or "he who has obtained his goal." The Buddha represents someone who is very clearheaded. In other words, he can *see* the forest from the trees and has a clear vantage point. He can assess importances and thereby achieve what he sets out to do.

Based upon what has been presented thus far, the expressions of *yin, jinn, ayin, og, and oc* all represent the eye. When we consider the aforementioned existential relationship to the godhead, it is ironic that the word *eye* is not only a homonym of *I* but that both words are intrinsically linked to the proposition of a quantum observer. Without an *eye* or an *I*, you have no quantum observer. While *eye* is usually thought to be limited to "seeing," *I* is actually more representative of the entire range of perceptions of the observer. The prospect of perception is not only part and parcel of the quantum observer, it is also the only means by which the quantum observer can evaluate and be evaluated.

Conventional physics as well as modern cutting-edge quantum physics is modified by the ability of the observers to perceive. When we consider the yin aspects of the female energies referred to previously, we can readily observe or conclude for ourselves that modern physicists are unable to comprehend a cohesive unified field theory because their perceptions are deficient. This yin aspect of perception, symbolizing the feminine energy spoken of by the Kabbalists, is indeed the unifying aspect of consciousness or anything that might be termed a "Unified Field Theory."

This feminine aspect of the unified field surfaces in the name *Eve* which equates to the word *eye*. The most obvious association of these words is that the *y* and *v* are convertible. In German, a *v* sound is not only pronounced as a *w*, it is written as one. The letters *y* and *w* are both convertible as vowels. It is also noteworthy that if you slice off the bottom of the *y* in *eye*, you get *eve*.

In addition to the above, *The Key* by Philip Cohane indicates that Oc or Og is the name of a god or goddess who replaced an earlier version that was known as Hawwah, Ava, or Eve. These names all relate to the magic land of Avalon, also known as the land of the Blue Apples of immortality. Once again, we are back to the fountain of youth and everlasting life.

We see this theme of Eve and the idyllic paradise of Eden emerging in the Norse religion where Odin sacrifices an eye in return for wisdom. In other words, through his eye, he obtains the secrets of the universe. The name *Odin* equates to *Eden.*

The Bible tells us that Eve receives the wisdom of the serpent and is kicked out of Eden, but it does not tell us the antidote for the serpent which was a key feature of the Egyptian religion and that is the cat. The cat represents felicity and emotions which are both maternal, empathic and positive. Although the cat was the key to the Egyptian religion, the word *cat* does not appear in *The Bible*.

The absence of feminine energy in this universe parallels Eve being cast out of the Garden of Eden. She was, however, cast out without the knowledge of the cat which also represents the gateway back to Eden, Avalon, or Og. The analogy of Eve being cast out is clearly symbolic of what happened to the original name for God which was, in fact, *IEVE* and pronounced as *Eve*.

In the Phoenician Paleo-Hebrew language of Canaan, the name of God was *IEVE*. If you compare the original writing for this word in Phoenician, you will find it hauntingly similar to how it is spelled and written in Arabic, Hebrew, Japanese, Chinese, and Sanskrit. When you strip away all of the ignorance caused by transliteration with regard to phonetics and their representative letters, *IEVE* was pronounced in the same way that we say *Eve*. In other words, the name for the Creator was *IEVE* or Eve.

The so-called Fall from Grace is very much evident in the name IEVE itself when it was transliterated into *YHVH, YHWH,* or *JHVH.* These words were pronounced with *avah* and *ovah* which mean "perverted, crooked or twisted." They are synonyms for evil as well. Someone was having a field day with the name of *IEVE,* and they were throwing away the key to understanding as well.

If for any reason, the preceding information disturbs you or makes you feel upset, do not distress. Just as the jinn are double-sided, so is the Creative Principle. You have to learn how to negotiate duality if you going to fully function in this universe. Duality is a part of the landscape. The key to understanding duality, however, is perception. Just as the feminine energy has been lost so has the ability to perceive. This applies not only to the ability to perceive the feminine but to perception in general which is, after all, a yin proposition. We can conclude from all of this that the universe is the way it is because we cannot perceive properly. We can further extrapolate upon this to say that the universe is the way it is because it is either incapable of or does not have the means of perceiving, filtering, and processing perceptions.

I did not realize it at the time, but my search for the lost tradition of Oc ended up in an all-out phonetic and etymological assault on the godhead. While I did not find a specific tradition of Oc, I arrived at the basic constituents of something that I consider to be far more valuable. In actual fact, I stumbled upon a magical formula which suggests a fountain of youth. More importantly, events and circumstances in life were presented to me that eventually enabled me to activate this formula. In other words, I discovered an actual fountain of youth. If that sounds too incredible to be true, I can understand how you feel. What happened to me, however, was indeed incredible.

I will begin my own presentation of what I learned with the formula I stumbled upon. It is arcane and very esoteric, but it works.

39

PERCEPTION

When we perceive, we are taking in information. When we express ourselves in language, we are reflecting back ideas that were previously taken in and processed. Expressions of an idea in different languages are reflective of an essence of what is being described or originally observed. That is why there is a commonality in certain words that goes back to a root idea. Sometimes this root idea is intertwined with other roots or concepts.

The etymology of the word *perception* is very important because it is the nexus point of all the potential problems that can and do surround the quantum observer or spiritual being. All problems he or she might have can be reduced to the nature of perception. The word *perception* derives from an Old Norse French word *percipere*, to perceive, which means "to take in or grasp." This is not much different from the modern French word for *perception* which is *perspicacité*.

These French etymologies are interesting for two reasons. First, they might be somewhat comparable to the original word in Languedoc, whatever that might be. Second, both words are close to *perspire* which comes from the Latin *persipirare* which means "to blow or breathe constantly" from *per*, meaning "through" and *spirare*, meaning "to breathe." The word *spirare* evolved into the Latin word *spiritus* which means "soul, courage, vigor, or breath." This data trail tells us that the very essence of the word *perception* is tied to the spirit or quantum observer as well as his/her breath. A look at other languages reveals some other interesting tie-ins.

In Icelandic, perception is referred to as *skynjun* which sounds like *sky jinn* or *scrye jinn.* To *scrye* means to divine or to see through the means of a crystal ball or stone. In Romanian and Dutch, the words for *perception* are *intelelegere* and *intelligens* respectively. These latter two words suggest that filing information and responding to it is also a key part of perception.

In the last chapter, I referred to an esoteric formula I stumbled across. This was discovered when I broke down the English word *perception* as *per+cep+tion* which also equates to *par+copt+shin.* As per earlier passages in this book, this can be equated to the following:

*par = pyr (*as in fire or pyramid*), pharaoh, or parthogenesis*
copt = blue, copper, Egyptian or "cat" if the "p" is silent
shin = spirit, heart, change, or tooth

Par represents the fire of the Shekinah Glory and its manifestation in the capstone of the Great Pyramid. It is lit by the pharaoh who is the interpreter between heaven and earth and sees both worlds. The pharaoh can also be considered to be representative of the quantum observer of the collective conscious. *Parthogenesis* is also important here because the pharoah can be either male or female. *Par* in this sense refers to a virgin which refers to *virtue*, meaning "power" or even "power of the *gin* or *jinn.*"

Copt represents the original blue Egyptians who built the Sphinx and were known as *fellas* (suggestive of feline) in Old Egyptian. They were the Moors, Mauresh, or cat-headed creatures. In later days, their descendants became known as Copts. The cat concept can also be seen in *perspicacacité*, the French word for perception where *cité* refers to *sidhe* or *cat*.

Shin is the secret word of Freemasonry which means "heart, change, spirit or teeth" and also refers to *Jesus* or the *Shekinah Glory*. My book, *Synchronicity and the Seventh Seal* gives a detailed treatise on the meaning of this word and its implications.

Ironically, the above breakdown includes most of the key threads which have already been discussed in this book and include: the Blue Race, the virgin birth, the cat, the pharaohs, and the elements of the Ark of the Covenant. These fit in with the two quantum observers implied in the analogy of the Olive Trees.

The two Olive Trees represent you and the godhead. We can call this godhead God, the Goddess, the All-Seeing Eye or the Creative Principle. The important point is that the End of Time is represented by two quantum observers: YOU and the godhead. To reach the End of Time, you need to be able to correlate or reconcile your perception with that of the godhead.

When it comes to humanity as a collective whole, there are other implication at work. In an ideal civilization, the pharaoh functions on behalf of the godhead as he or she can, like the cat, see into both worlds and thereby connect the heaven and the earth. He does this through the activation of the Sphinx which symbolizes the combination of the constellations Virgo (the virgin) and Leo (the cat). As a cat, the Sphinx is a gateway between the worlds. The Sphinx also executes a virgin birth which is symbolized by the fire of the Shekinah Glory or *shin*. This fire or Shekinah Glory resides within the capstone of the Great Pyramid. The pharoah's job is to maintain the fire and to keep the "Christ Consciousness" alive. He does this through the healing power of the Lion's Paw* (also represented by the paw of the Sphinx) which is the technique attributed to Solomon by which he could raise the dead.

Any of the above terms are interchangeable with other possible terms. It is not really a religious formula but one by which a pharaoh or a Christ can act as a healing modality or as a traffic cop between the heaven and the earth. This formula is the acme of perception whereby the entire universe, so to speak, is demonstrating self-referential intelligence and acting as a cohesive unit that is capable of self-correction.

What might seem much more relevant to you is that there is also a microcosmic aspect of this formula that applies to the individual. What is referred to as the qwa or kwa in Oriental martial arts represents the pyramid. This is a portion of the body below your waist that is viewed to conform to an upside down triangle or pyramid. The base of the pyramid would be at your waist. You play the role of the pharaoh in your own world by activating the sphincter (note the comparison to the word *sphinx*) and thereby lighting and then maintaining an energetic fire in the center of the qwa. This is a form of activating kundalini and begins with lifting

* It should be noted that studies have shown that the sound of a cats purr can actually heal bodily afflictions.

the sphincter or, more specifically, the anus. At the same time as you lift the anus, breathe deeply. Just as air is needed to maintain a fire, so is the breath needed to maintain this energetic fire.

What I have stated here might seem a bit too esoteric, but it is extremely important with regard to reconciling your perception with the godhead. All I have given you here, at best, is a realization or "intellectualization." It only becomes truly meaningful when you literally activate the breath, but we will get to that later. At this point, I only expect you to grasp this process with your intellect.

This formula represents perception, but most people have lost their ability to perceive to the full extent they are capable of. Keep in mind, humans only use a small percentage of their brains. The primary reason they are not fully able to perceive is that their brains are literally oxygen deprived. So is the entire body. Your lungs work at about five percent capacity and even lower in some cases. This is why the above analogy of the breath is mentioned. It is far more important than you realize.

The etymology of *Eve* plays into this principle very well. We can play around with the word *perceive* and view it as *per* + *c* + *eive*. If you make the *c* silent, you have "*par eve*" which can mean "the fire of Eve" or even refer to Eve as the pharoah. This word approach is not a stretch at all when you study the Hebraic derivation of *Eve* which comes from the Hebrew *chavvah* which means "living one" or "source of life." *Chavvah* is a particularly interesting word because it derives from two earlier words where the letters *y* and *v* are demonstrated to be convertible: *chavah* = breath and *chayah* = to live. The very essence of life is thus embodied in the name of *Eve* as breath and life go hand-in-hand. It is, after all, the act of breathing that makes one alive.

In practical human terms, the breath is the key to the entire formula. It sounds too simple, but it is true and will be explained in more detail later. At the time I stumbled upon the various associations connected with Og and Oc, I had no idea of what I have since figured out and written here. What is amazing to me is that, even though I did not know it, the elements of this formula were swirling around me and were starting to taking shape. This applied to the microcosm (myself) as well as the macrocosm. Before we get to that, however, there is another stopping point and this concerns my own personal journey into the Land of Og.

40

CERRIDWEN

The legend of Tir n' nÓg contains a very complex mythology that runs so deep into the collective unconscious that it is unlikely that it was concocted by one particular mythographer. As is typical with myths, it was arrived at by repetitions of various stories that were contoured and blended with different variations that best represented the expression of the collective soul of humanity of that geographical region at a particular time period.

The patron goddess of Tir na nÓg is Cerridwen whose cauldron was known as the "Cauldron of Regeneration." Through this magical cauldron, Cerridwen represents the mysterious process by which old life is renewed. All of this, of course, is a very adequate metaphor for a fountain of youth. This cauldron contained a substance known as Greal or Graal which Cerridwen concocted for her son Afagdu who was unsightly and dull. The Graal would give him inspiration, intelligence, wisdom, and knowledge, all things that Cerridwen was capable of dispensing.

The keeper of this cauldron was Gwion (meaning "white") who was a boy. As a keeper is also a jinn, we can consider him as the white jinn. While keeping guard of the heated cauldron, some of the Graal boiled up and spurted out with three drops landing upon the finger of Gwion. Feeling the pain of the heat, he took his finger into his mouth to ease the discomfort. He thus consumed the Graal whereupon he became enlightened of all things, past and future. Knowing that Cerridwen would be angry at him for taking the knowledge that was meant for her son, he feared for his life.

Gwion then turned himself into a hare and ran away, but Cerridwen turned into a greyhound and pursued him. Gwion then turned into a fish and swam away, but Cerridwen changed into an otter and kept up the pursuit. He then turned into a bird and she a hawk. Finally, he turned himself into a grain of corn, but Cerridwen became a hen and ate the grain of corn. Nine months later, the grain of corn gestated into a baby and Cerridwen had another son. When she realized it was Gwion, she cast him away in disgust. In his new incarnation, Gwion was rescued by a prince and became known as Taliesin who gave Mankind the Ogham language.

This entire story is rife with symbolism. The Graal symbolizes the Holy Grail which is really the cauldron of regeneration. The idea of placing the blood of Christ into the grail is symbolic of earlier menstrual rites of regeneration. In the personage of Afagdu, this legend also symbolizes the ignorance of the white race as Cerridwen was most often referred to as a white sow goddess. The knowledge instead went to Gwion, meaning white, who represents the redeemable aspects of the white race. Gwion, however, was trashed and created an independent tradition which is now obscure and lost.

Cerridwen was actually a version of the triple goddess and was represented in different ways. Her name is related to the Latin Ceres who was the mother of Persephone as well as central figure upon which the Eleusinian Mysteries were based. Ceres was a goddess of grains. At one point, the name of Cerridwen was influenced by the cults of Spain who had festivals in her honor. In Spanish, the word *cerdo* means pig.

In many respects, the archetype of the goddess Cerridwen contains carefully embedded elements of a key that you will not find elsewhere. This includes her relationship with bards. As the patron goddess of bards, she inspires them, censors them and exalts them to recognition.

The bards themselves are inextricably connected to her cauldron of regeneration. Myths and stories are the stock in trade of a bard. They are also the only means by which the mythos or consciousness of a population can restore itself. If the existing bards cannot tell adequate social truths for the time or era that they live in, they or other bards will have to go back to the drawing board and keep working until the social truths are iterated and conveyed.

This is a never-ending process and is indeed why she rules the bards. As the regenerator, Cerridwen will make sure that the right stories are told so as to produce the desired effect. Thus, when we consider Cerridwen, we are really talking about the agents of regeneration at work. They activate the bards who make a representation of Cerridwen or some other goddess or god.

The etymology of *Cerridwen* reveals more intrigue, particularly with regard to what we have already covered in this book. *Cerridwen* comes from *cerdd* which means at least two things: "artistic inspiration" and "pig." *Wen* means "white." Known as the White Sow Goddess, Cerridwen is also the White Lady of Inspiration and Death. With the theme of the sow so prominent in this goddess of Tir n' nÓg, it is obvious that the connection between *og* and *hog* is not an accident.

There is an even more mysterious correspondence at work in the name of *Cerridwen* when we consider *cerdd* and compare it to the word *aardvark*. *Cerdd* and *aard* are the same phoneme if you make the *c* in *cerdd* silent (just as you would not pronounce the *c* in the word Chanukkah). *Aardvark* is a very interesting word because it literally means "earth pig" which is equivalent to the Latin translation for *Jesus*. The actual etymology of *aardvark*, however, is a bit circular or inverted for our purposes.

Aardvark comes from the Dutch *aarde* (earth) and *vark* (pig). In Gaelic, *cerdd* refers to *pig* as while the Dutch *aarde* means "earth." This suggests that the pig is intrinsically tied to the earth (through the biochemistry of blood). The Dutch word *vark* is compelling because it contains *ark* and invites us to consider the role of the pig in Noah's Ark. *Vark* derives from *porc*, the Sansrkit word for *pig*, but it also connotes *orc* when the *p* is silent. The word *orc* was popularized by J.R.R. Tolkein, but it is also a regular English word that refers to a genetic monstrosity. Whichever way we look at it, there is no question that the legends of Cerridwen, the White Sow Goddess, persuade us to take very seriously the previously presented hypothesis with regard to pig blood.

As you can see, the correspondences between Cerridwen and Christ are amazing. Both are obviously archetypes of regeneration and everlasting life. These characteristics are also expressed in the land of Og itself. The entire association with these archetypes and the pig, however, contains a certain contradiction. As was said earlier, there is a Biblical story about Jesus casting evil spirits into pigs and thereby killing them. On the other hand, Latin and Italian transliterations of the name *Yeshua* deliberately convey "earth pig." The same can be said of Cerridwen who, in her mythical form as a white sow, is routinely portrayed as consuming the flesh of men. This is her most frightening aspect, but it is not her only aspect. She is also portrayed as a goddess who embraces positive elements.

As was presented earlier, the DNA of Mankind experienced either an evolutionary or deliberate alteration whereby it was amalgamated with pig DNA to the point where man could survive. It was an evolutionary construct that enabled the Blue Race to survive in a new environment. More importantly, and whether or not this is exactly what happened, something was lost in the equation and this loss was substantial. This loss includes the full use of the brain and other aspects of consciousness.

The theories presented here are primarily guideposts, and the most solid guidepost we have is that something noteworthy happened with regard to the DNA of the pig. Although we do not have all of the information, we are given yet another clue by the now familiar archetype of Cerridwen. To say that this clue is important is a great understatement because mythographers laid the foundation stone of this archetype with the most important mystery of our modern esoteric world: the "word" or letter *shin*.

Although virtually no one in modern society would recognize it, the mystery behind *shin* surfaces in various depictions of Cerridwen where she is pictured with a necklace of crescents which are actually representations of the teeth of a boar or a hog. These are referred to as moon-teeth as they are in the shape of a crescent and are sacred to her feminine aspect. These moon-teeth are the very reason why the Hebrew letter *shin* means "tooth."

The letter *shin* is the root of Shinar, the capital city of ancient Babylon. In that civilization, *shin* referred to the moon or crescent moon and this was eventually adopted as the symbol of Islam. *Shin* or *Shinar* also refers to the *shining* or the reflective (feminine) quality of the moon. In summary, *shin* referred to the feminine lunar current long before it was adopted by the Hebrews as "tooth," but the crescent teeth of the boar explain how and why it was adopted. The boar not only represented the highest level of sacredness, it contained a hidden secret which was symbolized in its tooth: *shin*.

Evolving into the centerpiece of Freemasonry, *shin* was the secret word that Hiram Abiff was killed for when he refused to reveal it. As an esoteric concept, *shin* is so definitive and expository of the universal mystery, including its hidden aspect, that it was only natural that it was "chosen" as the sacred and secret "word" of Freemasonry.

As Babalon refers to the "gateway of the lion," the fact that Shinar was the name of the capital demonstrates that the principle of *shin* was at the kernel of this ancient civilization that has been portrayed as the Gateway to God. The corollary is that knowledge of this mystery will propel you through the Gateway yourself.

Keep in mind that what is presented here is not just a matter for intellectual or esoteric edification. As per previous explanations of other meanings for *shin*, moon-teeth would also refer to *change, spirit,* and *heart*. These words speak for themselves. One merely has to study the five elements (*yod-he-shin-vau-he*) and how they apply to your own life and then move accordingly. If you want change in your personal life, you can apply the *shin* principle by looking into your heart and your spirit and the change needed will speak for itself.

Shin changes and catalyzes or "alchemizes" the other four elements so as to make all things possible. It is the essential component of regeneration. When Solomon resurrects Hiram Abiff, he does not say the magic "word" of *shin*, but rather uses the Lion's Paw or Lion's Grip. This is yet another analogy because the paws of a lion or sphinx contain five digits which are meant to represent the five elements or points of the pentagram known as pentagrammaton. This is a roundabout way of referring to the same principle.

As Cerridwen, through her moon-teeth, represents *shin* and the mysteries of Freemasonry, her mythical archetype has been cleverly arrived at. As a white sow goddess, her legacy was also imbedded into the occult mysteries of Exodus. She thus represents the essential mystery with regard to the paradigm of Mankind.

All of this makes Cerridwen a very compelling figure, but there is another aspect to her which literally makes the current of these pages you are reading come alive. This has to do with her connection to the bards. In the particular case of this book and its predecessor, *The Montauk Book of the Dead*, I am referring to the dream sequences in both books which all take place in the green backdrop of Tir na nÓg.

At the time those dream sequences were written, I was only vaguely aware of the Land of Og and had most certainly never heard of Tir na nÓg. As a writer, I arrived at the green backdrop and the concept of the Bard of Bards by employing the stream of consciousness. To my surprise, the environment I had created in the dream sequences literally began to talk back to me. The Blue Lady is a logical archetype when it comes to the Celtic tie-ins, but I had no idea that the elements of this book would blend together to the degree that they have or in the way that they have. The Blue Lady apparently has an agenda of her own.

THE DREAM — PART III

My relationship with the Blue Lady had either evolved into or was mimicking something along the lines of a love fantasy. Her nakedness and beauty had clearly provoked this sort of response. It was very clear, however, that there was much more going on here than met the eye or what might be termed "observable perception." When you reduce sex and its accoutrements to the lowest common denominator, it proves itself to be, primarily, a gateway. In the ordinary experiences of ordinary human beings, this gateway is most commonly expressed as the gateway into the universe.

"More than anything," said the Blue Lady, "the Black Virgin is symbolic of a gateway. She is much more than that; but first and foremost, she represents a gateway. The shape you know as the Vesica Pisces represents her yoni which is also a portal to other worlds. Out of this yoni comes the *shin* which is made manifest in the moonflower. This is the instrument of change and is why *shin* means "moon." It is not only the flowering of the feminine energy, it is the catalyst by which Creation flows into and out of the world."

"And the olive?" I asked.

"The olive is the instrument of this magical feminine force and it is also representative of a gate and the wisdom of such. Representing *aleph* or *alpha*, it represents the birth or the beginning.

"Now, she said, "go to the City of the Golden Gates."

As the Blue Lady said these last words, her body became translucent and I could see the Golden Gate Bridge in the city of San Francisco. This was not the City of the Golden Gates, I thought to myself.

"It is for <u>you</u>," she said. "Remember!"

I then remembered that I had decided to become a part of the Sea Organization in that city. Oddly, this decision took place on California Street, a name which would resonate strongly with the contents of this book. I spent my nights on California Street hovering over my body in an out-of-body state. The great exteriorization had first occurred on Olive Drive in Davis, but San Francisco was the gateway I would pass through on my way to L. Ron Hubbard.

"Remember!" she commanded once again.

I could now see myself in the year of 1982. I was on leave from the Sea Organization and had been visiting my friends in Davis. It was the second year in a row that I had done so. At that time, I was very happy with myself and had reached a peak with regard to various personal abilities, all of which had stemmed from my experiences with exteriorization in Scientology. On the other hand, the organization of Scientology had experienced severe problems on many fronts. As for myself, I was very happy.

For the second year in a row, my friends and I had attended a ball game at Candlestick Park on the eve of my departure. They would take me to a nearby motel after the game, and I would find my way to the airport the next day. At that time, San Francisco represented no special magic to me. It was only a way-station on the way home. I had forgotten about the magical experiences I had known ten years earlier. The City, however, did not forget me.

Having considerable time to kill, I deposited my luggage at a bus terminal. From there, I walked up and down Market Street to find something to do. As I recall, it was a Sunday and not much was open. There were many movie theaters but nothing appealed to me. Finally, I saw something that did, and it was a movie entitled *The Arabian Nights*. For a long time, I had wanted to learn about these tales. To a significant degree, it was L. Ron Hubbard himself who had inspired me in this regard. He sometimes referred to them as an inspiration for his work, particularly with his zest for what he termed "the incredible and fantastic." It was apparent to me that his impetus for creating the most advanced levels of Scientology was deeply connected to the phenomena described in the series of tales that are known as *The Arabian Nights*.

Walking into the lobby of a theater that had once been a proud establishment, it was observable that maintenance was no longer a primary concern. It was seedy. Entering the theater itself, I was taken aback. The house was about one-third full, but it consisted of men only and all were sitting alone. There were about two to three seats between each man. Maneuvering for an empty seat where I could sit alone, I could feel the soda-laden floor sticking hard to the leather bottoms of my shoes. As this was San Francisco, I hoped that the sticky substance on the floor was only soda. Besides these seedy conditions, there was a movie on the screen that was giving me encouragement to get up and leave. It was a version of Chaucer's *Canterbury Tales* and featured an angel escorting a man to hell or purgatory. The scene was replete with grotesque demons who were primarily defecating and urinating in many different ways and on particular people. I did not want to see this movie at all, but I knew from the schedule that it was almost over and I waited it out. To my relief, it soon ended. With some trepidation, I was now ready for the feature I had come to see.

Looking back, these very lonely men and the demons in the *Cantebury Tales* were acting as the gargoyles of the gate that might prevent me from experiencing what turned out to be a remarkable initiation and one that I would not fully appreciate for decades.

At this point in my life, I had experienced wonderful success with Hubbard's OT levels* (as discussed in *The Montauk Book of the Dead*). The sky was the limit as far as I was concerned, and I was convinced that something in *The Arabian Nights* would inspire me or clue me in on some aspect of the supernatural that would increase by own abilities. I was following my own intuition which I knew to be very accurate.

As it turned out, *The Arabian Nights* proved itself to be a very powerful aesthetic vehicle for me which would literally transport me into what might loosely be termed "the world of the gods." In Scientology, we called it "OT" or the state of Operating Thetan. It means that you as a spirit were trafficking with the creative forces of the universe. *The Arabian Nights* derives its power from its stunning depiction of the wills of various individuals. More importantly, these wills transfer and cross-correlate with the wills of others which include the spirit realm and Allah as well. Although the name *God* is utilized, it was very clear to me that Allah was portrayed as the supreme instrument of synchronicity.

The Arabian Nights is an Italian movie by director Pier Pablo Pasolini and was released in 1974. The characters speak Italian but there are English subtitles. The background features Moorish and Oriental architecture and reaches across the countries of Yemen, Iran, India and Nepal. The primitive conditions of the modern day

* In their most exalted aspects, the OT levels of Scientology induced a state of mind where literally anything could be accomplished, including miracles. The effectiveness and demonstrable results of these levels, however, were largely dependent upon the thoughts, skills and relative predisposition of the quantum observer concerned. There were no guarantees.

cities and dwellings give the impression that you are looking through a time capsule.

The film is very subtle as dreams are interwoven with astonishing tales which feature lust, base emotions, selfishness, trust, passion, compassion, and the highest nobility of the human spirit. It begins with a black Moorish slave girl being auctioned off in the market place. Oddly, the seller insists that she can only be sold to someone she would approve of. As the old and wealthy men bid for her, she rejects them all and insults them in the process. It is clear she will accept no one until she sees a young man in the crowd who is not even bidding. He has no money to speak of, but he is cajoled to bid and wins her. Admitting he has no money to pay, the slave girl gives him a bag of coins to pay the fee and she belongs to him. This is highly symbolic as the woman is enslaved yet she is directing the action and determining the outcome. In other words, her power is hidden.

As the couple begin to enjoy each other immensely, an old man who was rejected by her sets a trap. He hires a Christian to kidnap the slave girl and this succeeds. The slave girl suffers misadventures until she wisely uses her sensuality on her jailor in order to escape. Fleeing through the desert on a horse, her head is wrapped in a turban as she comes upon a Moorish city of old. The population of the city is waiting outside the walls for the next man to appear from the desert. As their king has just died, the next man to appear will be declared king. Due to the turban on her head, they assume the slave girl is a man and take her to the palace where she will marry the princess that evening. If she refuses, she will be thrown from the tower. In the privacy of the royal bedroom, the slave girl reveals herself as a woman but the princess promises to keep the secret and help her find her owner, the man she loves.

The movie then proceeds into various dream sequences with a pervading theme: "The truth lies not in one dream but in many dreams." In each vignette, the intent and integrity of the individuals concerned are the key instruments in how they make out in life. The margin between life and death is mystical but also very clear.

After various tales are played out, the distraught owner of the slave girl continues to seek her out. Earlier tales depict his frustrations and misadventures in trying to find her. Finally, he is so overwhelmed by his grief that he wants to die. Walking into the desert, he is stunned to come across a mighty male lion. He yields to the lion and asks to be killed as life is not worth living. The lion, however, has a different agenda and motions the man to follow him. Shocked by the lion's behavior, the man follows the lion to the city where his slave now lives. Having done his job, the lion goes on his own way. The man enters the city where he is soon arrested for violating a taboo that is worthy of death. Taken to the king for punishment, he does not know that the king is really his female slave who he has been seeking. She takes him to the royal bedroom where she reveals herself to him in secret. All is well.

Besides the statement that the truth lies in many dreams, there are many other subtle themes in this picture. The ending suggests there is not only secret goodness in the stewardship of this universe but that you can access it by being true to your heart and compassionate to others as well. In this movie, the winds of synchronicity were paramount. For some, it brought happiness; for others, death or misery. The lion also appears as not only a gate-keeper but THE monumental gate-keeper who delivers the resolution to the main players in the movie.

Perhaps the most important theme is that the slave possesses the determination of her own destiny. She not only chooses her owner but becomes king of the realm, all the time keeping the fact that she is a woman secret. While the more foreboding aspects of the female energy are not ignored, the movie also contains many scenes of extreme spiritual generosity where women conspire to do the right thing by acting on inspiration that is too seldom seen or contemplated in American culture.

For me, the more noble aspects of this movie resonated inside of me and touched me in a way that is not easy to describe other than saying it was supernatural. In other words, it touched the elemental or archetypal forces inside of me that were most closely connected to the creative principles which placed me in this universe in the first place. When I say "placed," however, I must make a subtle distinction. As a quantum observer, I was placed into this world through the birth process, just like all of you, but that does not mean I had nothing to do with the placing process. In Dianetics and Scientology, I had explored this placing process extensively as well as my reactions and considerations concerning it. I felt like I now had some power to say something about it.

I could not, however, change reality to the point where I could abrogate my entire life and start over. There is always the option of suicide, of course, but that has extreme consequences and was not even a slight consideration. I did not need to start over. The point is, however, I felt that I was in touch with the very elemental forces, guardian angels, or whatever you want to call them, that assisted or directed me into the human life I was now experiencing. These characters had placed me and were familiar with my life destiny and purpose from a higher plane. To me, this experience was sort of like going back to visit your parents just after you finished college and got your first real job. They are happy for you, but if you mention that you are not on the right track, they are likely to respond by helping you get on the right track.

As for myself, I was not on the wrong track but was merely woken up by the miraculous processes depicted in this movie of wills, jinn, and synchronicity. It was as if I had been waiting my entire life to see this movie and what it would unleash inside of me. The archetypal forces were at my disposal. How would I use them?

My wisdom in such matters was to just sit back and do nothing. I was too calm and collected to be sophomoric or manic about all this. When I returned home to Florida, I shared this experience with a couple of friends who understood and were happy for me. Other than that, life went on as usual — if a Scientology life can ever be considered usual.

Soon after returning, I was sort of "promoted" off of my job which was to prove to be a maneuver that would convenience the absolute downfall of Scientology management. I was put on full time training which only further enabled me to contemplate the lofty energies residing within me that had been inspired by *The Arabian Nights*. It was during this period that I was able to, in so many words, lift myself out of my entire life, peer into the future and decide what I wanted to do. Once again, the sky was the limit. I was not only in concert with the aforementioned energies I have spoken of, I was able to dictate what I wanted. This is somewhat akin to Solomon commanding the jinn, but I would not dare put it on that level. It is a parallel analogy only, and these jinn were more specific to myself.

At that point in my life, I am quite sure that if I decided to become a president of a major corporation, a member of a famous rock band, or an important politician, that I could have invoked the precise forces into my life that would have eventuated such a position. I supposed I could even have decided to become the richest person in the world. My decision process, however, was not so small-minded or selfish. In such a position, I knew that what I decided would last with me forever and such a position as I had reached should not be abused or taken lightly. Reflecting upon the more noble characters in the movie, I sought out the highest and most virtuous path I could manifest. Thinking of my parents and how they had died so violently, I was inspired to make a permanent resolution that would dissolve all hurtful mechanical conditions of existence. I was not only thinking of my parents but for all living creatures. My thoughts were for others as I was not in any personal pain and feeling quite well. I turned this resolution over to the forces of the universe and let it go.

Having contemplated these matters on the third story patio of the Heart of Clearwater motel, I went downstairs to where my car was parked. Looking up to my right, I saw the most spectacular and largest display of fireworks I have ever seen, at least in terms of one single skyrocket. This was not a fireworks display, however, because it appeared in what was probably no more than a second. It was as clear as day, however, and only for a short time. I knew it had something to do with paranormal phenomena, and I was careful not to deny that it had occurred. Soon after, a friend of mine named Cat came by, and I told her what I had witnessed.

"Oh yeah," she said. "I see strange stuff over there all the time." She was referring to an area over a vacant lot on Drew Street in Clearwater, not too far from Jack Russell Stadium and even closer to the GTE antenna structure. Years later, I would take a friend of mine to the area. He mentioned that he had once seen a UFO over the same area.

Over a decade later, the Montauk Shaman would explain to me what had happened, but she had no knowledge of this incident.

"You have gone to a place where your friends could not go," she said. "You have been there and have returned."

This is a paraphrase, but she indicated that I was here to accomplish great things and bridge worlds together. I should also add that she is so complimentary about me in general that it makes me a little cautious. She puts me on a pedestal, but she would be quick to add that I belong there. After all, she is enamored of the fact that I have been the biggest public advocate for the proper recognition of the Montauk tribe.

In any case, it is clear that the jinn were at work, and it was their job to change my life so that I could begin to accomplish what I myself had mandated. This would result in a rather sudden and unexpected marriage and my eventual departure from the Sea Organization and the Church of Scientology. My marriage would take me to Long Island where I would eventually connect with Preston Nichols and the legends of the Montauk Project. As soon as I met Preston, my life began to unfold in a series of magical associations and synchronicities.

What is probably more amazing is that the information revealed in *The Montauk Project: Experiments in Time* is only scratching the surface of what is mandated to be a very long and extensive process. As much change as that book created in the world, and I am rather tired of talking and writing about it, that change is only the beginning. The restoration of the Montauks is also a very key point and that still has a long way to go. We will be touching upon that later on in this book.

In the context of the dream, the Blue Lady spoke to me.

"You have now successfully recalled the time period where you sowed the seeds of your own fate."

"You brought me there," I said.

"No," she replied. "You brought yourself there. I have only assisted you in recalling your power."

The Blue Lady then stood back and stretched out her hands as if she was going to turn into a bird and fly away. She did not, however, turn into a bird. Instead, she began to whirl like a dervish until only a spiral of energy could be seen. When the spiral slowed down, she returned but in a different form. She was a white sow with protruding tusks and an array of pink teats. In her mouth was an apple.

"I am the sacrifice which made this world possible," she said. "I gave the blood to humans to make their lives livable."

"But something was lost in the process," I said.

"And that is why you are here," she replied.

The apple in her mouth fell to the ground and split in half so that a transverse cut of the fruit was made. A pentagram could be seen at the center of each part of the apple. Spirals began to swirl out of the center of each pentagram. One swirl enveloped her pig formation and disappeared. The other swirl eventually slowed down until it revealed the Blue Lady again. This time, however, she wore a necklace of crescent-shaped teeth. No longer naked, she wore the skins of a boar over her own blue skin.

"Now you are Cerridwen," I said.

"Yes, and it is time you discussed how you met me as Cerridwen," she replied.

"I only discovered Cerridwen as a result of my research into the Land of Og," I answered. "In writing this book, I discovered that she is just one aspect of yourself, the Blue Lady of the Lake."

"Tell your audience what else happened and how it all worked," she said.

41

DREAM MAGIC

As was stated earlier, *shin* represents the secret formula by which the universe is created and changed. *Shin* is a creative process. Dreams are a part of *shin*, and they represent the bridge between the world that is awake and the world that is asleep. To understand and interact with the creative process is very important for all living individuals because they are already a part of the Universal Creative Process which is sometimes called God.

Writing this book has been a living process as well as a creative one. The two words go hand-in-hand. Reading this book is also a creative process. In the process of writing it, however, the bizarre and phenomenal nature of this process became overwhelming as I discovered the archetype of Cerridwen.

The Blue Lady of the Lake has appeared in my dream vignettes because she was the perfect archetype which represented my creative and tailored rendition of the Land of Og. She appears in the dream sequences in this book as well as *The Montauk Book of the Dead.* These dreams are representative of the spiritual and energetic forces surrounding me when I wrote what I wrote.

Cerridwen came into my life in a most peculiar, significant, and interesting manner. I had heard the name before but had no idea of who she was or what she represented until writing this book. It was only through exploring the etymology of Ronald Reagan's name that I discovered that Og derived from Tir na nÓg. This opened up a lot of doors, and it was rather astonishing to learn of her correspondences with the pig, Jesus, and the white race.

As I first penned and studied the information in this book you have already read about Cerridwen, I just happened to be engaged in a profound spiritual exercise that is done in complete darkness. The exercise is designed to wake you up to your full potential and this includes accessing the dream state.

In the midst of this exercise, I was shocked to discover a rather profound portrayal of Cerridwen on a website that was describing a role playing game entitled *Teeth of the Moon Sow*. I do not know who the writers of the game are or what literary sources they were pulling from, but they conveyed the deepest and best rendition of Cerridwen that I have yet seen.

In their role playing game, they describe that Cerridwen, as the goddess of bards, held a great festival where bards were invited from all over in order to see who were the best. For me, this immediately conjured up the images I have already presented in the dream sequences of this book and its prequel. It was uncanny to say the least. Cerridwen was being substituted, so to speak, for my version of the Blue Lady. The two goddesses fit.

Possessing the power to destroy, foster, or enhance the position of a bard, Cerridwen would choose the ten bards she considered to be the best. They were then rewarded by her turning them into stones which are described as "teeth" or "moon teeth."

As I read this description, my eyes immediately focused on "moon teeth" because I clearly understood what was being implied, but I was more than a little surprised. There is no indication that the writers of the game have made the connection to *shin*. If they have, they have apparently remained silent. Mythology, however, is a self-regenerating process. As long as people write and tell stories, all truths will eventually resurface. Only the form of the stories and characters will change.

These "moon teeth," of course, represent the teeth of the moon sow. Stones represent wisdom, and by turning them into such, the chosen bards would receive the highest honor possible as their names would live forever. Out of these bards, the highest honor was given to only one who would be changed into the stone that would serve as Cerridwen's altar.

As none of the mythologies I have seen seem to be aware of the correspondences made in this book, it appears to me that the writers of this game have reached beyond themselves in their mythography. In any event, they have done a remarkable job of characterizing Cerridwen's most powerful aspects.

The writers of this game surpass themselves the most, or at least in terms of the most common myths of Cerridwen, when they describe the function of these stones or moon teeth as an acoustics chamber wherein a talented bard can stand in the center and manifest his dreams into literal reality. What can be accomplished in such a scenario is dependent upon the horsepower of the bard, but the potential is limitless. Essentially, the writers are describing a mind amplifier, but they do not use those words to describe it. It is nevertheless the same principle. This is the deepest aspect of the realm of Cerridwen, and it is a model by which you yourself can change reality.

What I have just described is only part of a role-playing game. I have never seen the game myself and do not play role-playing games. The game and the archetypes it depicts only came into my consciousness as a result of writing this living book.

As a result of what I was reading, I was now obliged to put myself in the so-called acoustics chamber of Cerridwen. This, however, happened by happenstance or synchronicity. It was not something I specifically willed. I was already in the midst of doing spiritual exercises which have to do with ancient Tibetan cave meditation. Instead of a cave, I was in a dark room. The specific exercise I was doing had to do with waking up the dreamer, but it is something you do while you are wide awake.

At the same time as I had been reading about a bard manifesting his dreams into reality, I was experiencing similar phenomena at the very same time. As I did my exercises, it occurred to me that my dream state was being activated in real life. The scenarios I had read about Cerridwen in the role playing game synchronized precisely with the scenarios depicted in my dreams with the Blue Lady. My research and writing were dovetailing precisely with my work in the dark room. This was an astonishing super synchronicity and something I did not expect.

My instructor for the cave meditation told me that it was a very powerful exercise and he was not kidding. I had suddenly found myself back in a similar state with regard to what I had described about my adventures with *The Arabian Nights*, but it was different this time. I now had over twenty-six years of experience.

The entire process was sort of the reverse of a lucid dream. In a lucid dream, you are dreaming when you suddenly become awake and are then able to direct your energy. In this instance, I was awake and began to connect to the dream state. This is a state of mind where you can literally create reality. It is exactly what happened to me in *The Arabian Nights* scenario. Testing it with small things, it was obvious that I could make another big decision that would change my destiny.

What was far more interesting to me, however, was the writing process itself. I had become my writing and it had become me. The Blue Lady I had written about in *The Montauk Book of the Dead*, through the personage of Cerridwen, had literally found her why into my psyche and had given me a gift I could not believe. It was as if the mythographers of *Teeth of the Moon Sow* had done her bidding as well as mine. The table had been set, and I was sitting in a state of consciousness where I knew I could literally manifest into being whatever I wanted. The only task for me was to simply choose what dream I wanted to manifest.

Standing in complete darkness, it was now time to make another decision. The original program to dissolve all hurtful mechanical conditions of existence was already in motion. I did not need to make major changes in my own life or career as these things were proceeding at their own pace. This was an opportunity to create something new that would, hopefully, augment the original program. There was no question that what I would create could or would have a powerful impact upon my readers. This made the decision quite easy, and it occurred in a matter of seconds. I simply decided that I wanted to empower the individuals reading this book. It is that plain and simple. That was all.

I did not even consider asking for money as such a request is shortsighted and can create a lot of problems. This not only includes the preoccupation of preserving and increasing it but an array of creatures who will want some of it and do anything they can to trick you out of it.

As you read the rest of this book, you will learn how my wish is coming true. Before I can put that in the proper context, however, it is appropriate that I fill you in on some other factors.

42

A QUANTUM TRAIL REVSITED

As I have already stated in this book, there was a considerable hiatus in my writing that lasted from 1997 until 2002, A significant amount of this lack of production had to do with recoils from the information I had already published. The olive synchronicities were always going on in the background and that was where my heart was, but I was unable to do any real writing other than my quarterly newsletter, *The Montauk Pulse*.

During 2001, I began to spend a lot of time with my psychic friend, Yonda, who is a very special person. I originally met her in 1991 when I began writing *The Montauk Project: Experiments in Time*. In order that I could have a visceral experience of what I was writing about, Preston advised me to go out to Montauk with a sensitive. When a friend of Yonda's heard about my quest, he put me in touch with her. Yonda's reputation was considerable and he thought she would be just perfect. She was perfect, but there was just one problem. Yonda had a boyfriend who was dead-set against her going out to Montauk or having much of anything to do with me. These were not issues of jealously but had to do with his own problems concerning the Montauk Project.

Yonda's boyfriend at that time was Michael, and he had originally been slated to write the book about the Montauk Project. He had already asked Preston, and I was just becoming acquainted to the scene. On an evening in November of 1990, I was visiting Preston's Space-Time Labs at an open-house event. There were several others there, including Michael. Preston demonstrated his music machine and mind amplifier. It was a wild night. By the end of it, Michael was frightened out of his skin. He could see that the stories and potentialities of what Preston discussed were more than mere legends. To him, they were viscerally real.

As the night ended, Michael expressed his edginess. I told him that if he ever changed his mind about writing a book on the Montauk Project then I would like to be next in line. He told me to go ahead because he no longer wanted anything to do with it. That story, in part, is how I came to write *The Montauk Project*. I did not jump into it however. I came to Preston's meetings at the Long Island Psychotronics Association and scoped out everything for about six months before negotiating a contract.

Yonda told me that Michael was so reactive about Montauk that he must have had something to do with it. He wanted her to have nothing to do with myself, Preston or Duncan. That explained his edginess. Due to these circumstances, Yonda and I parted ways before we really got to know each other. She did, however, say something very prophetic before we parted ways.

"This stuff is real, and you are in for much more than you bargained for," she said.

At that time, I was prepared to write Preston's fantastic story, but I neither believed it nor disbelieved it. As a matter of fact, I had not even been to Montauk at that point. Yonda's words, however, proved to be quite accurate. I certainly did get a whole lot more than I had bargained for. After that time, Yonda and I would occasionally run into each other but that was about it.

Nearly a decade later, I was going through the divorce process and ran into Yonda. She was no longer with Michael and told me that she was surprised to see that I was still alive. At the time she met me, she figured the Montauk goons would eventually knock me off. My ability to stay alive impressed her, and she became a very good friend. We started to hang out together, and she would sometimes visit me as well as my friend, Clyde, who lived with me during 2001. The three of us went out to Montauk, and the two of them began to do energy work at various points across Long Island. I usually did not go with them on these excursions.

I mention their energy work because it is tied to a very significant happening that occurred in 2001. Towards the very end of August, Yonda and Clyde went to Manhattan to do energy work.

Yonda was insistent on visiting the Twin Towers. Psychically, she picked up that something substantial was going to go down there. Weeks later, Clyde and I were travelling to New Jersey to transport a friend to her family in New Jersey. It was a most special day because the three of us had also decided to visit Ong's Hat,* New Jersey. Ten minutes into our trip, I heard a radio report that one of the Twin Towers had been hit. Next, we heard that the other tower had been hit. As we listened to various theories about a terrorist attack, I decided to make a mad dash for the Verrazano Bridge so that we could get to New Jersey and carry out our trip. I knew the bridges would be problematic. As we arrived in Queens, we could see the towers smoking and filling the Manhattan skyline. By the time we got to Brooklyn, both towers had fallen and the bridge was jammed. We turned around and went home. Yonda had been right.

During this time period, I wrote the original "parallel universe" story that begins my book *Synchronicity and the Seventh Seal.* Yonda and Clyde both read it and encouraged me to go with it and develop it. The *Seventh Seal* became the theme and title for the book as a result of my discussions with them. The book itself, however, was written for two primary reasons that ran parallel to each other. First, I needed to consolidate and summarize various synchronicities that had occurred in my research. Many of these concerned the Babalon Working. Secondarily, I had to exorcize apparent demons. By exorcism, I do not mean a ritualistic dramatization by a priest or shaman but more of a flushing of bad energy down the toilet. The demons, to their dismay, followed suit.

As a result of what I had written up to that point in my writing career, certain people had considerable problems. These were not

* Ong's Hat is an obscure location in the New Jersey Pine Barrens that was once the home of a rod and gun club that was frequented by physicists from Princeton. During the 1970's, a strange commune surfaced that not only retained the physics pedigree but added the alchemical mixture of hippies, Sufism, tantra, and hallucinogens. This commune allegedly was able to travel to parallel universes through mysterious egg-shaped devices. While the story sounds like science fiction, there are many tangible tie-ins which include scientific theory. The story of Ong's Hat was originally told in a popular e-book authored and complied by Joseph Matheny. Eventually, I collaborated with him and published a hard copy book entitled *Ong's Hat: The Beginning*. I should add that it is through the legends of Ong's Hat that I originally learned of the Moorish Science Temple who reportedly had an inside track on travelling in time. It is important to note that Moorish Science came into my consciousness through my interest in and pursuit of time travel.

my problems, but they were cluttering the environment and it was best to deal with them rather than ignore them. Ignoring usually works just fine, but things had gotten out of hand.

Essentially, various people were responding to the information I had presented in inappropriate ways. Some of this behavior manifested itself on the internet but certainly not all of it was online. Some of these problems emanated from so-called innocuous researchers who were "trying to discover the truth" about Montauk. Such people would pontificate but were under the influence of their own negativity in such a manner that they would reduce the subject to its lowest common denominator by emphasizing trauma-based mind control and sex. Sometimes, but not too often, I would be sniped at for having brought these matters to the attention of the public. More often, people would revel in this sewage as if they were pigs in mud.

In any event, I had to deal with the debris or residue of human beings whose "gray matter" had been stimulated into these matters. On a psychological level, it was as if I had demons roosting on my fence who were making noises and being obnoxious. It was as if all these creatures represented people who were listening to every word I had to say and we're expecting more. Their expectations, however, were determined by their own conditioned gray matter. It was apparent they wanted to hear about torture and trauma. If one is going to go anywhere in life, one has to move well beyond victimization and move in the direction of empowerment.

Writing *Seventh Seal* literally vanquished all of the negative energy referred to above. I tied up virtually every loose end I had been sitting on and presented it in a format that was unexpected. Further, the data was neither ghoulish nor terrifying. This is in stark contrast to what most writers have depicted with regard to the Babalon Working. Writing *Seventh Seal* freed me up considerably and enabled me to get on with whatever my next project might be. It was at this juncture that something very peculiar happened. It concerned Yonda and the mysterious playbill from The New Montauk Theatre, the one that inspired this book.

When I received the playbill originally, it was in a frame with a glass casing. Whenever a psychic was visiting, I would always bring it out and have them see what they could make of it. One hundred percent of the time, psychics came up with nothing.

One evening, when I had been showing the playbill to a particular psychic, the glass broke. This was not such a big deal in itself. I simply had to remove the glass and throw it away. It did, however, expose the original newspaper clipping to the air. In itself, this was not much of a problem either. What happened soon after, however, became a huge problem for me. The playbill had somehow become disconnected from the cardboard it was glued to and had disappeared. I was distressed.

Thinking I had already scanned it into my computer files, I searched my hard drive but could not find any trace of any such scan. Was I mistaken? The playbill was an integral part of the book I was to write, and this threw everything into a tailspin. For over a year, I looked for the playbill but could never find it. The cardboard stood out in my living room. Every time I passed it, I lamented that I had not recovered it with glass so that it would have stayed put. This was a recurring lamentation of mine.

One day, Yonda was coming to visit me. She had, of course, seen the playbill, but it had been quite a while since I had seen her. Clyde had moved and a year or so had gone by. Looking forward to seeing her, I cleaned up the house a bit in anticipation of her arrival. As I did, I could not help but notice that the playbill was now comfortably resting upon the cardboard. It had suddenly and unexpectedly manifested itself as if out of thin air!

There was no question in my mind that something very peculiar had happened. No one lived with me so no one could have put it back in place, let alone known where to have put it back in place. The damn thing had been missing.

I picked up the playbill and looked at it anew. Examining the data on the playbill very carefully, I wondered if there was something in the original reading of it that I had missed. Something, I felt, was calling my attention to the playbill. Continuing to peruse it carefully, I could not help but notice that the star of the performance was an actress by the name of Eva Tanguay. Who was that, I wondered? Prior to that moment, I had never even considered who she might be. To me, she was just some forgotten vaudeville performer.

When I first encountered this playbill, the internet was not so ubiquitous. At this time, however, considerable information was available by just typing a few keys on the keyboard. Yonda was a bit late so I went to the computer and did a search on Eva Tanguay. I soon found myself reading an article about her in an online version of the *Encyclopedia Britannica* that included a review of one of her performances. Reading the review, I became completely flabbergasted to see that it was written by Aleister Crowley.

I soon learned that Eva Tanguay was the most heralded and highly paid performer of the vaudeville era. Her voice was not considered to be exceptional nor was she considered to be a great beauty, but her vibrance and stage presence was electric. She could move an audience like no other. Eva Tanguay was also rather risque. At a time when nudity was a heavy cultural taboo, she was one of only a few women who performed the Dance of the Seven Veils. This dance is a highly esoteric dance that depicts the full unveiling of the goddess when the seventh veil is finally cast off. The context of this dance is completely lost in our culture, and it is not even closely equivalent to a conventional strip tease.

When Yonda finally arrived, we had a lot to discuss. Neither of us knew what to make of all this, but I eventually discovered that Eva Tanguay was a priestess of Aleister Crowley and they engaged in sexual magick together. Crowley, however, only makes a brief comment on Tanguay in his writings and laments that he did not do the right thing by her. He was not proud of how he had dealt with her. What I found significant, however, was that he had obviously worked with her around the same time he had worked with Roddie Minor, the woman who had engaged in the Amalantrah Working. In other words, Eva Tanguay crossed his magical path just before Crowley visited Montauk. He had apparently known her for more than a few years.

After writing *Seventh Seal*, I thought that the Crowley theme had been pretty much exhausted. I was glad to be done with it, but here it was, surfacing again. The playbill had already proven itself many times over to have been a remarkable oracle. Now I was learning that it seemed to hold many more secrets.

I began to find out what I could about The New Montauk Theatre, the establishment which was being advertized in the playbill. All these years, I had assumed that this theater had been located at Montauk, but I was wrong. There is an old theater at Montauk which is not far from the old Indian burial grounds. As it was built by Carl Fischer during the 1920's, it could not possibly be the same one.

The internet came to the rescue once again. I found out that there had been two Montauk Theatres. The original was at the location of 409 Flatbush Extension in Brooklyn. Flatbush Extension is at the northern end of Flatbush Avenue and is within walking distance of the Manhattan Bridge which leads to the borough of Manhattan. Due to changes in owners and various business problems, there was a name change in this theater and a new theater was constructed on Livingston Street. It was called The New Montauk Theatre and this is most certainly where Eva Tanguay performed as the Livingston Company is mentioned in the playbill. The history fits in perfectly.

Eventually, I would become close friends with a spiritual healer and psychic named Vicki. One day, Vicki was visiting me with another friend of mine, Sandy. Once again, I pulled out the famous playbill and sought their impressions. Oddly, they both picked up stuff. This was a first. Without knowing any of the story, Sandy picked up that Eva Tanguay was very significant and said that she had to do with the seven veils and Aleister Crowley. By this time, I knew about that association but had not said a word of it to either one of them. Despite her statement, Sandy did not know about the Dance of the Seven Veils. Vicki said that Tanguay had considerable goddess energy which Crowley tried to manipulate but was thwarted. Vicki was insistent that I should visit the area where the theater had been, preferably with her, because I would pick up something significant by being at the location. She was sure of that but was not sure of what I would pick up.

It took years for Vicki and I to meet up and go to Brooklyn together, but I will relay what happened there later on in the book. In the meantime, I visited the location of the original Montauk Theater with my friend, Penelope. There is still a vintage theater at 409 Flatbush Extension, but the property is now owned by Long Island University and is used as office space. It is a ghastly misuse of what should be declared a historic landmark. Livingston Street, the site of The New Montauk Theatre was not far away, but I forgot to bring the address with me and we did not visit that site.

Penelope and I then headed for the nearby Montauk Club which was only a very short drive away. Many years earlier, a reader had sent me an article telling me about this club. I eventually researched the history of the club and discovered that its namesake was deeply tied to the sovereignty of the Montauks who were once the royal tribe of Long Island. The name *Montauk* was chosen by reason of a complex voting procedure that included some disputes. The name that finally won out was *Montauk*. By design or otherwise, they had picked the name of the most powerful Indians on Long Island. The people who were members of the Montauk Club were known as the Tammany Hall political machine. They were the most powerful people in New York City and had taken their name from Chief Tammany of the Leni Lenape tribe of Delaware. The Montauks are also of the Leni Lenape tribe and both cultures consider the word *Montauk* to represent the highest aspect of the divinity. The New York politicians co-opted this name in the same manner that the Catholics co-opted *cat*.

In the late 1800's, The Montauk Club was the most prestigious social club in New York. Today, it is pretty much open to anyone who pays the dues. It is a social club that is ideal for those who live in Brooklyn and would like a nice place to entertain clients or friends. Rooms are available for parties and there is a restaurant which is open to club members and their guests.

When Penelope and I arrived at the Montauk Club, we could not help but notice a prominent and beautiful sculpted relief of the Montauk Indians that wraps itself around the top of what is a very quaint and beautiful building. The relief contains an element that would make most historians go nuts and that is the fact that a teepee is depicted. Conventional historians "know" that the eastern Indians, particularly the Montauks, did not have teepees. They lived in longhouses. The artist thought otherwise and sought to depict Indian life as it had been many years ago.

By reason of the grand design or otherwise, the mysterious playbill had put me back on the trail of the Montauks. It reminds me of the old saw that all roads lead to Rome. In my life, all roads seem to lead back to Montauk.

43

MONTAUK MEDICINE

After finishing *Seventh Seal*, I phoned Sharon Jackson, the shaman of the Montauks, in order to see what was happening with the tribe. Unfortunately, the tribal squabbles that had been going on for years had escalated and there was no unity whatsoever. The tribe was split into two main factions. One was led by Robert Cooper, a recognized tribal leader of the Montauks who had introduced me to Sharon Jackson in the first place. The other faction was led by Robert Pharoah, the son of Olive Pharoah.

I knew Robert Cooper pretty well and had even covered a civil suit waged against him by the former Chief of Police. At the same time I had been investigating dubious behavior by officials at Montauk, Cooper had made public comments about the police. Instead of simply acknowledging Cooper's first amendment rights, a punitive lawsuit was instituted. Hundreds of thousands of taxpayer dollars were spent defending Cooper because he was a town councilman at the time of the statements and they were made in the line of duty as far as he and many others were concerned. The police chief thought he was being defamed, but the lawsuit was eventually dropped as it had no legs to it. In any event, I had come to know Cooper and always liked him.

I only had the opportunity to meet Robert Pharoah on one occasion and that was at a powwow he had organized at Montauk. He was very pleasant and had done a great thing by getting the Montauks to meet on their own grounds at Third House. I have always considered him to be a very important figure.

In what I considered to be a rather odd irony, Sharon Jackson was in the Robert Pharoah camp and Gail Evening Star, my other good friend in the tribe, was in Cooper's camp. My two best friends in the Montauk Nation were on different sides. Personally, it was not my concern who was the tribal leader. I only wanted the Montauks to be united so as to get their land and culture back.

After listening to Sharon and realizing that these matters would never resolve if everyone remained on their same course of action, I made a suggestion to her. I told her that the men were never going to resolve these issues. The women are the ones who gave birth to the tribe and made it work in the first place. I suggested she get the women together so they could have their own meeting and take it from there. Sharon thought this was a great idea. Besides, she said, it is the women who keep all of the genetic records, and that is where so much of the power resides.

Sharon and Gail both have something very interesting in common and that is a great-grandmother by the name of Olive. They got together with others and eventually established a group which democratically elected a tribal council with a new spokesperson, Robert Redfeather. As so many of the tribe were now unified and the leaders were voted upon, there was no longer any room to argue.

As things developed, Sharon said she wanted me to become involved in tribal affairs. This was not something I asked for nor was I even sure what she was talking about. Her first step was to invite me to Coney Island on New Year's Day. It was the first day of 2006, and it was cold. For purposes of media exposure, the Montauks had been invited to attend an annual event that is held by the Ice Breakers of Brooklyn. The Ice Breakers are a group of swimmers who regularly take a quick dip in the ocean during the cold winter months. Every year, on New Year's Day, the media makes a big deal out of it and it is covered by all the local stations. What the media does not tell you, however, is that these swimmers are out there regularly. Some go in once a day and others go once a week, but virtually none of them do it once a year. They go in for only a short time, maybe ten minutes or twenty at the most, and then get out, dry off and get warm. Any longer can be dangerous for most people. The purpose is to increase circulation and many claim it really helps them.

The organizer of the Ice Breakers is Abraham Abraham, an Hasidic Rabbi who identified himself to me as a Cohen Priest. These are the most holy members of the priesthood who traditionally were the custodians of the Holy of Holies which contained the Ark of the Covenant. He was sympathetic to the Montauks and introduced them to the media. Speaking into the camera, he referred to them as a lost tribe of Israel.

I was also interviewed by Channel 12, Long Island's local cable news channel. The interviewer, however, was more interested in asking my impressions of Coney Island on this cold morning than he was in hearing about the Montauks, the pyramids or how I became involved with them.

As the early morning event came to an end, there were problems with the bathrooms. The public facilities were closed, but Rabbi Abraham had already arranged with the local restaurants to use their facilities. From the reports I received, the restaurateurs changed their minds when they saw the skin color of some of these natives. Although Brooklyn is as well integrated as any place in America, most of these restaurateurs were Russian. At the same time, many of the Montauks' cars were being ticketed by the police for parking violations. Usually, on a holiday, parking rules are suspended. All in all, these incidents were a prime example of the Montauks not being welcome in this world. What has been taken away, however, can always be regained.

In accordance with this last thought, the Montauks held another event several weeks later. An ancestral ceremony was to be held at a tribal cemetery in Copiague that would honor their dead. I was invited to attend and say a few words about the pyramids and the rich legacy of the Montauks. Keep in mind that most were not aware of the pyramids.

After the ceremony, I was saying good-bye to Gail Evening Star when she asked me if I was going to the festivities afterwards. Having no idea what she was talking about, she told me that everyone was going to gather for a meal and celebration. I told her I had not been invited.

"You are now," she said.

Sharon had deliberately wanted me to attend the party, but she did not bother to tell me about it. Had I not run into Gail, I would have gone straight home. Only by the narrowest of margins did I even end up where I was supposed to be. As I have learned over the years, Indian energy moves in strange and mysterious ways.

We all went to the V.F.W. building in Bayshore. V.F.W. stands for Veterans of Foreign Wars, and this establishment had a bar, tables for dining, and a hall for events. I arrived early and sat next to a man named Jessie. He was very nice but had some severe health problems he was dealing with. I liked him and offered what two-cents I could offer about his difficulties.

When everyone arrived, people were seated by families and groups when it was time to eat. I was placed at a table that was both in the center but to the side. When I returned from the buffet, another man was sitting at the table. He was Artie Crippen, and he was apparently very well informed and had a lot of interesting things to say about the Montauks.

As we sat there, Artie talked to the entire table and said that although the Montauks do not have federal recognition, every displaced Indian who has ever received recognition by the U.S. Government had accomplished this by proving they were related to the Montauk bloodline. This, he said, was by proving they were related to the Fowlers. The Fowlers are the preeminent name in Montauk history. Most tribes never kept any genetic records but the Montauks are an exception. They have kept better records than anyone, and they are virtually the only source of genetic records if a displaced Indian wants to prove his native roots. Despite this, the Montauks themselves are not recognized. It is one of the grandest contradictions one could imagine. As most of you reading this book are aware, this could not be by accident.

One of the most interesting things I would learn from Artie was that the name Fowler had originated when the early Dutch settlers transliterated the name *Pharoah* into *Fowler*. There were obviously much deeper threads at work when this occurred.

Artie was a delightful person to listen to and very informative. I told him a little bit of what I was up to and soon found out that he was the Montauk Medicine Man. His native name is Red Medicine. How come I had never heard of him? Once again, it was a prime example of things occurring in "Indian time."

When the dinner was over, Sharon had Artie speak to the entire group in order to introduce the Montauk Wellness Center. This is a wellness program instituted by Artie which is based upon his Native American heritage as a medicine man. He held up a bottle of a product called *AgelessXtra*® and said that it had literally saved his life. We were all invited to return in a week or two to attend the wellness program and see what it could do for us.

When it was time, I returned to learn about the wellness program. There were about twenty-five of us in attendance. I was the only one who was not a Montauk. Before we began, Sharon asked me to say a few words about the books I had written.

Summating *The Montauk Project* in only a few sentences, I quickly moved to my book, *The Pyramids of Montauk*, and opened it to the page where the pyramids are pictured. As I did so, I had a sudden flash. Artie must know about these pyramids! I took the opportunity to ask him in the middle of my talk.

"They were in Sag Harbor," he said.

Finally, and at long last, I received a report by someone who not only knew about the pyramids but knew where they had been. He explained that they did not survive the 1938 hurricane which completely devastated Montauk as well as other areas of Long Island. His data made a great deal of sense.

Artie also said that if one were to scuba dive under the water at Sag Harbor, one would find underground tunnels that were the remnants of ancient villages once occupied by the Montauks. I basically listened to Artie until my time was up. It was then his turn to speak but not about pyramids.

Artie spoke of the wellness program and said that it consists of three major avenues. The first is osha root, a plant that is indigenous to Montauk and is good for relieving pain and for detoxing the system. He gave us all a small bit to try. It should only be taken with a very very tiny nibble.

Once this was completely masticated, he had us try a small bottle of *AgelessXtra*® which he had passed out. The juice is the equivalent of about ten servings of fruits and vegetables in terms of its antioxidants. It also features herbs and ingredients that are patented to facilitate cellular renewal. Osha root is designed to get rid of dead cellular matter while the juice facilitates the production of new cells. The third prong of his wellness program is Chi Gong, an oriental technique which utilizes the breath and bodily motion. In Chinese, Chi Gong means "breath work." We all got up and did about fifteen or twenty minutes of these exercises which were led by Artie. They were simplistic but very powerful exercises and could also be done while sitting in a chair. This last aspect was very important as some of the Montauks were elderly. Anyone could do these exercises and benefit tremendously.

That is an oversimplification of the program, but it includes the essential ingredients of what we did. At the end, Artie gave me some osha root and a box of small *AgelessXtra*® bottles and said to try it for thirty days. He did not want payment, but I insisted on paying for that plus the additional juice I would need to complete the thirty day program.

I then found out that Artie had to leave. He had to get back to catch the Orient Point ferry as he lives across Long Island Sound. Learning this, I asked to take the two hour ride in order to follow up on the many things we had begun to discuss about the pyramids. This was the opportunity of a lifetime as far as I was concerned. Finally, there was someone who knew about the pyramids and their heritage.

As we rode to Orient Point, Artie explained much about the history of the Montauks as well as the local area. He said that there were several pyramids bedsides the ones in Sag Harbor. There were some near the beach in Southampton and also near Montauk Point. When and how those had been washed away is not known.

Long Island, he said, was once a mesa and the people were cliff dwellers, not unlike the Anastazi of the Grand Canyon. About 10,000 years ago there were some 30,000 people living in and around this mesa. This layout featured underground chambers beneath Montauk which included huge cats or sphinxes. So far, the Government has not been able to penetrate them.

Per this same oral tradition, there was also a strong connection between Egypt and Montauk. Before the breakup of the land mass known to scientists as Gondwanaland (when the various continents were all together as one land mass), Montauk and Egypt were adjacent to each other. There was also a connection between the people of both areas and this is how the word *pharoah* or *pharaoh* was transposed to North America.

Some seven hundred or more years ago, there was an Egyptian who had inherited the legacy of the pharaohs through the bloodline of his mother. Living under a repressive Islamic regime in Cairo, there was political pressure to assassinate him. He escaped to

America and settled at Montauk. His name was Montauk Pharoah, the name *Montauk* signifying the "highest expression of the divinity." Montauk Pharoah had a son who married at least thirteen native women, and their names became the namesakes of the so-called thirteen tribes of Long Island. This story explains not only why the Montauks were the ruling tribe but also how the name *Pharoah* or *Pharaoh* became integrated into their culture.

The arrival of Montauk Pharoah in America was not surprising to the natives because there is a longtime association between America and Africa that is not recognized by Academe. It is, however, common knowledge in native lore. This is why Montauk Pharoah was accepted as a leader. The entire area from Montauk Point to Mahwah, New Jersey was recognized as "Montauk" and all the sachems (chiefs) in the area would gather there at a meeting presided over by the Pharoah from Montauk Point. At one point, America itself was recognized by the name of Montauk.

It is also well known from the Moorish tradition that the Moors had an extensive legacy in America, a name which was transliterated from the original *Al-Maurikanos*, meaning "El Morroco." This also explains why an Islamic name like *sharif* became transliterated into *sheriff*. The word *Maurikanos* translates as "spirit of the cat" or "spirit of the cat king" where *maur* = *mauresh* (meaning cat-head or cat-king) and *kanos* is a word for "spirit," "power," or "fire." *Morrocco*, on the other hand, combines *mor*, *maur*, or *mauresh* with *occo* or *oc* which can be translated as "eye of the cat" or "eye of the cat-king." This is a blatant reference to Christ or King Felix. It should also be pointed out the jaguar, which is a virtual homonym for *hagar*, is the totem for the natives of Mexico as well as other vast regions of ancient America.

Montauk Pharoah also brought many tall people with him who were initiated into Freemasonry. These tall people primarily settled in Connecticut and became known as the Naragansetts. Some of these masons migrated westward and built the mounds in Ohio. That these people were known as pharaohs is substantiated by different sources. Chief Tecumseh Brown-Eagle of the Erie Mound Builders has sited historical accounts of locomotives using mummies found in the Ohio area for combustible fuel as they were far cheaper than coal or lumber. When the railroad men would hear a sudden pop from the fire, they were known to joke, "There goes another pharaoh!" There are also Jesuit documents indicating that the Ohio area was populated by pharaohs who spoke Hebrew.

I was learning an incredible new view of American history from Artie, but this was the only beginning. I would begin to look into things myself and find considerable corroborating information which academe has not only ignored but covered up. As intriguing as all of this is, it was foreseen long ago by certain native sages. Artie told me that they referred to this time and the unfolding of these revelations as the Second Coming of the Pharoahs. This includes the advent of universal healing as well as the restoration of the ancient culture of Montauk.

The medicine wheel on the back cover of this book was personally designed by Artie. It represents the Second Coming of the Pharoahs which includes the broad recognition of the brotherhood of Mankind. The colored feathers represent all the different races of people. The green feather represents the Little People as they are also recognized as part of this brotherhood. The full details of the medicine wheel will be discussed in *Medicine of Montauk*, a book I plan to write with Artie in the future. The following chapter will give a brief summary and touch on certain key points.

44

THE SECOND COMING OF THE PHAROAHS

When Artie was young, he had no idea that he would be a focal point of what would be known as the Second Coming of the Pharoahs. He began to get an inkling of what his life might become when he was attending an annual powwow with his family at the Shinnecock Reservation on Long Island. The Shinnecocks and the Montauks are two divisions of the same bloodline, and they are "cousins" in a sense. Artie's father was one-half Shinnecock and one-half Montauk.

At this powwow, two medicine men from the Lakota tribe of South Dakota arrived and created a commotion. To most everyone's consternation, they announced that their people had been waiting 33,000 for Artie to appear. He was the one who would inaugurate the Second Coming of the Pharoahs, an age that would usher in the return of great wisdom. Most of Artie's family were protective and thought these medicine men were nuts. A fight almost ensued. This was averted by Artie's grandfather, Arthur Emmett Crippen, the man Artie was named after. His grandfather calmed everybody down by simply saying that they should be allowed to talk to Artie. It was thus that Artie got to meet the two medicine men that would change his life. He refers to them as his spiritual fathers.

Artie's grandfather recognized that Artie was a very special and unique person. Perhaps that is because he was very special himself. Due to his contribution in facilitating the Second Coming of the Pharoahs, it is appropriate that he also be remembered in this book for some of his other accomplishments. Arthur Emmett Crippen was one of the best football players ever to play the game.

Arthur Emmett stood just a little bit over five feet and was built like a wall of granite. He was thick and fleet of foot, and it was virtually impossible to tackle him. As a result, his high school team would sometimes score over one hundred points in a game and literally slaughter the other team. This happened routinely and is unprecedented in high school or any other football league. For the entire duration of the National Football League, no team has ever scored one-hundred points in a game. When Arthur Emmett graduated high school, the NFL was not yet in existence so the professional leagues had a long way to go. Due to his skin color, which was dark, the pro leagues of those days and the colleges were shy to recruit him. You can find the results of his exploits, however, in write-ups of various games he played in. Artie, who is also athletic, obviously inherited much of this talent from his grandfather.

Even though Arthur Emmett gave the go-ahead for the Lakota medicine men to meet with his grandson, Artie was still too young for them to work with. All they could do at that point was plant a seed. When Artie grew older, he attended a trade school in Illinois and learned the trade of welding. During his first vacation, he travelled to South Dakota to meet up with his spiritual fathers.

When Artie arrived in South Dakota, he attended a gathering of medicine men from tribes across North America. The elders quickly recognized him but did not know how to designate him as he was something they had never seen before. Without having any formal training, Artie was given different "medicine tasks" to perform and either surpassed expectations or completed these tasks in record time. The result was that he became the youngest eastern native to have been initiated as a Sun Dancer of the Western Tradition, a designation which is the highest attribute that can be conferred upon a native medicine man.

The Sun Dance is a brutal endeavor that has been glamorized and popularized to some extent by New Age commercialism. There are some people who go around and say they are Sun Dancers. Nothing could be further than the truth. According to Artie's fathers, Artie is completely unique in that he has actually done the Sun Dance ritual according to prescription.

The Sun Dance is a long and arduous process which took about five years to finally complete. One has to prepare the body for great deprivation. Perhaps the most popularized version has to do with the piercing of the breasts with an element that is tied to a pole. One then moves in a circle around the pole to the point of exhaustion. According to tradition, this dance was taught to men by Jesus Christ in order that they might better appreciate and respect what a woman goes through in child birth. Whether you believe this or not, it should be pointed out that most native people share the tradition that Jesus actually visited the Americas. They knew about Him long before the missionaries arrived. These stories have been conveniently omitted by our academic tradition.

As brutal as this aspect was, however, it was not the most arduous for Artie or the others. The most difficult part was the fasting. This is the part that is cheated on by virtually everyone who does the Sun Dance. This particular fast is supposed to mean absolutely no water or food. As it puts the body in starvation mode, it is clearly not something your doctor would recommend. In recent times, dancers have been allowed to eat oranges to counter the harshness, but when they do so, they are no longer doing the ritual. To be blunt, the ritual is so arduous that nobody can do it. Artie, however, was the exception. There are two reasons for this. One, he is special. Two, he did the preparation and it took five years. There is much more involved than what I have described here. The main point you need to appreciate is that virtually no one does it or can do it according to the strictest prescription.

The climax of this ritual for Artie was when he was sent to the mountain for his fast. There, he would sit with no food or water for eleven days. Even though he had prepared for this for five years, it was still extremely difficult. He said that as soon as he reached the point of virtual death, the Great Spirit provided rain. This was a relief, and there was no rule against drinking rain water. Holding up his mouth, Artie let it pour in and this got him through the ritual. None of this, however, prevented him from passing out.

Everyone feared for his life and thought he was dead. When he woke up, however, there was a surprise waiting for him. Two eagle feathers had been placed in his hands. These were not placed in his hands by the medicine men or any other human. These eagle feathers were given to him by the Creator while he was on "the other side" and served as a testament to his experience. When he came down the mountain, the eagle feathers astonished some of the elder shamans. They knew what it represented and had been waiting their whole lives to receive eagle feathers but none had come. It encouraged some to be jealous but certainly not his spiritual fathers. They had foreseen his ability.

The Second Coming of the Pharoahs is the beginning of a brilliant time for humanity. As with any evolutionary process, however, there will be fallout but we do not need to focus on that. The beginning of this new era is being heralded with the release of this information. From one perspective, it could be said that it began with the expose of Preston Nichols' discoveries and the publication of *The Montauk Project.* If not, I would not have discovered the sacred aspects of Montauk and publicized them.

There is also a very old curse on the land at Montauk. Sharon Jackson discovered this in an old newspaper article from the *Brooklyn Times-Mirror* of November 26, 1933 which stated that it has been an accepted legend on Long Island, handed down by generations of Montauk Indians, that the lands of Montauk were cursed as "long as white men shall deprive Indians of their rights."

The Second Coming of the Pharoahs heralds the time when Indians will no longer be deprived, but it has not occurred yet. The release of this information is only the beginning. The next step is for the ancient culture of the Montauk Pharoahs to be restored. This will transpire, according to Artie's vision, through a healing center which will eventually grow into a great facility. He has seen it very clearly. This is not only a place where his ancient culture can be taught but where individuals can be made whole and well. The seeds for this began with our meeting in the V.F.W. and the wellness program. It is ironic, however, that this program actually began with me speaking about the pyramids and having a cultural exchange with Artie.

It is now clear to me that my own desire to fix the hurtful mechanical conditions of existence led me to Montauk and the Second Coming of the Pharoahs. It all fits into a bigger picture that was orchestrated from the outside. Learning all of this information has propelled me to investigate further, and I have come up with some very interesting finds that place a new light on Montauk, America, and its ancient history.

45

THE MORMON CONNECTION

Only a few months after meeting Artie, he invited me to a powwow of Montauk Indians that were meeting in Connecticut. This gathering was hosted by Artie and sponsored by the Corey family. Ed Mahon, a.k.a. Swooping Hawk, was one of the primary organizers. The purpose of this gathering was to serve as a naming ceremony for the Corey family who had been displaced and never acknowledged for their heritage as natives. They were indeed Montauks and had taken exhaustive efforts to prove it.

For Swooping Hawk, this began when he joined the Latter Day Saints in Utah and took the opportunity to study their vast genetic data base. There was no doubt about it. He and his family could prove without any doubt that they were Montauks. Artie and the Long Island Montauks welcomed them with open arms and consecrated them with native names.

When I arrived, I was struck by the fact that many of these Indians had blue eyes and blond hair. This is not what you would expect, but it should be pointed out that true natives are completely unbiased and non-judgmental when it comes to skin color and race. There is considerable misconception on what constitutes a native.

The Long Island Montauks already had the most extensive genealogical records of any tribe. Swooping Hawk and his family, however, with the help of the Mormon records, far surpassed that. They discovered that some thirty U.S. presidents, including Ronald Wilson Reagan, had Montauk Indian blood.

The implications of the above are rather staggering as it reinforces a theme which has continually reiterated itself in my life and research. Montauk has a knack for proving that it is far more important than myself or anyone else would ever have believed. This should not surprise us, however, if we take into account that the name *Montauk* itself signifies the highest expression of the divinity. It is a bizarre fact that, through the office of the President, we have been ruled by Pharoahs without even realizing it.

One of these presidents was Thomas Jefferson who was also part Montauk by reason of his ancestry to the Branch family. It is a well known historical fact that he journeyed to Long Island with James Madison to record and preserve the dying language of the Montauks. Historians generally think that the Montauks spoke Algonquian, and while this is true, it was spoken primarily as a trading language. They also had their own language which was more akin to what might be termed Reformed Egyptian. Jefferson claimed that he eventually lost the manuscripts for the Montauk language when a trunk of his was stolen and supposedly dumped into the Potomac River.

Based upon information I have read, my intuition tells me that this manuscript was either stolen by, came into the hands of, or was otherwise mysteriously associated with William Morgan, a man who was abducted from jail by Freemasons and literally disappeared. Morgan is most interesting because he is at the nexus point of many cross currents which include not only Freemasonry but the founding of the Anti-Mason Party and the foundation of the Mormon religion.

Like Thomas Jefferson, Morgan was from Virginia. After the War of 1812, he married a ravishing beauty named Lucinda Pendelton with whom he fathered two children. He named his son Thomas Jefferson Morgan. Morgan got into trouble after his application to join the Masonic Lodge in Batavia, New York was rejected. He then published a work exposing the secrets of Freemasonry which literally started the Anti-Mason movement in this country. Morgan was then jailed on trumped up charges by Freemasons with political power. Joseph Smith, the man who would eventually become the founder of the Church of Jesus Christ of Latter Day Saints, lived very close to Batavia. Smith and his family supported Morgan and signed a petition on his behalf.

Morgan was abducted from jail by Freemasons who pretended they were there to bail him out. Morgan never returned, but a body appeared and was oddly identified by his wife, Lucy, who knew it was not him. Morgan's own mother made it very clear that it was not her son. This, however, was after the formalities of declaring him dead has already been signed, sealed and delivered. There are rumors that Morgan became a pirate, but he never reappeared in the annals of history. His legacy, however, was never forgotten.

The Anti-Mason Party grew and became strong enough to the point where it became dangerous to be known as a Freemason. A key figure in all of this was a publisher by the name of Thurwood Weed who was the most staunch ally of the Anti-Masons. Weed is particularly interesting because he was born in the small town of Cairo, New York which was a Masonic strong point. It held the largest and most prestigious Masonic Lodge and most of our presidents visited it at one time or another. We know this because Preston Nichols, through happenstance and synchronicity, bought this old lodge when he moved from Long Island. Preston simply bought it as a house but found out the mysterious history afterwards. After he contracted to purchase the place, the Mormons tried to break the contract but were unsuccessful.

After her husband's abduction, Lucinda Morgan was deeply sympathized with and became the most famous woman in New York. She also found herself at the center of all the political intrigue surrounding the Freemasons. It is particularly odd that she eventually became the mistress or spiritual wife of Joseph Smith who, by that time, was a Mason himself. This history is as confusing as it is intriguing. I have only touched upon it here.

The Mormons fit into the history of the Montauks in the most mysterious of ways. When Joseph Smith was in his teens, he attended Moors Charity School with his brother Hyrum. Moors Charity School was in Lebanon, Connecticut and was established by Eleazar Wheelock, through the charity of Joshua Moor, in order that natives could be schooled in the English language, religion and European culture. Originally, Moors Charity School was only for natives. The campus eventually moved to New Hampshire and evolved into Dartmouth College. Anyone who can prove they are native to this day will be granted a scholarship to Dartmouth. There are still many Mormons in the area of the school.

Moors Charity School is not just interesting because of its name but also by reason of its first student who was named Samson Occum. Not only does *oc* appear prominently in his name, but Samson Occum married Mary Fowler, the matriarch and Queen of the Montauks. Although he was a Mohegan, Occum's marriage to Mary made him the spiritual leader of the Montauks.

A quick study, Occum learned to speak English impeccably and was a prime pupil. He became a Christian minister and visited England as an ambassador for Moors Charity School. Through his eloquence and diplomacy, he secured a fortune in donations for the school. His sponsor, however, betrayed him. This was Eleazar Wheelock who had promised to take care of Occum's family when the latter was in England. Wheelock neglected Occum's family but happily took the money that he had solicited. Not even thanked for his efforts, Occum parted ways with Wheelock.

As Occum was a Christian minister, historians often claim that he learned Christianity through Wheelock but that is not exactly the case. Artie explained that the Montauks routinely named their children after Biblical characters so as to maintain what they considered to be their historical connection to the bloodline of the Hebrews (who were also identified as Pharaohs per earlier passages in this book). This made their record keeping easier. The genetic research of Swooping Hawk and his family also bore this out. Occum, quite apparently, was no different as the Biblical name of Samson was given to him by his parents.

By the time Occum had parted ways with Wheelock, he had brought many Montauks to Moors Charity School. When Joseph and Hyrum Smith arrived at the school, Occum was long gone; but they would have had ample exposure to the Montauks and what Indian lore or history there was to share. In *The Book of Mormon*, Native Americans are said to have come from Israel. Although the Mormons are the only "white religion" to believe this, it is also recognized by many native cultures. In any event, Joseph and his brother did not stay at Moors Charity School much more than a year. Due to severe illness, they both had to return home. It should be noted, however, that in order for Joseph Smith to have been admitted to this charity school, he would have been of native blood. Smith is also known to have been related to witchcraft families from Salem, Massachusetts.

The trails of Samson Occum and the Mormons would eventually meet once again, and that was in the state of Wisconsin. After the Montauks suffered displacement on Long Island, Occum moved them to Brothertown, New York until they were once again displaced. From there, they moved to Wisconsin where a population of Montauk Indians has remained ever since.

Shortly before Joseph Smith was assassinated, he named his successor to be James Strang and instructed him to go to Wisconsin, not far from Burlington. Although Strang was the rightful successor to the Prophet of the Latter Day Saints, Brigham Young was a better politician and convinced the majority of Mormons to go with him to Salt Lake City. The Smith family, however, remained loyal to Joseph and went with Strang to Wisconsin.

The connections between the Montauks and Mormons are obscure, but the geographic juxtaposition of the two cultures is such that the relationship between the two cannot be ignored. Their common denominator is that they both recognize that the roots of Native Americans trace back to the Hebrews. While the Montauks had an Egyptian language and identified themselves as pharoahs, the Mormons based their religion on native writings that were referred to as Reformed Egyptian or Modern Egyptian.

I got a lot more insight into the Mormon connection when one of my readers put me in touch with a very interesting man named True Ott. True grew up as a Mormon and worked his way to the highest levels of the Church. When he discovered that they were not what he supposed them to be, he dropped out, but not before he came across some shocking information. This includes multiple reports of ritual sexual abuse perpetrated against parishioners of the Mormon faith. An investigation by one of their own bishops revealed that the abuse all traced back to the highest echelon of the Church. Instead of acting upon the bishop's data, the Church's hierarchy had him reassigned and silenced the whole matter. True also discovered that there were homosexual orgies at the highest level. The rank and file, of course, know nothing about this.

When he was still a dedicated Mormon, True was working at the Mormon center in Palmyra and was renting a room with an Italian lady in Syracuse. This lady just happened to have a brother who was a Jesuit priest. One weekend, the Jesuit came to visit his sister and had a little too much to drink. When True flashed him the sign of the nail,* the rather friendly Jesuit decided to tell him the real truth about the Mormon faith. According to the Jesuit, his order had visited the Ohio Valley in the 1620's in order to chronicle the history of a large tribe of "Indian Pharaohs" who wore pharaonic headdresses and possessed the accoutrements of Egypt.** The Jesuits learned everything they could about the history of these people and recorded it on scrolls which were kept in a cave. For some unknown reason, perhaps because they thought they were in league with the Jesuits, the Algonquins and Iroquois banded together and fought these pharaohs. As a result, the pharaohs and visiting Jesuits were completely wiped out.

Years later, a man by the name of Solomon Spaulding was travelling along Canute Creek and found these same scrolls which were written in Latin. The average person has never heard of Solomon Spaulding (the name Solomon suggests he was a Freemason), but he is of very keen interest to many who have vigorously debated the origin of the Mormon religion. Prior to the foundation of Smith's religion, Spaulding wrote a fiction book entitled "Manuscript Found" which, in many respects, is hauntingly similar to *The Book of Mormon*. It is not, however, identical. Many Mormon critics have asserted that Joseph Smith plagiarized or borrowed from this work in order to construct his book. Although scholars have debated this ad nauseam, none of them have ever heard the story you are about to read. You are amongst the first to learn of it, and it was told to me courtesy of True Ott.

Seeing that the scrolls he discovered were written in Latin, Spaulding could not read them. Instead, he took them to one of the most distinguished Latin scholars in his vicinity, a man named

* The sign of the nail refers to an Illuminati hand signal which refers to the nails used on Christ. There is a secret brotherhood between the Mormons, Jesuits, Bavarian Illuminati and many other Masonic groups. The sign of the nail is used at the top echelons as a password of sorts. True was just high enough to have learned this signal, but he was never a conspirator per se. At the very top of the steeple in Salt Lake City is the sculpture of a nail. It is meant to serve as a satanic "cover" symbol that triumphs the nailing of Christ.

** Although the dictionary etymologies appear to be different, do not underestimated the phonetic association between the word *pharaoh* and the Hebrew word *pharisee*. The latter is cited as deriving from *separate*, but this is not at all inconsistent with the word or concept of a pharaoh who is designated with the task of separating the traffic between the heavens and the Earth.

Sidney Rigdon. Rigdon not only knew Latin, he later became deeply involved with Joseph Smith. Spaulding, however, brought only fragments of the original scrolls when he gave them to Rigdon for translation. According to the Jesuit, Rigdon never had access to the entire contents.

In the early 1820's, and prior to Smith discovering the Golden Tablets, Rigdon moved north from Ohio to the Palmyra area and met with Smith. This is documented. It is possible that he fed Smith the actual information from the scrolls, but there is no certainty that this is the case either. It would stand to reason that he discussed what he learned with Smith. Mormon Elders have stated to the Moors that the original Golden Tablets were Washitaw tablets. The Washitaw are Moors whose Empress has been offered succor by the top brass at Salt Lake City. She has never accepted their offer, but they have shown a keen interest in her legacy.

After Solomon Spaulding passed away, his heirs forwarded his manuscript to a publisher in Pittsburgh in hopes of having it published. It eventually was and is entitled *Manuscript Found*. The heirs, however, not knowing what they really had on their hands, also delivered the original Latin scrolls to the publisher. It just so happened that the publisher was a Catholic and notified his own church. Catholic authorities came to Pittsburgh, took the scrolls and said, "Thank you for returning our property." To this day, these scrolls are said to be under seal of the Vatican.*

The uncovering of this information is just one more signal that the Second Coming of the Pharoahs is at hand.

* True Ott has written an entire manuscript on the above and his many adventures as a Mormon. I hope to publish his work when I can get around to it. He also has a Ph.D. in nutrition and has created some wonderful products that will help with the Montauk Wellness Center.

46

THE WELSH CONNECTION

Deciding to look more deeply into the various associations mentioned in the last chapter, I reviewed older material I had come across and compared it to the new data that Artie and others had supplied. One of these associations concerned a locale in Missouri which is known as Montauk. Local history indicates it was named after settlers who came from Montauk, New York. Digging a bit deeper, I discovered that this same area was once the home of the Mandan Indians who were known as Welsh Indians because they often had blue eyes and spoke Welsh. They are a puzzle to scholars, but they are believed to have arrived on a Welsh expedition to Mobile Bay, Alabama. The leader of this expedition, Prince Madoc, is of particular interest to my past research.

To most historians, Madoc has remained a mysterious and apocryphal character. Queen Elizabeth's court magician, Dr. John Dee, was Welsh and claimed to be a descendant of Madoc. Based upon this, the English Crown claimed America as their own. Dee claimed that his black obsidian scrying stone, which might be considered the most potent possession of the British Empire, was handed down to him by Prince Madoc who received it from the Aztecs. The Aztecs worshipped Quetzacoatl and Madoc himself has often been identified as this great "god-man." According to Aztec lore, Quetzacoatl had an evil twin brother called "Smoking Mirror" who had this same obsidian disk for a head or a foot.

These apocryphal legends are great in themselves, but they began to make a lot more sense to me when Artie explained that there was a component of Welsh people who settled at Montauk and became part of the tribe. This got me to thinking. If a contingent of Welshmen came to America, they would or could have easily stopped at Montauk Point. It is a perfect place to stop. Going to Alabama, they moved up the Mississippi and settled in various places, including Missouri. Mixing with the local Indians, they most commonly were known as the Mandan, a word which is the root for *Montana.* Migrating, the Mandan eventually made their way up the Missouri River to Montana. These Welsh Indians also migrated to other areas. To this day, there are so many place-names in Kentucky named after Madoc that they cannot be listed. There is something to this legacy.

As I put two and two together, it occurred to me that Prince Madoc might have been a much more potent character than anyone has ever imagined. The Aztecs thought of him as a god. When I took a trip to California and discovered there was a tribe of Indians called the Modoc, it made me think that if this man did not make it all the way across America, his legacy certainly did.

I then had what amounts to an ah-ha moment when I realized that the name *Madoc* could easily be a transliteration for *Montauk* or vice versa. As a historical character, Madoc sounded an awful lot like Montauk Pharoah. If Prince Madoc was considered the czar of America, it harmonized with what Artie had said about the entire American continent being known as Montauk.

A further investigation of Madoc revealed that commonly accepted Welsh history states that Madoc was the son of Owain Gwynedd, the King of Wales, who descends from Richard Mawr. Owain Gwynedd had at least ten children of which three, including Madoc, were bastards. The unmarried mother of Madoc is supposed to be named Brenda but there are also other names for his mother. The time period for Madoc is considered to be anywhere from the 1100's to the 1300's. These dates seem to fit in roughly with Artie's tale that Montauk Pharoah came to America approximately seven hundred years ago.

We are given a considerably more sober and intriguing account of the Welsh connection, however, through the scholarship of a British historian by the name of Alan Wilson. Studying Madoc since 1956, Wilson states that the accounts of Madoc living in the 1100's were fictionalized by Queen Elizabeth's advisers for the purpose of her making a legal claim to America as a descendant of the Welsh prince. Wilson states that much of the history of Madoc was misinterpreted (deliberately or otherwise) from writings in the 12th century which described his adventures in America. Citing extensive historical British documents, Wilson identifies Madoc as having lived during the inception of the Dark Ages when, in 562, debris from a comet rendered Wales as an uninhabitable land. This was the end of "Camelot." Forced to migrate, the Welsh moved in different directions. Madoc, who returned from his first trip to America, retrieved his brother, Arthur II, who followed with a 700 ship expedition. According to Wilson, Arthur II is the so-called historical King Arthur.

Wilson's scholarship indicates that Madoc's full name was Madoc Morfran (the name *Moor* appearing again) and that his brother-in-law was Ammwn Ddu. *Ammwn* is another way of spelling *Ammon*, the sun-god of Egypt. The Egyptian connection is given a further boost when we consider that Wales is known to its natives as Cymru. Sometimes the *C* is substituted with a *K* and it is written as Kymru. If you use a soft *c*, Cymru becomes "Sumeru," the mountain at the apex of Shambala. If you use a hard *c* or *k*, you have khumru which is very close to *khemet*, the native name for Egypt. *Khem* or *kheme* is Egyptian for black. To the Moors, Wales was known as the Khemet (Egypt) of the North.

Wilson's dissertations are extensive and, according to him, there is "copiously well-recorded" information stating that the farther of Madoc and Arthur II was King Meurig. In Welsh, the word *meurig* means "dark-skinned." There is another interpretation of *Meurig* as well and that is "Cat King"(*meu* = *mau* = *cat* + *rig* = king). The departure from Europe of this royal Meurig family coincides with the rise of the false Merovignian Kings and the eventual crowning of Charlemagne.

Wilson has brought very interesting points to light because the Welsh name of Khmru could easily have derived from Khemet (Egypt). More importantly, *Khmru* could easily be transliterated by Scottish people as *Khmrun*, or "people from Khmru." The spelling is convertible to *Cameron*, one of the names which triggered all this synchronicity in the first place.

These connections add up very nicely, but they do not end here. Due to place-names and local histories, it became glaringly obvious that the "Welsh Montauks" migrated all the way westward. Where some of this migration might seem preposterous geographically, it should be pointed out that oral tradition includes migration via underground tunnels. The Montauks, however, were not the only ones to migrate westward. I soon learned that there was a data trail indicating that the Knights Templar themselves came all the way to Mormon country in Utah.

Thanks to a subscriber to my newsletter, *The Montauk Pulse*, I was put in touch with a man in Utah who is not only conversant with the legends of Prince Madoc but has also had occasion to witness a multitude of Egyptian and Templar artifacts in that state. Treasure hunting in Utah has been very popular recently, but this man was in the center of it. This was long before Utah passed an antiquities act which prevents the taking of any artifacts. Prior to that law, he was able to secure a huge stone sarcophagus and several brass plates with Egyptian hieroglyphics.

In his words, there is no shortage of ancient Egyptian and Hebrew records as well as several tombs depicting the Knights Templar. The Templar artifacts include armor, swords, arched doorways and the like. They are pretty much "in plain sight" if one knows where to look.

One of the most spectacular archeological finds was near Manti, Utah in what is referred to as Noah's City. Besides being a real city that encompassed an entire mountain area, it featured brass plates with inscriptions depicting a massive flood. The plates, featuring "Noah" talking to people, were found in stone boxes and are in ancient Egyptian. They have been carbon dated as going back to 2,543 B.C..

There are many more finds and while this all might seem to be the discovery of the century, there is another factor at work. Certain members of the Ladder Day Saints took it upon themselves to bulldoze down the entirety of Noah's City. Fortunately, not all Mormons are so predisposed and one example is Wayne May. He is the editor and founder of *Ancient America* which has featured many articles on such topics and is on the cutting edge of these investigations. You can consult his magazine or the *Ancient America* website for further information. He is a Mormon but not a bulldozing one.

My own foraging through the *Ancient America* website led me to various cave paintings in America, one of which not only brought home an important point, it outdid all of the synchronicities I have encountered on this subject. A so-called Egyptian cave painting featured a sizable depiction of a human body crucified on a cross but the figure possessed the head of a cat!

Whether or not Prince Madoc was Montauk Pharoah, his namesake makes him a poster boy for the Moorish cause. Not only did his father's name, *Meurig,* represent a black cat, it indicates he was carrying the bloodline of the real Merovignians: the Moors or Cat Heads. Breaking down the name *Madoc* gives us *mau* (cat) + *doc* (channel) which equates to "channel of the cat." The etymology of his name is therefore in keeping with the king of the Aztecs, a people who worshipped the jaguar (once again a name seemingly derived from Hagar, the mother of the Arab people, or Ahaggar, the mountainous region of the Tauregs).

I also discovered an interesting irony when I was speaking to Artie one day. During a conversation, he happened to mention that Abraham Abraham (the Hasidic Rabbi who was the leader of the Ice Breakers) was the half-brother of Jessie, the man I met at the V.F.W. on the same day that I met Artie. In other words, Abraham Abraham was a Montauk Indian. This was a surprise to Sharon Jackson and most of the other Montauks. The connection between the Hebrews and the Montauks runs deeper than anyone might imagine. Artie knew it, and he has a unique way of networking between tribes and nations. This is what makes him a catalyst for the Second Coming of the Pharoahs.

What I have written in this chapter is an overview and a template for future researchers to work with. Much more will come to light over time. The bigger picture needs more detail. Artie's date of 700 years ago does not match up with Wilson's dates for Madoc and Arthur. It is possible, however, that Artie's dates are wrong or that there was more than one Montauk Pharoah.

We find another remarkable irony when we consider that this investigation began by associating the Montauks with the inception of the Mormon Church. In the beginning, Joseph Smith is studying along side the Montauks. In the end, his successors are orchestrating an audacious cover-up of their migration westward.

All of this information is fascinating, but it is just the beginning. It is more important, however, to cover the healing aspects of the Second Coming of the Pharoahs. This not only concerns the wellness program put forth by Artie, but what is suggestive of the fountain of youth as described in the legend of Tir na nÓg. As things turned out, my foray into the principles of Tir na nÓg went far beyond what Artie could teach me, but he was the catalyst.

47

THE FOUNTAIN OF YOUTH

Due to my own mortality, I had already discovered the need for a fountain of youth and was working on my own program before I met Artie. I could feel the pangs of age and could not help but notice my body atrophying in certain respects. Speaking to one of my friends, I was commenting on the sober and cold hard facts of aging.

"You shouldn't think that way or you *will* age," she said. "Be more positive."

I am a realist, and I thought her words were ridiculous. The results of my aging were not a result of attitude at all. It was clearly and simply a case of my body not being able to do what it used to do. After all, I had an excellent benchmark which would not let me lie and that is touch football, a game that I still play every Sunday during the fall and winter months. When you cannot run as fast and throw as far as you used to, you cannot lie to yourself. Many times, I went out and trained in an attempt to get back to my old playing capabilities. Running sprints and doing stretches, I did whatever I could think of to increase my athletic capacity, but improvement was nil. I was getting old. Nevertheless, I still played because it was fun. I could still make a play and do well but the frequency of my successes became less and less.

At age 52, I began to realize that I was seriously kidding myself. It was getting harder and harder to get myself out of bed on cold winter mornings and be on the field by nine o'clock. It got to the point where I was not even enjoying myself too much because of the physical exertion. I was no longer keeping up, but I could still play as we have players of all ages and capabilities. There were still players who were older or not as good as myself. Relying only on old habits and training patterns, I simply continued playing football every Sunday morning. When you have done something for over a decade, it is easy to just continue without thinking about it. Something was telling me, however, that it was now time to hang it up.

During a conversation with Joseph Matheny, he told me of a product that he had used with great success. It is called *Rejuvamax®* and is basically an HGH (human growth hormone) precursor consisting primarily of amino acids. Joe, who was forty-three at the time, told me that it did wonders for him. What particularly impressed me was his story that a twenty-four-year old at the local gym had challenged him to a boxing match. Joe thought the guy wanted to go three rounds, but the guy wanted to go twelve rounds. This shocked Joe as three rounds is enough to exhaust anyone, even if you are in good shape. Many professional boxers have a hard time in the later rounds. Due to the *Rejuvamax®*, Joe was not only able to go the distance but win the match on points.

Having boxed myself, I knew that fighting a twenty-four-year-old would be extremely challenging. People at that age have considerable energy. I was, however, hesitant to try the product because of the HGH factor. Joe, who is very astute at biochemistry, explained to me that there is a difference between a precursor and just taking HGH. With this product, one is basically consuming amino acids which stimulate the release of your own HGH. This is what is meant by the word precursor. Amino acids are just food and not a drug or foreign substance at all.

Old age is accompanied by a decrease in the amount of HGH that is released from your pituitary. It begins to seriously deplete by age thirty-five. This is the age at which most professional athletes retreat from the playing field. *Rejuvamax®* is merely a nutritional supplement that will counter this process and do it in a natural and big way. Deciding to try it, I purchased a can and could feel the difference within four hours. I was perhaps more sensitive than others in this regard. It made me sleep like a baby as HGH does affect your sleep. The biggest difference, however, was on the football field. Wow!

At this point in my touch football career, I had been pretty much going through the motions and was being ignored as a pass receiver. Showing little enthusiasm, I would mostly line up, go out and not be too much of a factor in what was going on. I was just happy to be getting exercise. *Rejuvamax*® changed everything and changed my life forever.

Within a few days of ingesting this product, I found myself on the football field with complete mental alertness. Although there were many benefits, my mental focus was probably the biggest difference. All of a sudden, I was going out for passes and finding locations where no one was defending. I caught about eight passes in a very short time. Oddly, no one covered me even though I began to be the biggest influence on the game. I could also run significantly faster. *Rejuvamax*® enables your body to recover faster from fatigue or exertion. I got better as the season came to a close. Every week that I went out, I was more eager to play.

Since that time, I have only improved and I am now age fifty-five. One thing I found out about this product, however, was that I should have been taking *Rejuvamin*®, a sister product which is for those who are under fifty-five. When I went off the *Rejuvamax*®, as you are supposed to every so often, I experienced fogginess. I called the inventor of the product, and he told me that I should be on *Rejuvamin*® until I reached fifty-five. As I found these products to be a little expensive, I also worked out with the manufacturer to buy them with a bulk discount so that I could offer them in the Sky Books catalog at a significant discount. I still take it every day with an occasional hiatus as per the instructions.

Having made tremendous strides with that product, I was then introduced to another. This is called *StemEnhance*® and was brought to my attention by my friend, Madalyn Suozzo. I met Madalyn during my research for *Montauk Revisited.* She is mentioned in the book and we have been good friends ever since. A healer and medical intuitive, Madalyn found herself in a panic when her breathing suddenly failed during yoga class. She was suffering from a leaky heart valve and was in deep medical trouble. Due to her good fortune, she has a friend by the name of Christian Dupreau. He has a degree in biophysics and was actually developing *StemEnhance*® at the same time. Although it had not been commercially released at that point, he gave her some and her heart problem cleared up within 24-48 hours. It was a miracle and she could not believe it. No medical bills either!

StemEnhance® consists of highly concentrated parts of blue-green algae which are designed to do four things: 1) act as an antiinflammatory agent; 2) promote a sense of well being in the brain; 3) increase the release of stem cells from the bone marrow; and 4) promote the circulation of the released stem cells throughout the entire body.

When I got a chance to meet Christian Drapeau and hear his presentation, he had some very interesting things to say about all the hysteria that surrounds stem cell research in the media. Essentially, embryonic stem cells are almost always rejected by the host because they are not the stem cells from that specific individual. Laboratory results are only successful when the patient's own stem cells are activated. These are referred to as adult stem cells, and they are released by the body every day. *StemEnhance*® makes an impact on an individual because it increases the production of stem cells. As the human organism is inherently an intelligent self-referencing system, the brain sends signals that tell the stem cells where to go. If one has a malfunction in one area of the body, the cells might go to another because that area is considered more essential to the vitality or survival of the entire organism. This is why *StemEnhance*® is designed to promote a sense of well being in the brain. It has been scientifically established that when the brain feels good, it will do a better job.

The vital organs of most adults are in need of vital repair by reason of insufficient diets and chemical abuse to the body. *StemEnhance*® is for repair and recuperation. It complements *Rejuvamax*® and *Rejuvamin*® and I take it every day.

With this history already going for me, I was ripe for the Montauk Wellness Program presented by Artie Crippen. I began the thirty day program that Artie put me on. This consisted of a very tiny piece of osha root, masticated well, which was followed by an ounce of *AgelessXtra*® mixed with water. Then it was fifteen minutes of Chi Gong exercise. I also took a second ounce of *AgelessXtra*® in the afternoon.

After doing this program for only a week, I could feel a tremendous increase in energy and vitality in my everyday life. People around me noticed the difference, too. My whole psychology improved markedly and I was now thinking young. The Chi Gong prevented pulled muscles and bodily injuries.

I followed this program for the entire thirty days. It was so wonderful that I did not even think about whether or not I wanted to continue. The Montauks and some of my friends were having similar success as well. As they needed funding for buying the juice, I helped to sponsor that and became a distributor for all of these products which are now offered in the Sky Books catalog.

After the thirty day program, Artie invited us all to World Tai Chi Day in Waterford, Connecticut where he encouraged us to meet his Chi Gong teacher, Roosevelt Gainey. Out of the many people who attended the program, I was the only one who took the three hour drive to attend World Tai Chi Day. I did not know what I was in store for, but I expected to learn some more exercises.

When I arrived, there were a host of different instructors who advocated different disciplines. The event is held outside and it is a colorful and festive atmosphere. I was surprised, however, to see that there was considerable focus on the martial arts aspects of Tai Chi and Chi Gong. I did not expect this. In fact, I was taken aback a bit. I was not really too interested in the martial arts.

Looking around for Artie Crippen, I could not find him. Not knowing anybody, I stood amongst a good-sized crowd and listened to the master of ceremonies who had gathered everyone together. Right behind me, I heard two people talking quietly. It sounded like one of them mentioned Artie's name.

"Do you know Artie Crippen?" I asked.

"He is my student," said Roosevelt Gainey. "He's late."

By the principle of synchronicity, I had placed myself right next to the man who was to eventually become my teacher and have a profound impact on my life. This was the exact same thing that had happened when I met Artie. He had been placed right next to me at the dinner table.

Introducing myself to Roosevelt, we exchanged a few brief words. He soon had to go as all the various instructors were going to their respective stations where they would give free demonstrations all afternoon. The organizers encouraged us to listen and learn from each instructor.

Listening to Roosevelt that day, I learned more about the martial arts in twenty minutes than I had learned in my entire life.

He explained that the time of secrets is over. For years, he said that teachers had piece-mealed out their teachings. These were hierarchal systems where the most powerful teachings were reserved only for family members so that the family could stay in power. Outsiders were kept ignorant. This, he said, was changing. On that particular day, Roosevelt did not emphasize the fact that he is one of the main reason it is changing, but I would learn that later.

Roosevelt then demonstrated a technique that is sometimes called the one-inch punch. As guys much larger than him would charge his body, he would make a motion with his hand that was barely visible but it would send the guy flying. At that point in my life, it was the most impressive thing I had ever seen demonstrated in the martial arts.

When Artie showed up, I got a chance to meet his wife, Cat and some of his other friends. I also met Brenda who is Roosevelt's primary facilitator. She had a remarkable story to tell. Almost dying at a weight of about 200 pounds, her life was literally saved by learning and practicing Roosevelt's brand of Chi Gong. She is now slim, good-looking and practices every day.

Brenda told me that I could attend a seminar being given by Roosevelt in Suffren, New York but that was a bit too far away for me and my schedule did not fit with the date. There was no flyer of course schedules so I was not able to connect with them at that point. I was also very busy with assisting Artie's program.

By this time, Sharon Jackson had an IRS approved 501-3C corporation for the Montauk Wellness Center. This means that it is a nonprofit corporation and that the IRS will accept donations as tax deductible contributions. We did a lot of work and finally found a building. The building was going to be donated, and we had access to funds from the Government in order to renovate it . At the last minute, someone else offered money for the building and we lost it. It is still possible, however, that the Montauks might rent the building.

None of this deterred me, and I simply declared that the Montauk Wellness Center was alive and well. It did not need a building. I began to teach people what I learned from Artie and received mostly positive responses. If I did not know the answer for someone, I would find somebody that did. Artie even did some successful Chi Gong instructions over the phone.

After attending the Corey family powwow in Connecticut, I took Artie with me to Michigan. We were both going to speak at Mary Hardy's annual event held during the summer. It is a long drive by car, and we got a chance to talk. For me, it was a real education. This drive was where I learned about his Sun Dance experiences. Of equal interest was his own background in the martial arts.

Although Artie is Shinnecock and Montauk by reason of his father, his mother is a Chinese immigrant from Hong Kong. You would not necessarily see the Chinese in him when you first meet him, but it is there. He said that members of his immediate family have no consistency whatsoever in the racial descriptions given on their driver's licenses. Officials arbitrarily list some as Asian, some as black, some as native and others as white.

Artie was exposed to martial arts at a very young age and is quite accomplished himself. One of his early influences was Bruce Lee, the famous Chinese movie star who used to come to the powwows held on the Shinnecock Reservation. Natives and Chinese have much more in common than most people might think. To Artie, Bruce was "Uncle Lee" and that is what he knew him by as a kid. One day, Artie attended an exhibition held at Madison Square Garden where Bruce Lee allowed a man to hit him as hard as possible with a baseball bat. The principle at work in such a circumstance was that Lee would encircle his body with chi (life energy) and the bat would literally bounce off of him.

Before Bruce Lee was ready, the person with the bat swung, hit him in the head and knocked him down. When Lee eventually recovered, he told everyone the man had not followed his instruction and had swung too soon. He would now demonstrate it properly by making sure the man waited until his energy field was built up. Given the signal, the man swung hard and hit Bruce Lee again. The bat bounced off without any injury for Lee.

The demonstration worked but it had adverse effects. According to Artie, this injury caused the aneurism in Bruce Lee's head that led to his death. There are many theories as to how Bruce Lee died. He took drugs to relieve pain from his head injury, but the generally cited cause of his death is the aneurism.

Artie went on to study the martial arts, but as is the case with many martial artists, Artie ceased to practice and acquired some bad eating habits. He became seriously overweight and turned into a walking time bomb. In other words, he was walking a path towards death. During this period, he was walking through a park in New York City and could no longer move. His breath was short and he felt as if it was about to expire. In the park, he saw a martial arts class and stumbled as he literally fell into the arms of Roosevelt Gainey and asked for his help. Roosevelt then uttered words that Artie would never forget.

"You're a maggot, but I will help you," he said.

These words were music to Artie's ears, and Roosevelt added him to the long list of people whose life he has saved. Teaching him Chi Gong, Roosevelt got Artie back on track. He has maintained his health and martial arts disciplines ever since.

As we travelled together, Artie impressed upon me how special Roosevelt Gainey is. In all of his vast years of studying the martial arts, Artie said that he had never met anyone who has as much knowledge of the human body or the martial arts. He told me that Roosevelt could and would walk into any martial arts studio he wanted to and simply say, "I am here to correct your martial arts." The response, as might be expected, was often negative. A demonstration would then ensue whereupon Roosevelt would send the teacher of the dojo flying. The result would be a new student for Roosevelt. When I first heard this, it sounded intimidating and a bit of an extreme claim. I now know that it is the truth.

Artie also explained to me that Roosevelt is an outcast in the world of martial arts. He is an outcast because he is not conforming to long established traditions of keeping the truth secret and only for the privileged. Many a time, Roosevelt has been approached by different Chinese people who have told him not to teach what he is teaching. It is meant to be kept secret. Roosevelt's response to this is rather uniform. "Try and stop me," is the response. The reason he can teach what he is teaching is that he is exercising his own will and that includes empowering others. He is also standing up to millennia of traditions and secrecy.

Although Artie himself has been accepted at the highest level as a medicine man, he is also an outcast in many respects. Medicine men, after all, are not your typical people. They are mysterious and traffic in the non-ordinary. Many people in Artie's own tribe would be much more comfortable with Artie if he acted more like Donald Trump and was the squire of an estate. In other words, he does not inspire confidence as having made it in the white man's economic system.

It should be no surprise that I fit in with these outcasts very well and almost too well. I did not go seeking them out, however. They came to me through the process of trafficking with the mysterious frequencies of synchronicity that resulted in the writing of this living book. Do not underestimate this process. You are interested in it and have already experienced something like it yourself. If not, you would not have gotten this far in the book. There will be, as we continue, an opportunity for you to participate in the beneficial aspects of this experience.

As we continued our thirteen hour drive, Artie and I shared our life stories. This is more than I can hope to relay in this book. One thing he talked about that is relevant to this discussion has to do with a martial arts tournament that is called the Octagon. This is a gathering of martial artists where disciples of various disciplines display their skills and see who is superior. There are many masters who come and go. Artie then made a comment to me that I felt was a bit off. He mentioned that Roosevelt was getting older and intimated that he might not do so well against some of the top competitors in these tournaments. It had to do with age, not skill or fighting savvy. I do not know why this comment seemed off to me because I had only met Roosevelt once at that point and was completely new to this subject. Despite the obvious fact that I had been experiencing the ravages of old age myself, the comment just seemed off. Perhaps it was my intuition or maybe it was just my unbridled enthusiasm for the youth I had already regained with the *Rejuvamax*® and *AgelessXtra*®.

I can now tell you from my own experiences with Roosevelt Gainey that if he had been sleeping in the back seat while we were talking, that comment would have woken him out of his slumber. He would probably have grabbed Artie, looked him in the eye, and said something on the order of, "You don't know what you are talking about, you maggot!"

My intuition would later be confirmed by Roosevelt himself. He is not aging in the manner that Artie had thought for he has truly discovered the *real* fountain of youth. Everything I have talked about in this chapter is valid and was a <u>tremendous</u> boon to my own health and vitality. It literally changed my outlook as well as my tangible ability to play sports. Much to my own surprise, however, this was only a warm-up act. A fountain of youth was something that I had never sought out. After all, Ponce de Leon and several others had come up empty-handed. The principle of synchronicity, however, had something else to teach me.

And by the way, please do not feel bad for Artie for being referred to as a maggot by his teacher. Artie was so grateful to Roosevelt for all the help he has received that he one day gave him a big surprise. Working at the Mashatucket Reservation which houses the Foxwoods Casino and Hotel, Artie saved up his money and arranged for Roosevelt to have the nicest suite in the place. It was very impressive. When Roosevelt was taken to the suite, he was surprised and pleased with what Artie had done.

"None of my students have ever done anything like this for me," he said. "You are no longer a maggot. You're a fly!"

The maggot analogy is very funny, but it is also symbolic of humility. If one is going to tackle a subject that is either impossible, incomprehensible, or staggering to the human mind, one had better assume a humble state and get rid of one's preconceived notions. To ordinary human beings, the prospect of a real fountain of youth is either laughable or absurd. It is completely foreign to the way you were brought up and became acclimated to your body. To change your condition would therefore require a drastic change in your viewpoint. That is what we will address next.

48

HUMILITY

In the first part of the book, I warned you that there would be many circuitous twists and turns. I compared it to a labyrinth. If you have followed it this far, it is likely that you were either impressed or interested in some of the information presented. What follows is the most important.

When I was a junior in high school, I was taking a required class in government. The teacher said that as all government is based upon philosophy, we would study nothing but philosophy for the first quarter. Each of us were to pick a particular philosophy and write a paper on it. Most of the students chose to study the "canned" gay philosophers such as Socrates and Plato. For most, it was just a robotic assignment to get through the class.

To be different, I chose Taoism. This was such a radical departure from what was expected, I sought out the teacher and wanted to make sure that it was all right with him. To my pleasure, he approved my choice. Although I knew of the Tao, I knew very little about it. From my previous Oriental studies in school, I was far more familiar with Buddhism and Shintoism. Taoism was presented as something of an alternative religion that did not have too many followers and was rather obscure.

Instead of this assignment being a robotic exercise, I found it to be very interesting. The school library did not have a copy of Lao Tzu's *Tao Te Ching* nor were there many texts on Chinese philosophy, but I did find a helpful work that quoted many passages from Chang Tzu and was very easy to understand.

The first thing you learn about the Tao is that it cannot be expressed in words. If it can be described, it is not the Tao. The best one can really do is allude to the Tao. It is non-assertive yet all things emanate from it and depend upon it. The Tao is greater than all things because it does not seek to be great.

These are just a few of the catch phrases, and I cannot expect to write a full treatise on the Tao. Many of you are already familiar with the concept anyway. The main doctrine of Taoism is called *wu wei* and this is the principle of causing things through non-action. In other words, you can accomplish more by being non-assertive. This principle is seen in water which yields to most anything yet can penetrate the hardest stone.

I took the Tao to heart after doing that paper in school. Eventually, I found a copy of *The Tao Te Ching* and it became my favorite book. There was one problem, however. Upon reading it, I felt completely divorced from nature. I was surrounded by the tumult of the Sixties revolution and the war-cry against corporate America. Whether one agreed with these agendas or not, they brought home the fact that civilization was very far from a natural ideal. Personally, this book caused me to see my various flaws, but they were overwhelming. I felt like a fish out of water. Worse yet, there was no school of instruction for this new philosophy. Those who went to college were obviously going in an opposite direction. They were buying into civilized madness which included a job, two kids, and a house in the suburbs. I did not desire any of these things nor an education into ignorance. Under such circumstances, my introduction into the Tao began as a self-help book. It was most certainly something that I never discussed with anyone.

For me, there was still a semester of high school to finish, and I did not have to worry about the pressures of life. As was covered extensively in *The Montauk Book of the Dead*, my path led directly to Scientology where I began to thrive. It was in Scientology where I encountered Taoism for the second time.

In a book entitled *The Phoenix Lectures*, Hubbard explained the doctrine of *wu wei* and stated that Taoism is a distant cousin to Scientology. He further stated it was the most civilized philosophy on the planet and was a great inspiration in developing Scientology. Unfortunately, he also said that Taoism was lost in obscurity. It was therefore a hidden or dead philosophy.

Hubbard's stated enthusiasm for Taoism not only touched me, it gave me the go-ahead to deeply embrace the philosophy I had already come to know. Consequently, I used the doctrine of *wu wei* and other aspects of Taoism to negotiate my way through the literal madness that organized Scientology could be at times. This philosophy is no small part of the reason why I transmuted my experiences in Scientology into a wonderful afterlife. After all, I was never competing with anyone.

My respect for the Tao was such that when I wrote *Montauk Revisited: Adventures in Synchronicity*, I deliberately placed a tribute to it on a page that otherwise would have remained blank. On the reverse side of the dedication page and opposite the table of contents, it states: "There is a mystery that underlies all other mysteries and we call that the Tao."

There was no question in my mind that all of the incredible synchronicities that were being generated in my life were a result of the Tao. That was, after all, the Great Mystery. All of the whiz-bang electronics and enchanting theories of time travel were subservient to and only a manifestation of the Tao. It is, after all, the Mother of All Mysteries.

It was only after writing *The Montauk Project*, however, that I was brought in touch with an actual Taoist tradition. A friend of mine had introduced me to a Taoist Holy House in Queens where I was sponsored to meet a Taoist master from Taiwan who I would "receive the Tao" from.

The master, who speaks only Chinese, explained that the Taoist masters went underground for thousands of years due to the insane political climate that has infested this planet. This reclusiveness, which Hubbard mentioned but was puzzled about, was done in order to stay alive and keep the knowledge safe. In recent times, however, Taoist masters are coming forward to teach their knowledge and save as many people as they can. In their tradition, one saves the person by administering the Tao to them. This is a sacred ceremony, and those of us who receive it are asked not to talk about it. The obvious reason is that it would profane what is meant to be sacred. I will say only one thing, however, and that is that it has something to do with the third eye.

I have gone to the Holy House throughout the years and have even sponsored people to receive the Tao. The Holy House features lectures about the Tao, and I have met new friends and old friends while visiting. It is always a nice experience. It is also a wonderful opportunity to experience a different culture.

I have told you about my experiences with the Tao for a couple of different reasons. First, it tells you what the underlying principle behind my life and writing career has been for all of these years. Second, it demonstrates that I had a somewhat extensive background with the Tao prior to meeting Roosevelt Gainey. Besides being a Chi Gong instructor, he is also a Taoist priest.

When I first read *The Tao Te Ching*, I was disappointed that there was no school of instruction. That problem is now solved. It just took me thirty-five years to find the right teacher. This is not a bad thing, however. In Chi Gong, slower is better. Do not be in too much of a hurry. We are literally living in a sea of eternity.

It is important to state that Roosevelt Gainey is not an ordinary Taoist priest nor is he an ordinary Chi Gong instructor. I am very lucky to have encountered him, but I should also state that is was not really luck. All of the Taoist spiritual work that I have done over my life led me to the various synchronicities I have experienced. This includes my Scientology experiences which were extensive. I received immense help from L. Ron Hubbard. I, however, was always the director of my life. I used the Tao wherever possible. I would eventually learn that synchronicity is the precursor to the Tao. At long last, courtesy of the Montauk Medicine Man and my other adventures in synchronicity, I arrived at the Taoist school which will some day be my alma mater.

I will now share my experiences with regard to the fountain of youth and some of the best secrets I know.

49

REAL RESULTS

After doing Artie's wellness program for one year, I attended World Tai Chi Day once again. This time, I would be very careful to spend all of my time with Roosevelt Gainey. Listening to anyone else might not have been a waste of time, but that was the way I looked at it.

Roosevelt's demonstrations were even superior to the previous year. This time, he was explaining that there are three different types of force: obvious, hidden, and mysterious. Obvious force speaks for itself. It is striking someone with a body part. Hidden force is far more subtle. It is utilizing the body, but the source of the force or power is not obvious. Hidden force synchronizes the motion of the body into a power-packed movement. This was the technique used in the one-inch punch I had witnessed the previous year. Mysterious force is even more awesome. Roosevelt demonstrated this by having someone hold up their hands in a grappling posture. Standing three or four feet away, the person completely collapsed and went down to his knees. He was not touched either. I had never seen anything like this before. It should also be added that the person this was demonstrated on was not a student of Roosevelt's so there was no question of it being staged. I bring this last point up because so-called masters in the martial arts have accused Roosevelt of staging his demonstrations. He does not. The accusations are either a result of the demonstrations being too incredible to be believed or the fact that the so-called masters often feel shown-up when they are exposed to something they cannot do.

I then heard him say something that I did not know about the martial arts, at least his brand of it. For every exercise you do that has a martial benefit, there is a health benefit and vice-versa. In other words, if you study his brand of Chi Gong for health, you are also going to enjoy an increased ability to defend yourself. Unfortunately, too many people who study the martial arts are more interested in physical power. They will, nevertheless, receive tremendous health benefits if they do their workouts.

This year, I got a chance to talk to many of his students. It was one in particular, however, who opened the door for me to come to class. Her name is Sharia Jones-Bey. We were talking about various subjects, and she handed me her business card. Being very cognizant that her name ended in "Bey," I asked her if she knew about Noble Drew Ali and the Moorish Science Temple. As a matter of fact, she had grown up attending it. This was a very neat coincidence because most of Roosevelt's students do not have this background. When I learned this, I went to my car so that I could give her a copy of *Synchronicity and the Seventh Seal* which features information on the Moors and Moorish Science.

As we continued to talk, she told me about the class schedule. Had she not mentioned it, I would have been in the dark about coming to Chi Gong class. Thus it was that Moorish Science opened the door for me to attend Roosevelt's class. I also spent time with Jimmy Haggerty who had been studying with Roosevelt for about a year and a half. His story was very dramatic.

As a steel worker, Jimmy had fallen off of a two story building and was badly injured. Three vertebrae were crushed and his hand looked like a catcher's mitt. It just so happened that one of Jimmy's coworkers was Roosevelt's nephew who told him to come to class. The result was miraculous for Jimmy. His hand recovered and so did his back. I should add that Jimmy works at his Chi Gong exercises longer and harder than any of the other students I have seen. The more time you put in, the better the result.

This caused a bit of trouble when he was playing around with a student from another school. This student was a very accomplished black belt who had been studying martial arts for over thirteen years. Roosevelt's techniques are so superior that Jimmy, who did not even have two years of experience, was throwing this guy right and left. It did not go over well with the black belt. In actual fact, this sort of thing happens frequently with Roosevelt's students. In Jimmy's case, he had no intention to piss the guy off or show him up.

When people hear stories like this, they will often show up to class and expect miracles to happen without doing anything. Too often, big strong men show up and are taken to task by women who are old enough to be their mother. Such people often leave and never come back. One has to park their ego and be humble in order to learn. There are countless stories, but I will now share my own.

After hearing so many stories and seeing actual results, I found out that a class would be held the next morning. It started at seven o'clock in the morning at Kaiser Park in Coney Island. After dinner, I realized that if I wanted to get to class on time, I would have to drive over three hours to get home from Connecticut, get some sleep and then wake up about five-thirty.

Everyone who fails to come to class has a good excuse, and I had an excellent one. I had forgotten to wear a hat that day and my head became badly sunburned. It hurt like hell, too. While sleeping that night, I woke up in pain and drenched my head with aloe vera gel. This relieved the pain for an hour or so whereupon I woke up in pain once again. This routine continued throughout the entire night. Despite the rather excruciating pain, I was determined to go to class. I arose without much real sleep and took the forty-five minute drive to Coney Island. Keep in mind that it was a Sunday morning and there was virtually nobody on the road. I wondered if anyone would be there.

My first day was not spectacular in terms of results, but I learned to "push the tree" with Jimmy. In Chi Gong, there are three basic tools you use: the tree, a towel, and a medicine ball. The tree gives you power, the towel gives you strength, and the medicine ball gives you dexterity. I will not say too much about these exercises as they really have to be demonstrated in person.

If you read *The Tao Te Ching*, it says that you should strengthen your bones. This is what one is doing when they are pushing the tree. It should be done with the entire skeleton. Muscles can only withstand three or four hundred pounds of pressure while bones can withstand four tons. That is an amazing scientific fact and one that enables little Oriental people to throw big "strong" Caucasians. Squeezing a towel builds incredible strength in the tendons and ligaments in your hands. With this exercise, you could easily choke an attacker who has grabbed you.

There are all sorts of exercises you can do with a medicine ball, but a very important one is to roll it against the tree with your forearms. One can also do this on a table or on the ground. It not only builds strength but increases agility when engaged with another person's arms or hands.

Beginning these exercises was great, but it was not revelatory to me in terms of the fountain of youth principle. I was just getting stronger and beginning to feel really good. I put in a lot of time and did these exercises every day.

A few weeks into my training, I began to get a very practical idea about the fountain of youth. When Roosevelt was showing one of his younger students how to do a particular exercise, I commented that I was too old to do that one as I could no longer touch my toes.

"That has nothing to do with it," he said as he took me over to a bench where he proceeded to show me a towel stretch.

After doing this towel stretch for five or ten minutes, I was now able to touch my toes. I could not believe it. It was almost as if I was young again!

I was so impressed that I wondered if he could do something about my throwing arm. I had hurt my arm very badly the year before when I was suddenly and unexpectedly recruited to play quarterback. My arm, which was already floundering due to age, was not warmed up and I threw it out. As a result, I could not throw a ball for more than ten yards without severe pain.

Telling Roosevelt about my condition, he showed me how to do a windmill in order to work out all the calcium or other junk that had accumulated in my rotator cuff. He said to do it one hundred times a day for twenty-two days. In a very short time, my arm had recovered fully. Between that and other exercises I was learning, my arm was better than it had been in years.

Although I had expected to get healthier and stronger by doing Chi Gong, I never thought it might revive my athleticism. I now took on the subject of running. Since I was very young, I was a fast runner. I was never fast enough to win a track meet as a sprinter but I was often the fastest on a sports team or in my class. In athletics, however, track people are not always so good. I was best at sports like football, rugby or soccer where one utilizes the skills of slowing down, speeding up and running laterally.

The towel stretches I had already learned did wonders for my legs. The tendons and ligaments were firming up and this made running far easier. I also learned accelerated running. This is where one starts off running as slow as possible and then gradually increases to a full sprint. When full speed is reached, one then gradually slows down. This enables the heart to clock the body and makes for better performance. It also conditions the joints to get more performance. For me, the results were spectacular. When we started football season, I soon found myself dodging and jumping around people for half of the entire field in order to score a touchdown. I had not run like that in almost ten years and I was completely flabbergasted.

While this may or may not sound spectacular to you, it was. In our world, fifty-four-year-old men do not often perform like that, particularly when they were over the hill a year or two earlier. I literally could not wait to play each week as I wanted to see how much I could improve.

I should also add that there is no professional sports trainer or so-called expert in sports medicine who could have gotten the same results for me. Doctors and professional sports people are oblivious to these techniques. If they taught them, players would not have the injuries they do. They would also perform better.

My ability to perform continued to increase until one Sunday in November. I had a friend staying with me from out of town, and I invited him to come play with us. He watched from the sidelines on one particular play where I caught a short pass. I then dodged three players. As my friend watched, he said that he did not think I would get around the first guy. After I did, he was sure I would not get around the second. The same for the third.

This last feat was very significant because, in the last few years, I could not have dodged my way around old men on the field. These men were slower than I, but I had lost my lateral running skills and the ability to shift my hips. All of a sudden, everything had changed. That was the good news.

The bad news was that I did not realize the situation I was in. I was operating at a peak capacity that I had not known in many many years. I felt like a twenty-eight-year-old again. Not feeling any limits, I was tearing around people like there was no tomorrow. Feeling one-hundred percent, I was trying to operate at one-hundred-and-twenty-five percent. This was a mistake. I created so much torque on my hips that my gluteus maximus and several other muscles were pulled. Some tendons and ligaments suffered as well. The general area of injury was in my lumbar area where I had suffered three herniated disks in a car accident a couple of years earlier. I had to be helped off of the football field.

I could hardly walk for the next three days. Fortunately, my friend who was visiting was able to take care of necessities for me. I was lucky to have him with me. I did, however, continue on with my daily Chi Gong regimen.

Recovery was slow, but I did recover. I was able to play again after only a couple of weeks but I wore a back brace and did not play at full tilt. One of my fellow students then taught me a very important lesson. When you reach a new peak, you should play at eighty percent strength. This will enable you to build your dexterity slowly. Full exertion can be dangerous, particularly when you are older and not yet in prime shape.

One of the most important things I have learned in Chi Gong is that I have to remember that I am not Superman. Sometimes the actual things you are able to accomplish are amazing. This has to be tempered with reality. One needs to find a balance point.

My recovery from the injury was such that I also healed a long term pain and discomfort that was generated from the herniated disks. Before the football season ended in March, I enjoyed another surprise. On a snowy day, I ran after a player who was dashing for a touchdown. This player, who is at least fifteen years younger, is either just as fast or a tad faster than myself. On this day, I chased him from afar and actually caught him from behind. No one, especially myself, could really believe it. When I told Roosevelt about, he told me that it was due to the new exercises I had been doing in class. They are designed to strengthen the legs. In other words, you can run a lot faster with steel girders for legs as opposed to toothpicks. I had no idea it could be that much faster.

At this writing, I am looking forward to another football season. The sky seems to be the limit, as long as I remember that I am not a superhero.

50

CHI GONG

Every human being on Earth is on a march towards death. It begins when we are born and is to be expected. If one follows the typical behavior pattern of typical people, you will be right in step with the life expectancy of the average citizen. Stepping off of this treadmill requires that you make a radical departure from your fellow human beings. This does not mean that you disengage from society, but it mandates a definite change in your lifestyle. I found myself routinely getting up at five in the morning and either beginning my workout or going to class.

Although improving your diet and exercising is a very important part of Chi Gong, the most radical change required of you will be that of your breath. Previously in this work, Chi Gong was defined as "breath work." *Chi* means "life" or "breath" and *Gong* means "work."

Most of you in the reading audience are breathing without any conscious effort as you go through the day. For those of you who practice yoga or other disciplines, you might be breathing somewhat differently. Even so, this is probably relegated to the specific time when you are doing your disciplines. In any event, you are not breathing anywhere near your full capacity.

It is a scientific fact that most people breathe with five percent lung capacity or less. Why? What are we supposed to do with the rest of our lung capacity? One of the reasons we do not breathe to the fullest extent we can is that no one has told us any different. It is just accepted by our thought processes that we should limp along as substandard breathers. Our brain certainly does not go into a panic if we breath at five percent capacity, and this is a very key point which opens the door to further understanding.

It has been stated many times that human beings operate with something on the order of ten percent of their brain capacity. Although this is broadly recognized, it is never recognized that this has everything to do with our lung capacity. In order to function, the brain needs oxygen. Fill your lungs to capacity and your brain is going to change substantially. Keep in mind that breathing is literally the act of animating a body. If you control your breath, you control your life. By running your body at five percent capacity, you will be capable of five percent of your potential longevity. Maybe the ages given for Methuselah and other Biblical characters were based upon actual solar years after all.

Roosevelt learned that ancient men were far more capable than the best athletes of today. In the New York Public Library, he was given books from the 1800's which stated that men of old were once fully capable of defeating a giant beast on their own. This meant a mastodon or a sabre-tooth tiger. The reason these men could take down a beast single-handedly was due to their breathing capacity. In other words, they were utilizing all of their lungs when they took in oxygen. As the brains of their descendants developed, pure physical strength receded from every day life. As they physically degenerated, it took several men with spears and other weapons to subdue a large beast.

This might sound preposterous to you, but you should admit to yourself that you have little experience in such matters. Have you ever known anyone who breathes at full capacity? Of course you do not. I would be in the same boat had I not met Roosevelt Gainey and learned these things from him. You should also understand that the prospect that breathing results in increased strength has to do with the laws of physics. It is not mumbo-jumbo.

Your lungs have five lobes, but most people use less that one. By breathing long enough and continuously enough, you can eventually fill these lobes to capacity. Reaching this level is quite an accomplishment, but it is no place to stop. One keeps breathing. If you do, you will then begin to fill ten chambers of the body. This is another level all together. When you fill all five lobes and all ten chambers, oxygen literally begins to pour out of your system.

The technique required in these matters is to gradually and slowly fill up your lungs and body as if you were very slowly inflating a balloon. If you have ever seen the air let out of a full balloon, you will begin to understand the power that a human body is capable of. When you employ tendons and bones, it is even more powerful. It takes a lot of practice and hard work to inflate your body to such an extent. That is why Chi Gong means breath *work*. You actually have to work at it.

It should also be pointed out that 99.9% of all Chi Gong instructors in the world neither know nor teach these methods. It is unique to Roosevelt Gainey and his Taoist System of Living Arts©. What I am telling you here is unprecedented with regard to the human condition and exploration of such. You literally have no benchmark with which to compare it. To you, it is only a theory at this point. I have only arrived at these secrets as a result of the elaborate journeys I have undertaken in this life. As of this writing, I am approaching fifty percent lung capacity. I have a long ways to go, but I have come very far. It would be a crime against myself not to continue. As spectacular as it all sounds, I am actually understating everything.

Many of you, quite wisely, will want to know where to begin. The first step begins with your next breath. Simply take a breath and notice everything you can about that breath. Next, just be aware of your breathing and the various mechanisms your body employs in conducting the act of breathing. I will give you more to do in a bit, but that is your first step.

Breathing is the most important step, but there is more to the equation. The act of breathing brings oxygen into the lungs which then transfers into the blood. The blood vessels, however, are not the only way oxygen gets into your body. There is also something in your body which is called the fascia and it connects your entire body. When you cut open an uncooked chicken, you see can see a viscous white matter which seems to connect everything. This is the fascia. It connects your muscles, your organs, your bones, your tendons, your ligaments and everything else.

The fascia brings oxygen to all of the body. It laces itself through the ligaments, tendons and literally brings oxygen into the bone marrow. This is why the Chinese refer to Chi Gong as bone marrow washing. When your bones have oxygen, they become strong and generate adult stem cells. These stem cells travel throughout the entire system and heal the body.*

When you were born, the fascia originally emanated from the naval and this is its source. The entire fascia of the body can be manipulated, massaged or healed through the naval. The in-out function of breathing originated in the naval even before the lungs were developed. Breathing therefore includes the naval. It is already occurring naturally in your body but on a reduced level. You want to cultivate and increase its ability to literally make the fascia come alive.

You will sometimes see the fascia come alive in a martial arts movie. An actor will sometimes flex his body into one impressive tendon sheath which looks like a mass of sinews and muscles. This is a genuine example of one who has put in long hours turning their body into a formidable weapon.

In Chi Gong we are building up or conditioning the fascia, the ligaments, the tendons, and the bones. Muscles are simply there to assist these more senior support systems. If the fascia, ligaments, tendons and bones are conditioned, professional athletes will not need to retire at age thirty-five or forty. They can last a lot longer. If you were to tell them this, however, they would probably not believe you. After all, what I am saying here has been a guarded secret for millennia so of course they would not know it.

All of this raises a very intersting question. If this knowledge is true, why do you not hear of martial arts masters living exceptionally long lives? There are at least a couple of good answers.

First, if there are Chi Gong practitioners who have lived for centuries, they just might not want to advertise it. Second, most accomplished martial artists do not really emphasize or fully appreciate the longevity or health aspects of what is being said here. There are many true stories of masters who could accomplish phenomenal physical feats but either drank to excess or smoked their tail off. It is common. Such individuals are too physically oriented and lack an adequate spiritual or health quotient. You might not believe this, but it is true.

* This is complimentary to *StemEnhance®*, the product I referred to earlier in this book. As there is no limit as to what you can accomplish with Chi Gong, it raises the question of whether or not one should take supplements. The body needs all the help it can get so I do both. One, of course, has to actually do the work to get the full benefits.

Longevity has everything to do with the optimum functioning of your internal organs such as the heart, liver, pancreas, spleen, and kidneys. The more oxygen in your system, the better these will function. From this perspective, it is a no-brainer that increased lung capacity will extend your life by leaps and bounds. The equation is too simple to be believed, but it is genuinely that elementary. All answers are basically simple, and this one is hiding in plain sight yet virtually no one does it.

Practicing Chi Gong will strengthen your internal organs and make you much more formidable for purposes of health as well as self defense. In this regard, Roosevelt had an addendum to add to Artie's story about Bruce Lee.

Shortly before Lee's death, he had occasion to meet with an elder martial artist who was heralded as a great teacher and master. As was typical of Lee's showmanship and one-up-man-ship, he struck him unexpectedly and hurt the elder. This was not only rude and disrespectful, it angered one of the elder's students who then administered an intense Chi Gong blow to Lee.

When you build up your Chi Gong, you become powerful. When you strike another in combat or with bad intent, it is a direct assault on your opponent's internal organs. Conversely, if you receive a blow, the power of your internal organs will enable you to withstand it.

In the case of Bruce Lee, he was dealt a severe blow that resulted in his demise. The aneurism and other conditions only precipitated his premature death. There were other complex factors surrounding Bruce Lee, but these are not so important. For all of his incredible skill, he ended up living a very short life. What is important is that your best bet for longevity is increasing the strength of your internal organs. This is done through the breath.

In Chapter 39, entitled *Perception*, I relayed an esoteric formula about the breath. Specifically, I stated how the pharaoh lights the fire of the capstone by activating the Sphinx. This is an analogy for mainting a universal or planetary equilibrium. A fire, of course, is maintained by an air flow or oxygen. More importantly to you, this analogy can be applied to yourself by lighting the fire in your own pyramid (situated at the root of your gestation point) by breathing. It is one of the most valuable things you can ever learn.

Earlier in this chapter, I told you to be aware of your breathing and the various mechanisms associated with it. If you did so, now revist what you previously experienced. It is now time to begin your next step. It sounds easy, but it is not as easy as it might sound. It begins with your next breath. Breathe in as slowly as you can, breathing in through your nose and inflating your lungs like a balloon. You are trying to take in a long, slow and continuous breath. When you reach full inhalation, exhale through your mouth and make the exhalation as long, slow and continuous as possible. Play with this breath until you are comfortable with it.

Once you are comfortable with the breath and are doing it as per the above instructions, repeat it as many times as possible. Some people get tired after a few breaths and some might get tired after twenty or thirty. The reason for the tiredness is that after you breathe in, your body responds by exhaling. This includes toxins that are within your system. As the food and environment of most people is quite toxic, there is a lot to get rid of. The body has a natural repulsion to toxins. Artie Crippen recommneds the osha root to help the body detoxify. Breathing will accelerate the process. You want to work your way up to one hundred long, slow and continuous breaths per day. Once you have done that, you want to do it three times a day. This is an arduous process for the average person, but it is extremely rewarding.

If you have the discipline to accomplish the above, you are well on your way towards becoming a disciple of Chi Gong. Take it at your own pace. Even though the above will take a chunk out of your day, Roosevelt has a good philosophy about time spent on Chi Gong. Look at it as if you are tithing to yourself instead of a church. A church might require one-tenth of your income. Chi Gong requires one-tenth of your day which comes out to two hours and twenty-four minutes.

As you go through life, integrate this breathing into your day-to-day activities. If you can breathe in massively for eight hours a day, Roosevelt says that you will eventually kick into into the natural mode of our ancestors. Mastondons and sabre-tooth tigers will no longer be so intimidating.

51

RETURN OF THE JINN

In the previous chapter, I provided you with secrets that have been guarded for millenia. It is all common sense if you think about it but it is scientific as well. As I have demonstrated already, however, scientists are limited by their perception. Increase your capacity for oxygen and you will broaden your horizons.

There is, of course, another component to life besides science and known information. Those are the darker areas of the horizon which include the twilight of sunset and the darkness of night. As challenging as these areas can be, we get a clue in how to deal with them when we consider the etymology of the word *oxygen*. The dictionary hypothesizes that the word comes from *ak* and *gen*. They translate *oxys*, the Greek word for "sharp" or "acid" as deriving from the Indo-European *aks* or *ak*. *Gen*, or course, refers to genesis or generation. If they studied Egyptian, they would know that *ak* means light. It also translates as *oc* or *og* and this brings us back to Tir na nÓg and the fountain of youth. Oxygen thus refers to the generation of light and the decay of ignorance.

As straightforward as the above etymology is, do not dismiss for one second that *gen* is also convertible to *jinn*. The jinn represent the gargoyles who will either bless or prevent your passage into the realm of Tir na nÓg and the adventures of eternity. I can think of no way to better demonstrate this principle than what happened when I introduced some of my friends to Chi Gong.

When I first lectured on my Chi Gong adventures at one of our monthly Montauk meetings, the crowd was very impressed. Never before have I had so many people come up to me and tell me that it was the best lecture I had ever given. I was relaying many of the things you have just read in this book. Everyone heard about a remarkable path that would not only prolong their life, it would make them feel better and handle so many of their physical problems. Although they were delighted by what they had heard, none of them took the effort to show up to class. They are all locked into their routines which are orchestrated by jinn keeping them in their sleeping state. If it is not a sleeping state, it is certainly one that is going to keep them moving rapidly on the march to death.

When I told Roosevelt about this, he had a further explanation. There is a difference between realization and actualization. People love to hear about such exploits as they are truly miraculous and create a sense of euphoria and an exalted state of consciousness. Actualization, however, is a totally different ball game. It requires dedication and hard work. People are entrained and conditioned to be entertained. They are seldom encouraged to do things, particularly on the level of Chi Gong. Just because I have broken out of the trance of "old age" or whatever you want to call it, it does not mean that others are going to break free from it. There are some that will, but there are too few who will wake up. Keep in mind that waking up is not good enough. One has to actually get out of bed and start earning one's keep in the Chi Gong world.

Despite the above, I was able to bring one person to class. This was Madalyn Suozzo who is a remarkable healer herself and has studied with energy masters from all over the world. As she respected my viewpoint, she was happy to learn something while visiting the East Coast. After only a few minutes in Roosevelt's presence, she could not believe what she was experiencing. Despite her extensive experience with masters in both the field of healing and the martial arts, she had never seen anything like this.

"He is the only one I ever met who knows how to be in a body!" she said.

Madalyn was so impressed with what she had learned, she wanted to promote Roosevelt's work on the West Coast where she lives. When she got home, she actively promoted a weekend workshop for Roosevelt in Marin County.

At the same time as she was promoting him in California, he was arranging to have his own workshop in New Jersey. This was only for select students from his classes. Impressed with her own healing ability, he specifically selected Madalyn to attend.

In the midst of all of this, I was at Mary Hardy's conference in Michigan. Mary's home is on a lake and is not conducive to good cell phone reception. My cell phone does not work there at all. I cannot receive or make calls. For some mysterious reason, I was able to receive a call on my cell phone from Madalyn. She was very upset that Roosevelt was not returning her calls as she needed to make flight arrangements to attend his seminar. I, however, was more preoccupied with the oddity of why she was the only one who could get through to me on my cell phone. Oddly, I received a couple of more calls from her on my cell phone. All I could offer her was to say that I would give her some alternative phone numbers for Roosevelt when I returned home.

En route home, I called Madalyn when I reached a restaurant where my cell phone worked. I let her know that I expected to be home by the end of the night and would give her some phone numbers then. Getting home, however, was not quite that easy.

That same evening, I planned to visit Sleepy Hollow on the way home and see a lady who was helping me with another project. As I forgot her number, I visited the local library in order to obtain it. Once there, I realized that this was an opportunity to look up some information on the Montauk Indians. Although I did not have a long time to read, I did see indications that Franklin Roosevelt was a Montauk Indian and that his family was also tied to the Van Tassel clan. I was in town, however, to visit my friend.

Unable to find her number in the directories provided, I headed out to her house. I had been there before but did not recall the exact address. My memory would have to serve. Unfortunately, my transmission failed at the exact point of the famous Sleepy Hollow bridge. I struggled to get the car to a parking place and knew that I was stranded for the night in Sleepy Hollow. Unfortunately, I could not get through to my friend and had to make hotel arrangements.

A failed transmission is not only a major dent in one's budget, it means that one will be without transportation for several days. I was a good ways from home and phoned friends in order to resolve the problems this mishap generated. The car would have to be fixed locally, and I would take the train home to Long Island.

Sleeping in a hotel that night, my dream state was penetrated and I suffered a magical attack. There was no doubt about it, but I was surprised. Since I had been practicing Chi Gong, this sort of thing did not happen. It was a rare occurence in any event.

When I got home the following afternoon, the first thing I did was call Brenda, Roosevelt's assitant, and let her know that Madalyn had not been able to get through. Not long after that, I heard from Roosevelt, and he insisted that I attend his seminar which was to be held that coming weekend. I was pleased but very surprised to be able to attend as this was an exclusive seminar. Madalyn was selected as she has obvious abilities and wanted to become one his teachers. Roosevelt said that a lot had been going on and he would fill me in on the details later. He was also willing to arrange transportation for me to New Jersey.

As it turned out, Madalyn paid for airline tickets to fly to New York, but she never arrived. The entire situation had become too stressful for her, and she forfeited the airline money. For myself, however, things worked out smoothly. My car was repaired in time, and I drove to New Jersey myself. When I arrived at the workshop, I was immediately put on healing exercises. There was instense healing and energy work going on, and I would only get to find out what had happened with Madalyn during breaks or when there was a spare moment. The focus of the workshop was on healing and not personal drama.

I eventually learned that as a result of Madalyn's promotion of Roosevelt, there had been a rather severe psychic attack on all three of us. Her action of putting a notice on the internet attracted attention that none of us needed or wanted.

Thanks to the principles of synchronicity, a Taoist Circle of Masters were meeting the same weekend of the psychic attacks. Roosevelt is a member of this circle and asked them all to simultaneously work on our behalf. Whatever they did worked, and I had no reason do doubt him.

Roosvelt then explained to me that a coven once offered him a briefcase full of money to teach them his powers. He said it was tempting, but he declined the offer as it was unethical. The coven eventually raised the offer to one-hundred thousand dollars in cash, but he declined that, too. This coven and their related entities were not too happy about other people learning his work.

The long and short of this episode was that Madalyn completely backed away from learning any more about Roosevelt's teachings. I found this surprising as she had wanted to become one of his top teachers. Perhaps the psychic attack worked on her. In any event, the jinn did their job. She is not going to follow this path, at least for the immediate future. Prior to this incident, Madalyn and I had been pretty much best friends. She made it clear we are still friends, but we hardly ever talk anymore.

When I told Roosevelt my sadness over Madalyn, he explained that Chi Gong will create profound changes in your life. Madalyn was obviously not ready for this training. One of my other friends, who is a practitioner of Chi Gong, said that Chi Gong will really stir up your stuff. This friend also said that Chi Gong is not for everybody.

I disagree with this last statement. Good nutrition and routine exercise is not for everybody either. If you ignore them, however, you are putting yourself at extreme risk. I think you get the idea. There is no question in my mind, however, that most people are not ready to walk this particular path.

In any event, there was an upside for me. Had it not been for all of this kerfuffle and nonsense, I do not know that I would have received Roosevelt's phone call and been invited to the seminar. It was the opportunity of a lifetime. Not only did I learn many of the stories I have shared with you, I became much more accomplished at Chi Gong. The jinn are positive as well as negative. One has to learn how to negotiate these pathways. It begins with being receptive or yin to the circumstances that are presented to you. Do keep in mind that far too many people are receptive to indoctrinations and modalities that will undermine their actual ability. If not, grocery stores and media would not be the way they are.

Although the jinn had definitely treated me well in the previous circumstances, I would soon realize that some of these forces were familiar and had been planted in my life years before.

52

VIRTUE

When on a research trip many years ago, I had occasion to go into a sauna. It was a rather large sauna, and there were other people inside. Somebody brought up the subject of tantra, and before I knew it, I had struck up a conversation with a beautiful lady. She soon came over to sit down across from me so that she could hear me better. At some point, I realized that she was completely naked. Before that, I had no idea that I had entered a "clothing optional" sauna.

The woman basically needed an ear to talk to as she was very frustrated with her husband's sexuality. She said it all began when he had studied the work of Mantak Chia, a very popular author who writes on Taoist sexuality, healing, Chi Gong, and multiple orgasms for males. He covers many other topics, too. The husband, who was within earshot, came over as I began to engage him in the conversation as well.

I was already familiar with Mantak Chia who used to teach on Long Island. He is highly revered throughout the New Age community and his work has been lauded by all sorts of people. My interest in him had only to do with the fact that his name was *Mantak*. When I phoned him, he was kind enough to pick up the phone and answer my questions. I basically wanted to know what the name *Mantak* meant and how he had acquired it. Telling me that the name was given to him, he said that *Mantak* is a Tibetan word which means virtue. Besides that, it also means clarity, understanding or bright light. *Chia*, by the way, means beast.

Mantak Chia eventually left Long Island and returned to his native home of Thailand. For many years, he came back to the United States and did workshops. Most of his focus was on huge retreat centers he had established in Thailand and Central America.

When I saw that he was coming back to New York for some weekend workshops, I decided to attend one on Iron Shirt Chi Gong. I gave him a copy of *Pyramids of Montauk*, which included his name, and had a pleasant conversation with him. Attending the workshop for two days, I did many postures that were designed to activate the various meridians in the body. I thought the exercises were kind of neat. It left me with a sort of glowing energy you might say. I not only felt it but many of my healer friends commented on it when they saw me soon afterwards. Although I wanted to continue the exercises, it never happened and I lost interest. He eventually stopped coming to America.

When I heard about the problems this couple was having, I just listened to everything they said. The husband was trying hard to apply Mantak Chia's techniques, but his body just short-circuited. I already had acquired some knowledge about multiple orgasms for males and understood what he was talking about. Although I had not read Mantak Chia's books, it was pretty clear this man had screwed himself up and wrapped himself up around a telephone pole as far as his sexuality was concerned. I basically had to deprogram him (conversationally) from what he had read. At the end of our talk, he was very grateful and was going to start off on a new foot. I did not keep in contact with him or his wife.

Our bad report does not deserve judgment or condemnation for anybody. It is just a report. This report, however, started a long and slow process which eventually resulted in revelation. I would later receive privileged information, through a confidential source, about Mantak Chia's personal state of well being. At class one day, I happened to mention this information to Roosevelt. What he had to say, I will not repeat but he was not enthusiastic about Mantak Chia's teachings.

He then explained to me that he had once tested the Iron Shirt Chi Gong that Mantak Chia teaches. When Roosevelt placed his index finger on one of Chia's students, the man simply crumbled in pain. He had no idea what Roosevelt had done. This brand of Iron Shirt Chi Gong did not stand up to a rudimentary test.

Keep in mind that this was not a casual student of Mantak Chia's but a regular and devout student. It is quite clear that this man's internal organs were not sufficient to withstand a little energy poke in the ribs. This was not a punch mind you, but a very slight touch with an emission of energy. The whole point is that if one is learning Iron Shirt Chi Gong, one should expect to have an iron shirt that is capable of withstanding an energetic force.

Doctors and scientists study the phenomena around Mantak Chia as if it were some great mystery. He is lauded by practitioners across the world. As far as I am concerned, this is just one more example of people following anyone that sounds good and knows more than they do. Mantak Chia does know a lot and has been hailed as a healer, but my experience with both teachers tells me that Roosevelt's Taoist System of Living Arts© is far superior and more practical.

I would compare the two systems between training for the Olympics as compared to the Special Olympics. I make this analogy not to be funny but because it brings home a vital point. People in the Special Olympics have a physical handicap of some sort. By whatever karmic reason under the sun, their status in the physical plane has been compromised from what is considered the status quo. In Chi Gong, it is vital that the spiritual, mental, emotional, and physical bodies all be in alignment.

According to reports Roosevelt has received, Chia's work has opened up students to advanced levels they are not ready for. The two examples I've given in this chapter are not the only ones. Although I do not have the time or inclination, I could write an entire novel (based on exact truth) on how a student of Mantak Chia's virtually rose from the dead to befuddle some of the characters in this book, and I am not talking about my Chi Gong friends. One does not blame Mantak Chia for this, but the jinn are prone to exploit those who open up without proper grounding.

There are, of course, no guarantees with any teacher. You have to pick and choose wisely. Personally, I would be wary of anyone who refers to themselves as a master. Too many times I have seen people defer to a wise master from the East who ends up vampirizing their vital life force. Roosevelt Gainey does not allow his students to refer to him as a master. He says that anyone who believes he has truly mastered life is a fool. Instead, he calls himself the head student. People sometimes promote Roosevelt as a master or grand master, and that is unavoidable in his profession but he disdains the title.

As for masters, he has an open challenge to anyone in the martial arts. If you are truly a master, he invites you to spar with him and see how you hold up. So-called masters will not take the challenge which tells us pretty much everything we need to know about them. If someone were to overcome him in a sparring session, he would then become their student. That is how he learned what he learned in the first place.

Some Taoists feel that Roosevelt's challenging mentality is not yin enough for them. They have relayed stories to me about how taking it on the chin is only due to one's karma. In this regard, it might also surprise you to know that Roosevelt's most powerful principles were handed down as a feminine (yin) tradition. If one yields to the vital breath and makes the body a yin receptacle for oxygen, they will acquire significant power and strength. Ironically, this is seen in the etymology of the word *mantak* or *virtue*.

> **virtue** *vertue* < *OFr.* vertue, *virtue, goodness, power* < *Latin virtus*, manliness, worth < *vir*, man: see werewolf

Most people think of virtue as chastity or moral excellence. While these are definitions for the word, the etymology derives from power. Virtue is strength. When we consider this etymology, keep in mind that *vir* or *man* are words that originally derived from or referred to the female. Incredible strength means health.

According to ancient Chinese history, Confucius had occasion to meet Lao Tzu. Finding Confucius rude and inappropriate, Lao Tzu at first refused to take him on as a student. When Confucius went home with his tail between his legs, he mentioned to his fellows that he did not know what to make of Lao Tzu and referred to him as a dragon. In this respect, I should tell you that if Roosevelt Gainey is not pure dragon, he is as close as I have seen. To me, this is a refreshing indication that I am one step closer to the Tao.

53

THE LEGEND

What I have told you in these short chapters is far more than one of Roosevelt's typical students will learn when they come to class. They could even remain in class for years and not hear some of these stories. On the other hand, they might learn a lot of other things and hear different stories. No class is ever the same.

One day, fairly early on in my training, I had asked Roosevelt a question. He took me to some geometric diagrams that have been drawn in chalk at the park.

"The circle squared," he said. "You need to square the circle."

I could not believe my ears in lieu of what I have written about this principle in previous chapters of this book. He was explaining how to maneuver the body and relate it to the infinite patterns of geometry that exist within and around the body. Squaring the circle can make for a very effective punch or maneuver. He then demonstrated how all of his movement conforms to the patterns of infinite geometry.

This also applies to what he calls Infinite Mind. This refers to infinity itself and is pure thought or essence. He teaches from Infinite Mind and not from a rote series of instructions. Infinite Mind rolls through the universe and deposits itself wherever it happens to. In this sense, one is opening up to the pattern of heaven itself when one studies Chi Gong with him.

Earlier, I mentioned that Roosevelt Gainey teaches a unique system of Chi Gong. When I attended his seminar, I learned how he came to study it.

One day, he was looking out from his apartment in Coney Island and saw an Oriental man working out on the beach. As the man was doing martial arts exercises, Roosevelt wanted to see what he was up to. At that time in his life, he had earned many black belts in different disciplines. Having a very muscular frame, he was working towards becoming "Mr. Black America."

Soon after sparring with the Oriental man, Roosevelt soon found himself turned upside down against a building and realized that he was coming straight down on his head. At the last minute, the Oriental man brought his hand down and rescued him from having a serious injury.

As far as Roosevelt knew, he was an accomplished martial artist with few or no rivals. This man, who was tiny by comparison, cleaned his clock and did so effortlessly. Roosevelt went home, put all his belts in a bag, and became this man's pupil. It changed his life forever.

His teacher, C.C. Liang, spoke to him only in Chinese. After about five years, they were in a bar together and Liang ordered a drink in fluent English. Unbeknownst to Roosevelt, C.C. Liang was a translator at the U.N. and spoke at least five different languages. Communication became much easier.

After six years, Liang brought Roosevelt to his cousin and had him fight his best pupil. When Roosevelt won, Liang was pleased to show up his cousin and told his pupil that he was all done with him. Insisting that he wanted to learn more, Roosevelt continued to study with his teacher for another six years.

C.C. Liang learned his martial arts from his Chinese mother. His father, who was a Korean, used to abuse him. Although his mother was highly skilled in martial arts and could have easily subdued the father, she never did so. This was due to the Chinese cultural habit of self-effacing respect to others. Instead, she taught her son Chi Gong so that he was able to defend himself. This tradition that I have been expounding upon was handed down from female to female over thousands of years. C.C. Liang was the first male to receive instruction in it.

Essentially, Roosevelt learned that muscles are nowhere near as important as tendons, ligaments and bones. These are what can do real damage. As I have already stated, breathing not only strengthens these body parts, it also strengthens the internal organs. When you see muscle-bound people, their internal organs are usually shot. This makes them extremely vulnerable in martial combat. Bad diet also contributes greatly to the breakdown of internal organs. Just like everything else in your body, they need oxygen and lots of it.

From his teacher, Roosevelt learned that all of the incredible accomplishments he had achieved from his previous martial arts training were relatively worthless by comparison. What he had learned previously, of course, would not have been worthless at all in terms of defending oneself. When you compare the essence of the breath, however, there is no comparison. It is very powerful and can do wonders.

If you hear Roosevelt talk about his teacher for very long, you might get the impression that he learned everything from him. This, however, is certainly not the case. He was a gifted healer well before he ever met him. In other words, he had special abilities. As he is also dyslexic, this has enabled him to focus and see things in four-dimensions. This is accompanied by an incredible memory. Despite the dyslexia, he has learned to overcome this and reads quite a bit.

Before meeting his teacher and before the pyramid craze of the Seventies, Roosevelt was lecturing on the powers and properties of pyramids to scientists in Brooklyn. When I told Preston about Roosevelt's exploits in this regard, he had heard of him.

On many occasions, I have been subjected to demonstrations where Roosevelt utilizes the principles of mysterious force described previously. Many times I have seen him drop somebody from twenty or thirty feet. There is no touching involved. I have seen it so many times that it no longer surprises me.

One time, I asked him about the use of such force and how it would or could subvert the legal purpose of a restraining order. In other words, this sort of phenomena is not really covered by our existing laws. Telling me that several students have asked him this question, he relayed a real life experience of his.

Standing on a subway platform beneath Chinatown one day, he saw something very odd. It was an older Oriental man who was careening over the side of the platform. He was moving like a yo-yo on a string. As he careened, it was remarkable that he did not fall into the pit where he could be potentially crushed by a subway train. Continuing to watch this spectacle, Roosevelt looked over to the other side of the platform where he saw one of his own students manipulating the energy of the man.

"Why were you doing that?" he asked the student.

The student replied that he just wanted to see if he could do it. That was all.

Roosevelt responded by letting him know that he was cut off from further training for four years and that he was not to talk to any of the other students. It is all about synchronicity, he said. If he had not been at that particular platform at that particular time, he would not have noticed his student misusing energy.

If you mess around with this stuff, you are going to have to answer to a higher power. Such a power might act much more kindly to you than Roosevelt would under such a circumstance.

There are many more stories I could tell you, but I think you have gotten the point, at least on a level of realization. I hope that my words in this book will encourage you to actualize some of these things. You can begin with the breathing exercises I have already explained. It is hard work. If you actually do it, you will have done something that many of Roosevelt's other students have not done. Roosevelt would not only respect you for doing such, he would be able to see that you have done the work.

There are many more stories, but stories are not the point. It is most important you begin breathing, and I have already given you your first step. From there, Infinite Mind will take over the process. You will then have your own stories.

If you would like to inquire about the Montauk Wellness Center and receive instruction in Chi Gong, you can write to *skybooks@yahoo.com.*

54

OLIVE AND OMEGA

After reading this book, some people might get the idea that I have accomplished something great and have emerged into some form of paradise. This is not quite the truth. I have accomplished something great in terms of finding a competent teacher who can and has assisted me in accessing Taoist principles. It is also true that I have made some remarkable breakthroughs with regards to my own health, athleticism and potential longevity. That is the good news. On the other hand, I have never been confronted by so many challenges. Even so, I treat my Chi Gong work outs as priority. It assists me with the various challenges.

As I write this, I have been studying The Taoist System of Living Arts© for one year and four months. That is not a very long time in one sense, but it is a very long time in another. I have practiced hard every day during that time and I look at it like investing in the financial markets.

If you or someone had invested one hundred dollars a month for yourself in a mutual fund since you were born, it would have accumulated into a tidy sum by now. If one thousand dollars a month had been invested, it would be a small fortune or a sizable fortune, depending upon your age. If you spend one-tenth of your day doing Chi Gong, you will be investing in your own longevity as well as your physical strength. The path towards longevity requires work and that means breath work.

Part of my work, of course, includes writing and the various paths of synchronicity I tread. As I studied Chi Gong, I discovered the tales of Cerridwen and Tir na nÓg. If they are not real in themselves, they are certainly reflective of the principles of reality. The same could be said for the olive.

As I shared my olive stories with one of my psychic friends, she told me that there are olive trees out at Montauk. I thought she was nuts as olive trees do not take kindly to the cold and Montauk goes below freezing in the winter. Looking further into these matters, I discovered that Montauk is indeed home to a tree which is known as the Russian olive or Asian olive. It is a very hearty tree that grows in China and Russia. The Russian olive bears a fruit that is reddish and very high in Vitamin C. While the leaves of this tree resemble those of the olive, the fruit is quite different.

When I asked Artie Crippen about the Russian olive, he knew exactly what I was talking about. He said this tree is not indigenous to Montauk but was brought over by the Chinese many years ago. They traded the seeds of the Russian olive to the locals in exchange for other goods. As these trees are not indigenous to Montauk, they have devastated other plant life. In certain areas, such as the area near the Walking Dunes, they have literally taken over.

Several months into my Chi Gong classes at Kaiser Park, I finally got someone to come to class with me besides Madalyn. His name is Michael, and he is an expert in biology. One day, he pointed out to me that the trees where we do our Chi Gong are Russian olives. I was amazed. The very area where I had learned my Chi Gong was right under the watchful eye of olive trees. It is a fitting end to this book, but it is not the only ending.

I mentioned earlier that I have many challenges in my life, and most of these are quite mundane. In the background, however, there lurk some very interesting threads which are weaving their way into my life. These present new challenges altogether, and one of these concerns my old friend David Anderson who once had a Time Travel Research Center on Long Island. You can read all about various details of his research on the Sky Books website (*skybooksusa.com*). As this book comes to a close, David is making good on an old pledge of his to invite me to Romania where he still has a research center.

Considerable intrigue has been added to my trip to Romania by reason of another project that has surfaced in that mysterious country. This concerns a book entitled *The Enemy Within*, by Radu

Cinamar, a member of "Department Zero" of the Romanian Secret Service. Department Zero is named such because it does not officially exist.

The Enemy Within is a true story about a mysterious area in the Bucegi Mountains, not far from an ancient megalith known as the Romanian Sphinx. This area is not unlike the Bermuda Triangle as several people have mysteriously disappeared while climbing in this region. After the American military discovered anomalous phenomena in this area with their own advanced satellite imaging technology, a joint collaboration was undertaken with the Romanian government.* Eventually, with the help of the Americans, the area was penetrated and a very mysterious hall of records was discovered. Instead of ancient artifacts, the chamber consists of geometric shapes that facilitate holographic projections. This includes a projection hall which is capable of showing the entire history of the planet Earth.

I have contracted to publish this book, and it will be ready in early 2008. The English version of the book will be entitled *Transylvanian Sunrise*. According to the Romanian publisher, who has also published the Romanian translation of *The Montauk Project*, the story of the hall of records is indeed true and has been independently verified. As soon as I agreed on a contract to publish this book, I was surprised to receive an email from David Anderson who I have not seen for five years. He was inviting me to a cultural tour of Romania and also to participate in Atlantykron 2008, an annual conference of scientists, writers, and artists.

The timing was so bizarre that I could not help but wonder if there was a connection between David Anderson's time travel research, all of which has been very secret for the last five years, and this mysterious hall of records which seems to be an outpost that was created out of this time line. These represent great mysteries, and I cannot hope to answer them at this time. Hopefully, my trip to Romania will answer these questions.

As I prepared for my trip, I heard from one of my readers who is already familiar with my olive synchronicities. To my surprise, she informed me that the entire country of Romania was formed over a dispute that occurred on the Mount of Olives.

* Romania has just recently joined NATO and is being welcomed into the European Union. America has recently established new military bases there.

Earlier in this book, I mentioned that there was a chapel on the Mount of Olives that was built upon the very spot where Christ is supposed to have ascended to heaven. It turns out that the keys to this chapel eventually ended up in the hands of what we now know as the Russian Orthodox Church. For some mysterious reason, and perhaps as a pretext to wage war, the French and English wanted access to this chapel. Apparently, they did not think the Russians deserved sole access to this holy site. In any case, this seemingly silly dispute over a church escalated into the Crimean War, a horrible conflict that gave rise to the Charge of the Light Brigade and the glorification of Florence Nightingale as the founder of modern nursing. When the spoils of war were divided up, new boundaries and nationalities were created. Out of this, the country of Romania was formed. It seems apparent that I cannot escape the synchronicity of the olive even if I would want to.

The olive theme returned once more when my friend psychic friend, Vicki, came to Chi Gong class. As we were in Brooklyn, we decided to go to Livingston Street and see where the second version of the New Montauk Theatre (from the playbill) had once stood. Years ago, she said that if I went to the area, I would find out something. It would be best, however, if I went with her. When we arrived, there was no indication of a theater. The property had been converted into a cineplex at some point, but that was also long gone. There was no vestige of anything worth pursuing except for what Vicki had originally said when she suggested we go to the actual site. She said we would find something. Vick then pointed to a couple of prominent buildings and said we should visit them They were both beautiful buildings.

After parking the car, we walked to the buildings and discovered that one was a Methodist church while the other was the Brooklyn Opera House. Both were interesting in and of themselves, but there was no special significance with regard to the mysterious playbill that had directed us there. As we walked back to the car, Vicki pointed to a triangular area with a statue.

"That is the place we need to go," she said. "That is the spot."

As we arrived at the area, I looked at the statue. It was a general from the Civil War.

"Stand in front of the statue," Vicki said. "That is the exact spot, right in front of the statue."

Standing right in front of the statue, I looked down and saw the name "Fowler." Although I did not know it, we were in Fowler Square, named after General Edward Brush Fowler.

"It's right there," I said, pointing to the name of Fowler.

I then explained to Vicki how the name of Pharoah was transliterated by the Dutch into Fowler. The name Fowler signfies Montauk royalty. Vicki had led me to the place, but I was the one who would understand. Pursuing the mystery of the playbill once again led me back to the fundamental truth of the Montauk Indians. The Fowler or Pharoah line is used by the Government to prove that alleged or supposed Indians are real Indians. The Fowlers themselves, however, are denied this privilige.

Edward Brush Fowler was a Civil War hero from Brooklyn who led his "Red Legged Devils" during the battles of Bull Run. As it turns out, he was married in the Methodist church that Vicki directed me to. Fowler was an accountant by profession but was very well connected in New York City politics. While the biographical write-ups I have seen on him do not indicate that he was a Native American, the name Brush is a dead give-a-way. The Brush family were involved in controversial land deeds with the Montauks. The Brush family later intermarried with the Montauks, and it is a prominent name amongst the tribe.

That this trip with Vicki led back to land deeds is not an accident. Earlier in this book, I reported on my discovery that the land deeds of Montauk were replete with 666 references. As Aleister Crowley identified so strongly with 666, perhaps it is not so unusual that his magical partner, Eva Tanguay, was a key part of the package that was handed to me by Kenn Arthur.

There is an alleged relative of Eva Tanguay by the name of Richard Tanguay who has very strange resonance with the occult side of the Montauk legacy. Richard Tanguay was closely associated with both Jim Morrison and Mick Jagger, two colleagues of Preston Nichols from his days in the recording industry.

Jagger wrote a song about his days at Montauk. It is entitled *Memory Motel* and is named after a motel of the same name. Although I have never been able to verify it, that hotel was said to house a mysterious entrance to the Montauk underground. Jagger was also a member of the O.T.O. under the tutelage of Kenneth Anger. He produced a satanic video or two during those days and was deeply influenced by the darker aspects of occultism.

Jim Morrison was also deeply obsessed with Aleister Crowley. When he died in France, no one was allowed to see his body. This included his family. According to Preston Nichols, Morrison was then sent to New Jersey by his handlers while record sales boomed. He was messed up and virtually brain dead. Preston, who had always been able to handle Jim during his prime recording years, was called in to try and help him in his incoherent state.

Richard Tanguay comes into the picture as he was known to have impersonated Jim Morrison in concerts with the other members of the Doors. Jagger was said to have been involved in these productions as well. In any event, Tanguay, Jagger and Morrison were all connected to each other in some strange way.

All of this represents the dark under belly of Montauk and the 666 connection. In whatever form this darkness comes, it is representative of or parallel to the forces or jinn which have denied the Montauks their rights and sacred land. This is why it came to me in the package that included Mount Olive. The associations are endless as they are a part of Infinite Mind.

What is significant about the Brush and Fowler connection is that it represents the Second Coming of the Pharoahs, and this is the new paradigm on the horizon. When the rights and the land of the Pharoahs are acknowledged and returned, the Second Coming of the Pharoahs will be fully activated.

As was said earlier, the pharaoh represents the mediator between the heavens and the Earth. This is the same as a stargate. If we refer to the esoteric formula presented earlier in this book, the pharaoh's job is to light the fire of the pyramid by activating the energy of the Sphinx. Is it not then ironic that my next journey will take me to visit the Romanian Sphinx? This, of course, is not a coincidence. While I do not know the full ramifications of all this, it is a prime example of synchronicity, the precursor to the Tao.

A sphinx not only represents a bridging of human and animal DNA, it represents the guardian of a sacred temple. The circumstance of a sphinx near this hall of records corroborates the truthfulness of the story and also represents the riddle of man. What is Mankind and where is it going?

The consciousness of Mankind is controlled and influenced by jinn who have also limited the functioning of the Montauk

Pharoahs. The traditional role of the pharoah is to bridge the world of the heavens with that of the Earth. He or she is an arbiter or traffic cop in this regard. Restoring the holy site of Montauk is an obvious step in accelerating and improving this process. Although I am not the pharaoh, I will fill the vaccuum and do my best to act as a steward until the rightful heritage of the Montauks is restored.

My trip to see David Anderson in Romania is also highly significant in this regard. He is providing me the means to visit the Romanian Sphinx itself. His ties to the hall of records in the Bucegi Mountains is both mysterious and unknown at this point. Between him and the adventures of Radu Cinemar, however, it is obvious that they are at the gateway of where "heaven" meets the Earth. As I activate the energy of the Sphinx, so to speak, my next few years will be involved with unveiling this mystery and publishing and writing on the phenomena that is encountered.

With regard to the matter of a stargate, it will also interest you to know that the word *alien* is etymologically connected to *olive*. *Alien* means "strange, foreign, foreign-born, or exotic" amongst other definitions. It refers to something that is unfamiliar. The etymology of *alien* actually derives from the Latin *alius* which should tell you something very pertinent. This is the same as the English word *alias* which refers to an alternative or, more importantly, false identity. If we examine the etymology of *alius* or *alias* further, we will see that it refers to *else* or *other*. The word *else* derives from the Old English *elles* as in *el-land* which refers to "foreign land" but might better be described as the land of the elves. *Elles* relates to the Greek *allos* which means "other." Not only does *El* relate to God, but these eytmologies suggest that God is a foreigner. More importantly, *elles* and *allos* are virtually the same as the Greek *elaia* or *olive*.

If Cairo was a stargate and Egypt was also known as the Land of the Olives, it is understandable that Isis was known as the Queen of the Olives. It is therefore quite suitable that Olive Pharoah would have been the matriarch of the Montauk Pharoahs and the guardian of a stargate as well.

I would like to thank Olive Pharoah and Louise Boyd for their contributions in unveiling the living memory of the universe and providing us with a gateway.

The end is always a beginning.

Author's Note

If you are interested in contributing to the Montauk Wellness Center or otherwise helping the cause of the Montauks, please send an email to me at *skybooks@yahoo.com* or write via letter to Sky Books, PO Box 769, Westbury, NY 11590. Those who are interested in a Chi Gong workshop in their local area with either "Red Medicine" Artie Crippen or Roosevelt Gainey can also make contact as per above.

Those who would like to receive updates on Peter Moon's adventures with David Anderson and the groundbreaking events that are occurring in Romania should subscribe to the *Montauk Pulse* newsletter as described below.

ALSO BY PETER MOON

THE MONTAUK BOOK OF THE DEAD

The Montauk Book of the Dead is a tale of the intrigue and power which hover over the most sacred kernel of our existence: the secrets of life and death. The personal story of Peter Moon reveals fascinating details of his years aboard L. Ron Hubbard's mystery ship and gives an inside look at one of the most controversial figures in recent history. This includes how L. Ron Hubbard clinically "died" only to discover that he could "remote view." From this state of consciousness, termed "exterior," he was able to access what he termed the answers to all of the questions that had ever puzzled philosophers or the minds of men. Transcribing this into a work entitled **Excalibur**, still under lock and key to this day, he developed one of the most controversial movements in history: Dianetics and Scientology.

Over 400 pages..........................ISBN 978-0-9678162-3-4 ***$29.95***

SYNCHRONICITY & THE SEVENTH SEAL

Peter Moon's consummate work on synchronicity begins with a brief scientific description of the quantum universe and how the quantum observer experiences the principle of synchronicity, an expression of the divine or infinite mind. Exploring the influences of parallel universes, personal experiences of the author go deep into the magical exploits of the Babalon Working and the various antics and breakthroughs of the various players and that which influenced them. These characters include the legacies and personas of Jack Parsons, Marjorie Cameron, L. Ron Hubbard and Aleister Crowley. Eventually, pursuit of synchronicity leads Peter Moon to a most intriguing and mysterious encounter with Joseph Matheny, an adept who has not only had similar experiences to Peter, but has his own version of a space-time project known as Ong's Hat. Matheny has not only had incredible synchronicities himself, he created one of the highest forms of artificial intelligence known to man, a computer known as the Metamachine which is designed to precipitate and generate synchronicities. These many synchronicities lead to the books climax, a revelation of the true Seventh Seal. The proof is delivered. No theologian nor anyone has even tried to counter the claim.

Over 400 pages................................ISBN 0-9678162-7-0 ***$29.95***

THE BIGGEST SECRET EVER TOLD

The Montauk Project: Experiments In Time chronicles forty years of research starting with the "Philadelphia Experiment" of 1943 when the Navy attempted to make a destroyer escort invisible to radar only to have it teleport out of this reality with accompanying psychological disorders and physical trauma to the crew. Forty years of massive research ensued culminating in bizarre experiments at Montauk Point, New York that actually tapped the powers of creation and manipulated time itself. *The Montauk Project* is a first hand account by Preston Nichols, a technician who worked on the project and has survived threats on his life and attempts to brainwash his memory of what occurred.
160 pages, illustrations, photos and diagrams....................$15.95

THE ASTONISHING SEQUEL

Montauk Revisited: Adventures in Synchronicity pursues the mysteries of time brought to light in *The Montauk Project* and unmasks the occult forces behind the science and technology used in the *Montauk Project*. An ornate tapestry is revealed which interweaves the mysterious associations of the Cameron clan with the genesis of American rocketry and the magick of Aleister Crowley and Jack Parsons. *Montauk Revisited* carries forward with the Montauk investigation and unleashes a host of incredible characters and new information.
249 pages, illustrations, photos and diagrams......................$19.95

THE ULTIMATE PROOF

Pyramids of Montauk: Explorations In Consciousness awakens the consciousness of humanity to its ancient history and origins through the discovery of pyramids at Montauk and their placement on sacred Native American ground leading to an unprecedented investigation of the mystery schools of Earth and their connection to Egypt, Atlantis, Mars and the star Sirius. An astonishing sequel to the *Montauk Project* and *Montauk Revisited*, this chapter of the legend propels us far beyond the adventures of the first two books and stirs the quest for future reality and the end of time as we know it.
256 pages, illustrations, photos and diagrams..................$19.95

SkyBooks	ORDER FORM

We wait for ALL checks to clear before shipping. This includes Priority Mail orders. If you want to speed delivery time, please send a U.S. Money Order or use MasterCard or Visa. Those orders will be shipped right away.

Complete this order form and send with payment or credit card information to: Sky Books, Box 769, Westbury, New York 11590-0104

Name	
Address	
City	
State / Country	Zip
Daytime Phone (In case we have a question) ( )	

☐ This is my first order ☐ I have ordered before ☐ This is a new address

Method of Payment: ☐ Visa ☐ MasterCard ☐ Money Order ☐ Check

\# — — —

Expiration Date Signature

Title	Qty	Price
The Montauk Pulse (1 year subscription).....................$15.00		
Subtotal		
For delivery in NY add 8.625% tax		
Shipping: see chart on the next page		
U.S. only: Priority Mail		
Total		

Thank you for your order. We appreciate your business.

SHIPPING INFORMATION

United States Shipping

Under $30.00 ....add $5.00	Allow 30 days for delivery. For U.S. only: Priority Mail—add the following to the regular shipping charge: $4.00 for first item, $1.50 for each additional item.
$30.01 — 60.00 ...add $6.00	
$60.00 — $100.00 add $8.00	
$100.01 and over .add $10.00	

Outside U.S. Shipping

Due to excessive shipping costs for foreign orders, please email us at skybooks@yahoo.com prior to your order so that we can properly estimate the cost of your shipment.

For a complimentary listing of
special interdimensional books and videos —
send a $1.06 stamp or one dollar to:
Sky Books, Box 769, Westbury, NY 11590-0104

FUTURE BOOKS

Transylvanian Sunrise
by Radu Cinamar

Medicine of Montauk
by Peter Moon and Artie Crippen